THE GOLDEN SHEEP

(1)

KAORI OZAKI

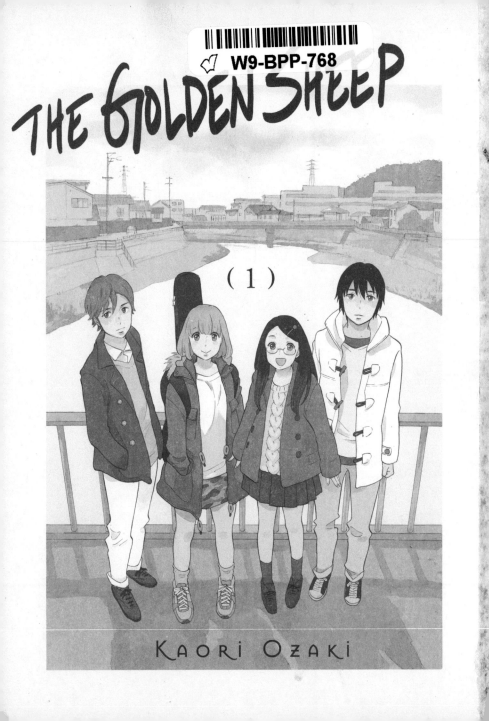

contents

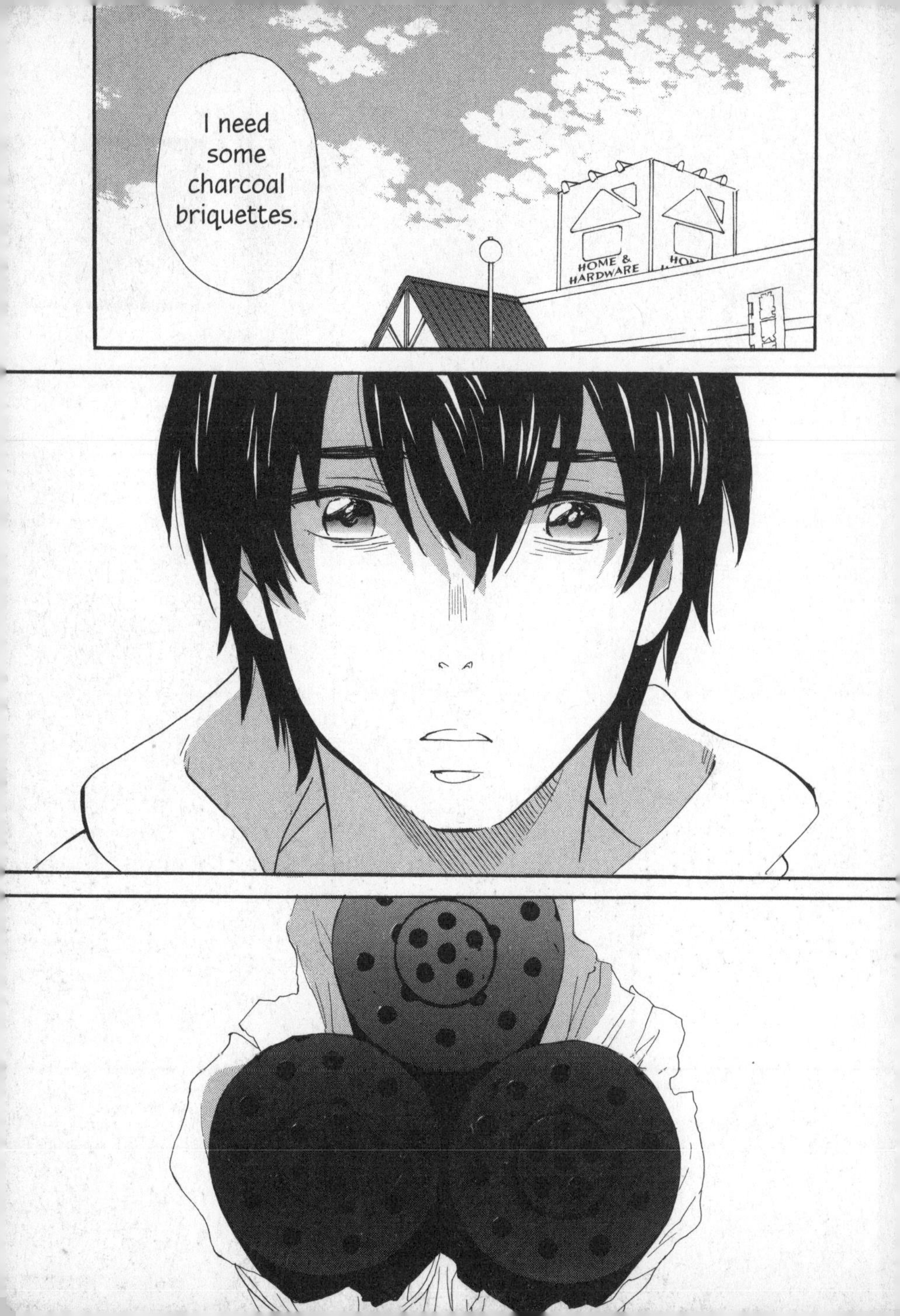
I need some charcoal briquettes.
HOME & HARDWARE

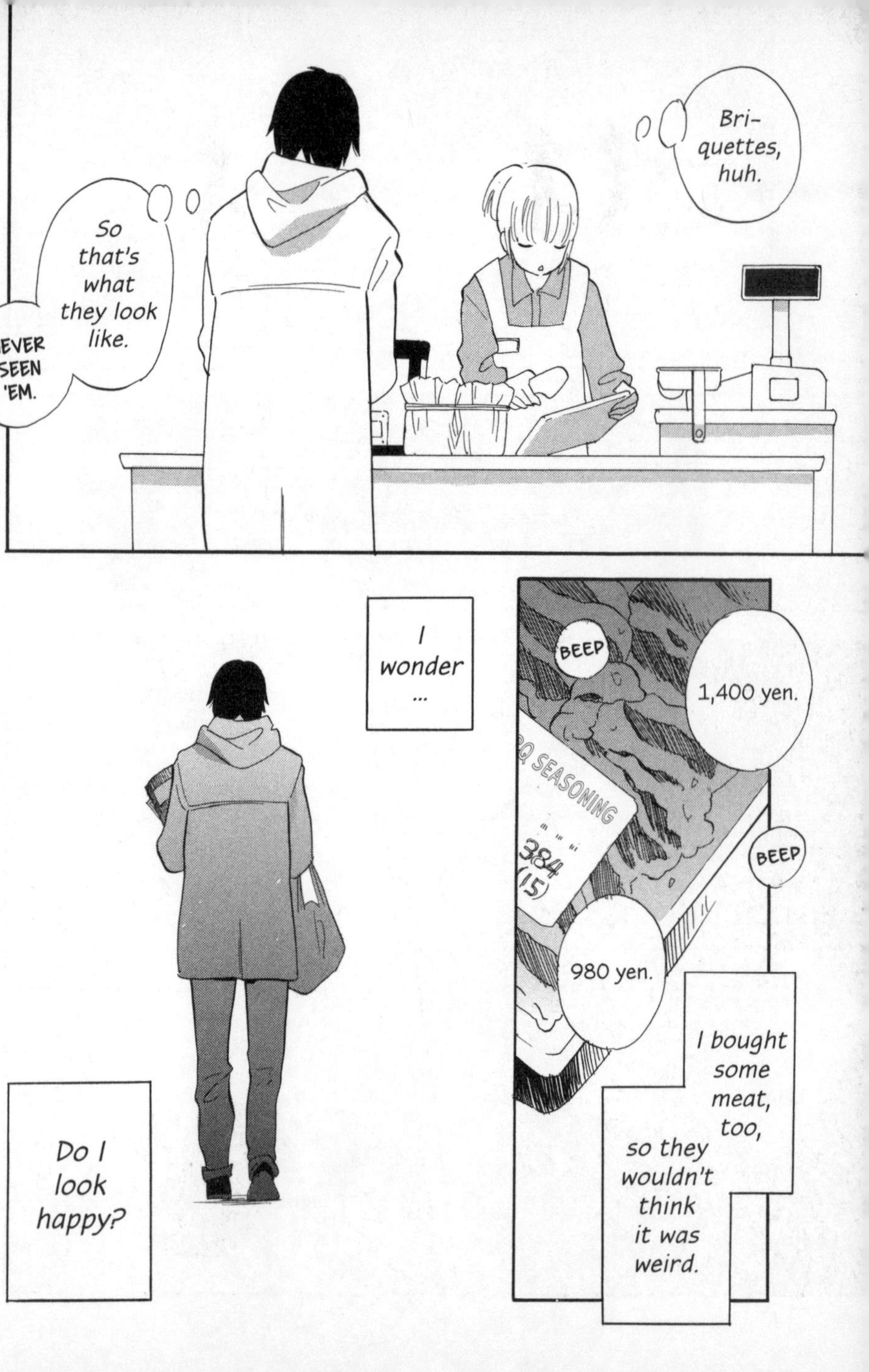
Bri-quettes, huh.
So that's what they look like.
NEVER SEEN 'EM.
BEEP
1,400 yen.
BEEP
980 yen.
I bought some meat, too,
so they wouldn't think it was weird.
I wonder ...
Do I look happy?

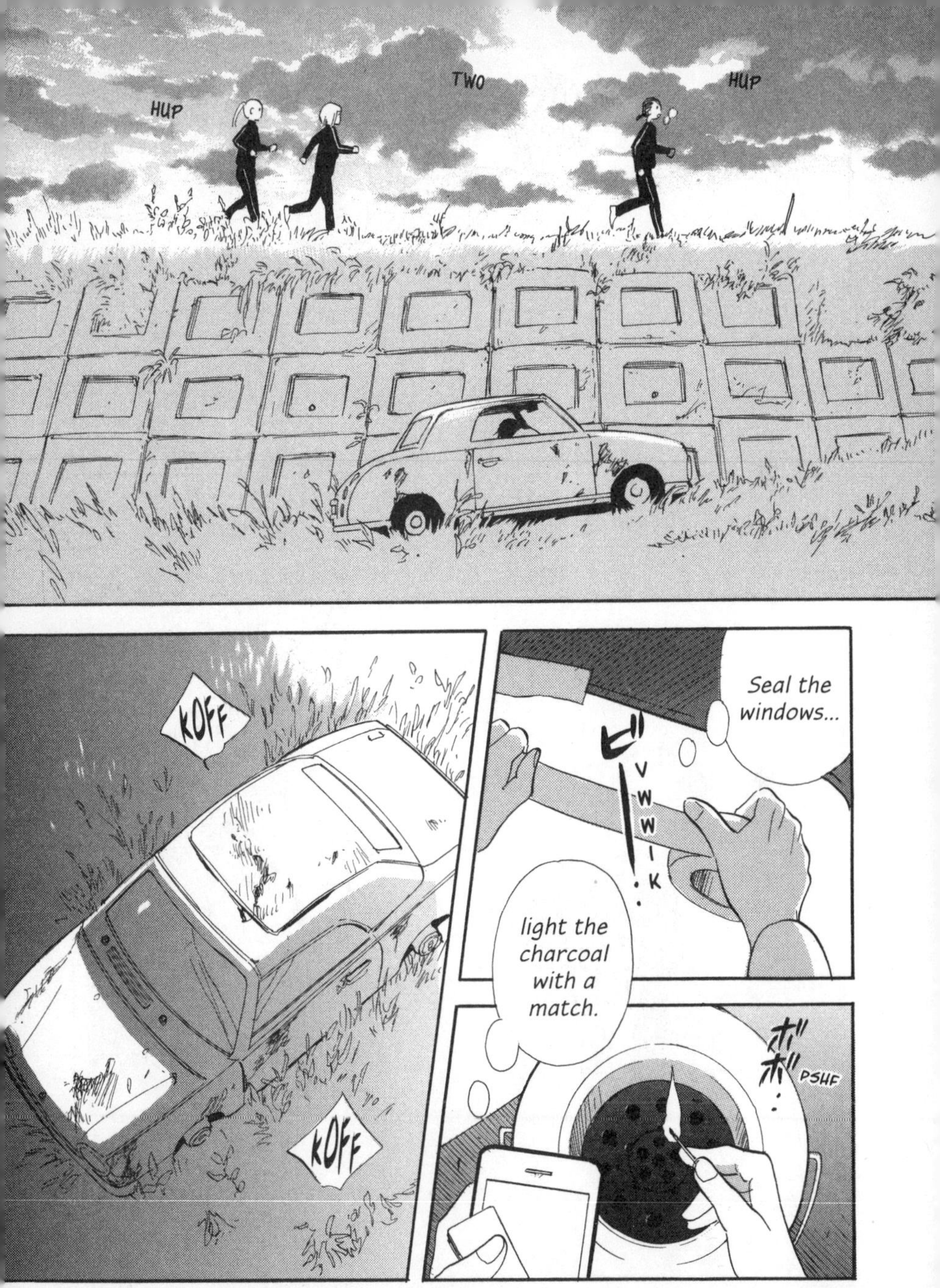
HUP
TWO
HUP
Seal the windows...
ビ
VWWIK
light the charcoal with a match.
ボボ
PSHF
KOFF
KOFF

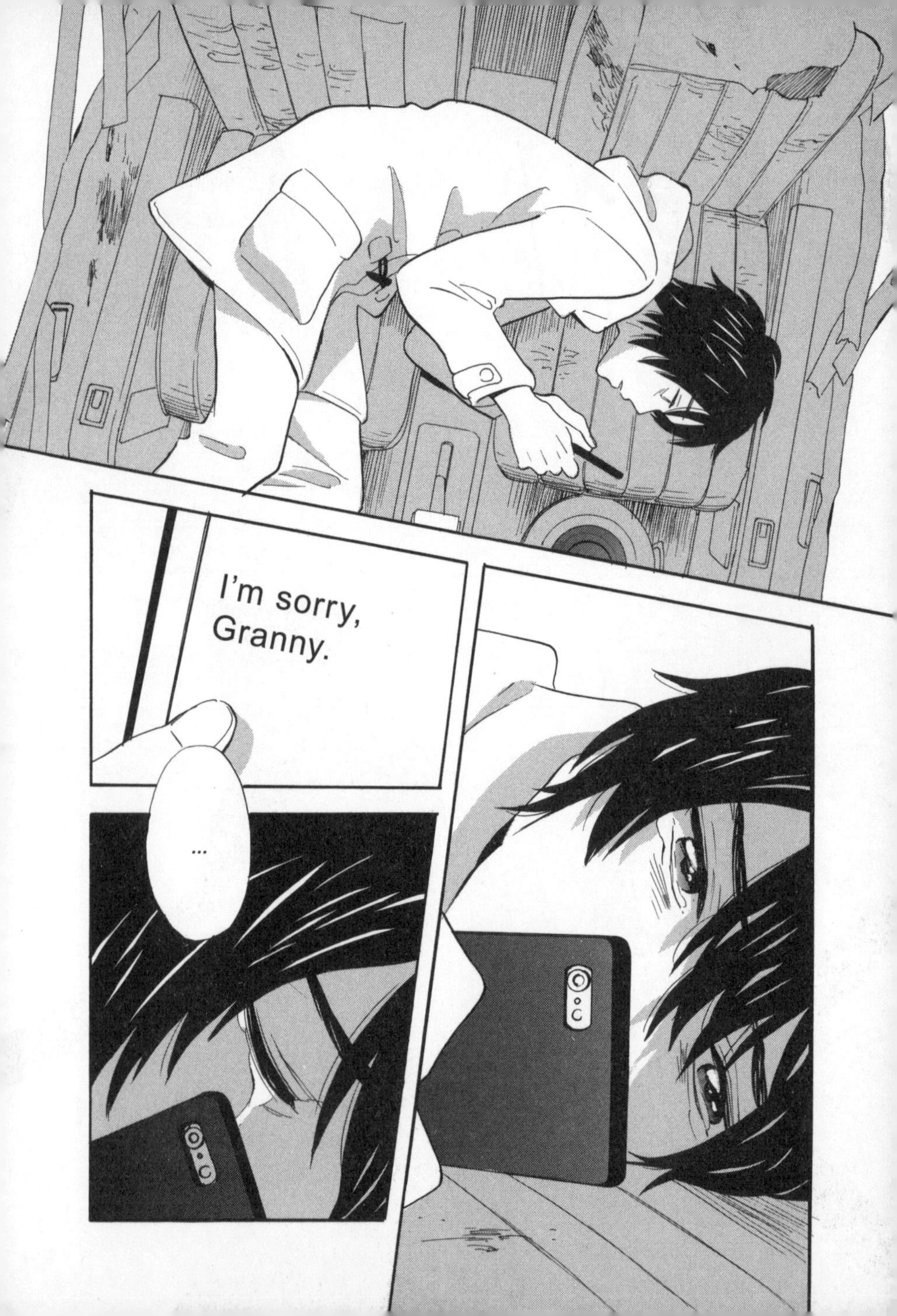

I'm sorry, Granny.
...

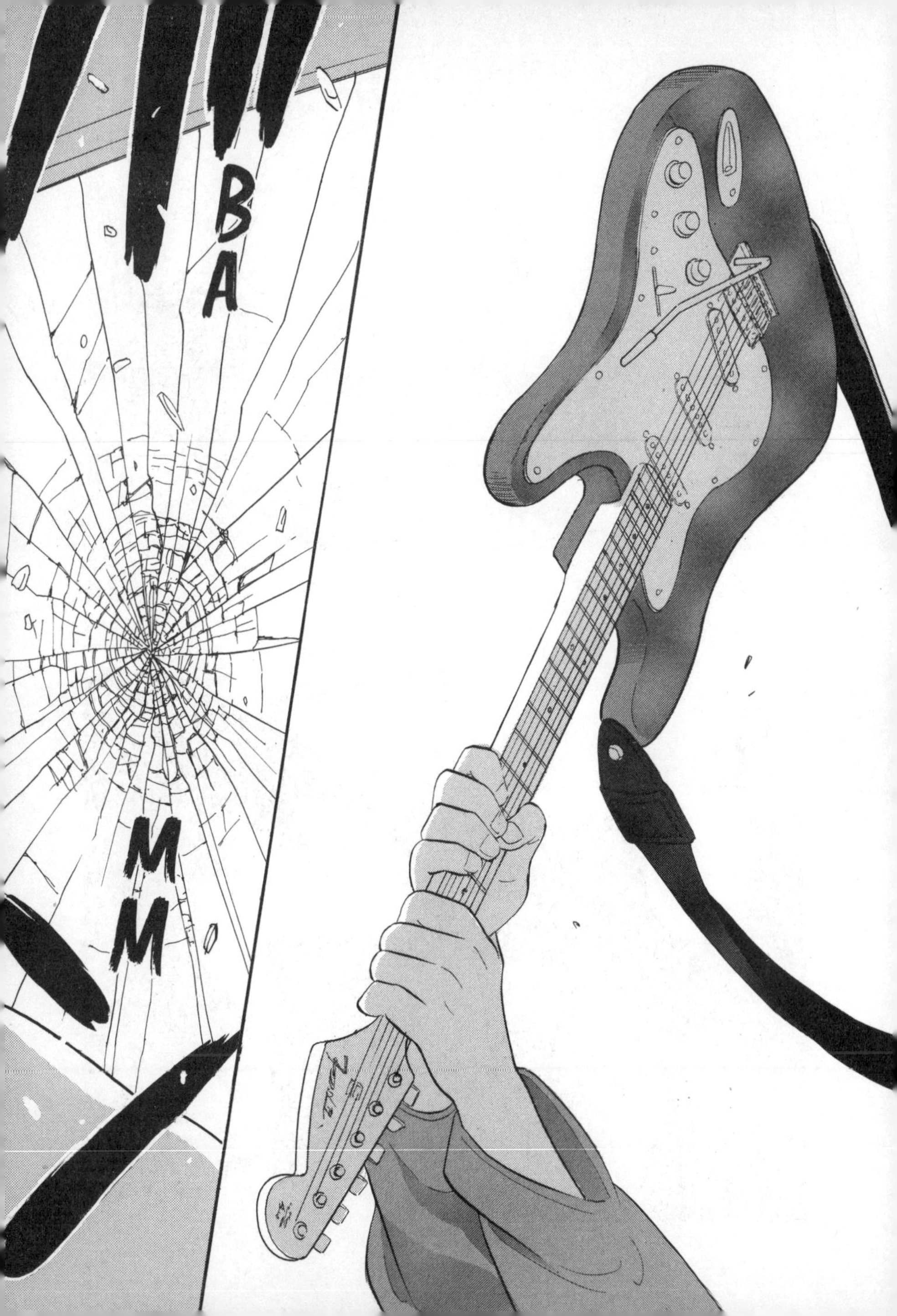
BAMM

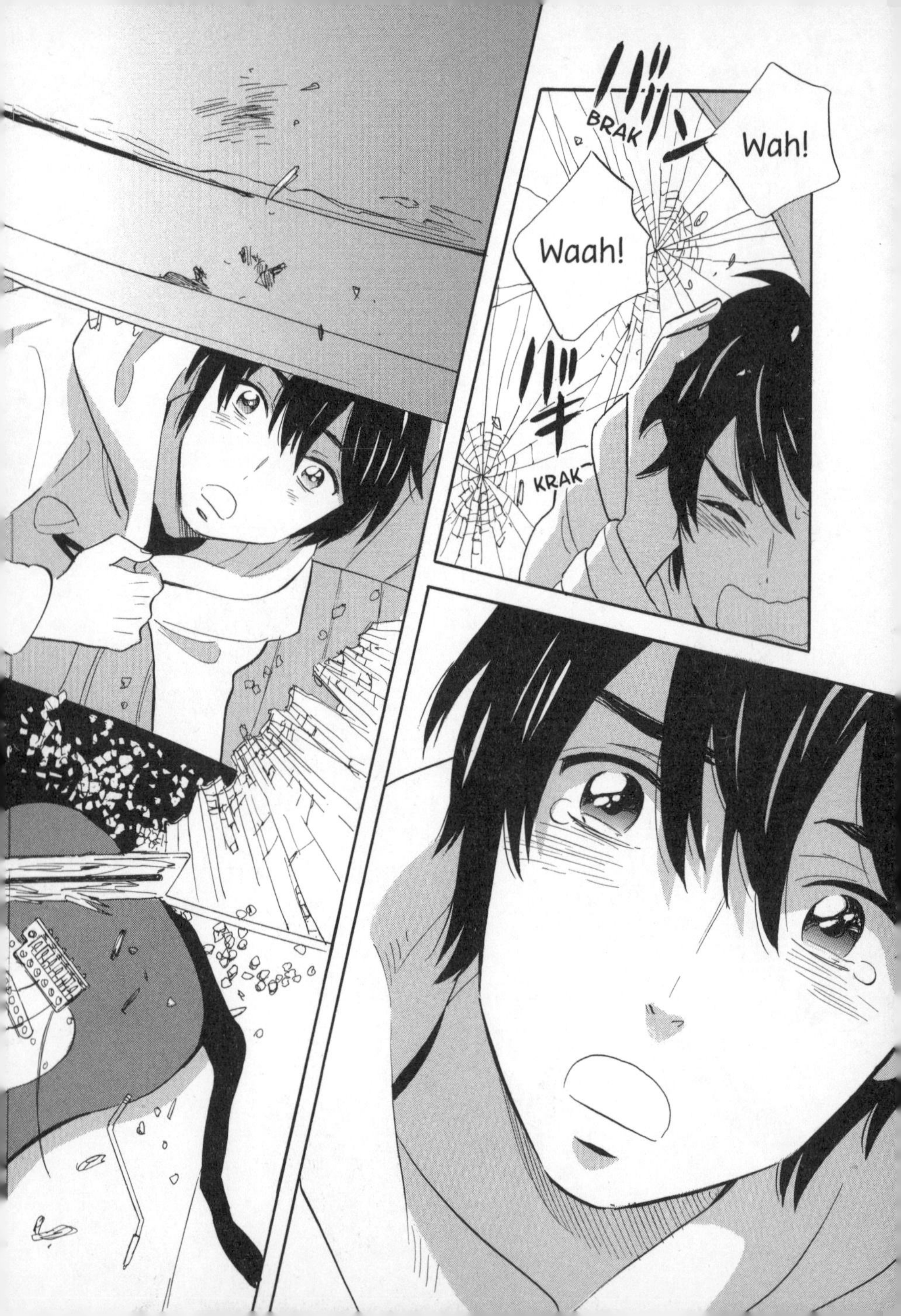
BRAK
Wah!
Waah!
KRAK

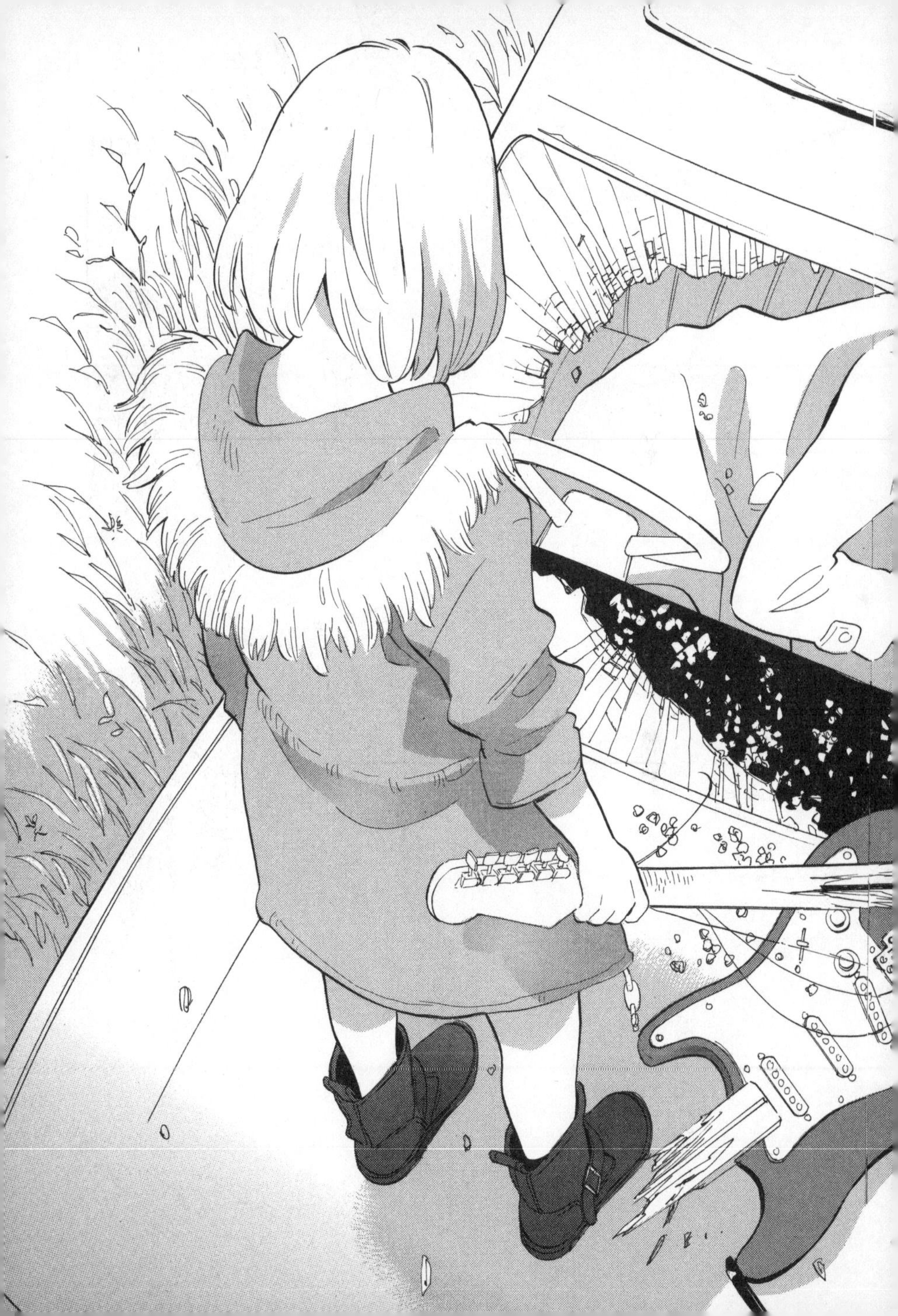

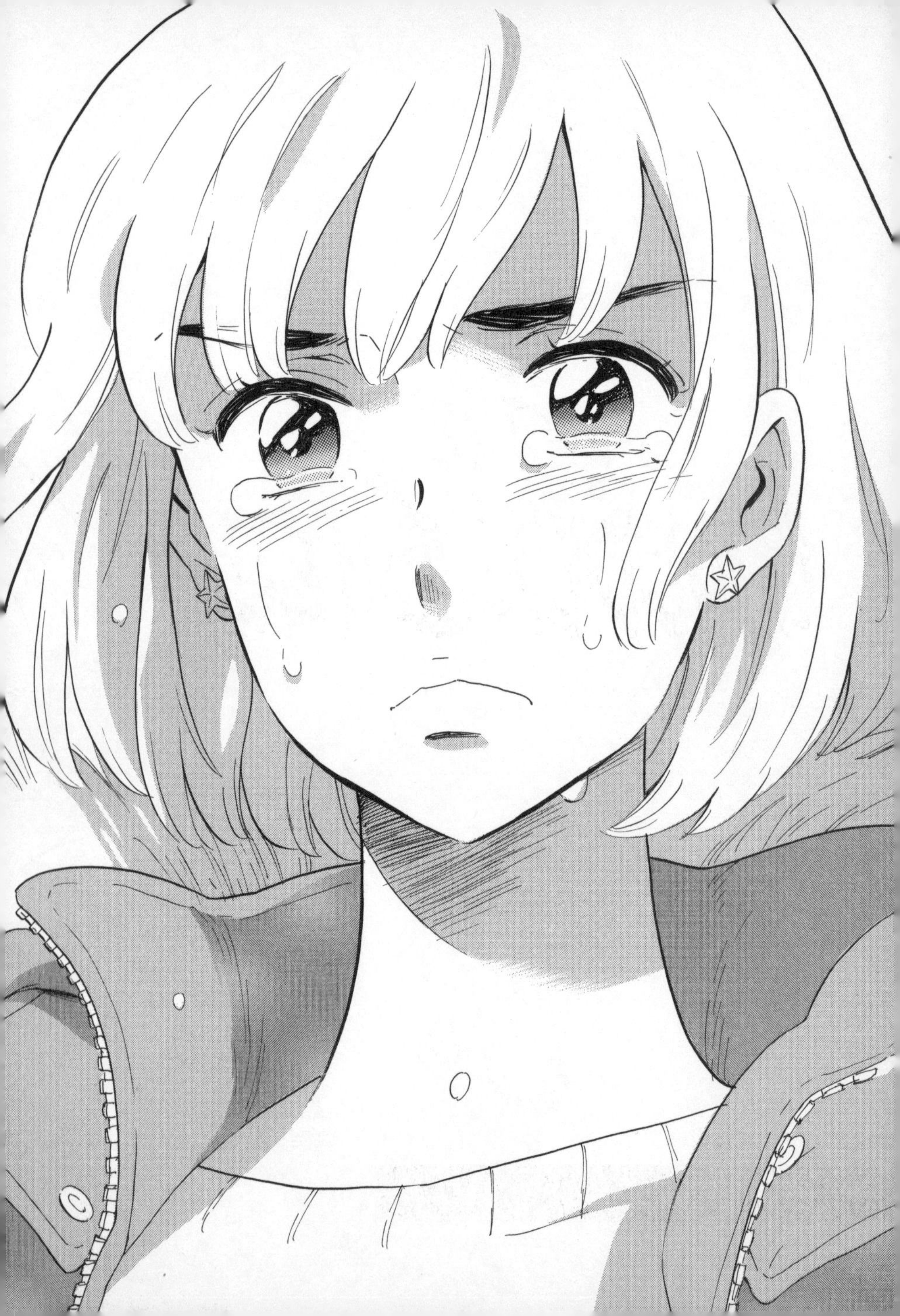

THE GOLDEN SHEEP

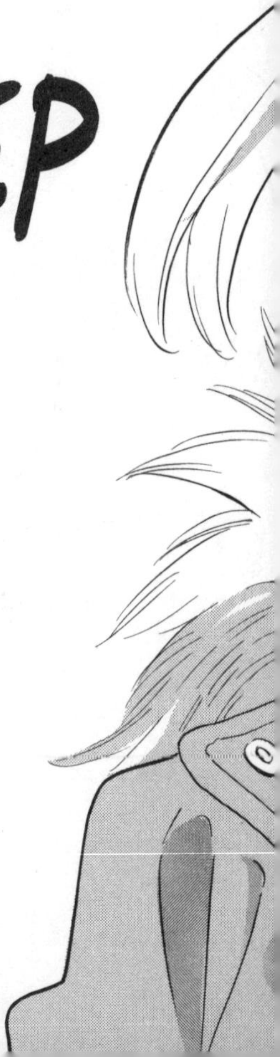

(CHAPTER 1) SHEEP PARK

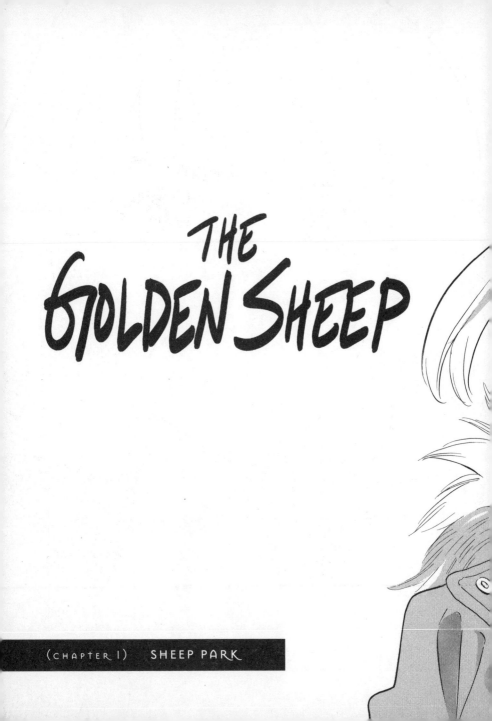

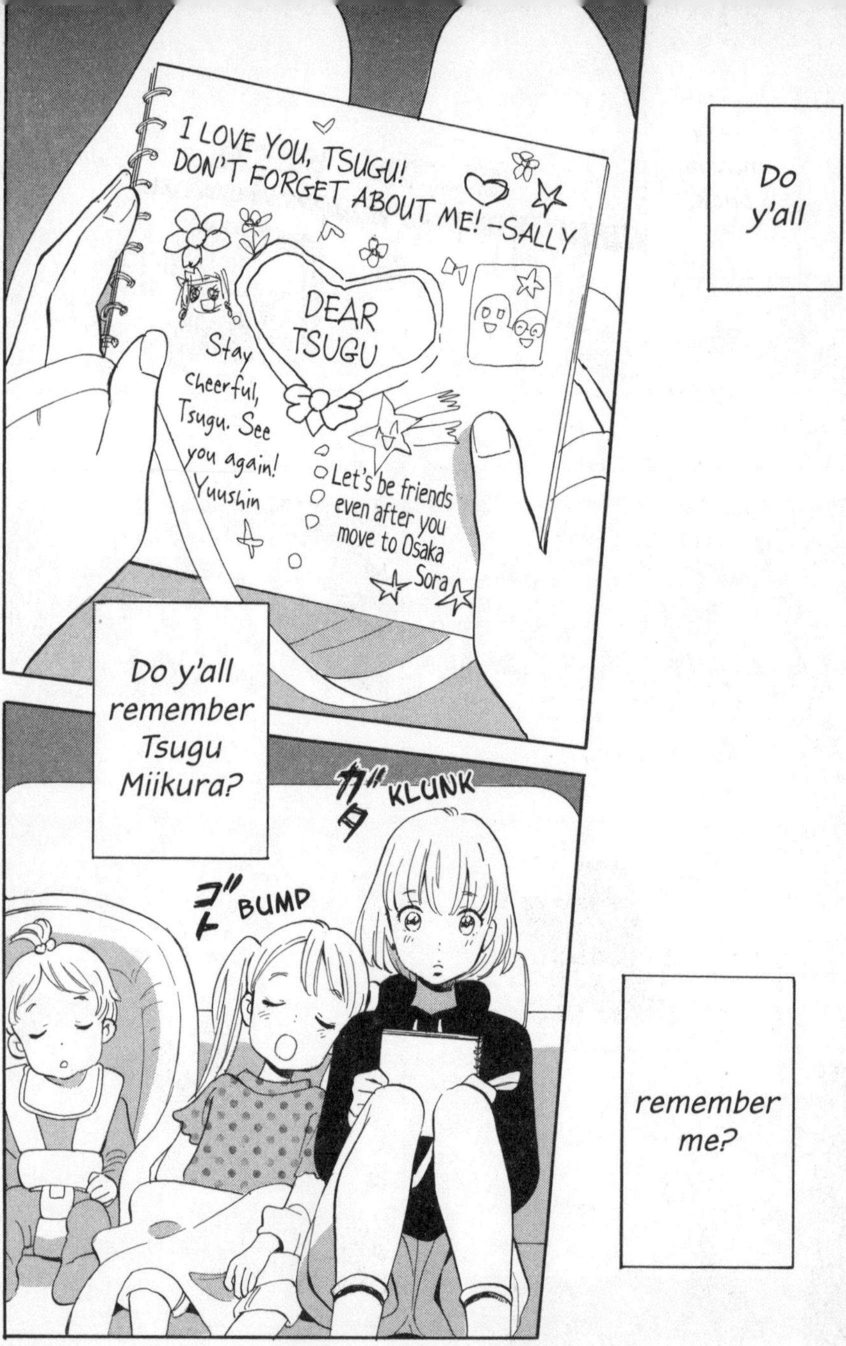

Do y'all
I LOVE YOU, TSUGU! DON'T FORGET ABOUT ME! -SALLY
DEAR TSUGU
Stay cheerful, Tsugu. See you again! Yuushin
Let's be friends even after you move to Osaka Sora
Do y'all remember Tsugu Miikura?
ガタ KLUNK
ゴト BUMP
remember me?

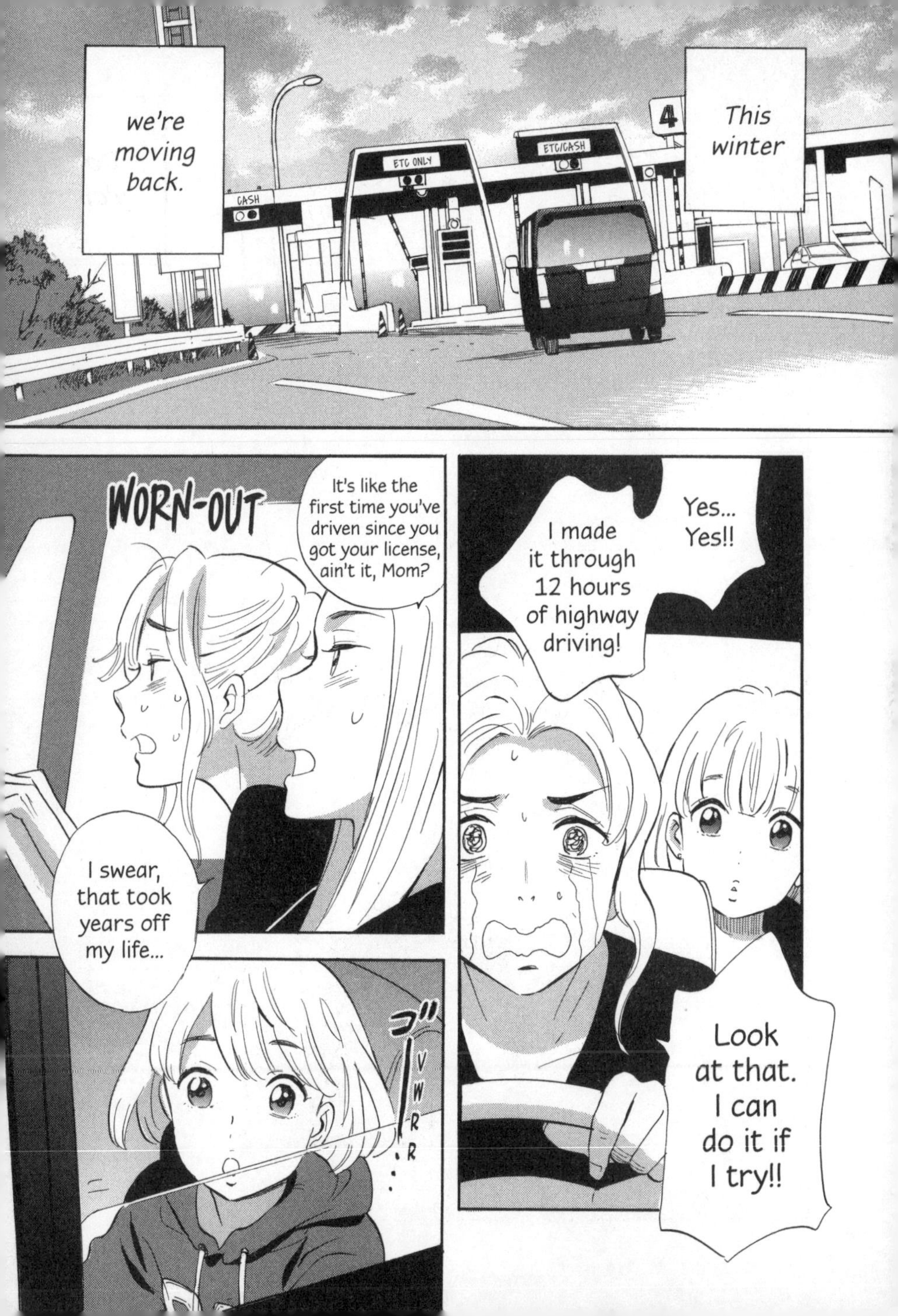
This winter
we're moving back.
Yes... Yes!!
I made it through 12 hours of highway driving!
Look at that. I can do it if I try!!
WORN-OUT
It's like the first time you've driven since you got your license, ain't it, Mom?
I swear, that took years off my life...
VWRR

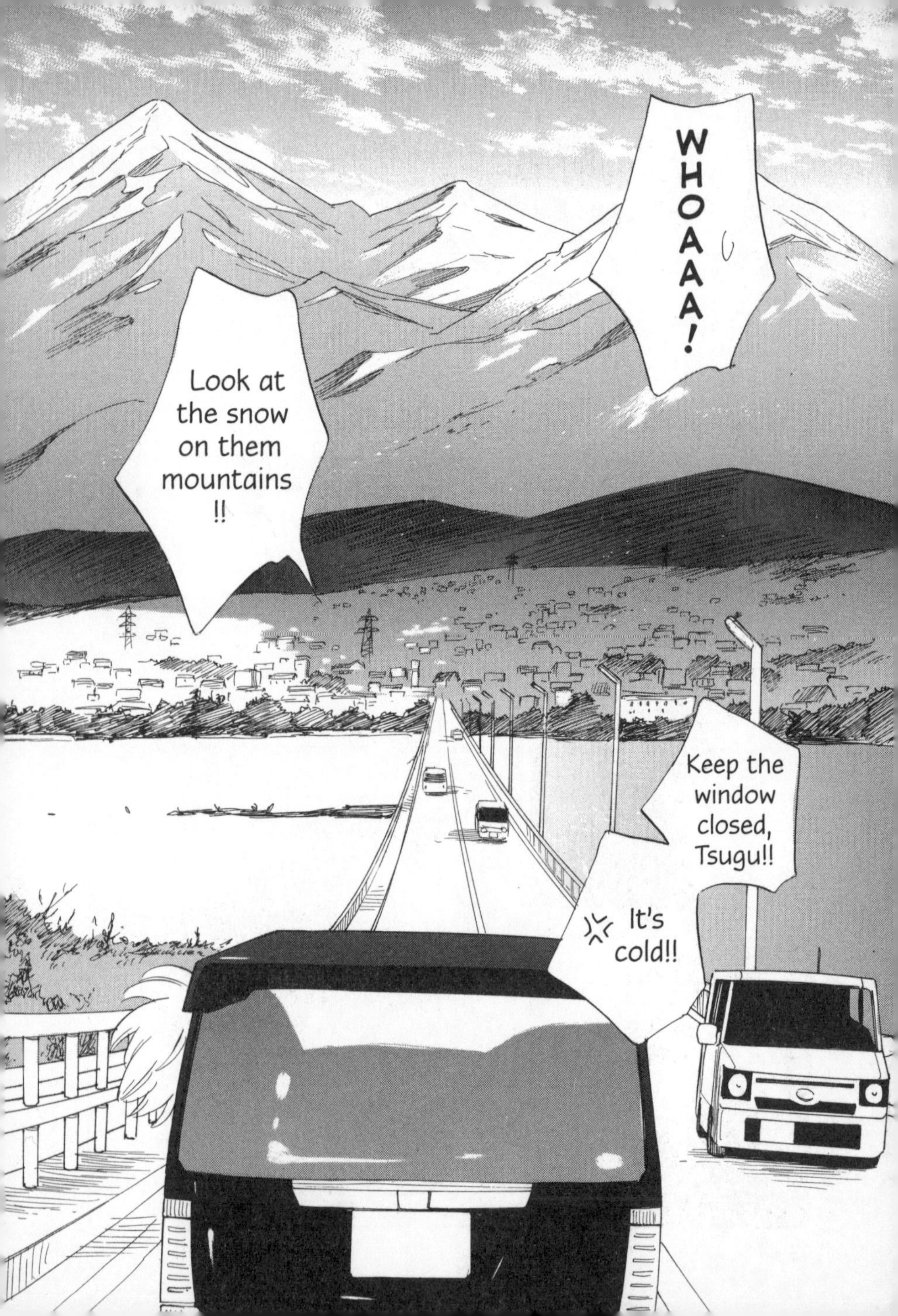
WHOAAA!
Look at the snow on them mountains !!
Keep the window closed, Tsugu!!
It's cold!!

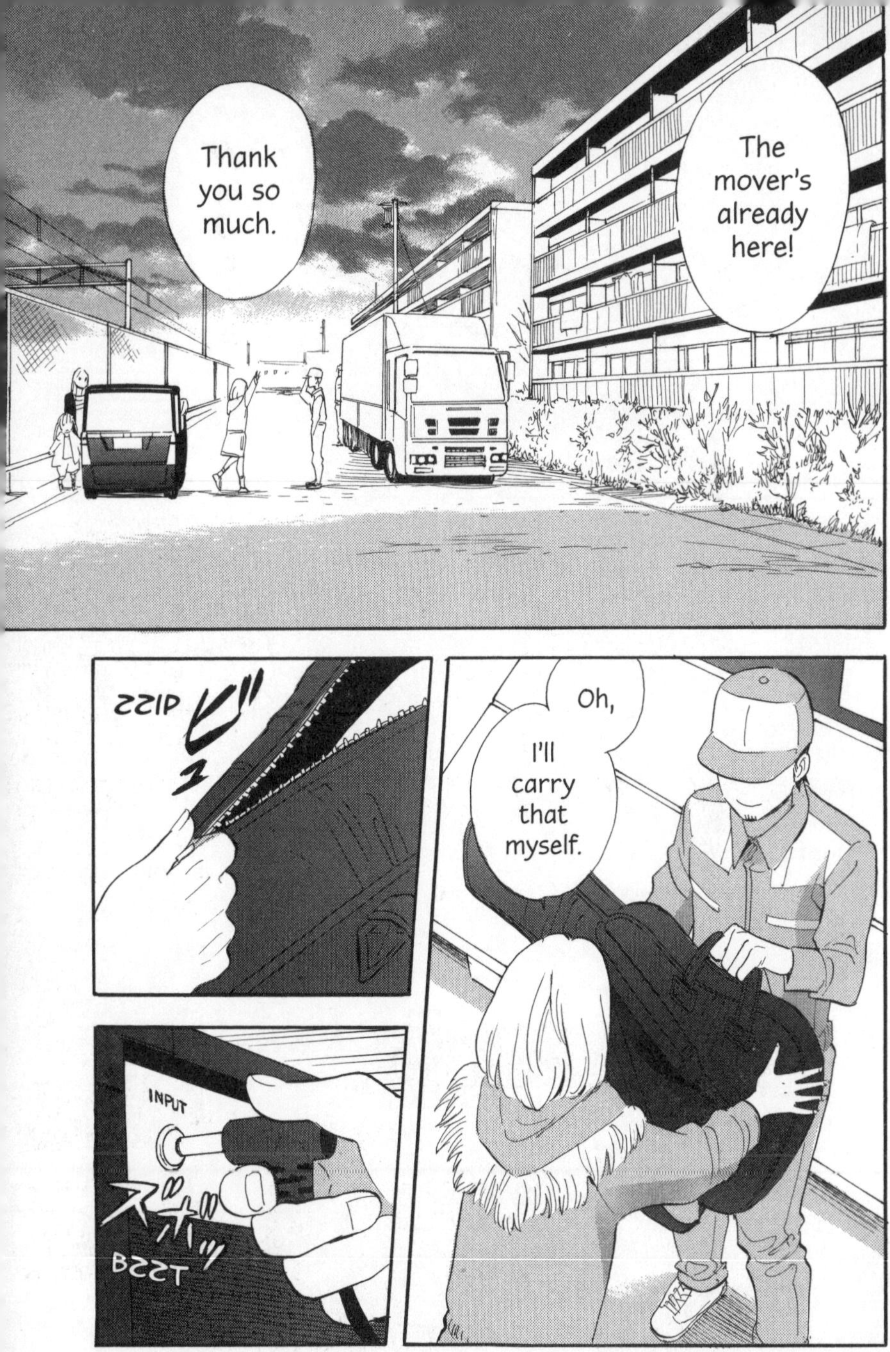
The mover's already here!
Thank you so much.
Oh,
I'll carry that myself.
ZZIP
INPUT
BZZT

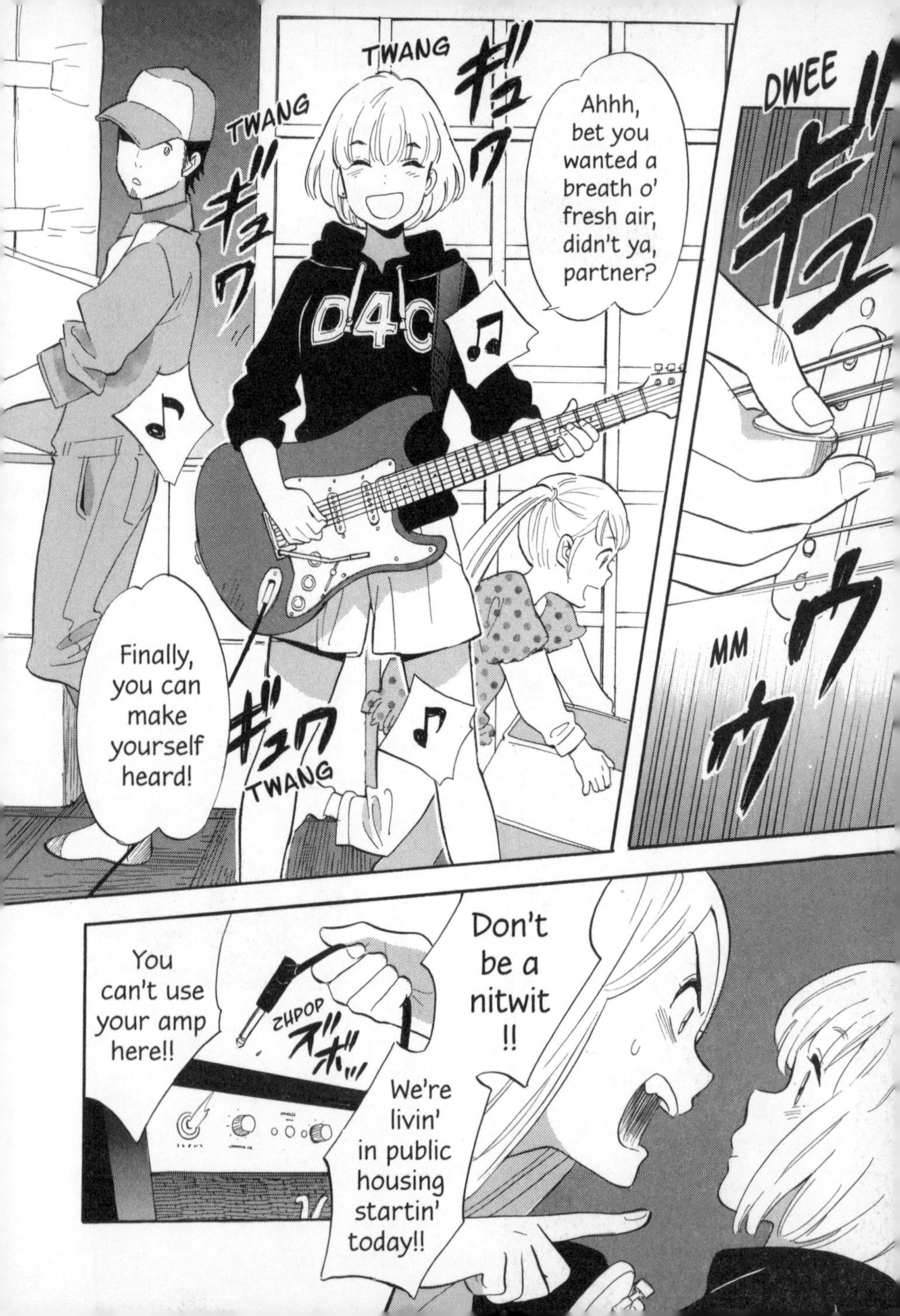
DWEE
MM
TWANG
Ahhh, bet you wanted a breath o' fresh air, didn't ya, partner?
TWANG
Finally, you can make yourself heard!
TWANG
Don't be a nitwit !!
You can't use your amp here!!
ZHPOP
We're livin' in public housing startin' today!!

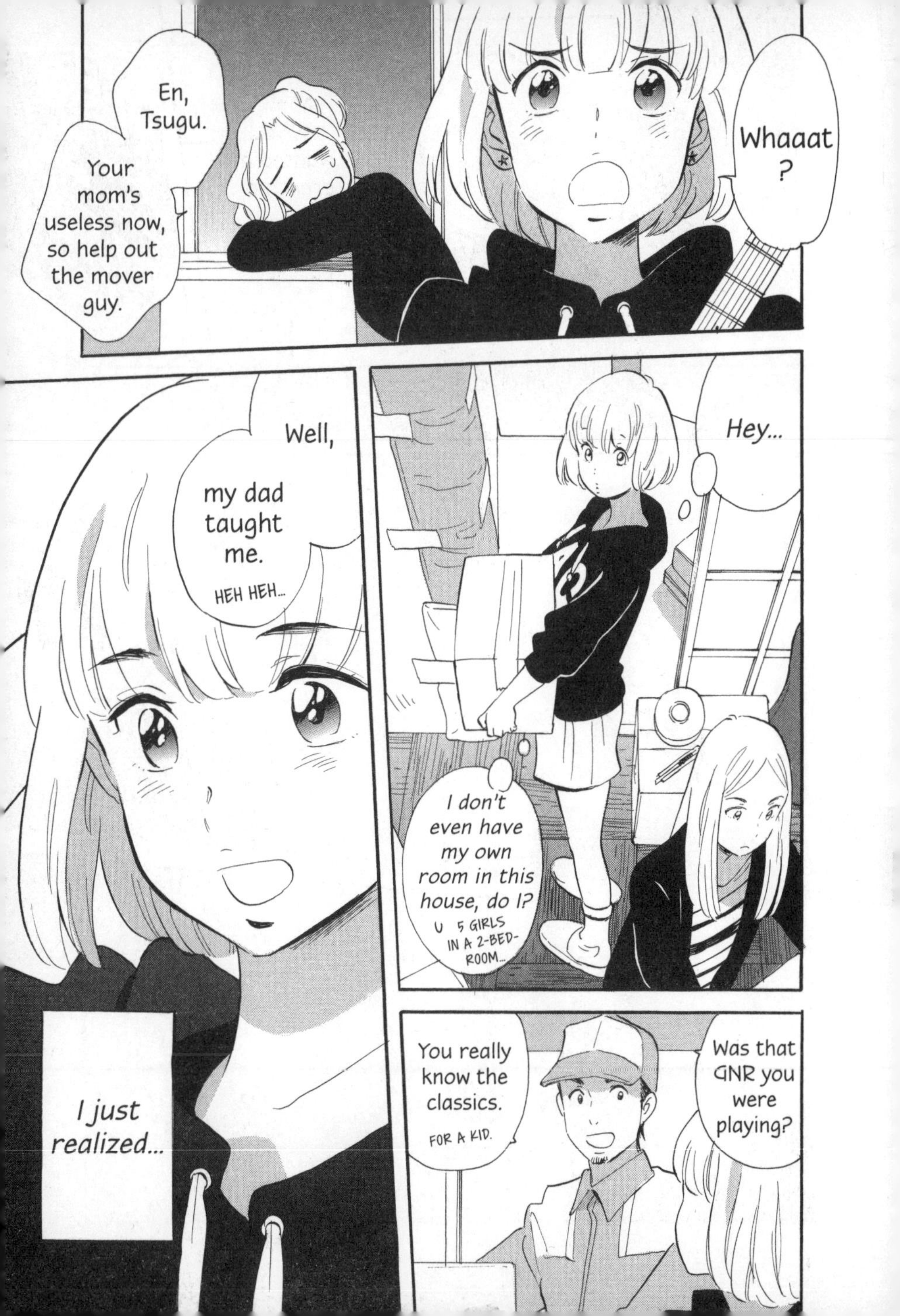
Whaaat ?
En, Tsugu.
Your mom's useless now, so help out the mover guy.
Hey...
I don't even have my own room in this house, do I?
5 GIRLS IN A 2-BED-ROOM...
Was that GNR you were playing?
You really know the classics.
FOR A KID.
Well,
my dad taught me.
HEH HEH...
I just realized...

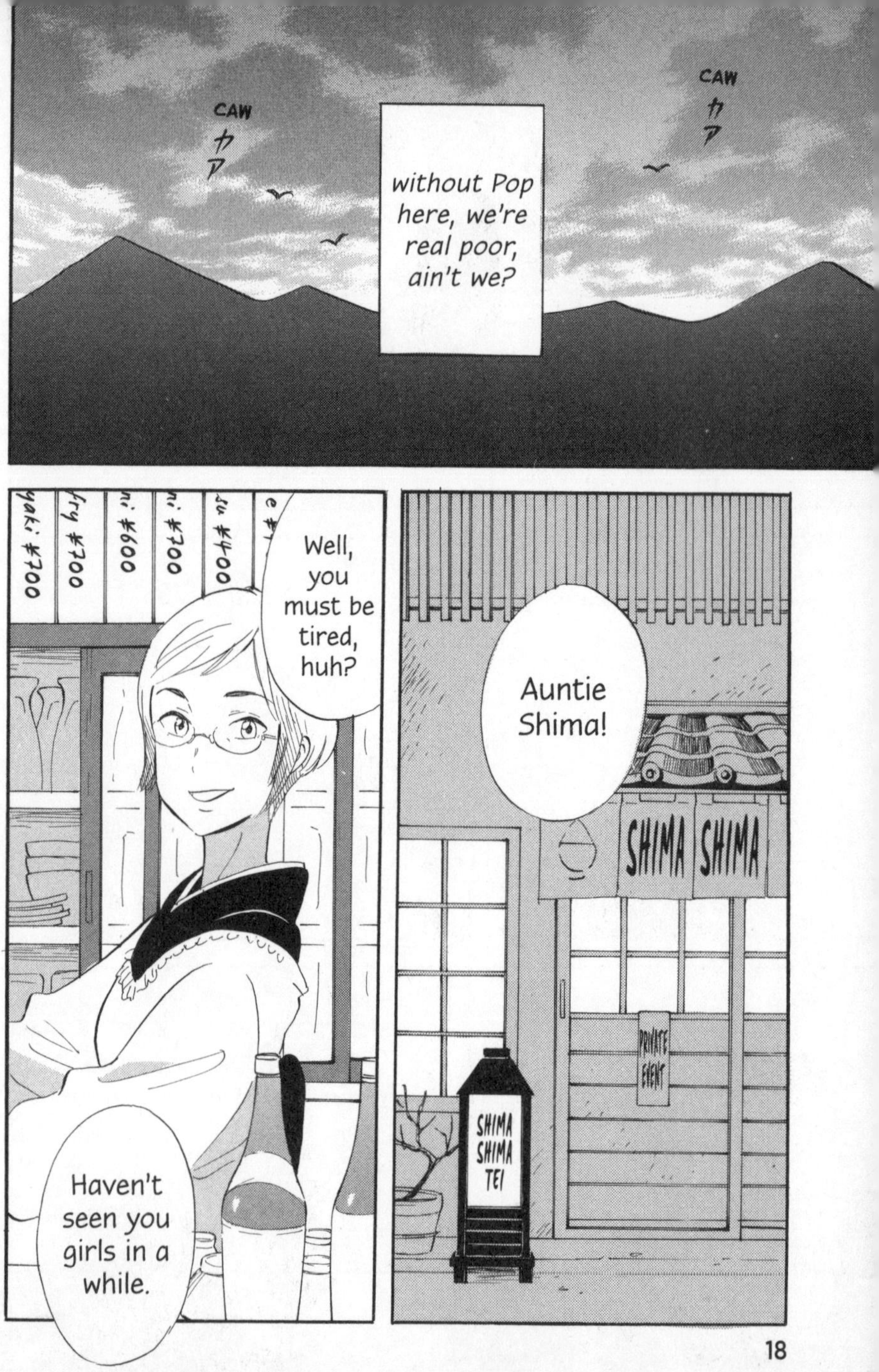
CAW
without Pop here, we're real poor, ain't we?
CAW
Auntie Shima!
SHIMA SHIMA
PRIVATE EVENT
SHIMA SHIMA TEI
Well, you must be tired, huh?
Haven't seen you girls in a while.

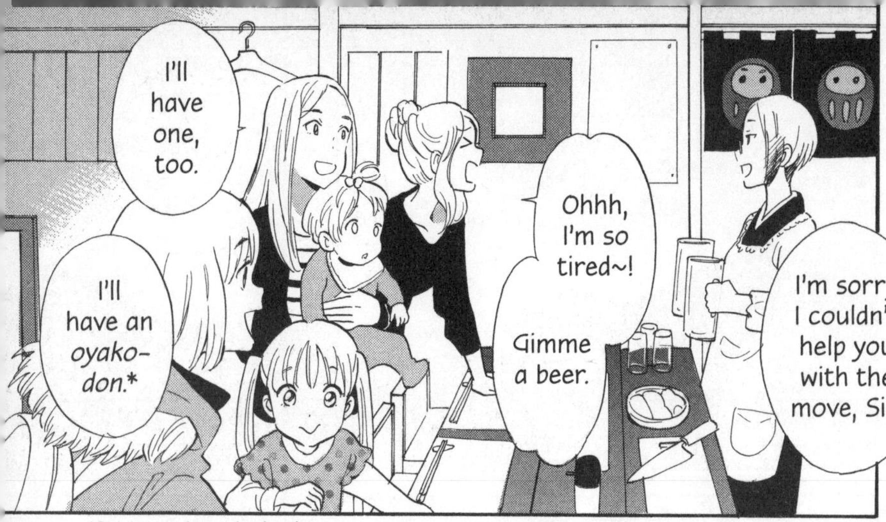
I'm sorry I couldn't help you with the move, Sis.
Ohhh, I'm so tired~!
Gimme a beer.
I'll have one, too.
I'll have an oyako-don.*

*Chicken and egg rice bowl

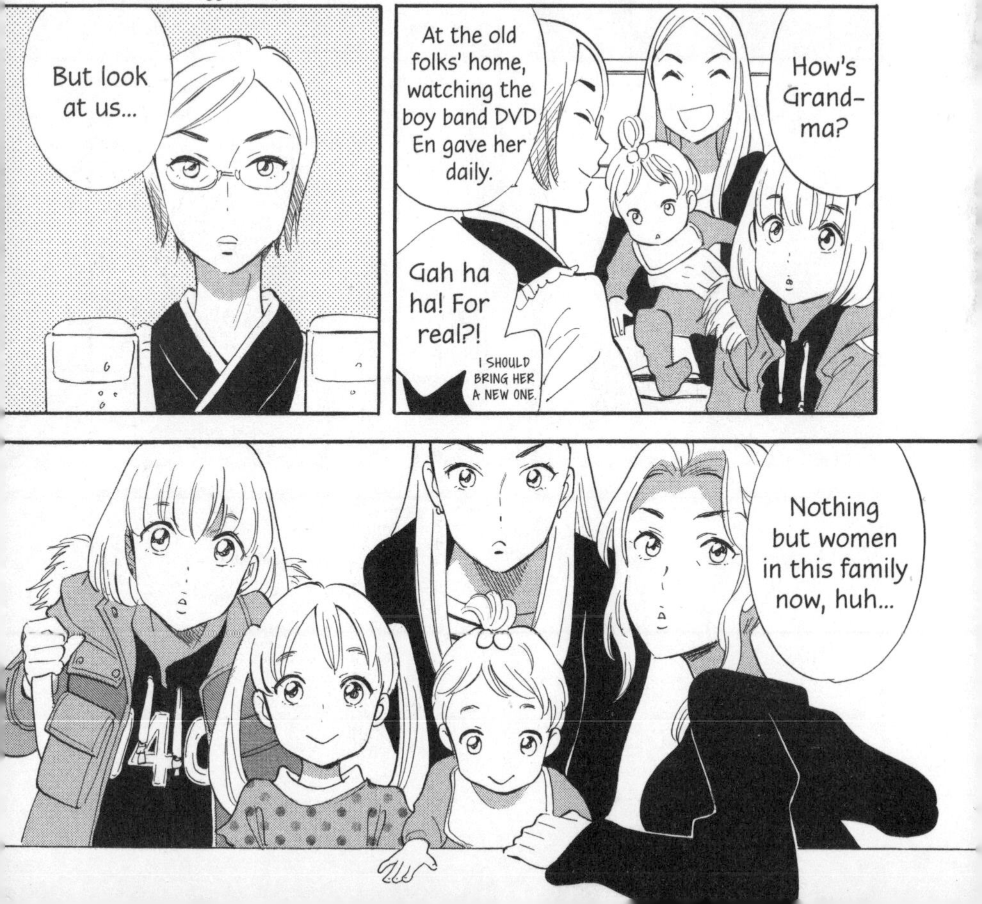
How's Grand-ma?
At the old folks' home, watching the boy band DVD En gave her daily.
Gah ha ha! For real?!
I SHOULD BRING HER A NEW ONE.
But look at us...
Nothing but women in this family now, huh...

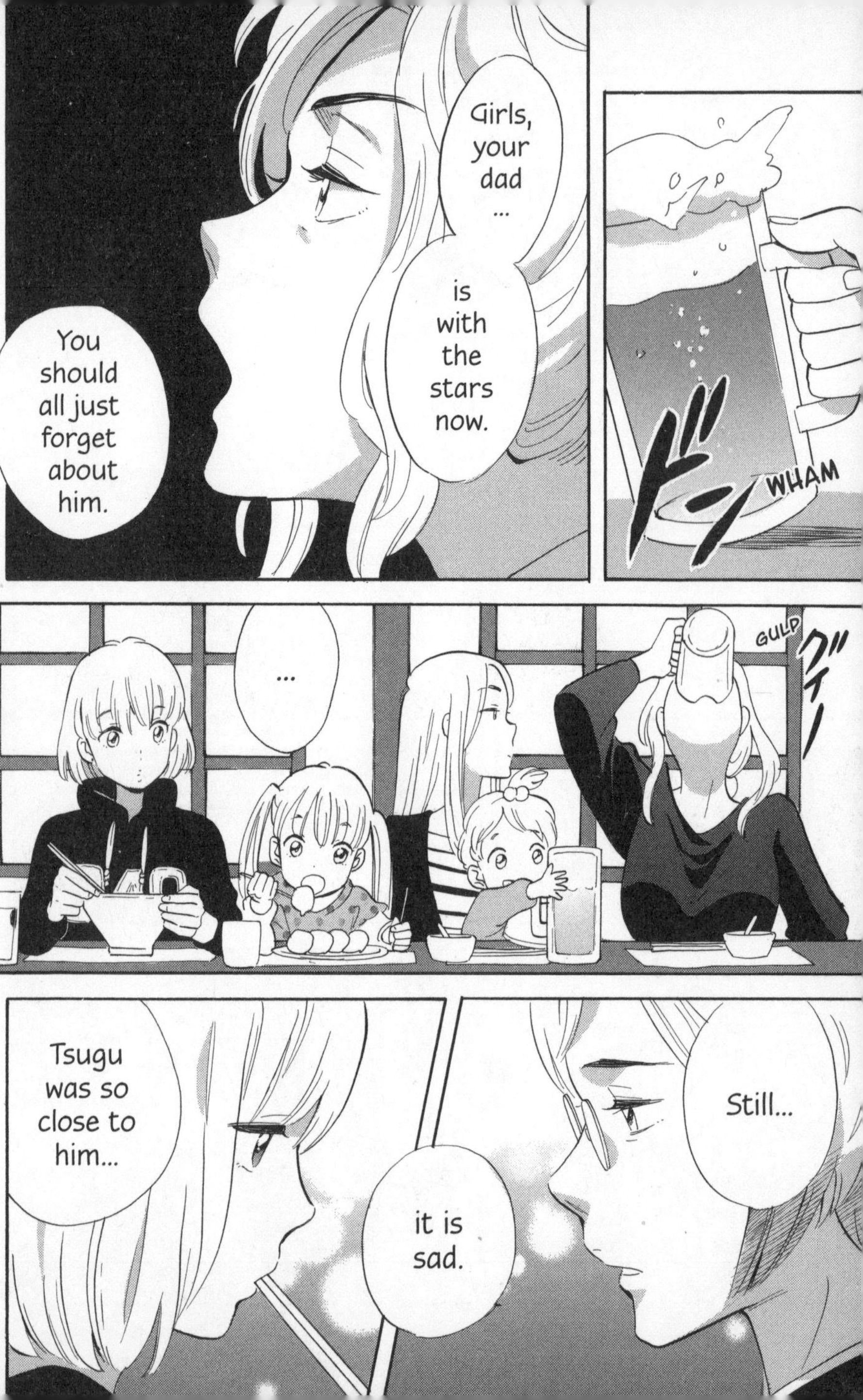
WHAM
Girls, your dad ...
is with the stars now.
You should all just forget about him.
GULP
...
Still...
it is sad.
Tsugu was so close to him...

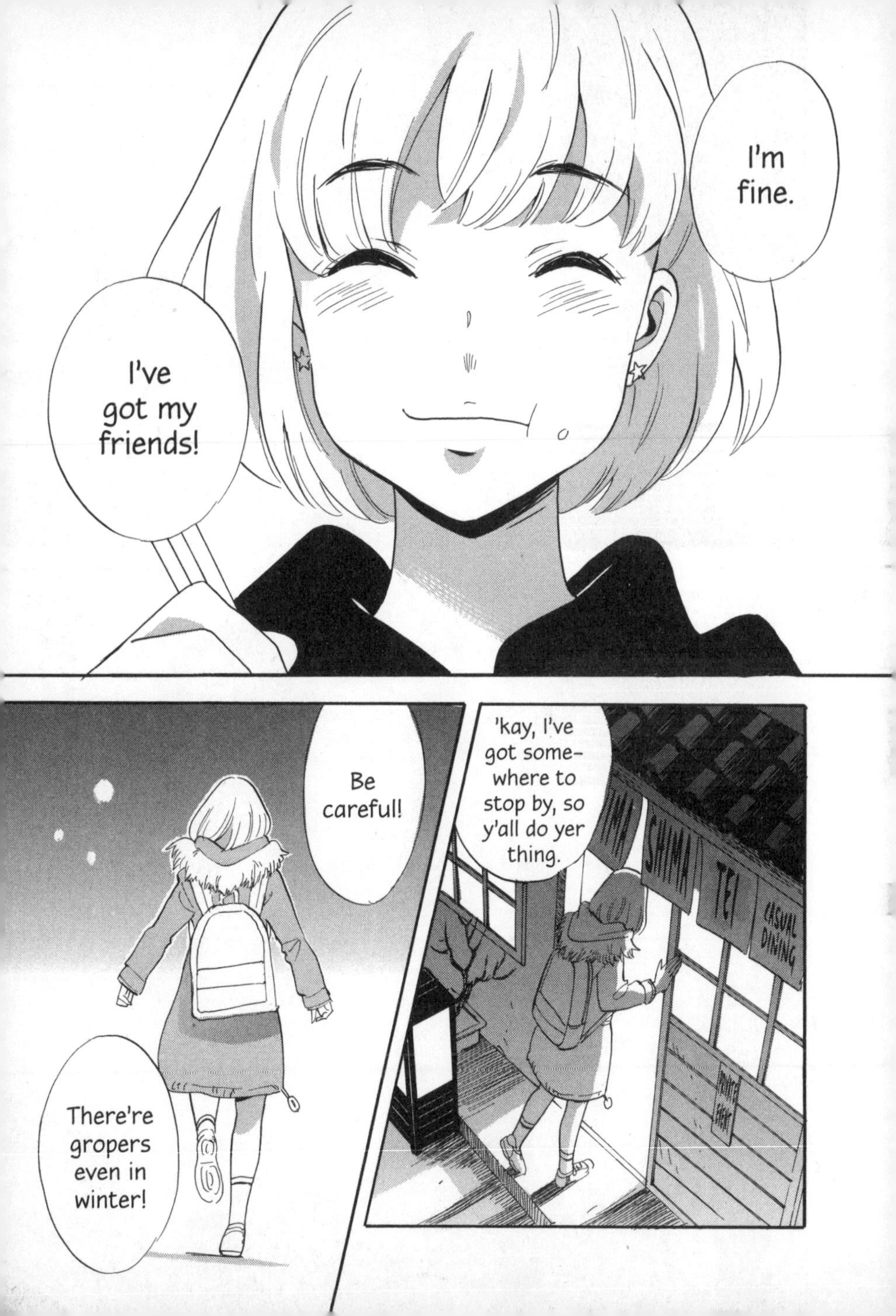
I'm fine.
I've got my friends!
'kay, I've got some-where to stop by, so y'all do yer thing.
SHIMA
TEI
CASUAL DINING
Be careful!
There're gropers even in winter!

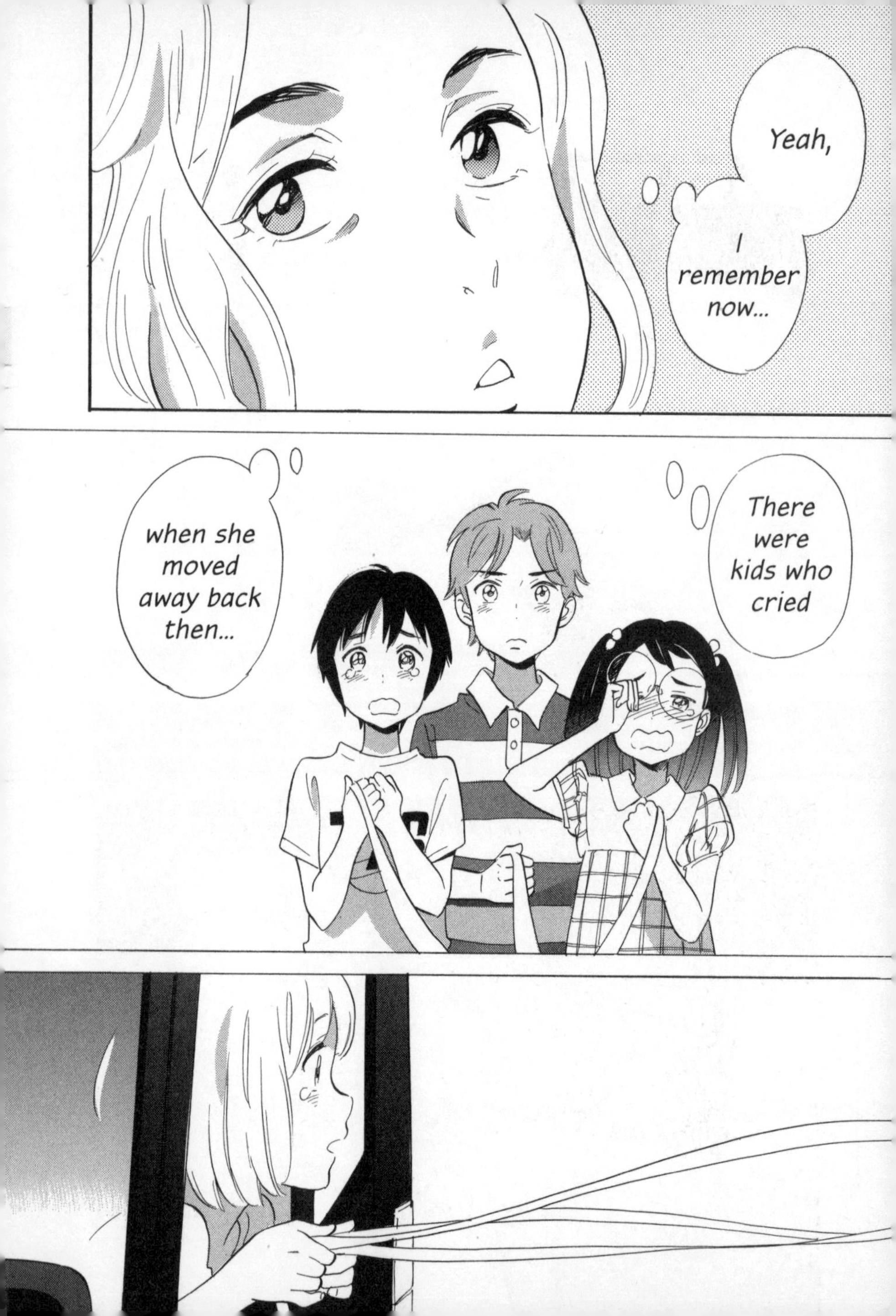
Yeah,
I remember now...
There were kids who cried
when she moved away back then...

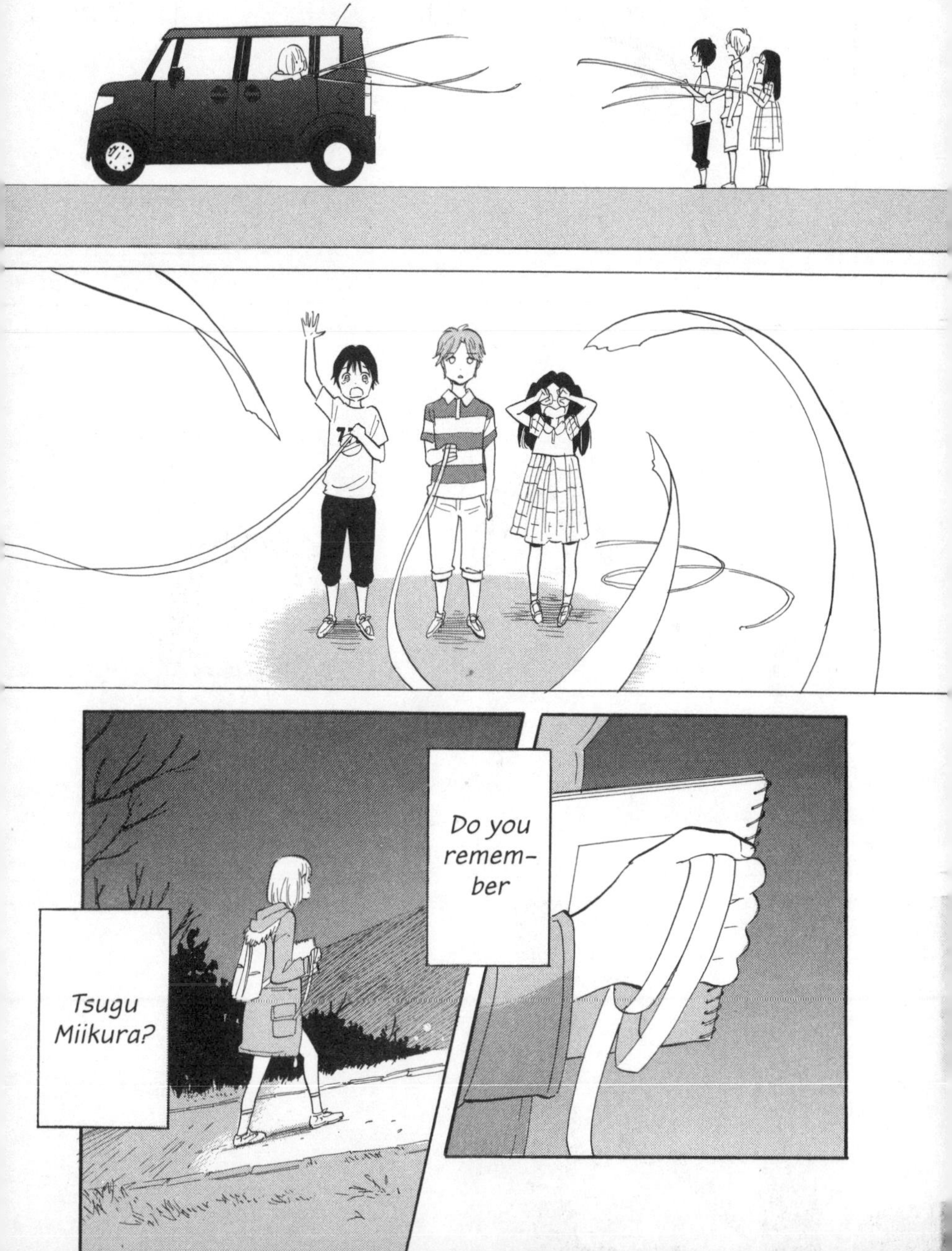
Do you remem-ber
Tsugu Miikura?

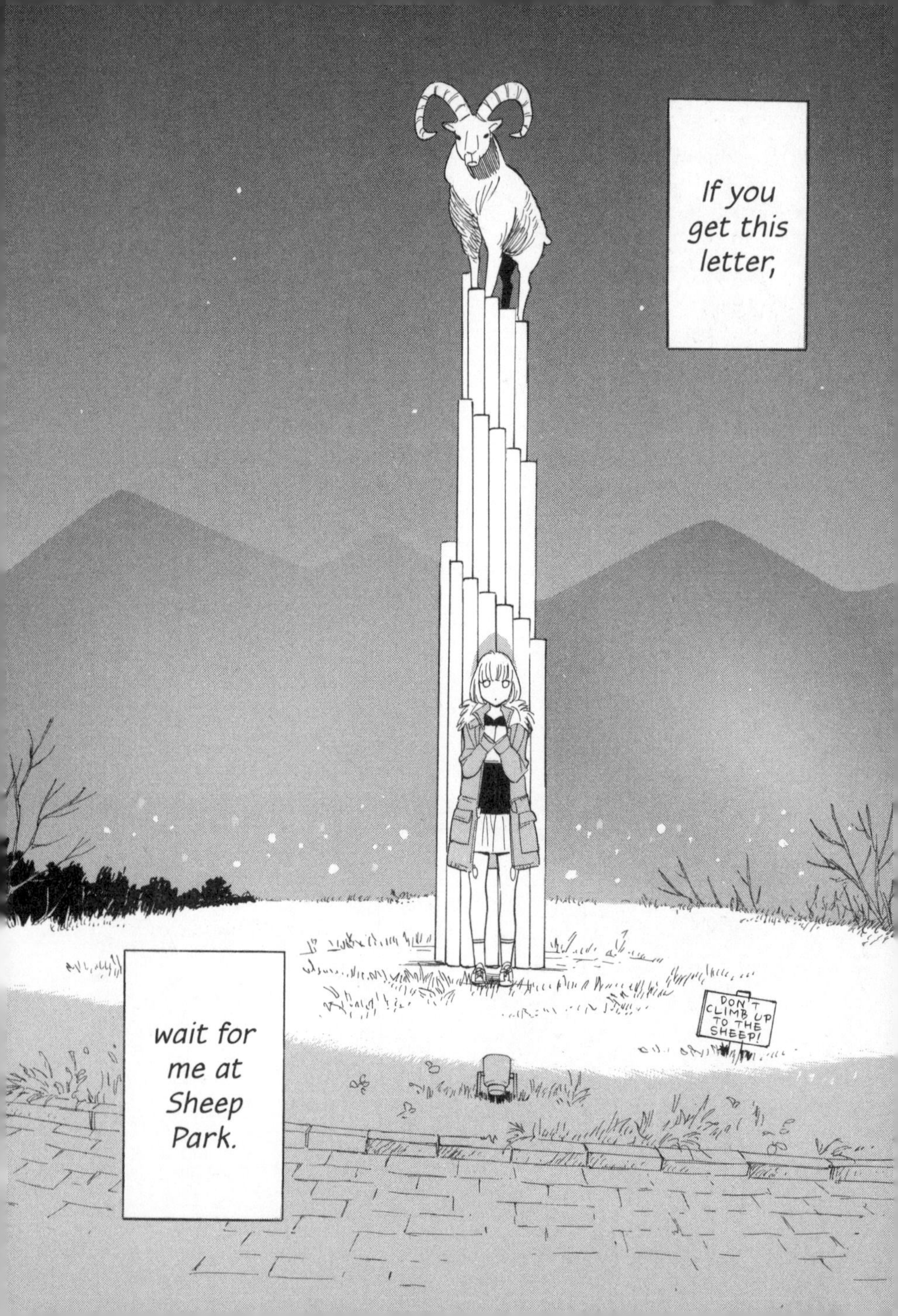
If you get this letter,
DON'T CLIMB UP TO THE SHEEP!
wait for me at Sheep Park.

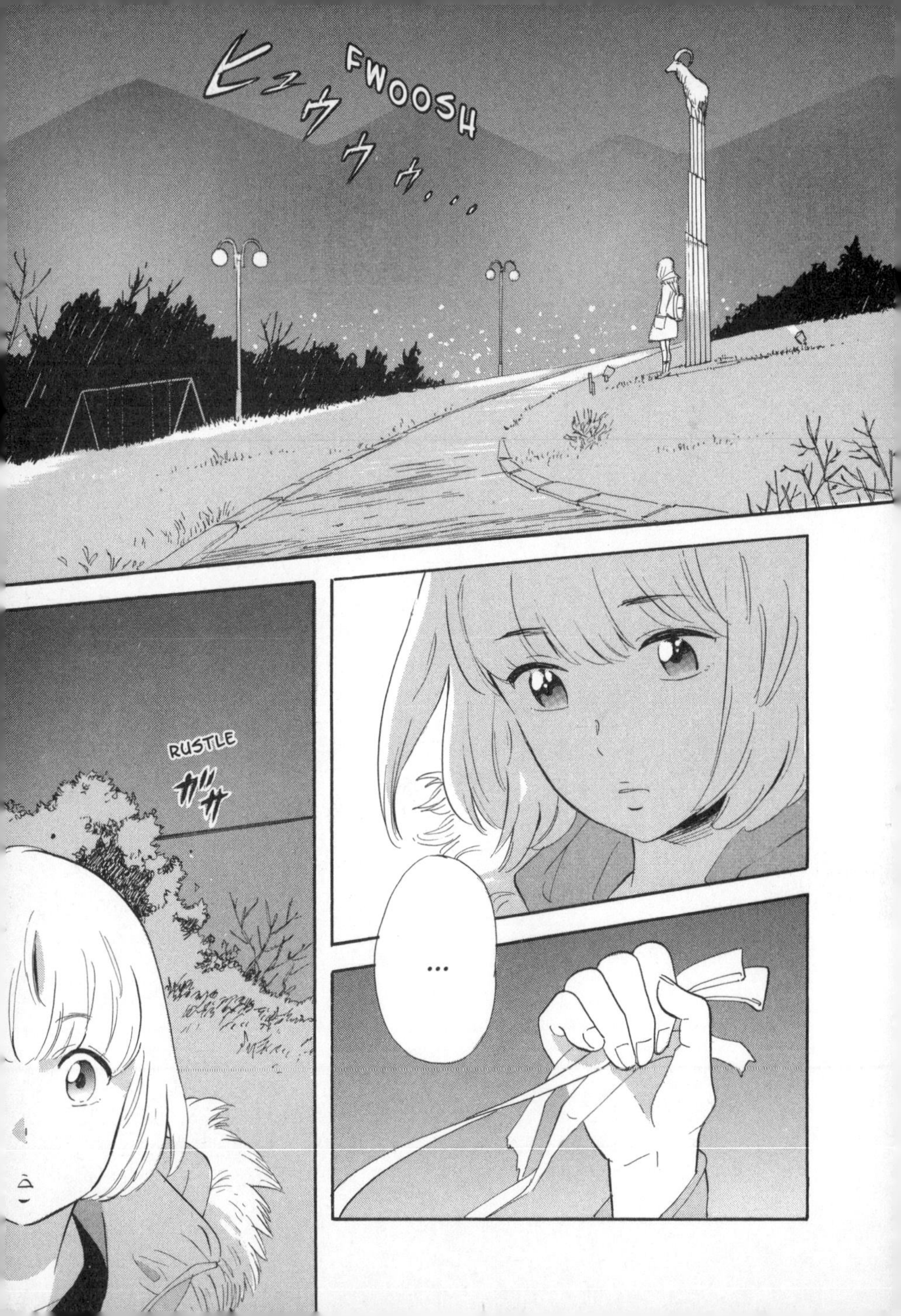
ヒュウウウ…
FWOOSH
…
ガサ
RUSTLE

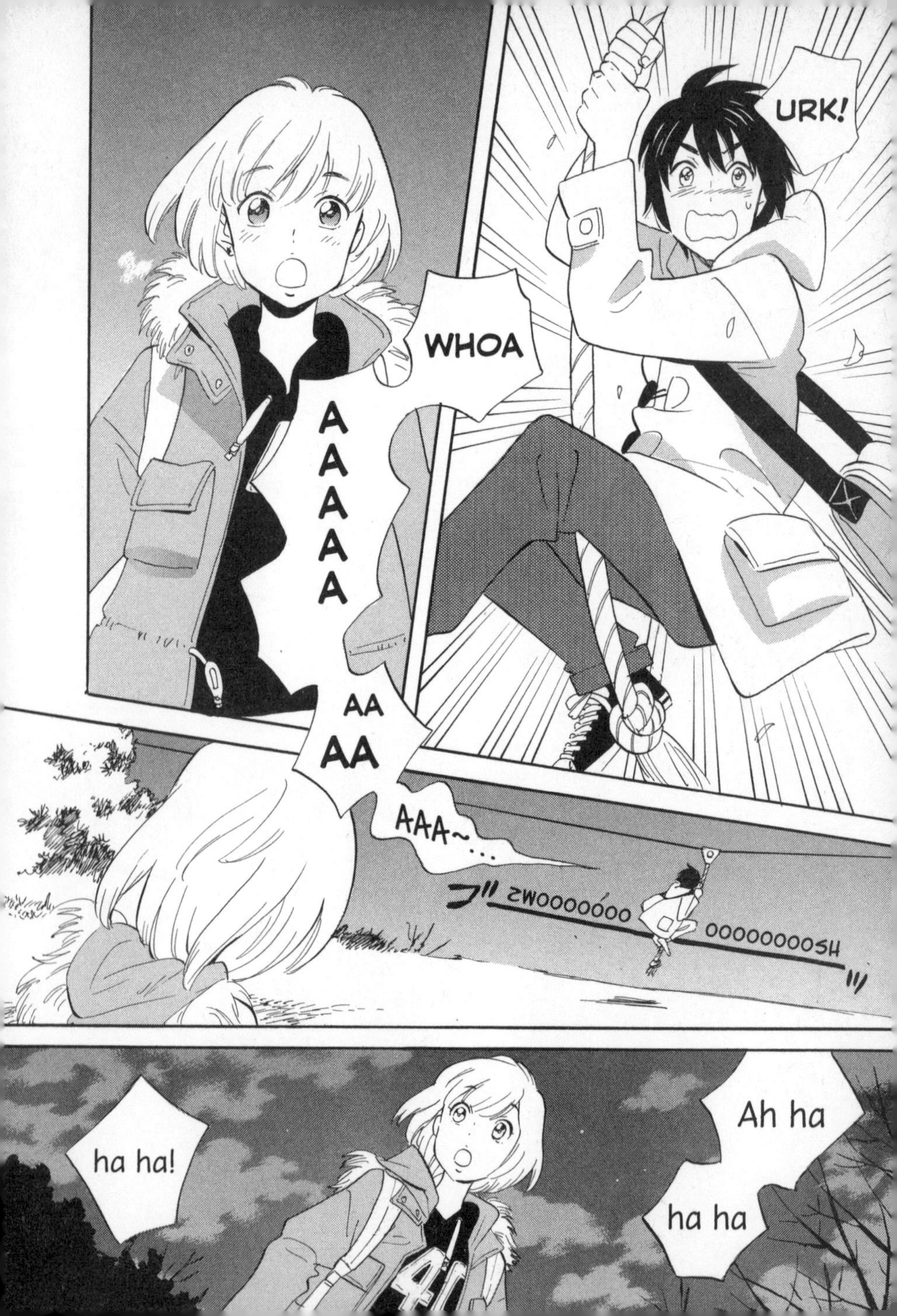
URK!
WHOA
AAAAA
AA
AA
AAA~...
ブ
ZWOOOOOOO
OOOOOOOOSH
Ah ha
ha ha
ha ha!

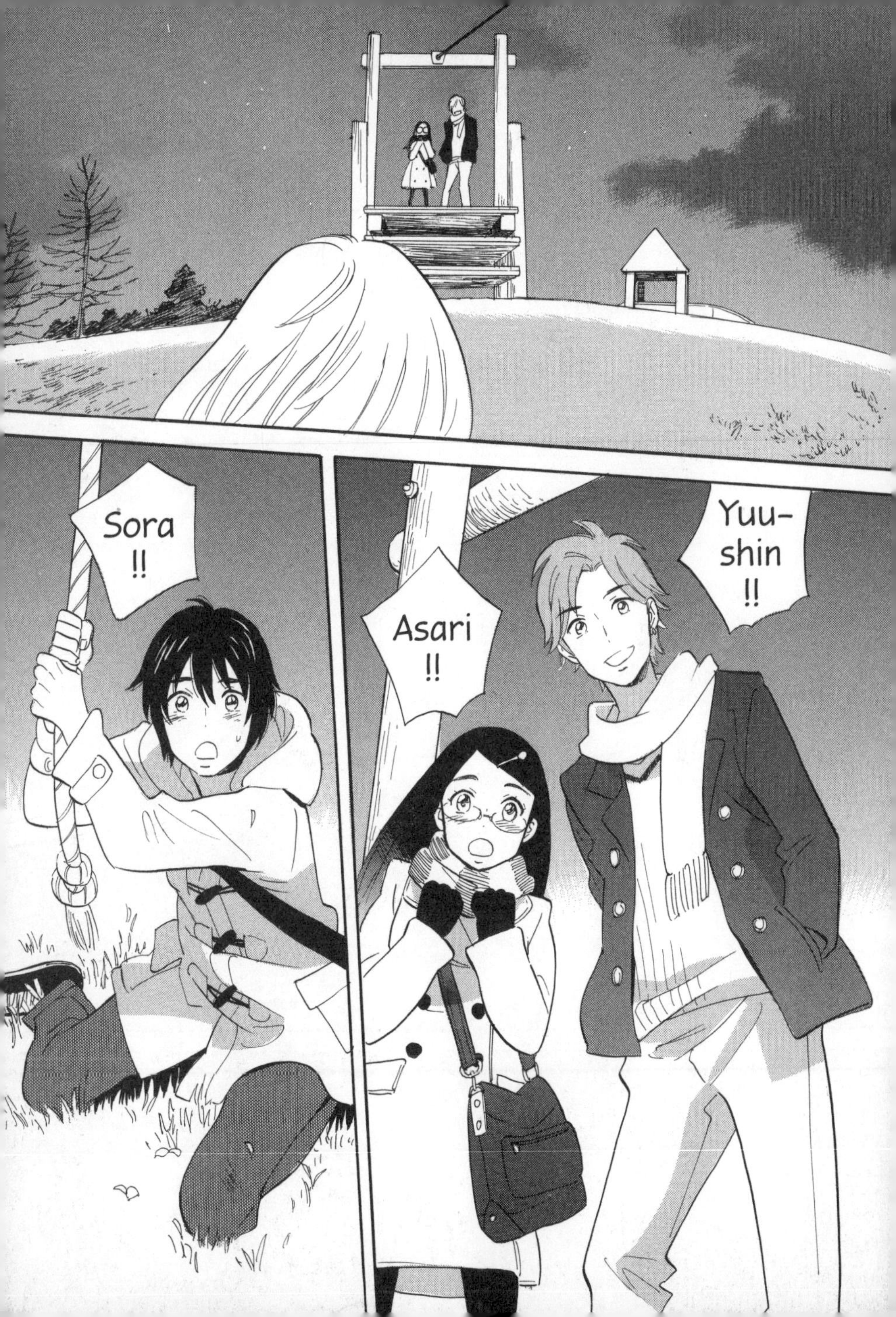
Yuu-shin!!
Asari!!
Sora!!

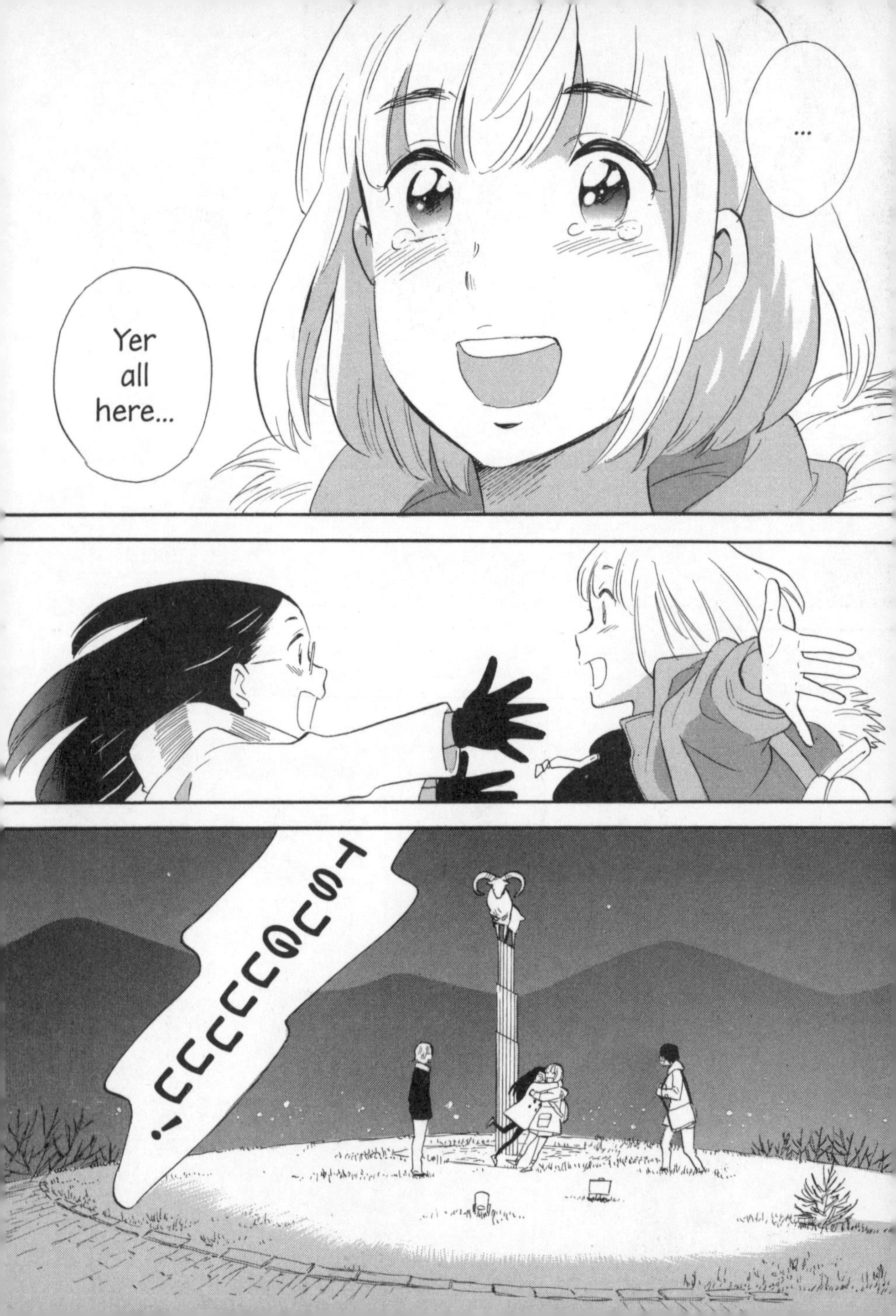
...
Yer all here...
TSUGUUUUU!

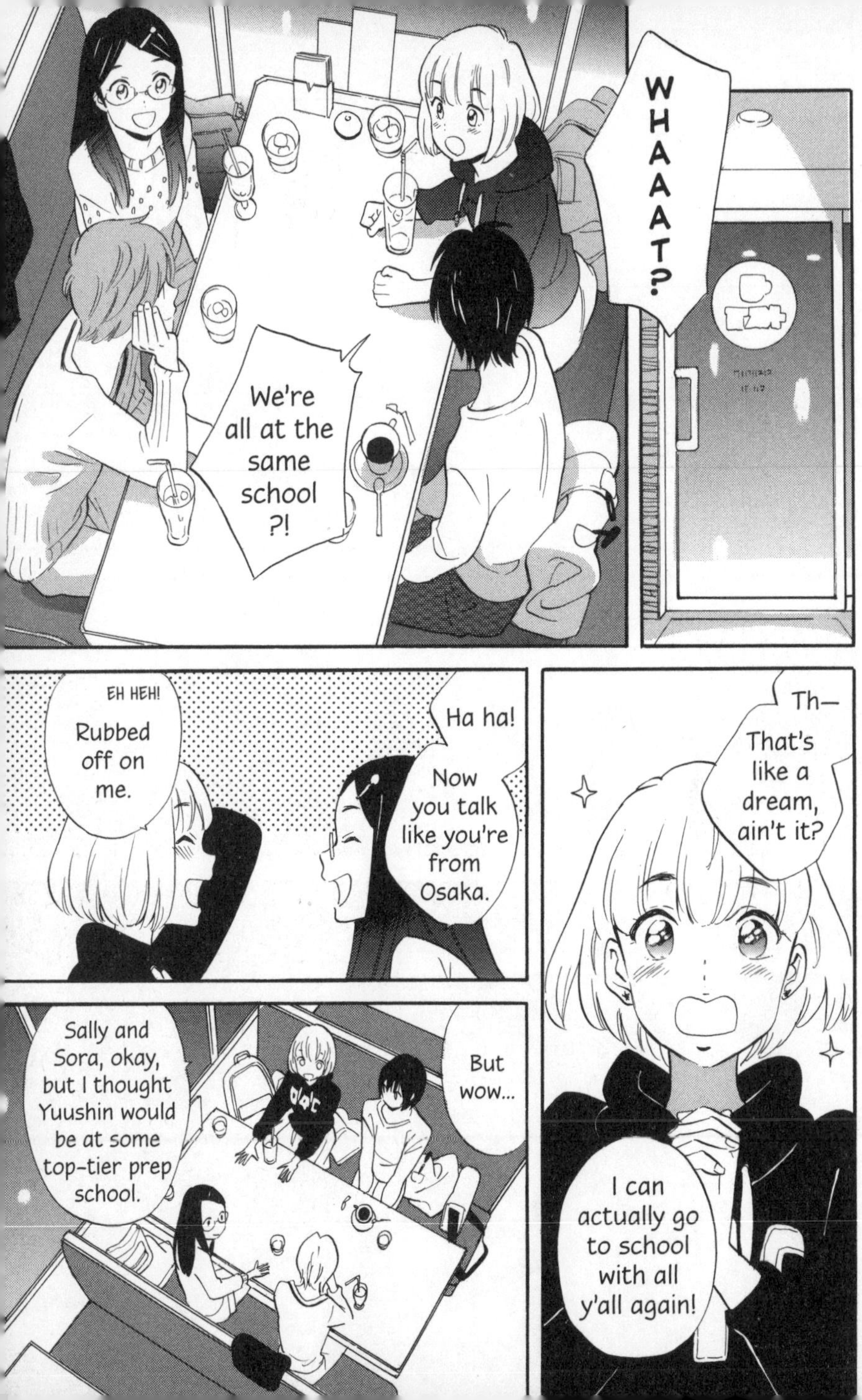
WHAAAT?
We're all at the same school ?!
Th— That's like a dream, ain't it?
I can actually go to school with all y'all again!
Ha ha!
Now you talk like you're from Osaka.
EH HEH!
Rubbed off on me.
But wow...
Sally and Sora, okay, but I thought Yuushin would be at some top-tier prep school.

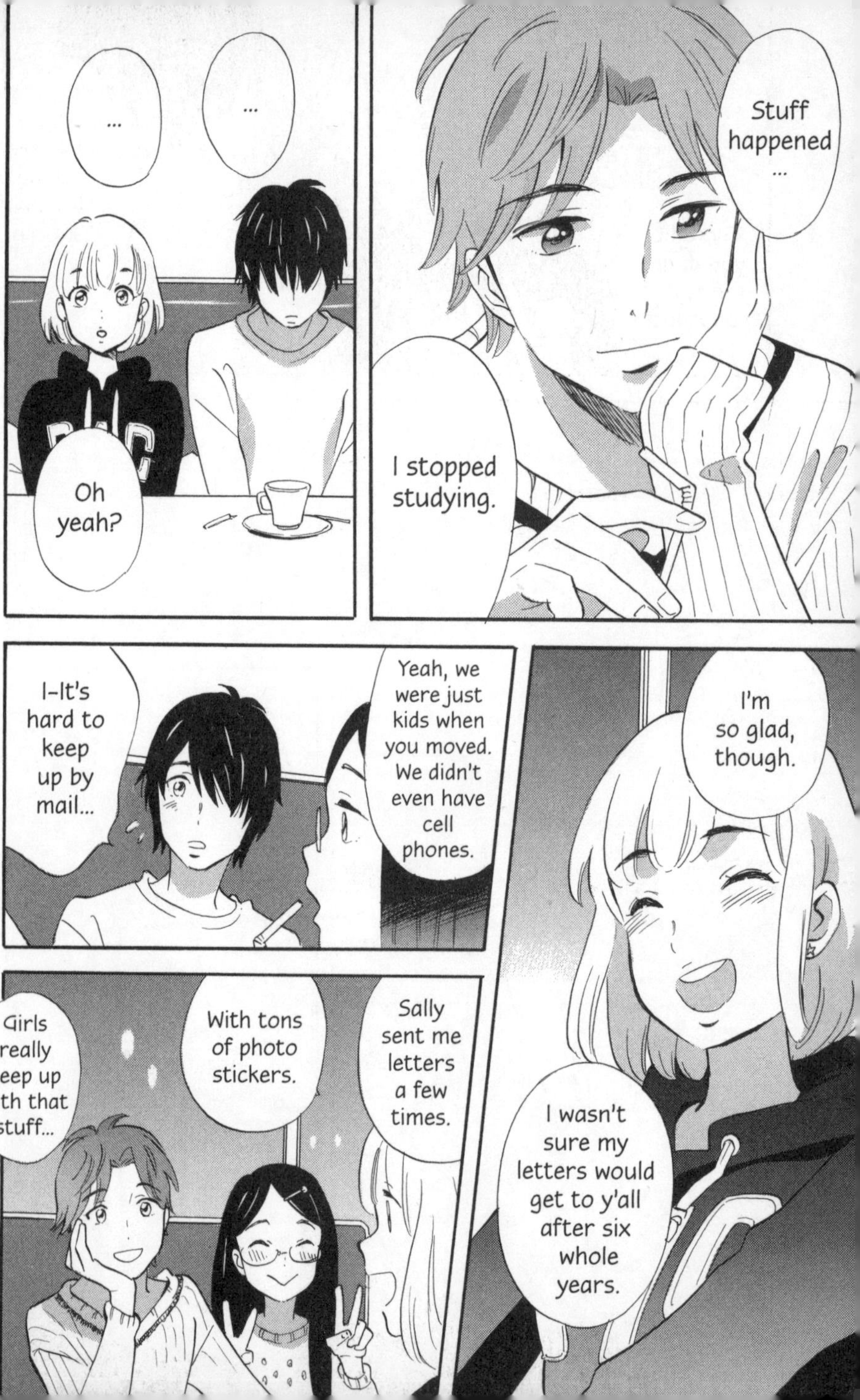
Stuff happened ...
I stopped studying.
...
...
Oh yeah?
I'm so glad, though.
I wasn't sure my letters would get to y'all after six whole years.
Yeah, we were just kids when you moved. We didn't even have cell phones.
I-It's hard to keep up by mail...
Sally sent me letters a few times.
With tons of photo stickers.
Girls really keep up with that stuff...

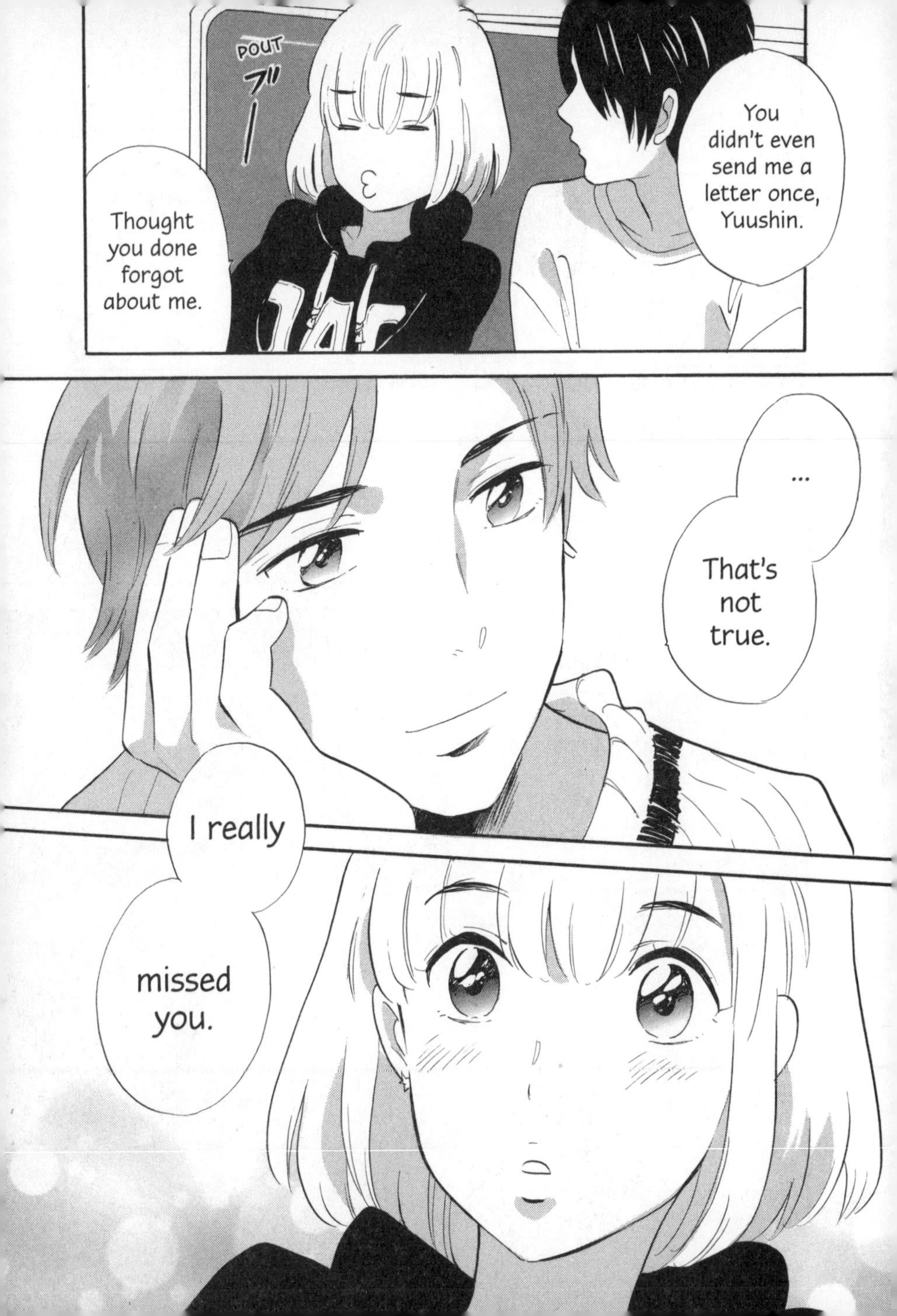
You didn't even send me a letter once, Yuushin.
POUT
ブー
Thought you done forgot about me.
...
That's not true.
I really missed you.

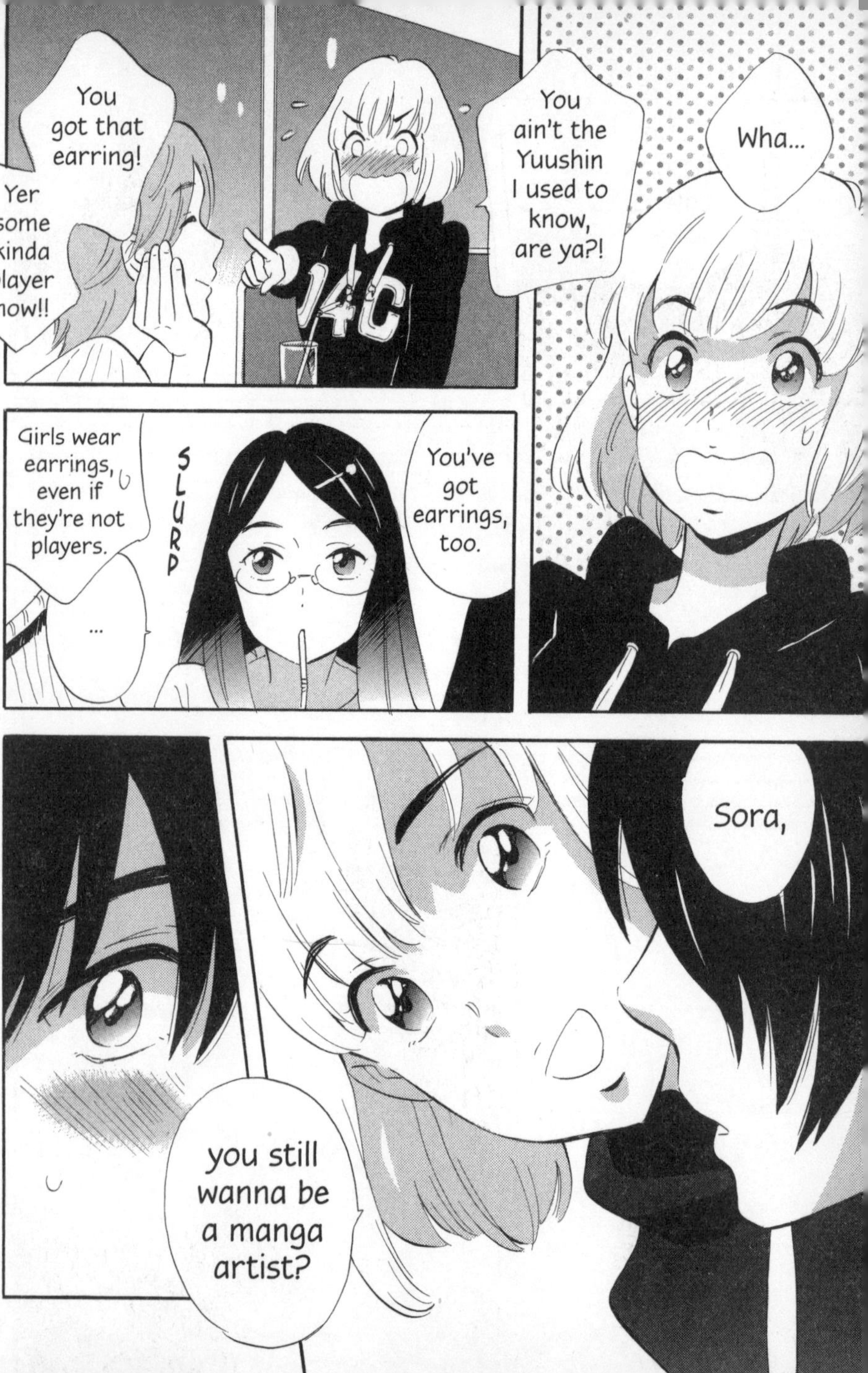
Wha...
You ain't the Yuushin I used to know, are ya?!
You got that earring!
Yer some kinda player now!!
You've got earrings, too.
SLURP
Girls wear earrings, even if they're not players.
...
Sora,
you still wanna be a manga artist?

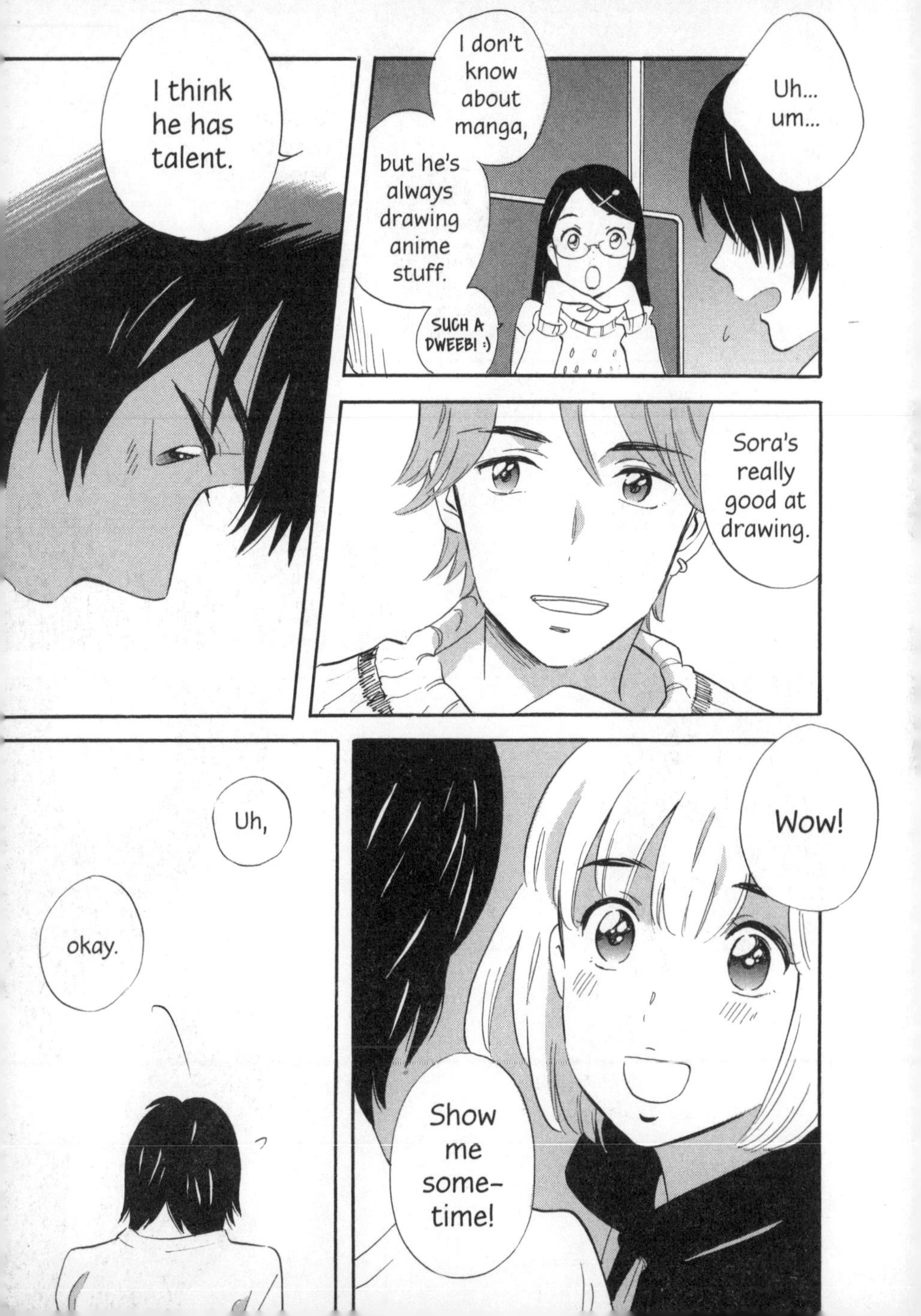
Uh... um...
I don't know about manga,
but he's always drawing anime stuff.
SUCH A DWEEB! :)
Sora's really good at drawing.
I think he has talent.
Wow!
Show me some-time!
Uh,
okay.

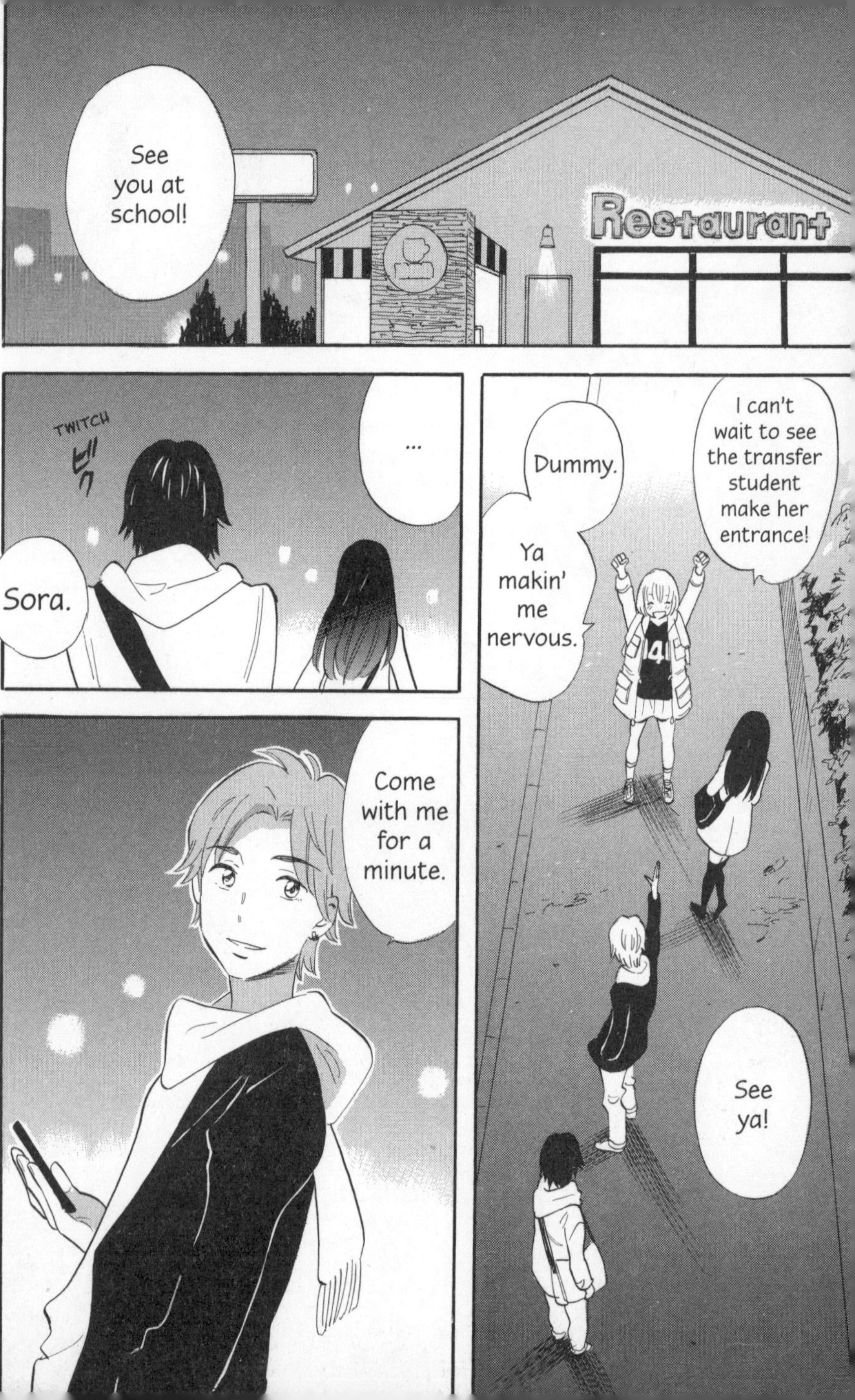
See you at school!
Restaurant
I can't wait to see the transfer student make her entrance!
Dummy.
Ya makin' me nervous.
See ya!
...
TWITCH
ビク
Sora.
Come with me for a minute.

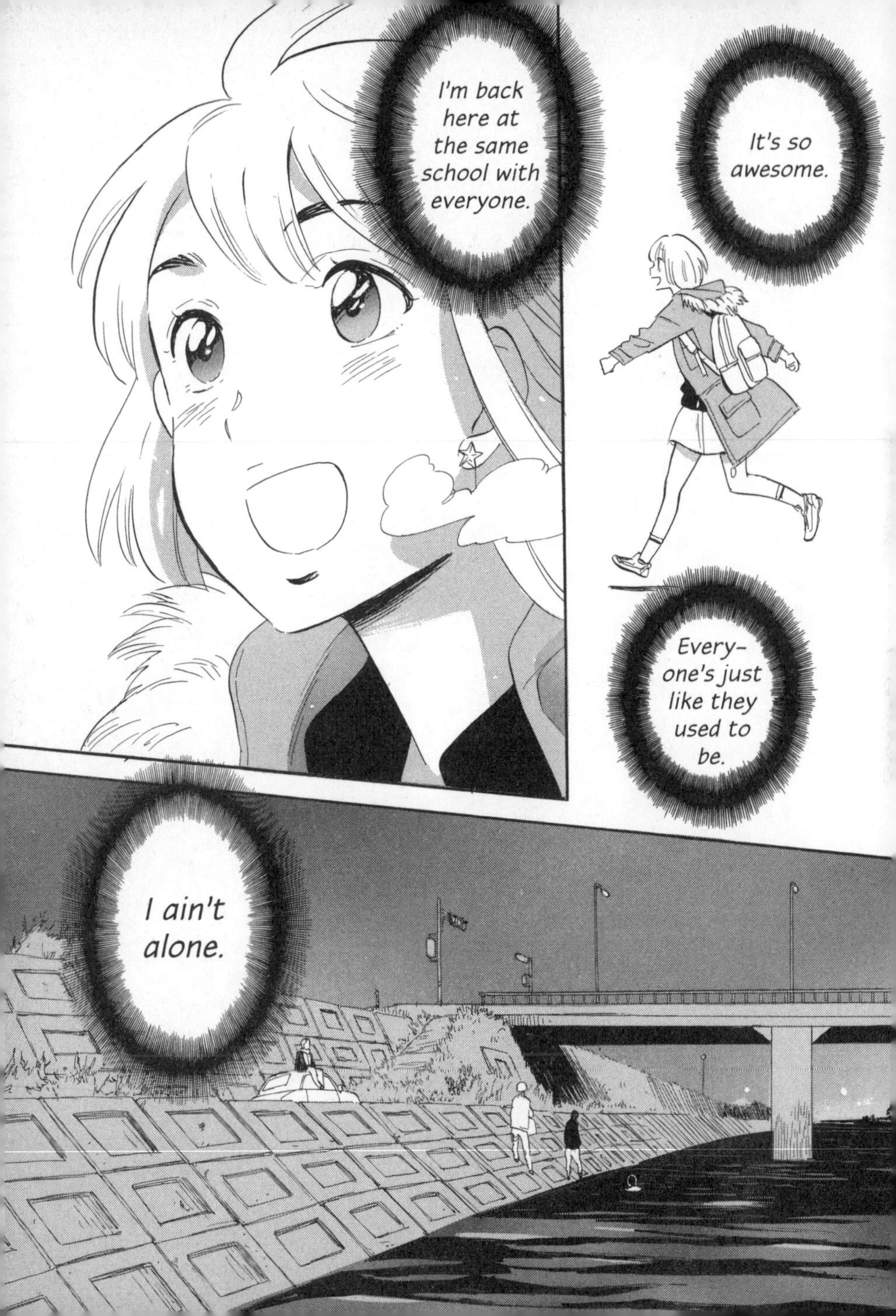
It's so awesome.
Everyone's just like they used to be.
I'm back here at the same school with everyone.
I ain't alone.

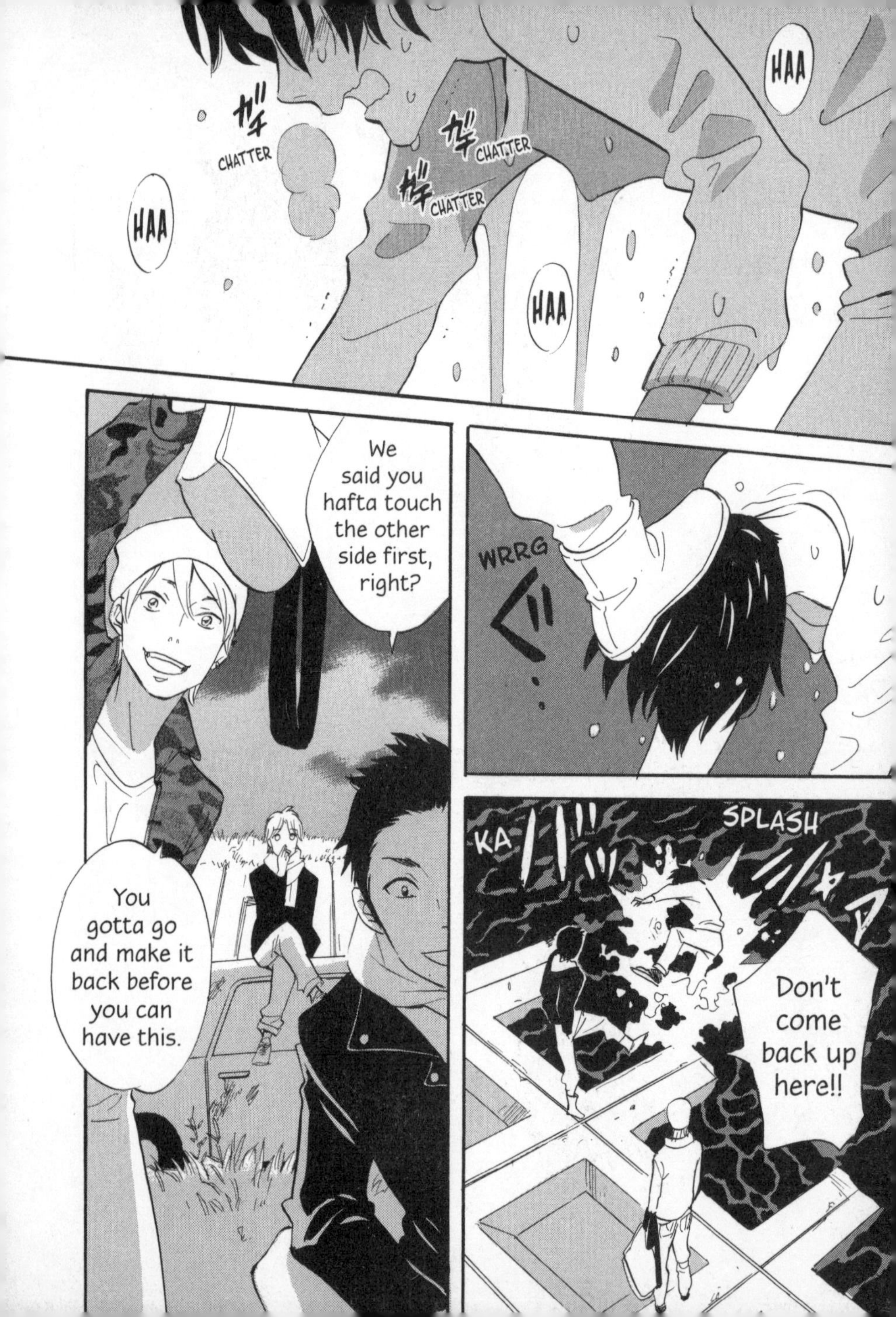
HAA
ガチ CHATTER
ガチ CHATTER
ガチ CHATTER
HAA
HAA
WRRG
KA
SPLASH
Don't come back up here!!
We said you hafta touch the other side first, right?
You gotta go and make it back before you can have this.

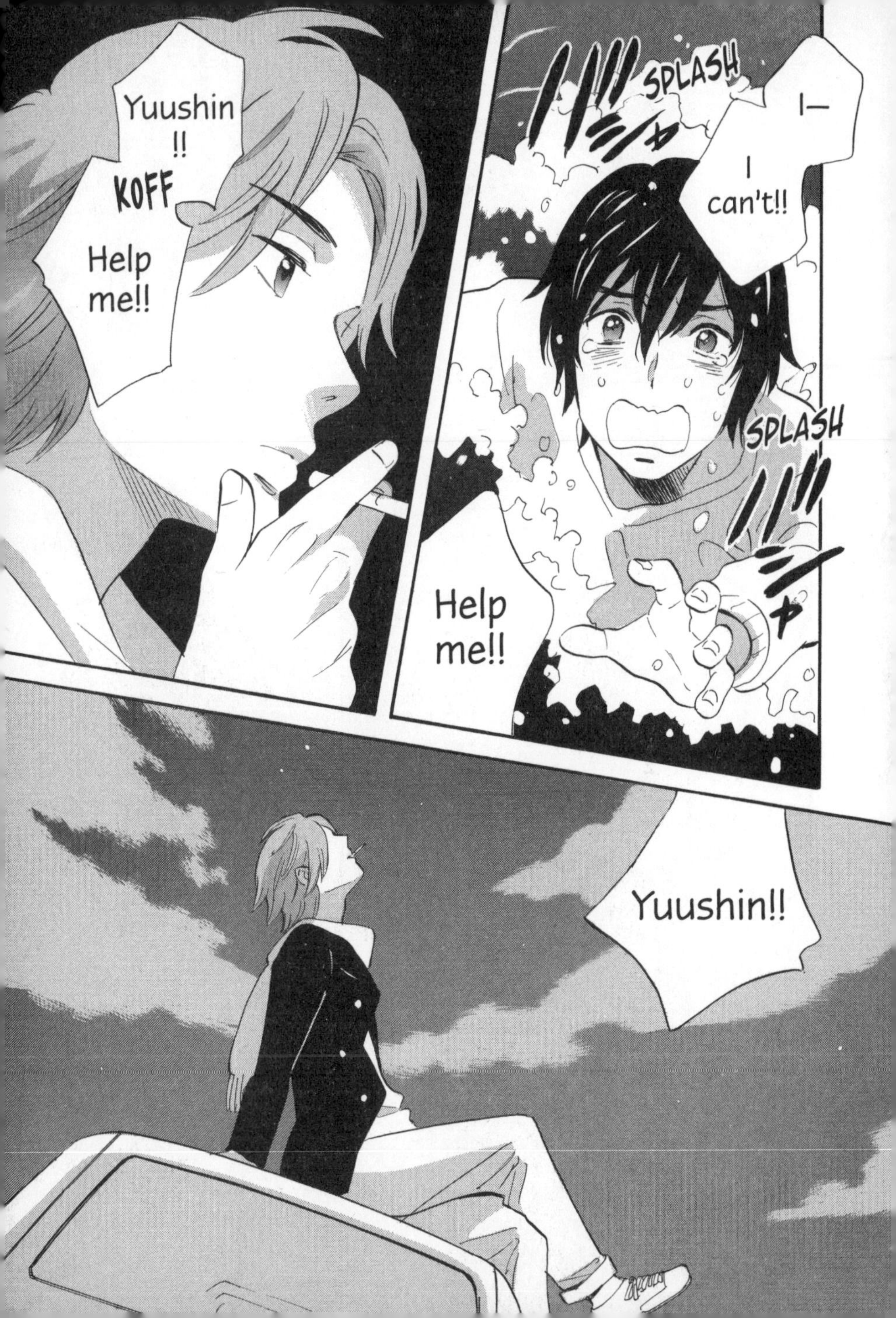
SPLASH
I— I can't!!
SPLASH
Help me!!
Yuushin !!
KOFF
Help me!!
Yuushin!!

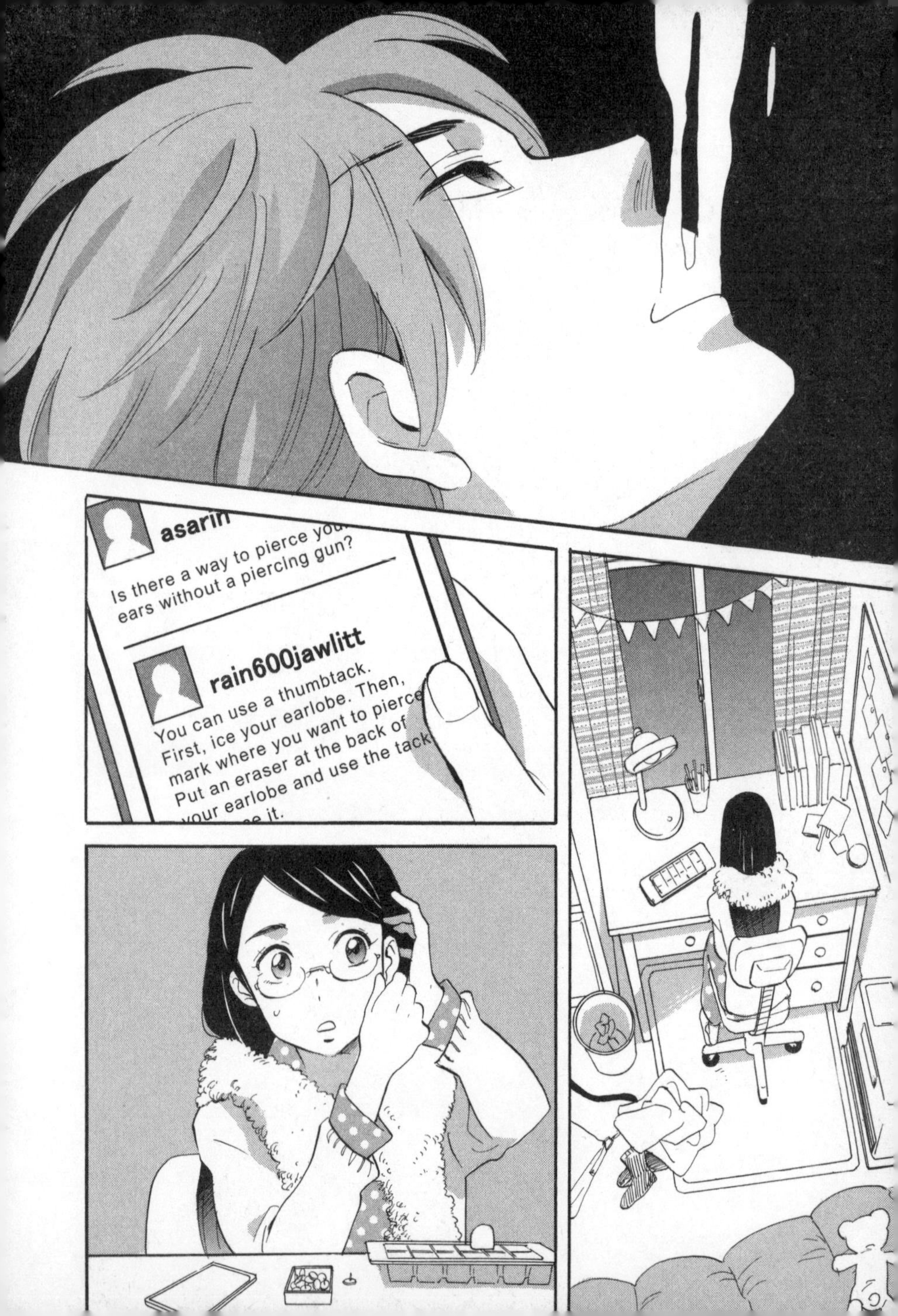
asarin
Is there a way to pierce you
ears without a piercing gun?
rain600jawlitt
You can use a thumbtack.
First, ice your earlobe. Then,
mark where you want to pierce
Put an eraser at the back of
your earlobe and use the tack

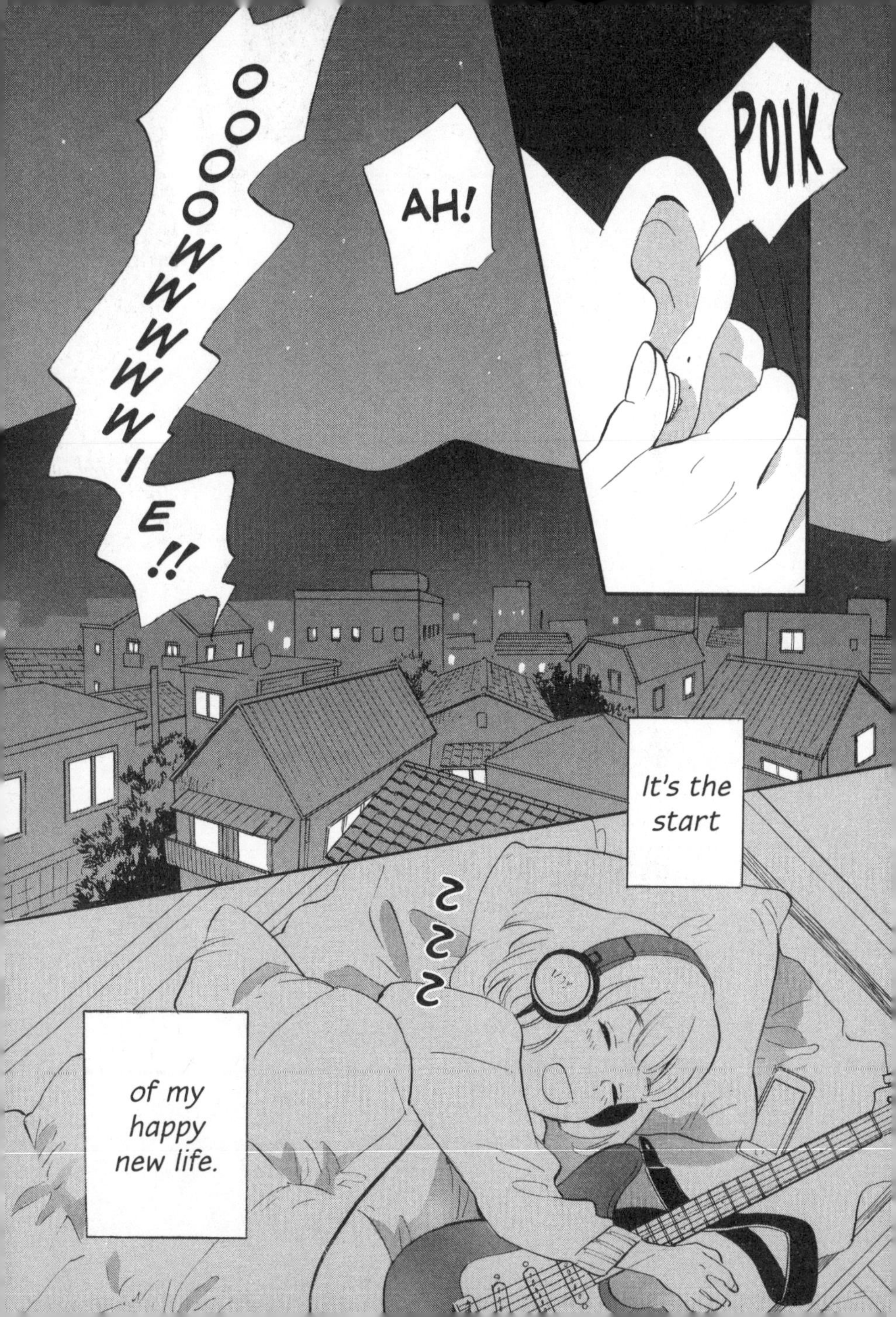
POIK
AH!
OOOOWWWWWIE!!
It's the start
ZZZ
of my happy new life.

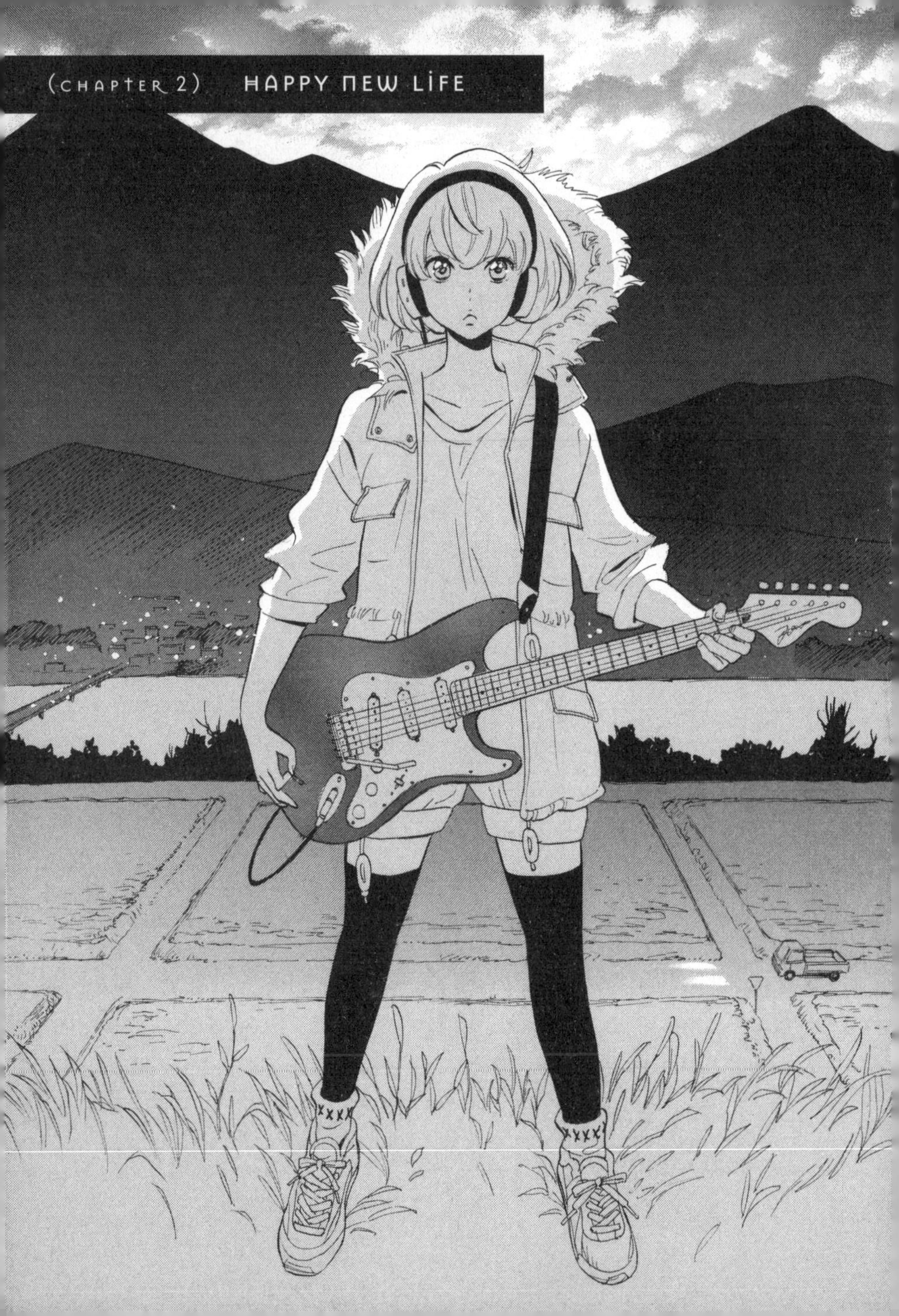
(CHAPTER 2) HAPPY NEW LIFE

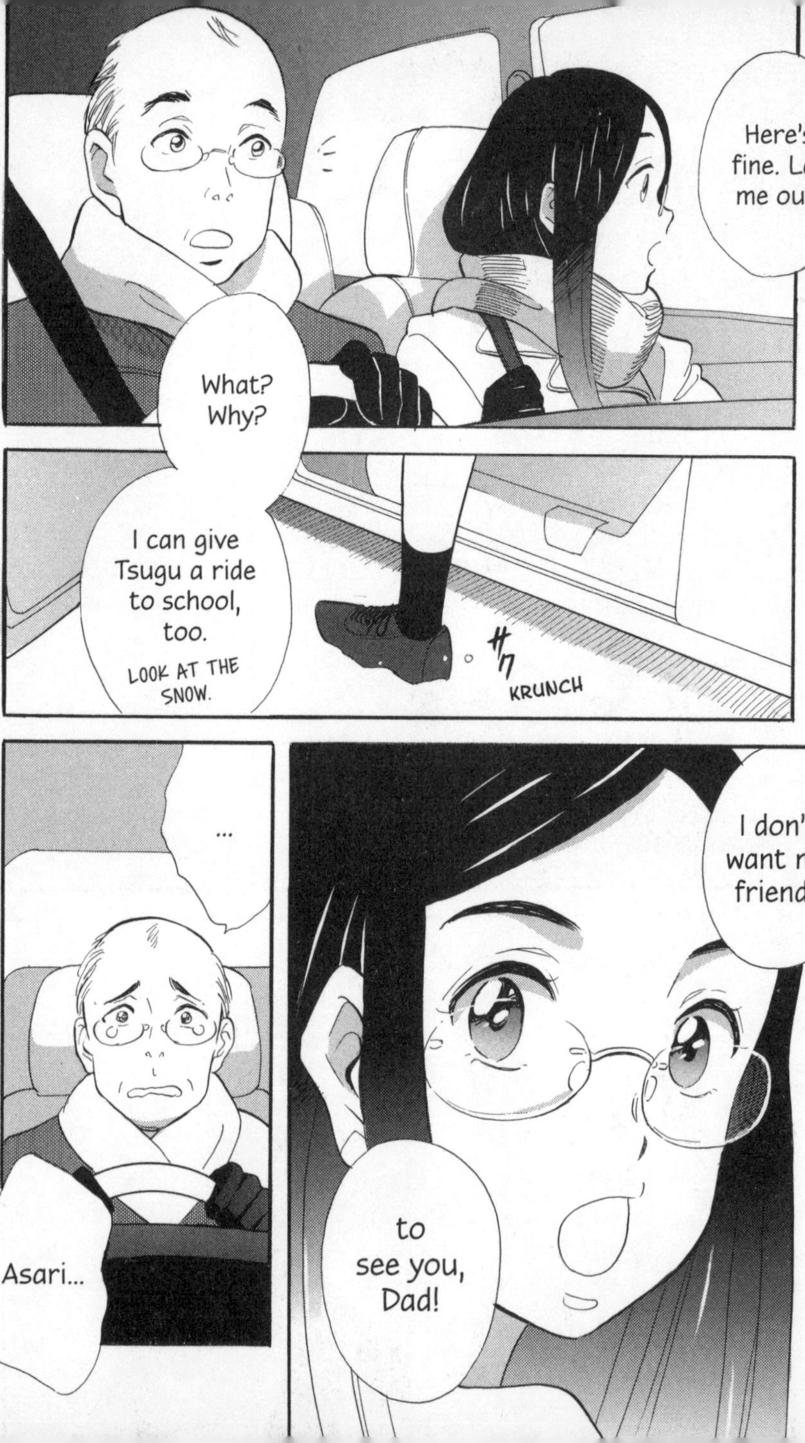
Here's fine. Let me out.
What? Why?
I can give Tsugu a ride to school, too.
LOOK AT THE SNOW.
KRUNCH
I don't want my friends
to see you, Dad!
...
Asari...

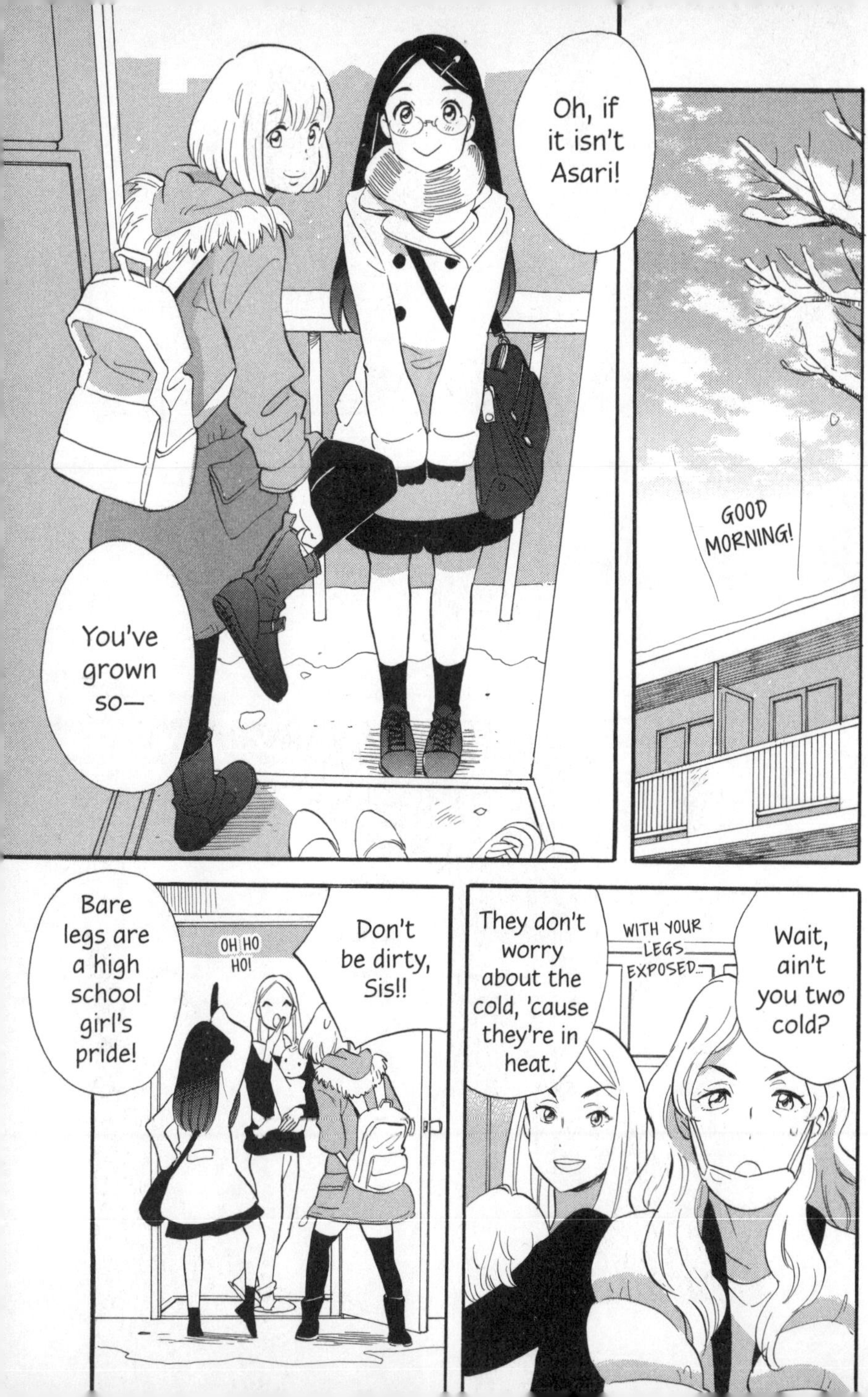
GOOD MORNING!
Oh, if it isn't Asari!
You've grown so—
Wait, ain't you two cold?
WITH YOUR LEGS EXPOSED...
They don't worry about the cold, 'cause they're in heat.
Don't be dirty, Sis!!
OH HO HO!
Bare legs are a high school girl's pride!

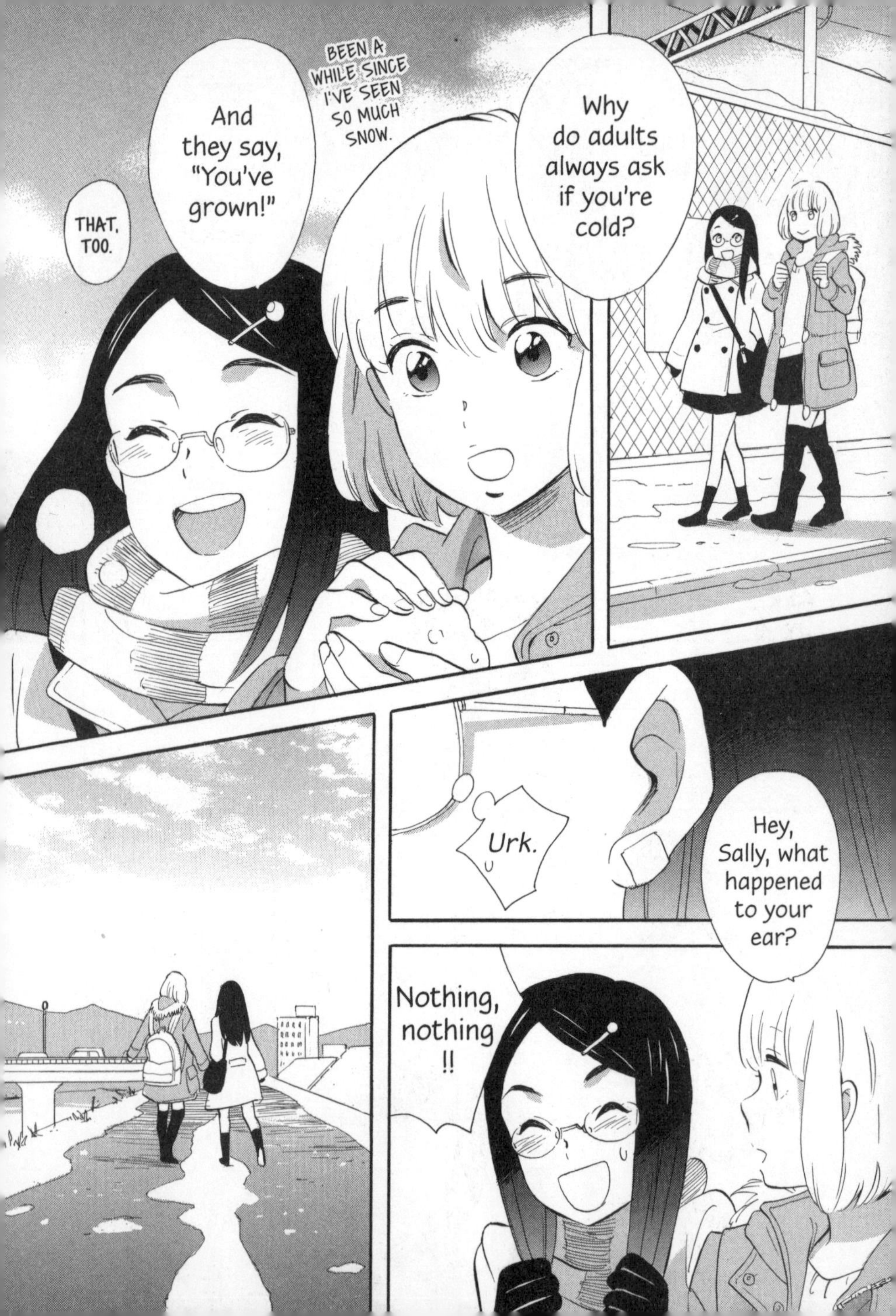

Why do adults always ask if you're cold?
BEEN A WHILE SINCE I'VE SEEN SO MUCH SNOW.
And they say, "You've grown!"
THAT, TOO.
Urk.
Hey, Sally, what happened to your ear?
Nothing, nothing !!

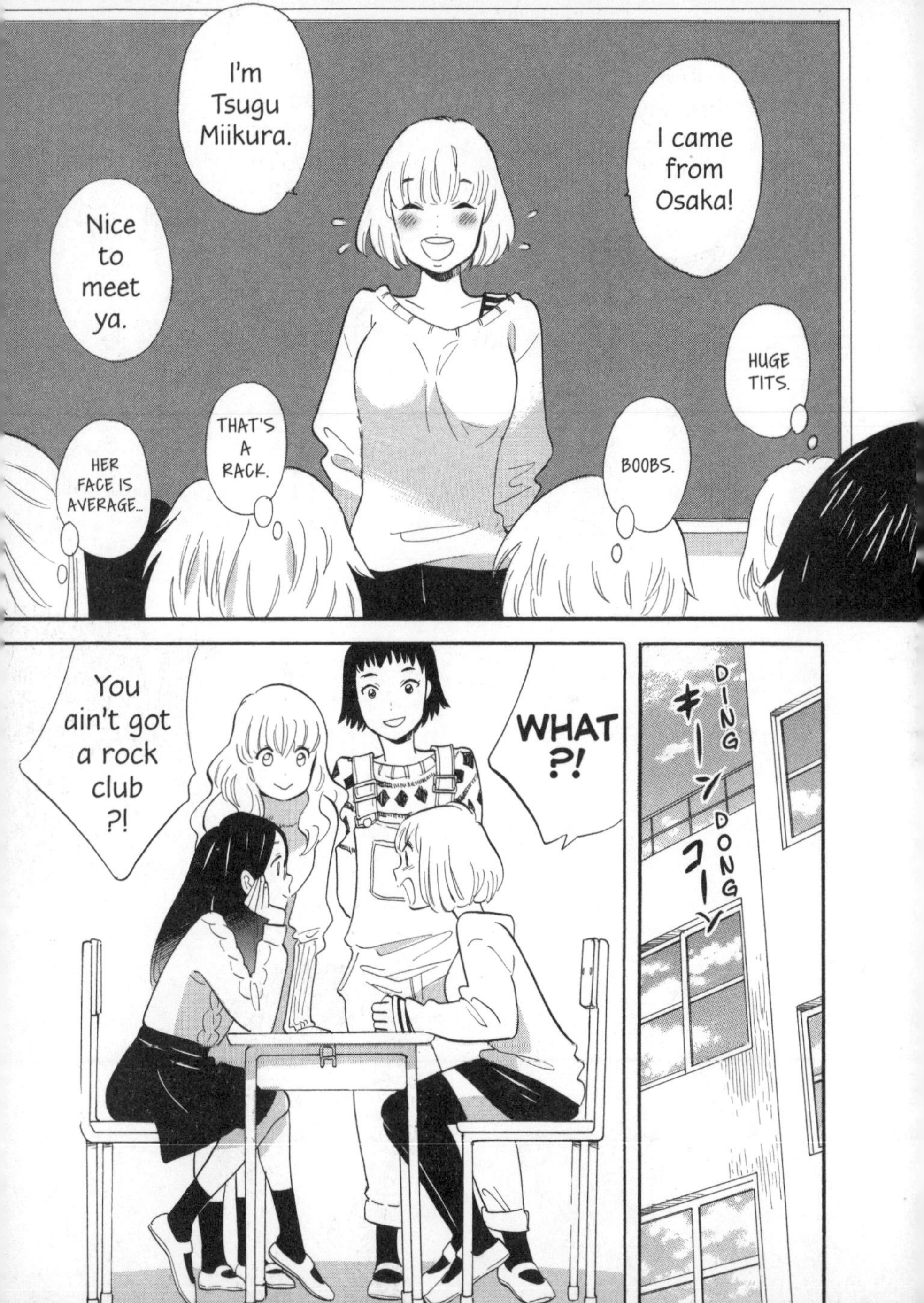
I came from Osaka!
I'm Tsugu Miikura.
Nice to meet ya.
HUGE TITS.
BOOBS.
THAT'S A RACK.
HER FACE IS AVERAGE...
DING DONG
WHAT?!
You ain't got a rock club?!

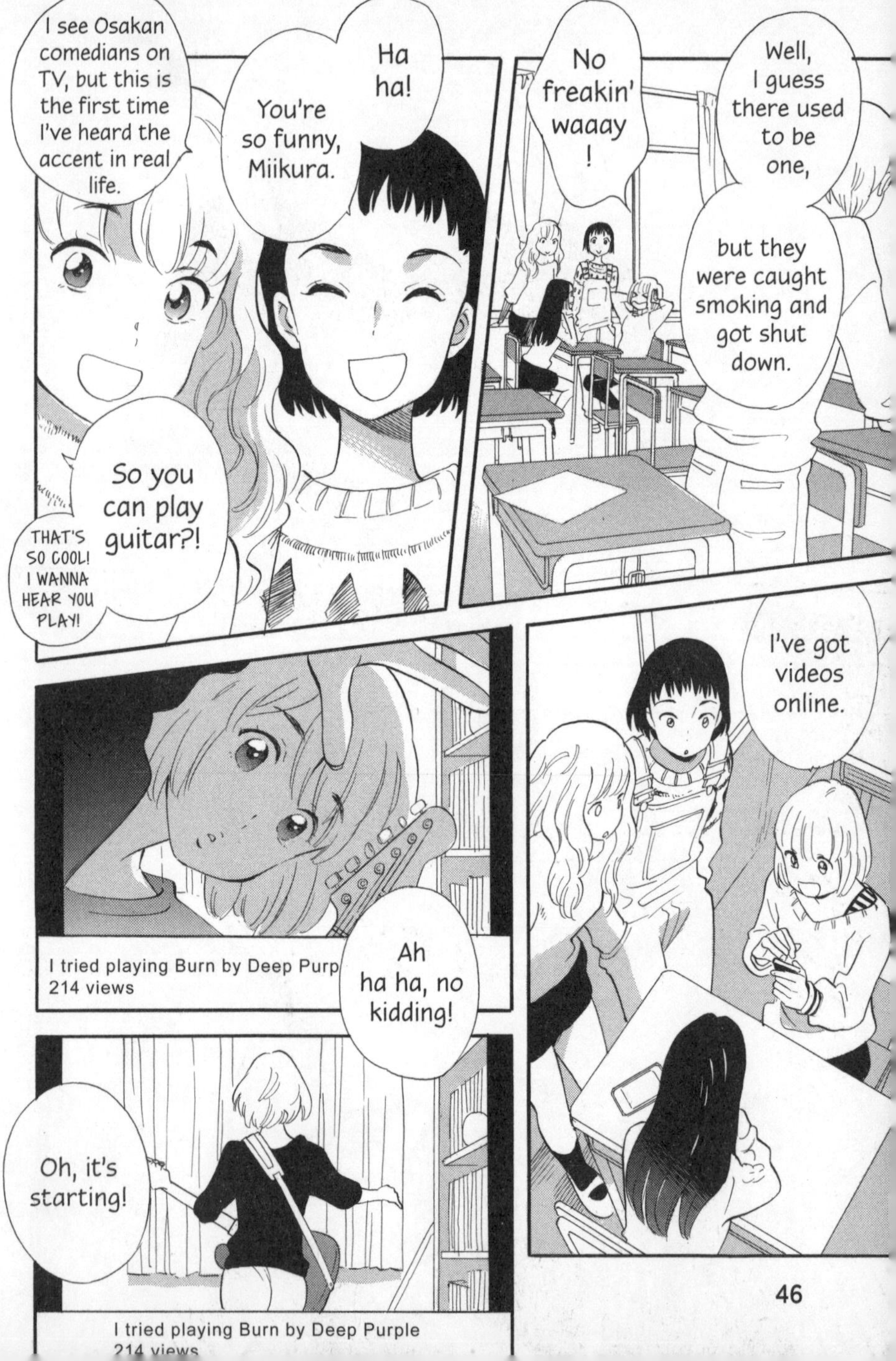
Well, I guess there used to be one,
but they were caught smoking and got shut down.
No freakin' waaay!
Ha ha!
You're so funny, Miikura.
I see Osakan comedians on TV, but this is the first time I've heard the accent in real life.
So you can play guitar?!
THAT'S SO COOL! I WANNA HEAR YOU PLAY!
I've got videos online.
I tried playing Burn by Deep Purp
214 views
Ah ha ha, no kidding!
Oh, it's starting!
I tried playing Burn by Deep Purple
214 views

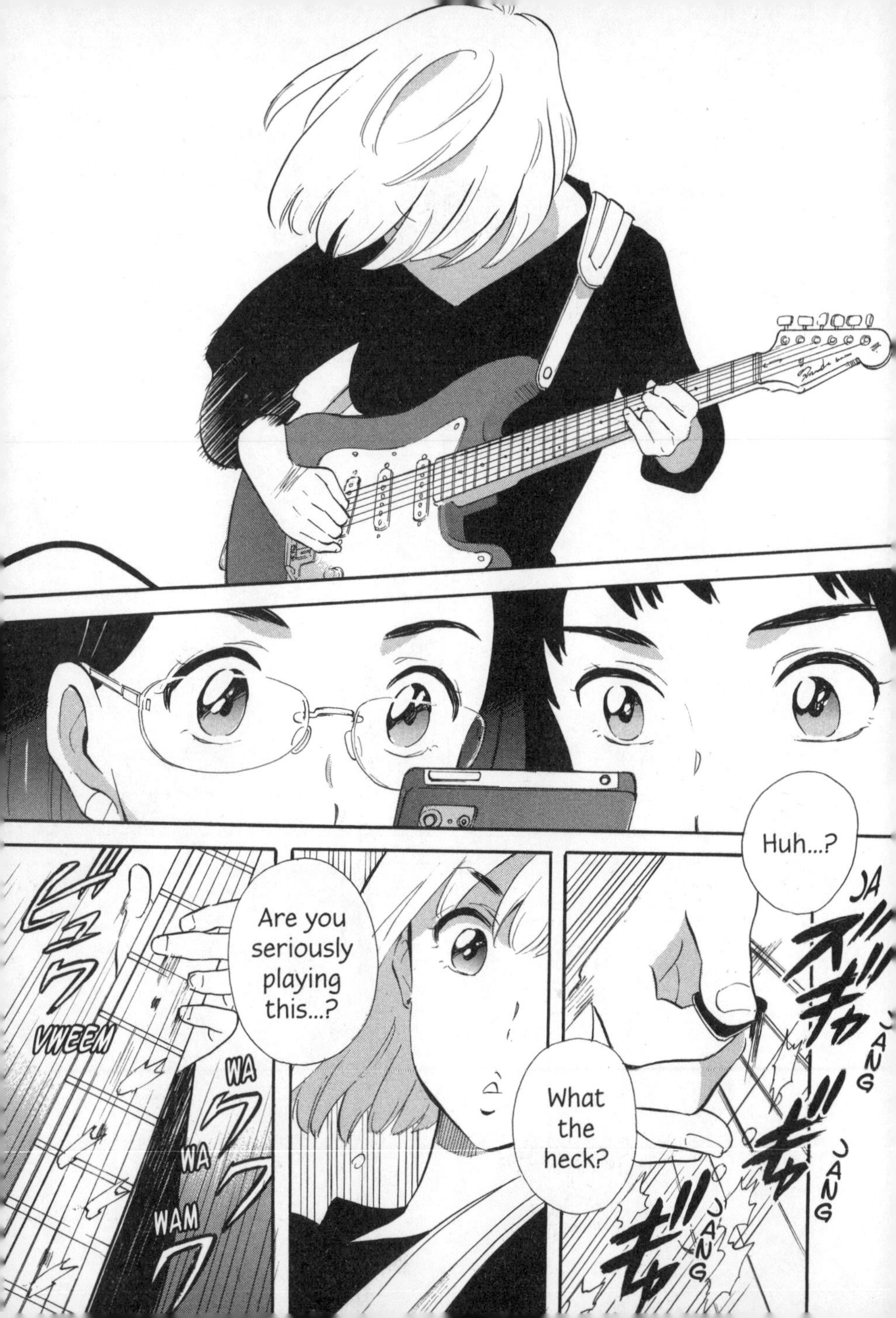

Huh...?
JA
JANG
JANG
JANG
JANG
Are you seriously playing this...?
What the heck?
VWEEM
WA
WA
WAM

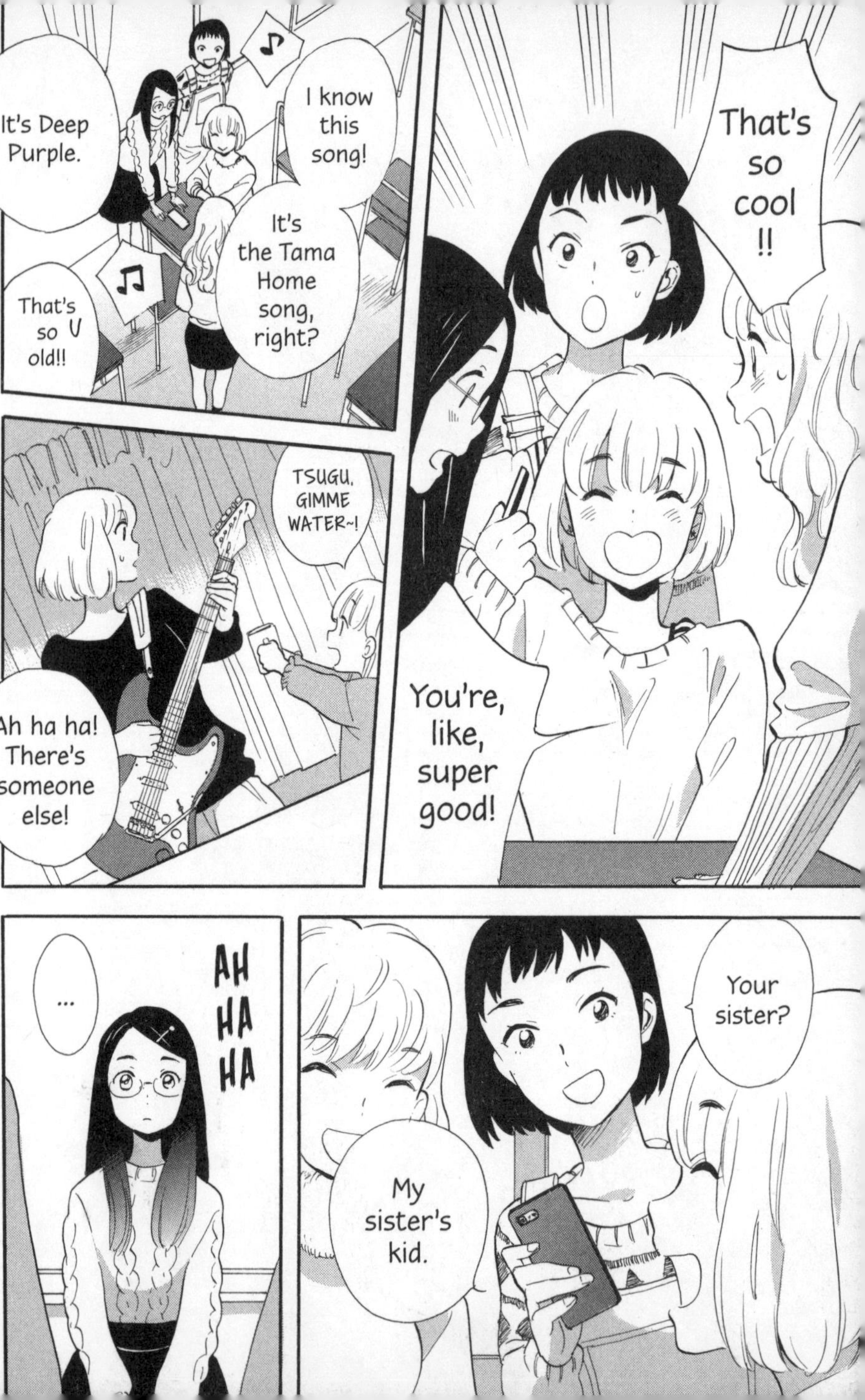
That's so cool!!
You're, like, super good!
I know this song!
It's Deep Purple.
It's the Tama Home song, right?
That's so old!!
TSUGU, GIMME WATER~!
Ah ha ha! There's someone else!
Your sister?
My sister's kid.
...
AH HA HA

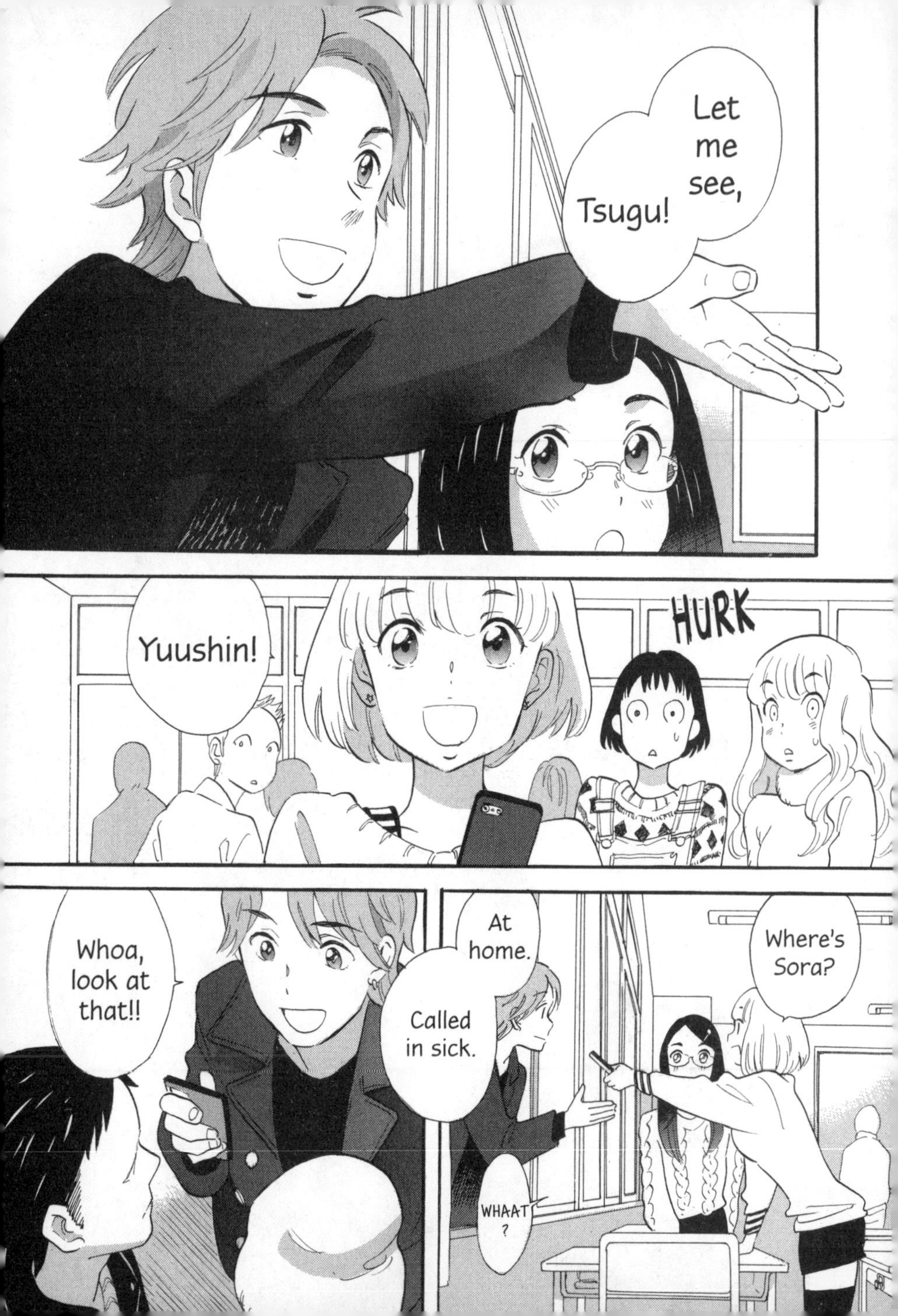
Let me see, Tsugu!
HURK
Yuushin!
Where's Sora?
At home.
Called in sick.
WHAAT ?
Whoa, look at that!!

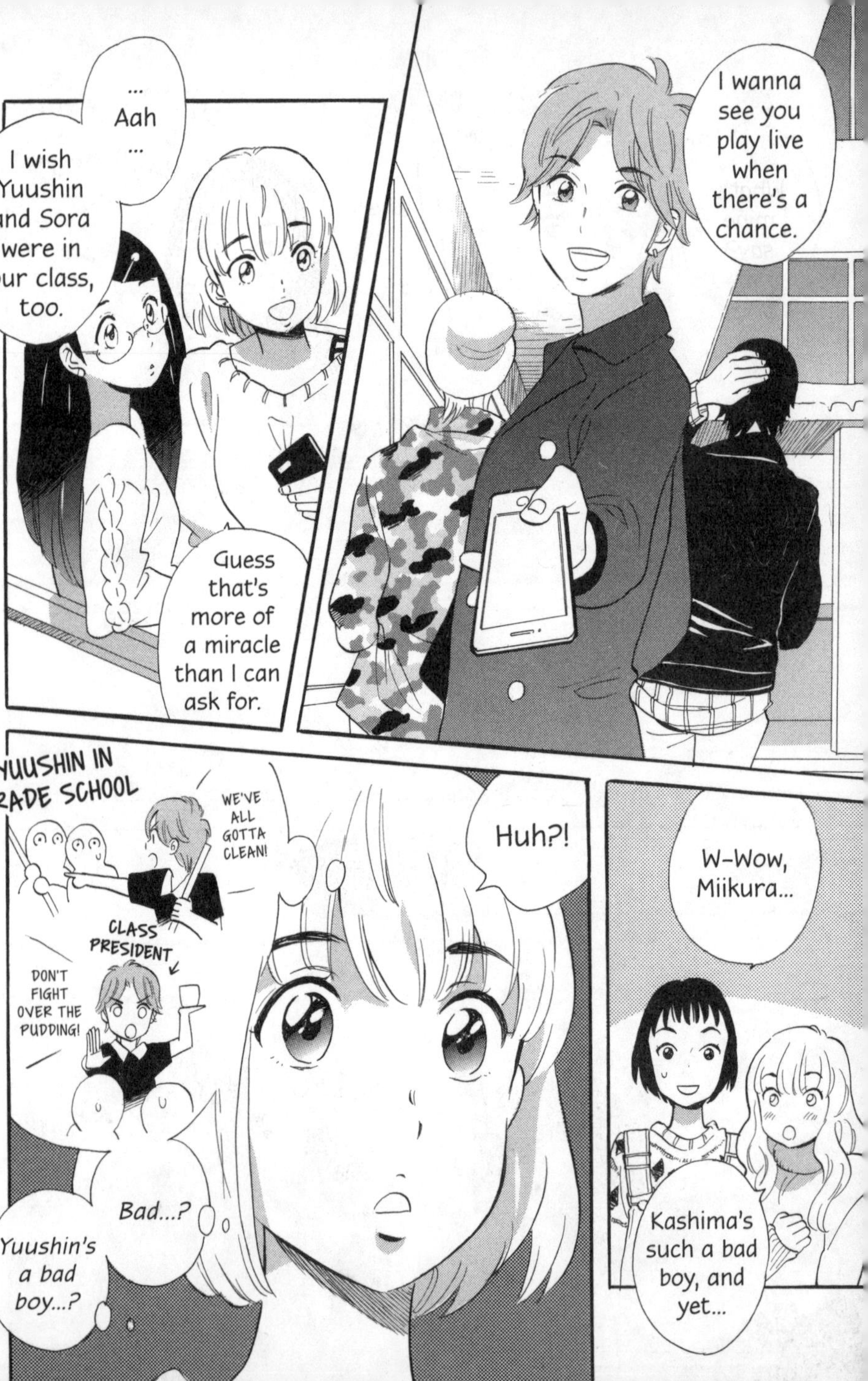
I wanna see you play live when there's a chance.
... Aah ...
I wish Yuushin and Sora were in our class, too.
Guess that's more of a miracle than I can ask for.
W-Wow, Miikura...
Kashima's such a bad boy, and yet...
Huh?!
YUUSHIN IN GRADE SCHOOL
WE'VE ALL GOTTA CLEAN!
CLASS PRESIDENT
DON'T FIGHT OVER THE PUDDING!
Bad...?
Yuushin's a bad boy...?

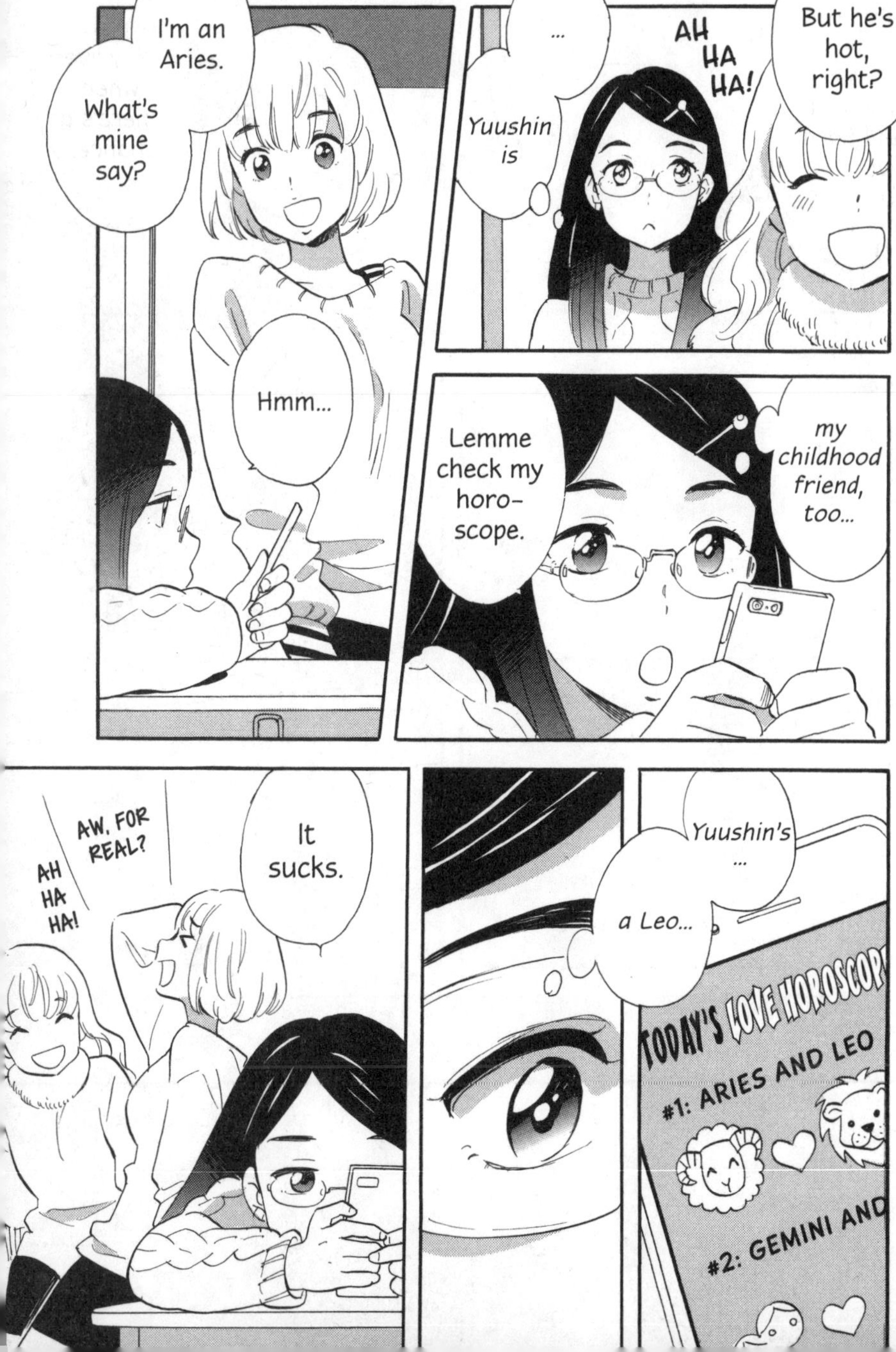
But he's hot, right?
AH HA HA!
...
Yuushin is
my childhood friend, too...
Lemme check my horoscope.
I'm an Aries.
What's mine say?
Hmm...
Yuushin's...
a Leo...
TODAY'S LOVE HOROSCOP
#1: ARIES AND LEO
#2: GEMINI AND
It sucks.
AW, FOR REAL?
AH HA HA!

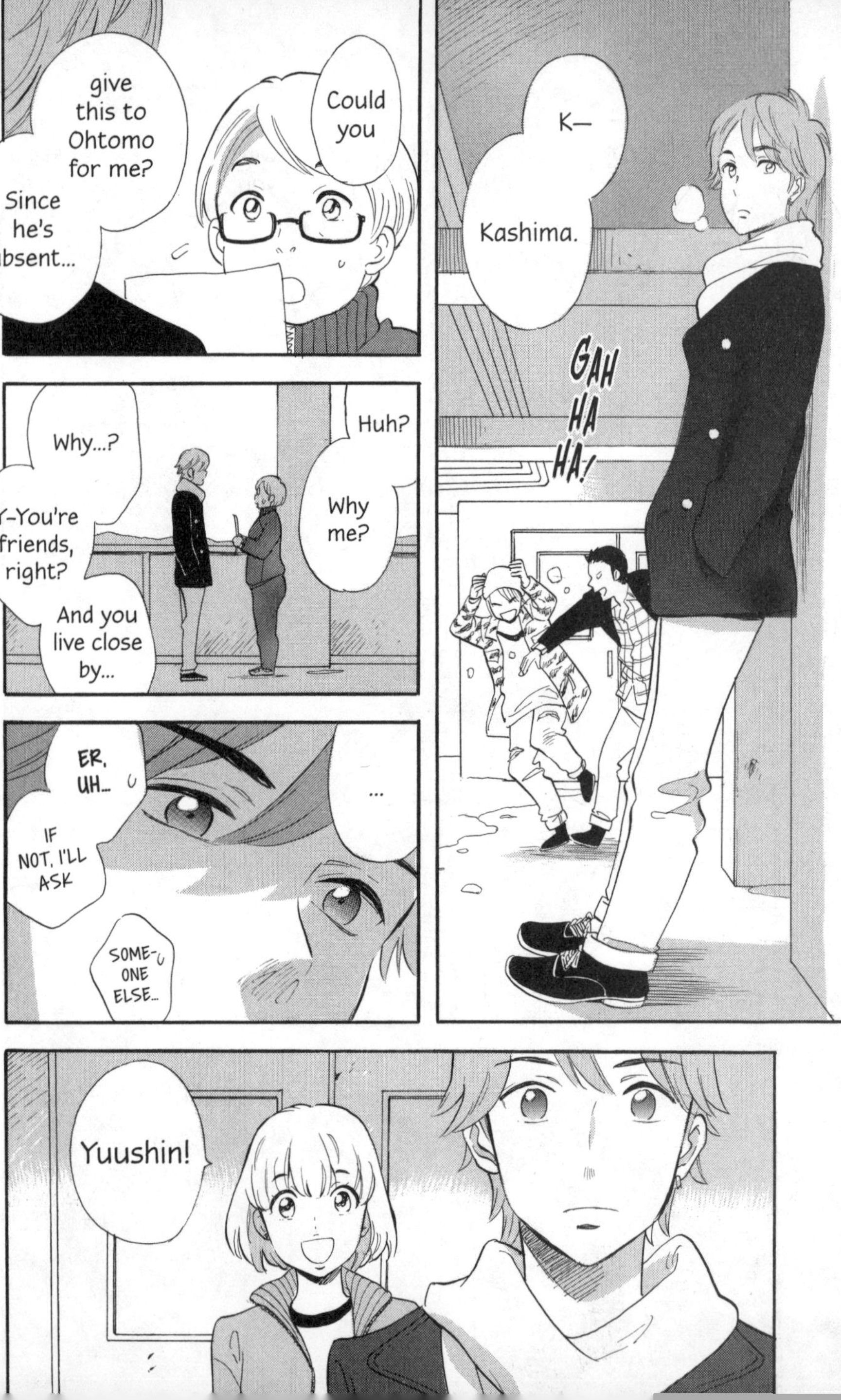
K—
Kashima.
GAH HA HA!
Could you
give this to Ohtomo for me?
Since he's absent...
Huh?
Why me?
Why...?
Y-You're friends, right?
And you live close by...
...
ER, UH...
IF NOT, I'LL ASK
SOME-ONE ELSE...
Yuushin!

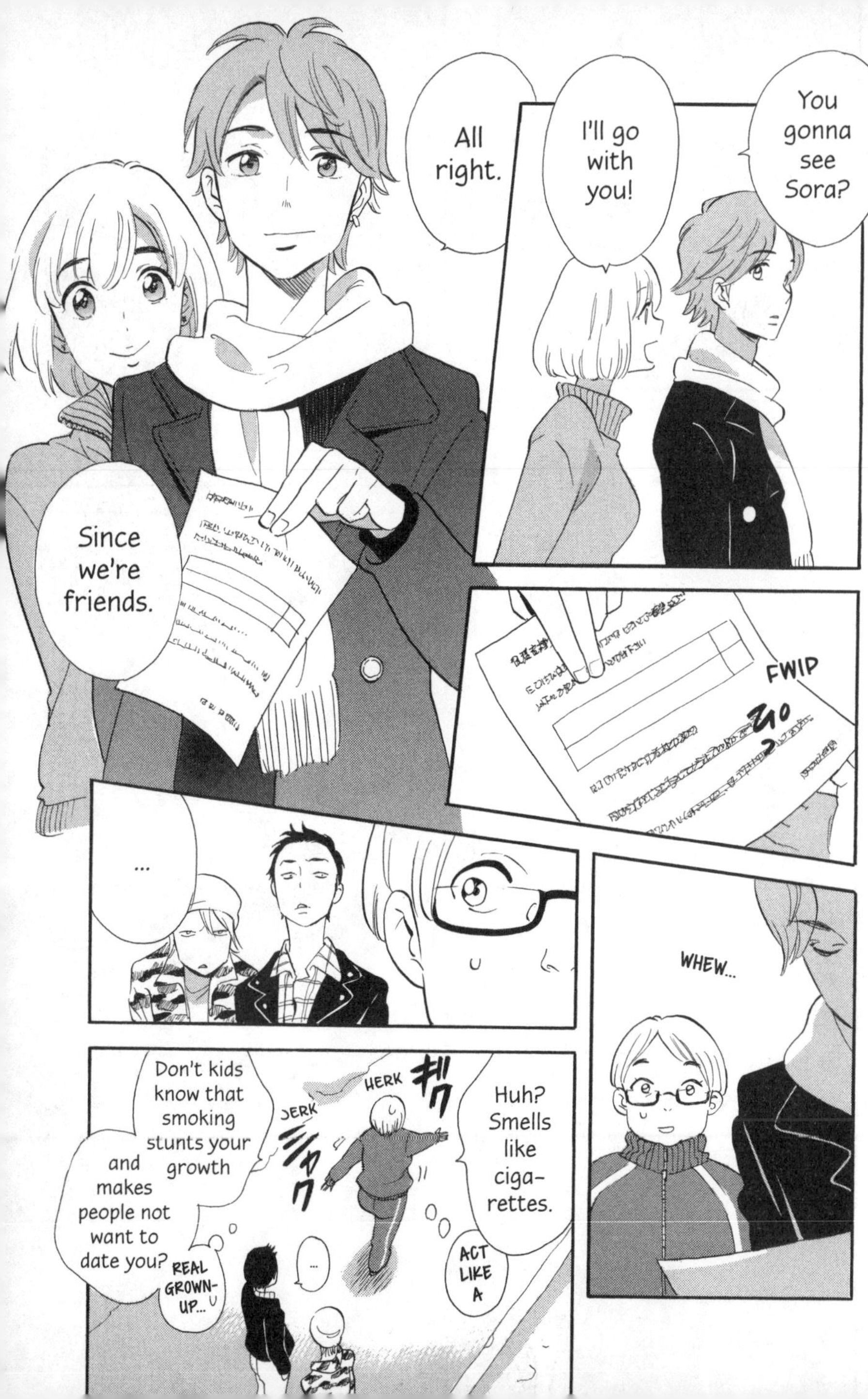
You gonna see Sora?
I'll go with you!
All right.
Since we're friends.
FWIP
WHEW...
...
Huh? Smells like ciga-rettes.
HERK
JERK
Don't kids know that smoking stunts your growth and makes people not want to date you?
...
ACT LIKE A
REAL GROWN-UP...

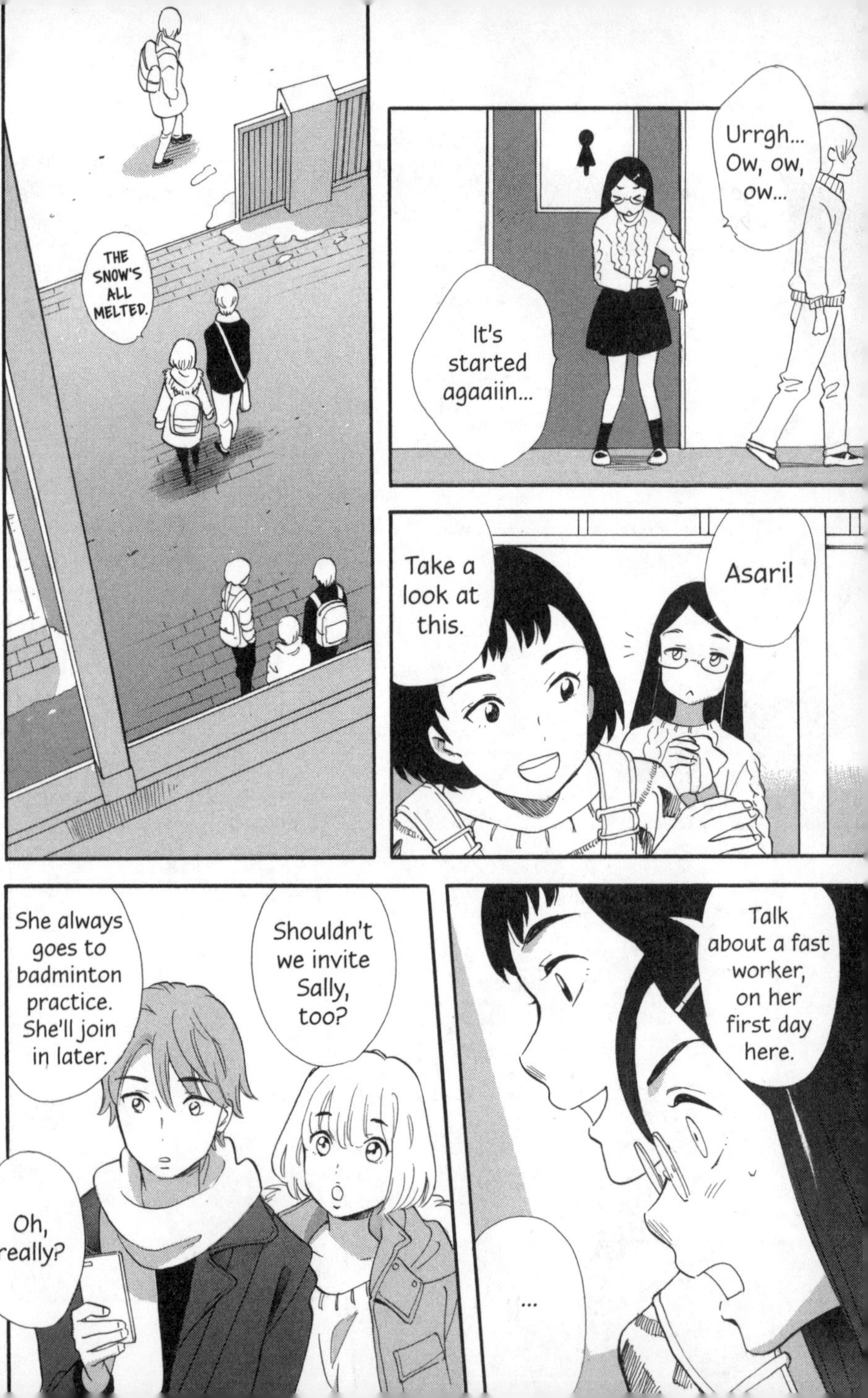

Urrgh... Ow, ow, ow...
It's started agaaiin...
Asari!
Take a look at this.
THE SNOW'S ALL MELTED.
Talk about a fast worker, on her first day here.
...
Shouldn't we invite Sally, too?
She always goes to badminton practice. She'll join in later.
Oh, really?

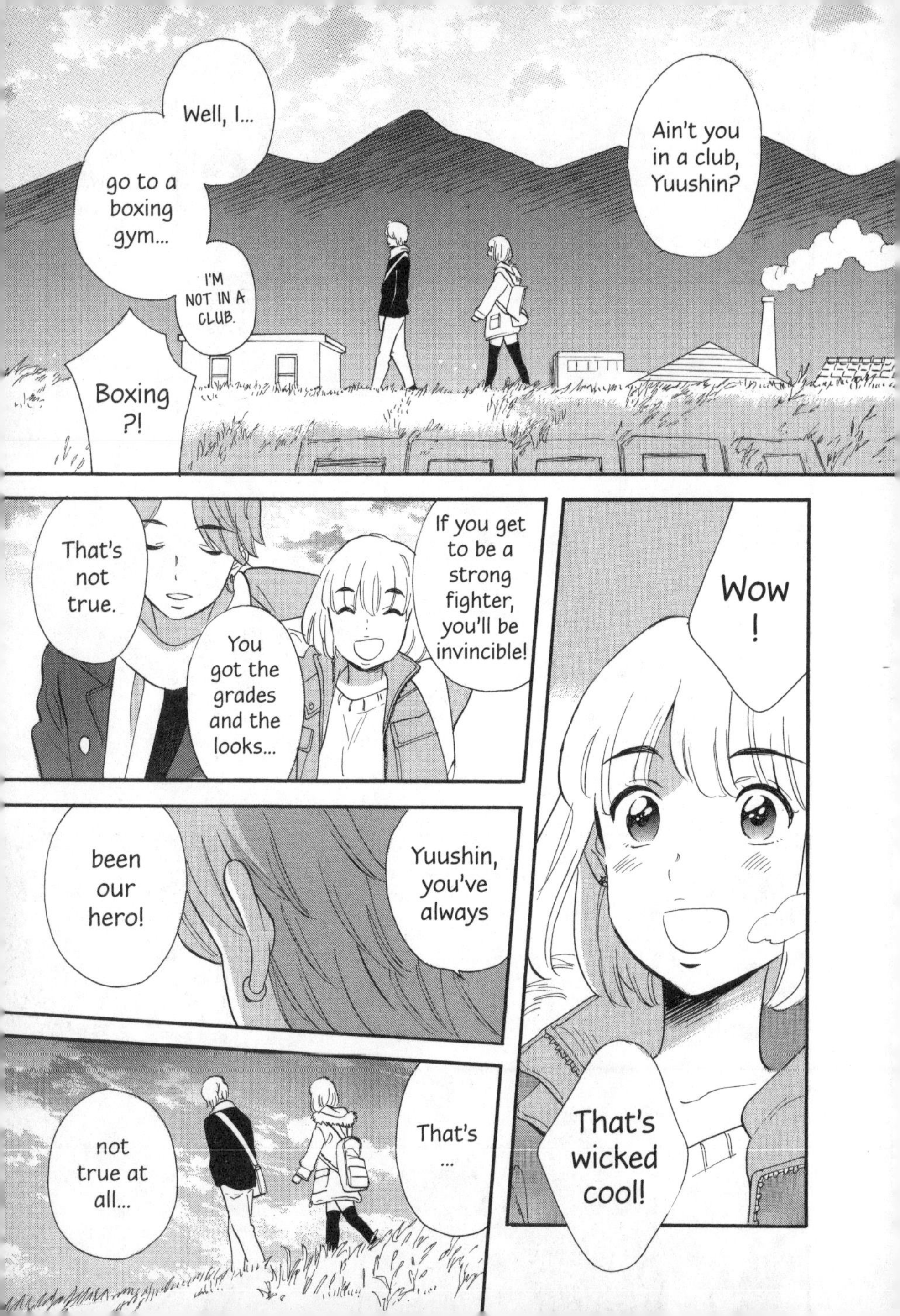
Ain't you in a club, Yuushin?
Well, I...
go to a boxing gym...
I'M NOT IN A CLUB.
Boxing?!
Wow!
That's wicked cool!
If you get to be a strong fighter, you'll be invincible!
You got the grades and the looks...
That's not true.
Yuushin, you've always
been our hero!
That's...
not true at all...

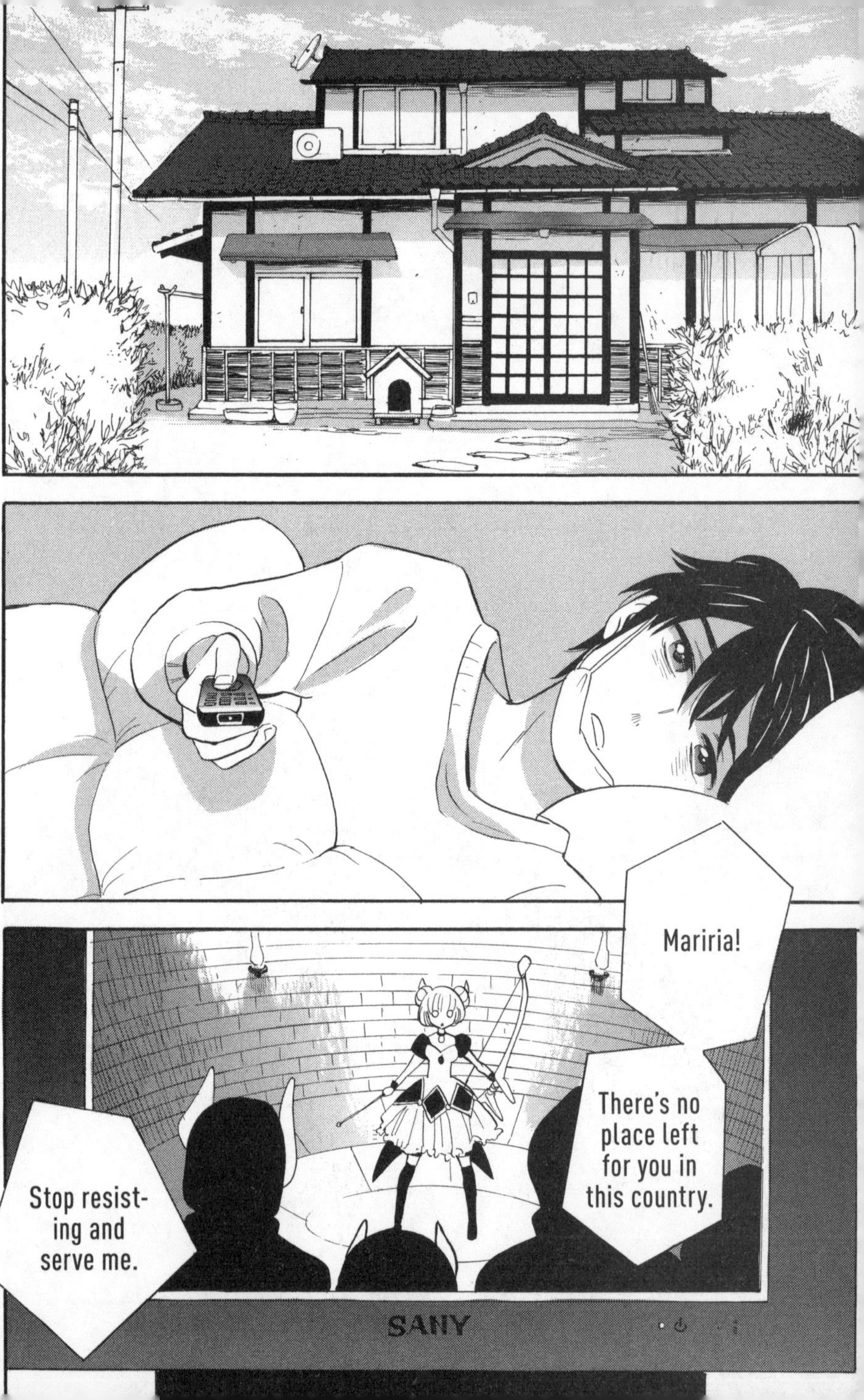
Mariria!
There's no place left for you in this country.
Stop resist-ing and serve me.
SANY

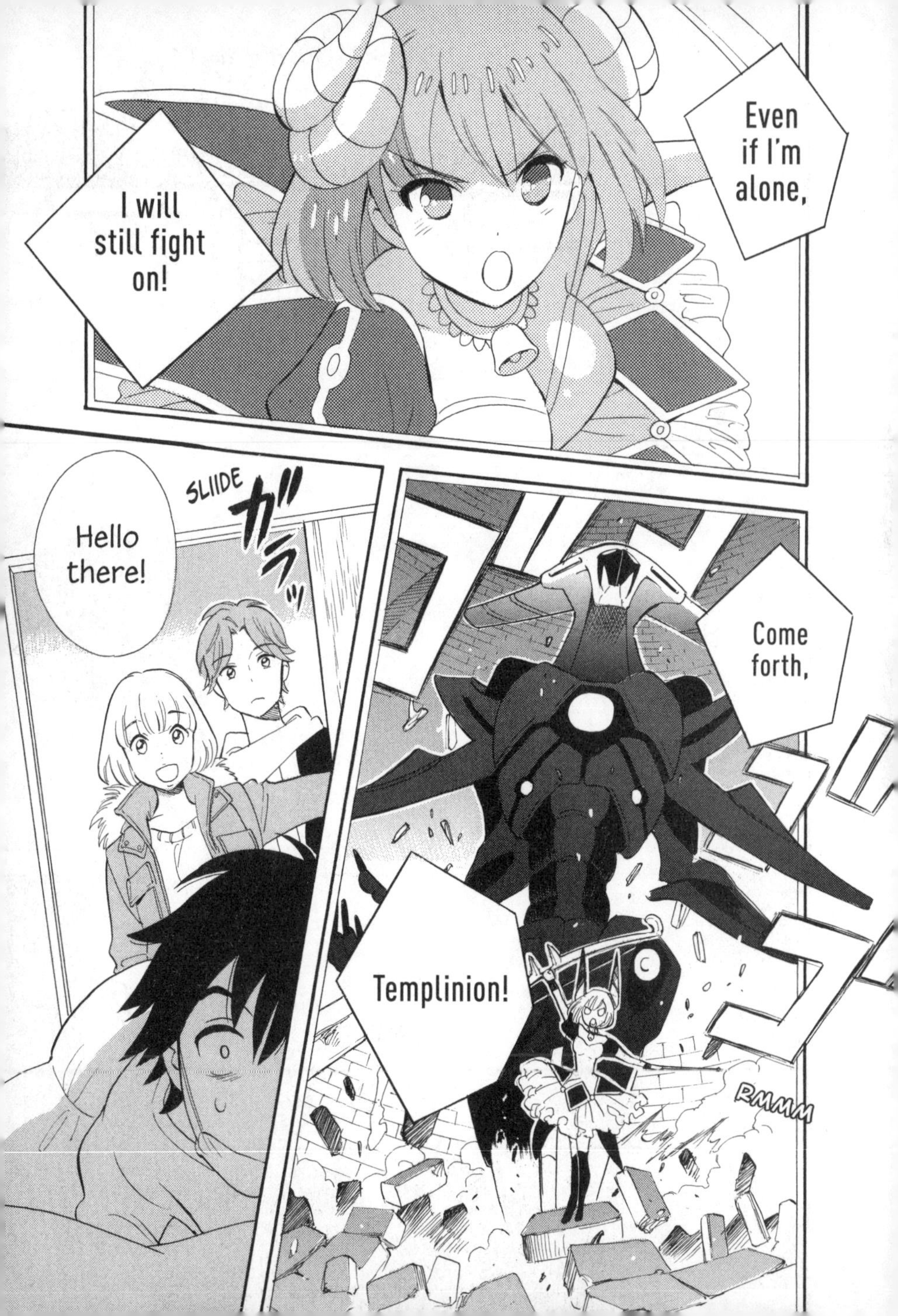
Even if I'm alone,
I will still fight on!
Come forth,
Templinion!
RMMM
SLIIDE
ガラッ
Hello there!

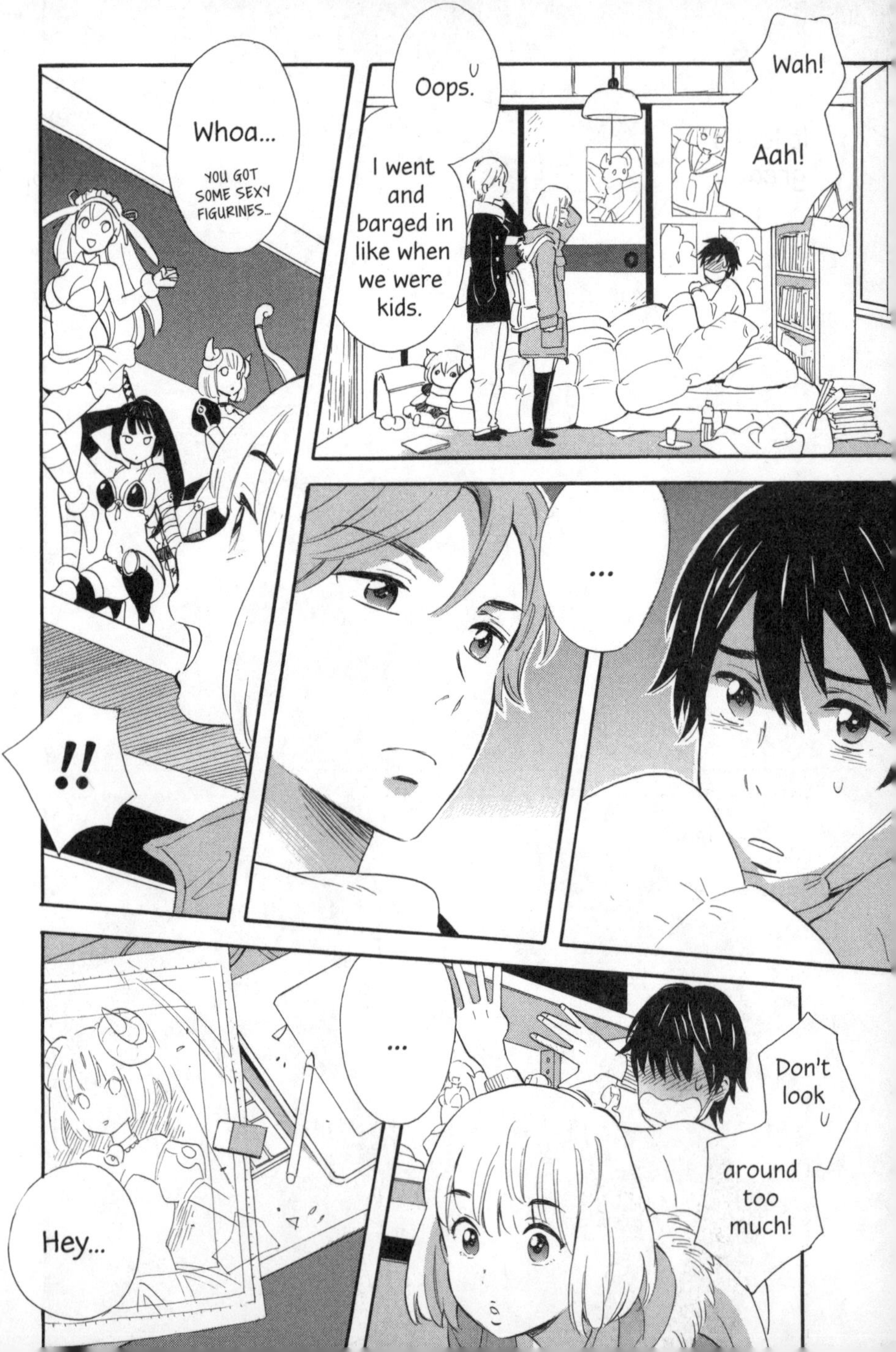
Wah!
Aah!
Oops.
I went and barged in like when we were kids.
Whoa...
YOU GOT SOME SEXY FIGURINES...
...
!!
Don't look around too much!
...
Hey...

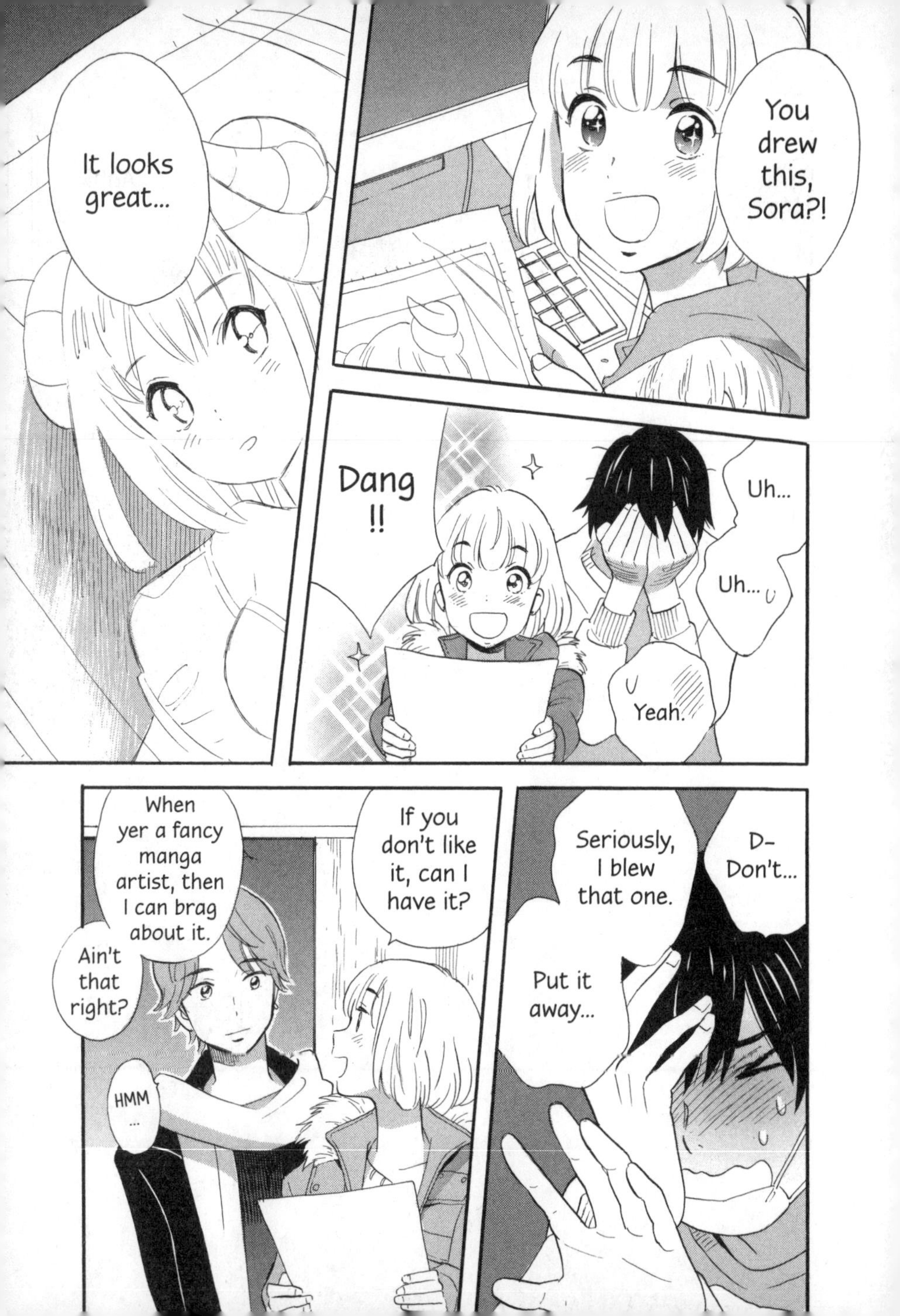
You drew this, Sora?!
Uh...
Dang !!
Uh...
Yeah.
It looks great...
D- Don't...
Seriously, I blew that one.
Put it away...
If you don't like it, can I have it?
When yer a fancy manga artist, then I can brag about it.
Ain't that right?
HMM ...

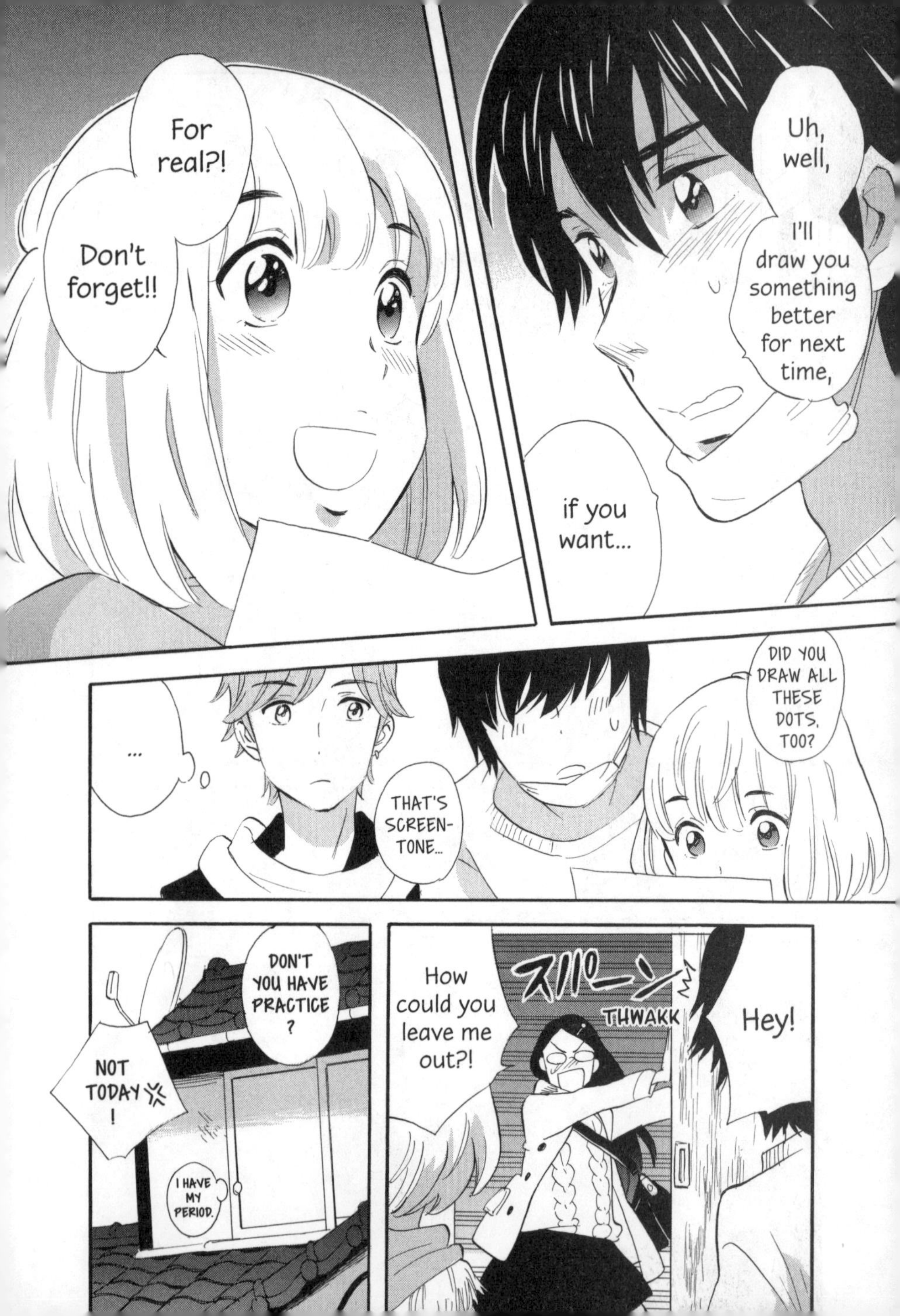
Uh, well,
I'll draw you something better for next time,
if you want...
For real?!
Don't forget!!
DID YOU DRAW ALL THESE DOTS, TOO?
THAT'S SCREEN-TONE...
...
Hey!
スパーン
THWAKK
How could you leave me out?!
DON'T YOU HAVE PRACTICE?
NOT TODAY!
I HAVE MY PERIOD.

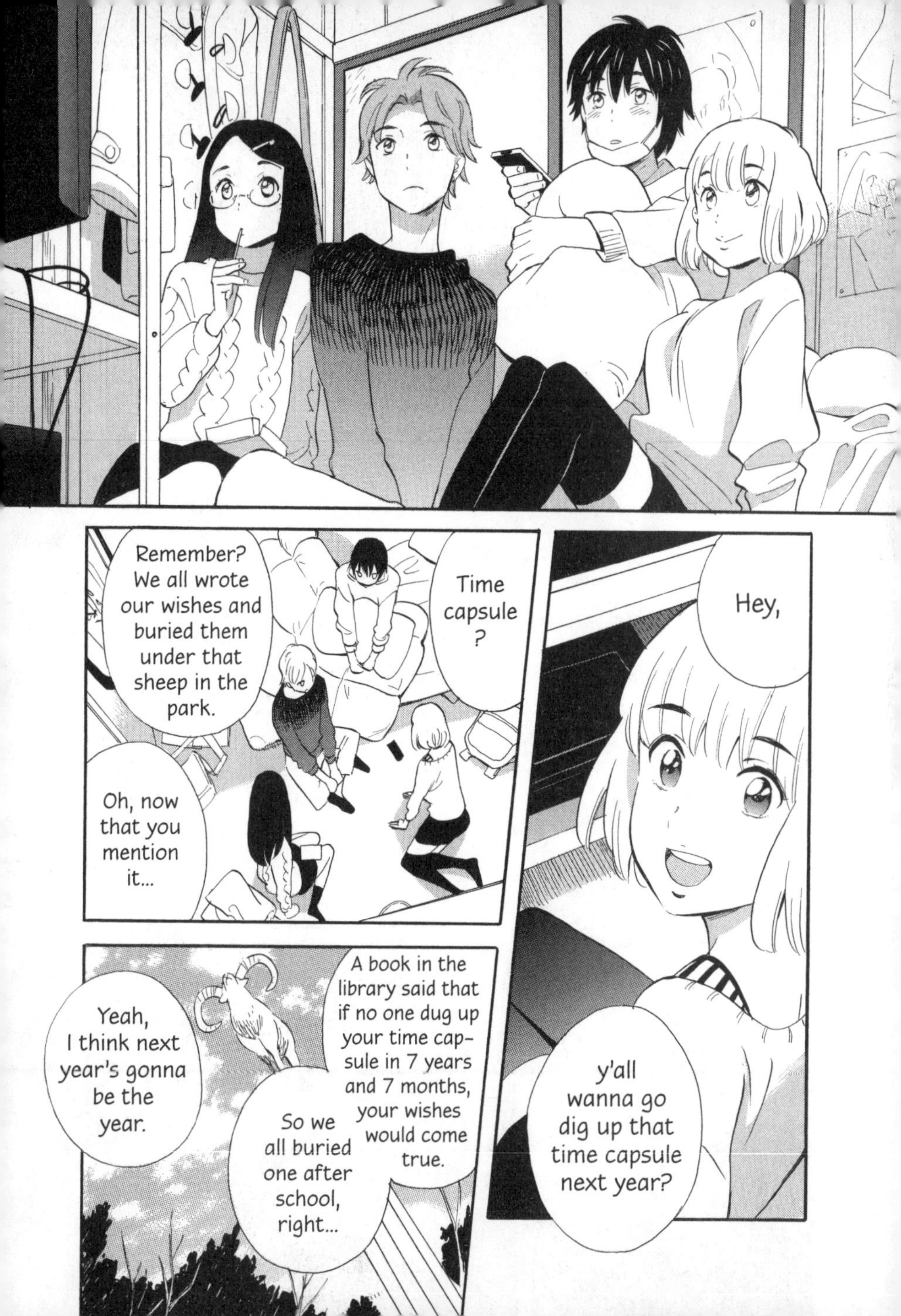
Hey,
y'all wanna go dig up that time capsule next year?
Time capsule?
Remember? We all wrote our wishes and buried them under that sheep in the park.
Oh, now that you mention it...
A book in the library said that if no one dug up your time capsule in 7 years and 7 months, your wishes would come true.
So we all buried one after school, right...
Yeah, I think next year's gonna be the year.

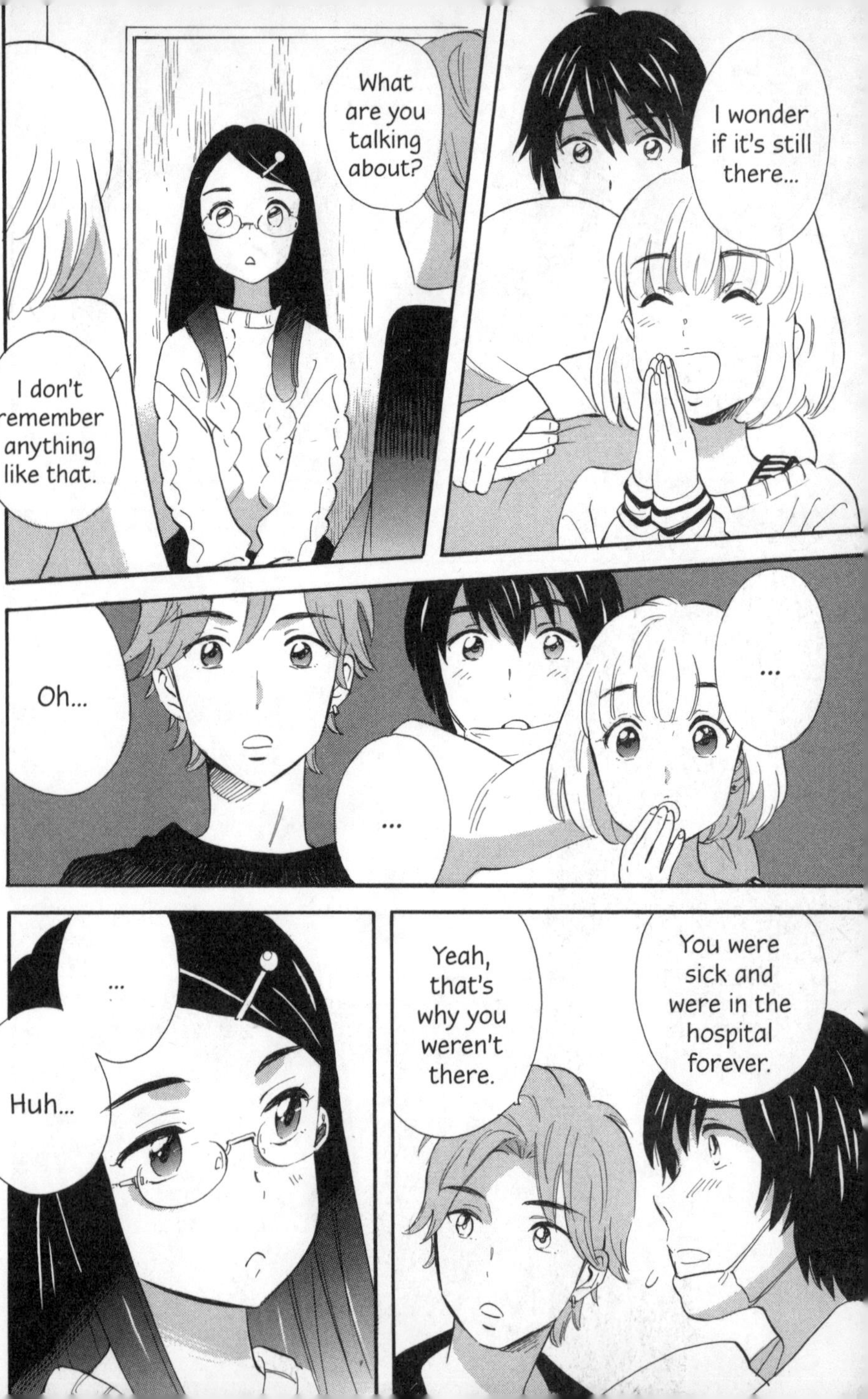
I wonder if it's still there...
What are you talking about?
I don't remember anything like that.
...
...
Oh...
You were sick and were in the hospital forever.
Yeah, that's why you weren't there.
...
Huh...

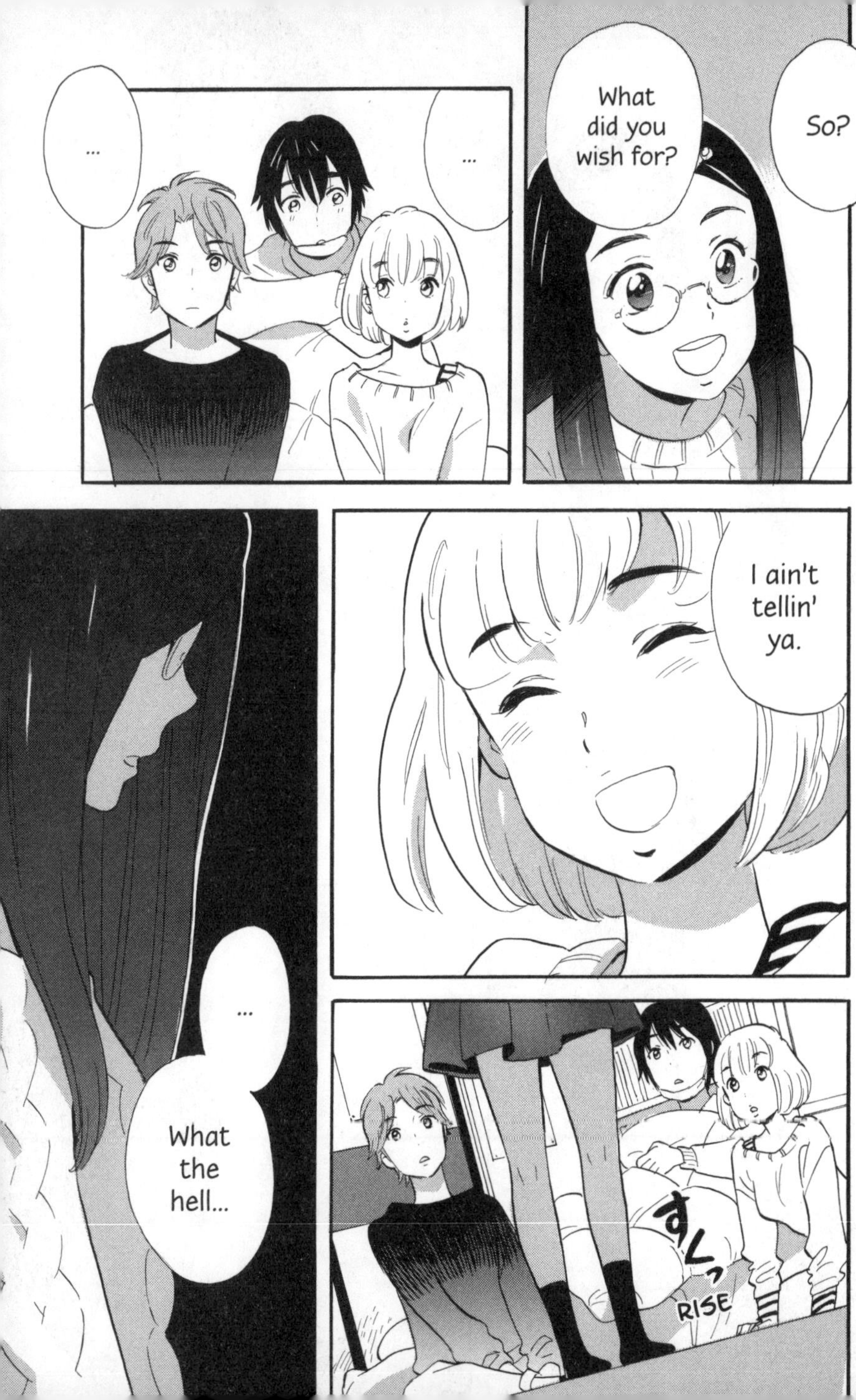
So?
What did you wish for?
...
...
I ain't tellin' ya.
すくっ
RISE
...
What the hell...

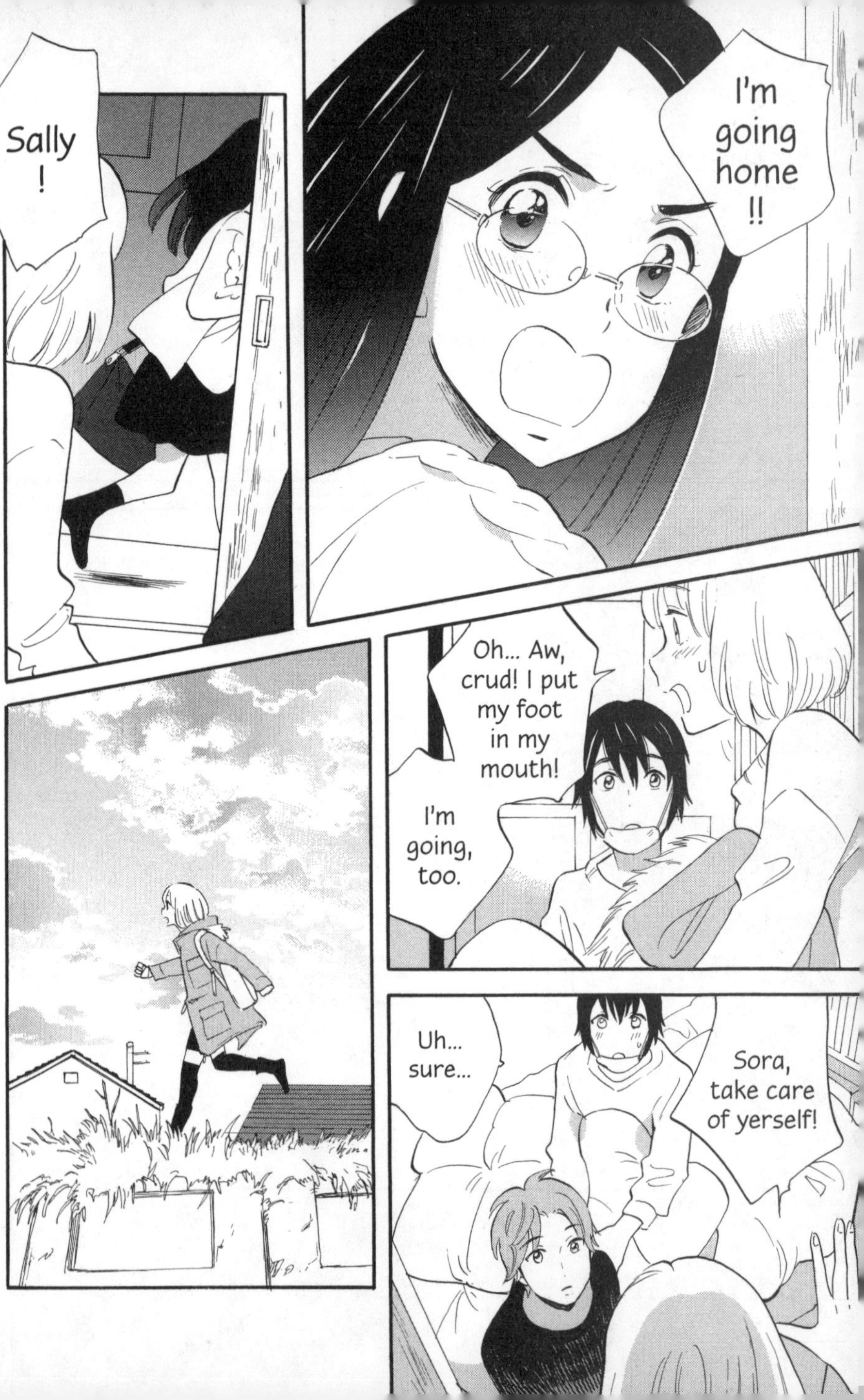
I'm going home !!
Sally !
Oh... Aw, crud! I put my foot in my mouth!
I'm going, too.
Sora, take care of yerself!
Uh... sure...

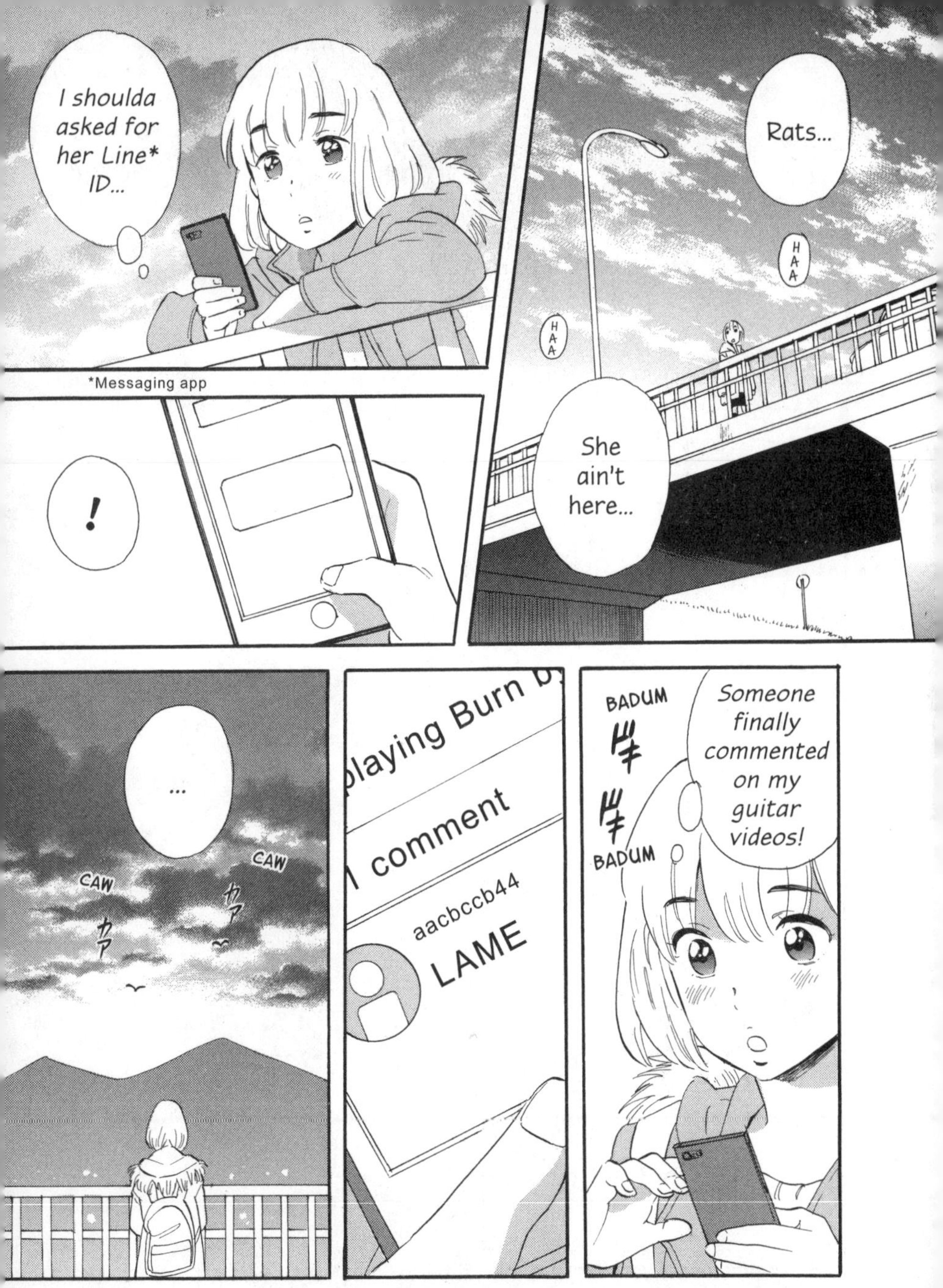
Rats...
HAA
HAA
She ain't here...
I shoulda asked for her Line* ID...
!
BADUM
BADUM
Someone finally commented on my guitar videos!
playing Burn b
1 comment
aacbccb44
LAME
...
CAW
カァ
CAW
カァ

*Messaging app

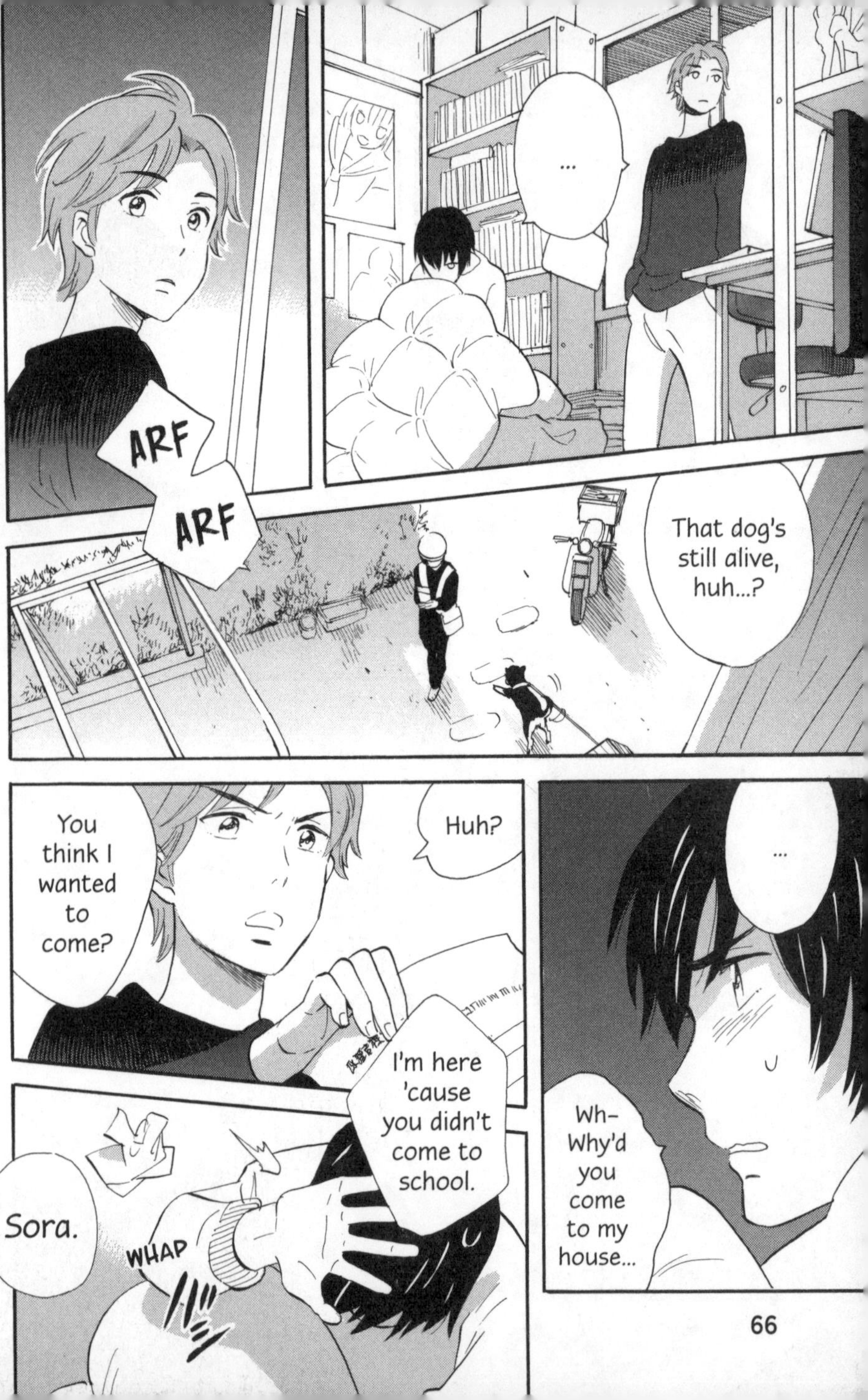
...
ARF
ARF
That dog's still alive, huh...?
...
Wh- Why'd you come to my house...
Huh?
You think I wanted to come?
I'm here 'cause you didn't come to school.
Sora.
WHAP

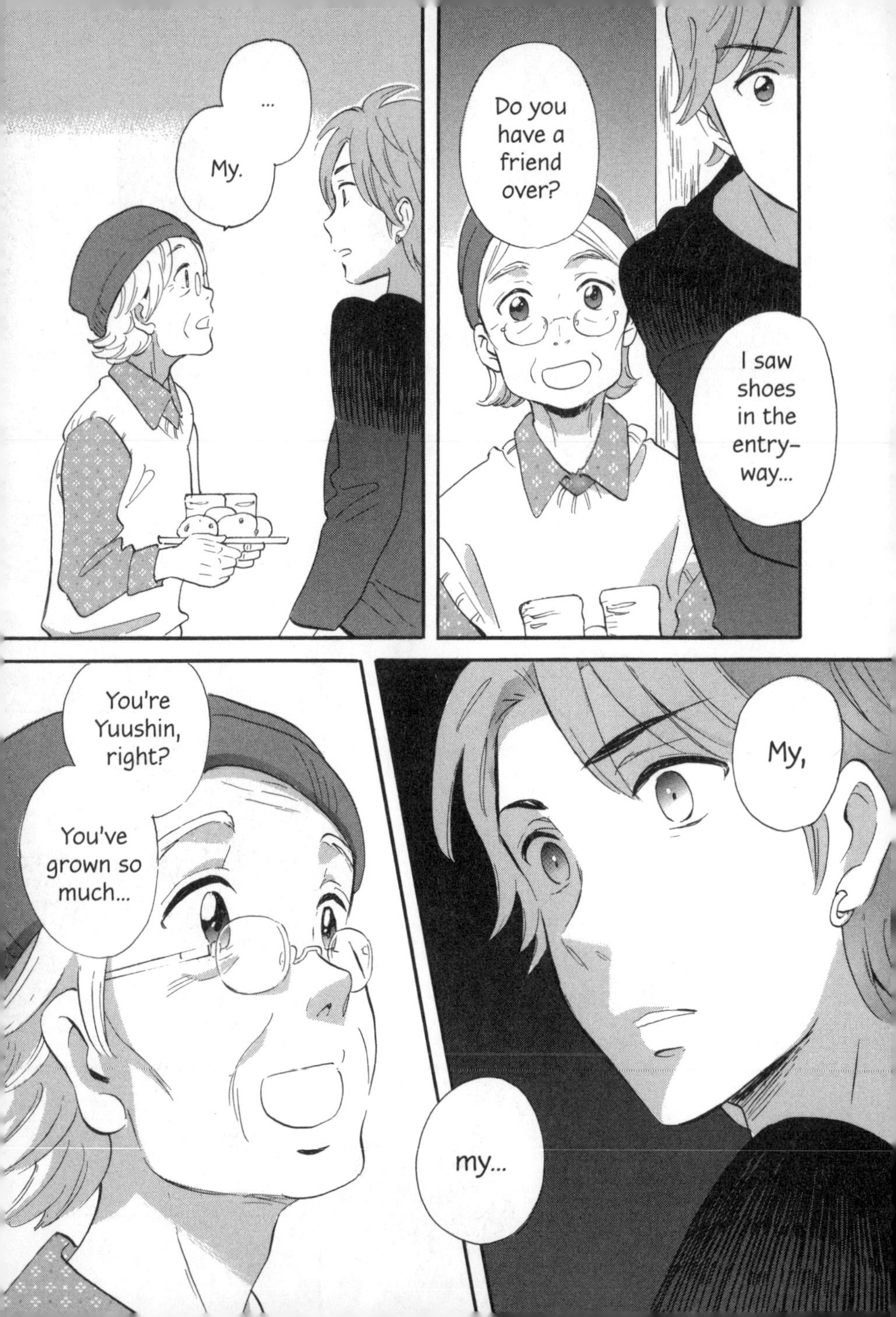
Do you have a friend over?
I saw shoes in the entry-way...
...
My.
My,
my...
You're Yuushin, right?
You've grown so much...

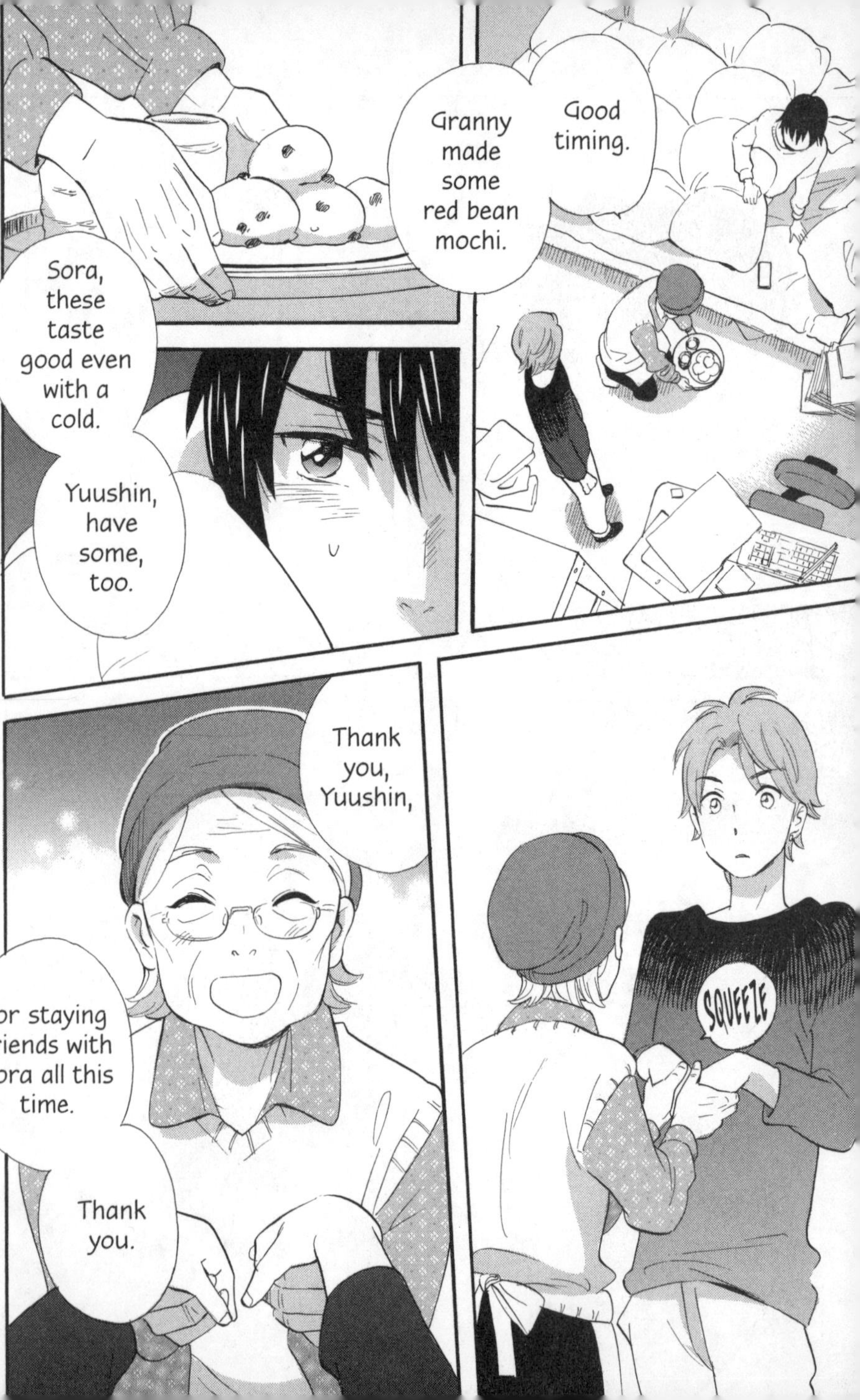
Good timing.
Granny made some red bean mochi.
Sora, these taste good even with a cold.
Yuushin, have some, too.
SQUEEZE
Thank you, Yuushin,
for staying friends with Sora all this time.
Thank you.

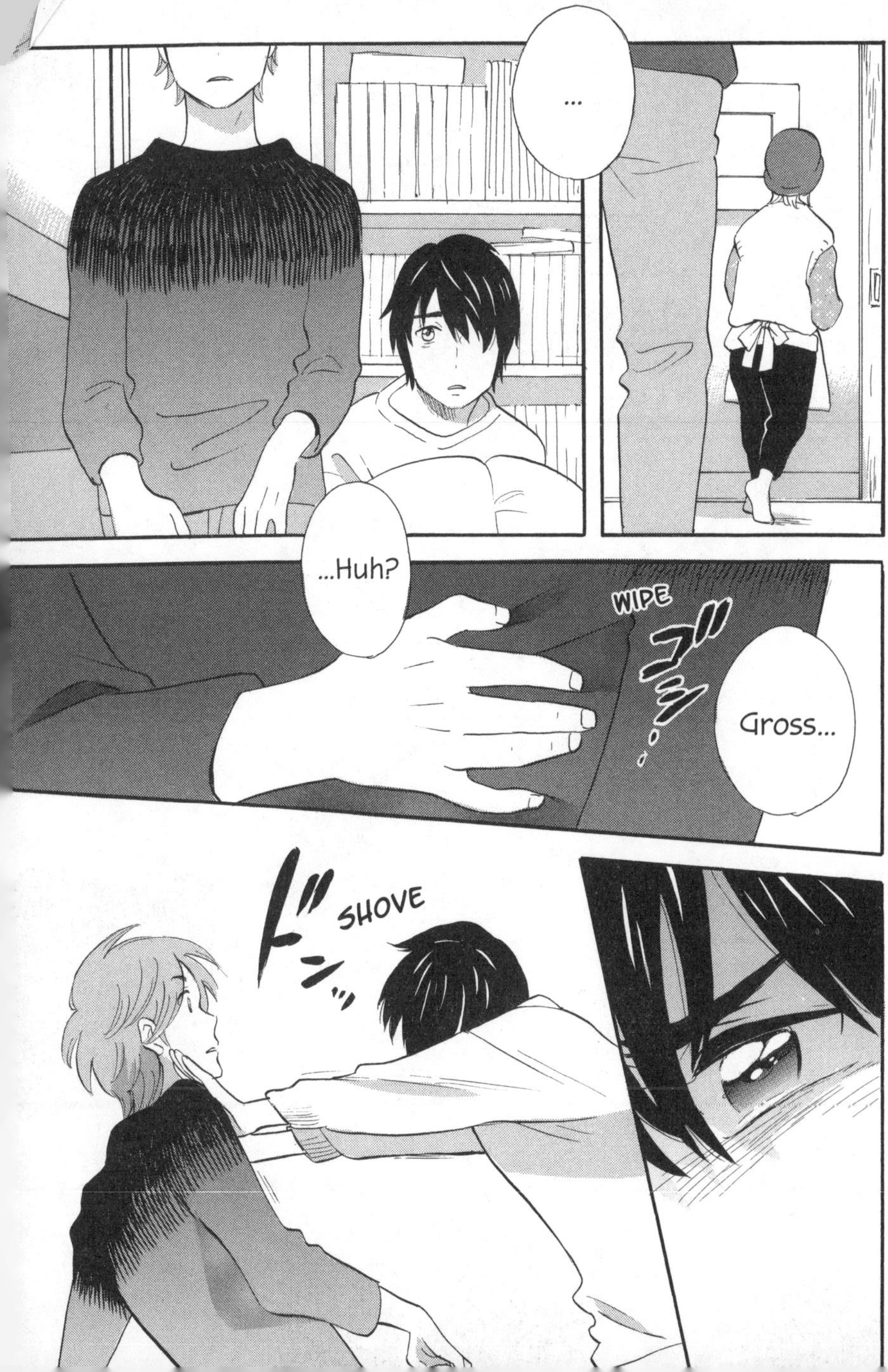
...
...Huh?
WIPE
Gross...
SHOVE

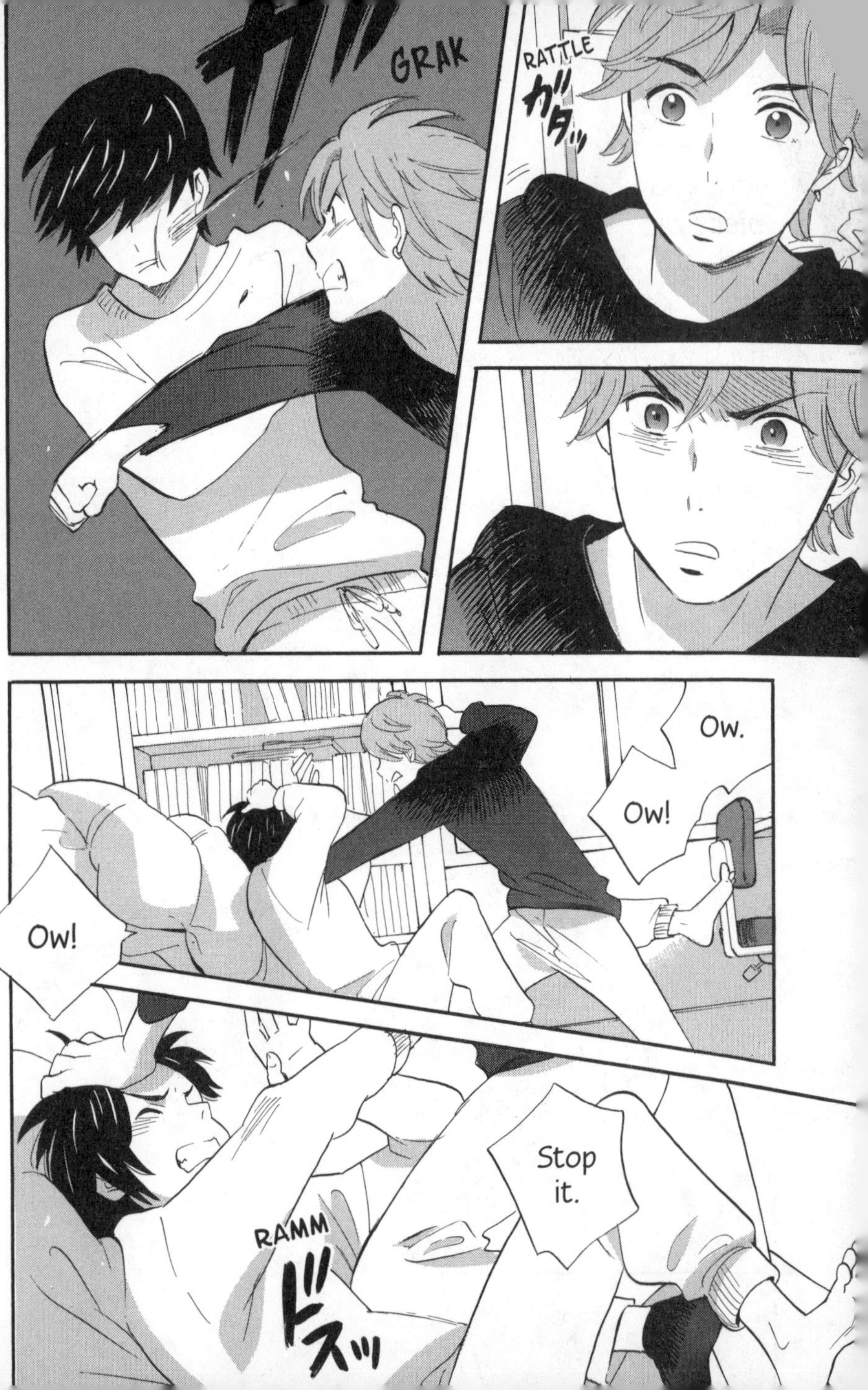
RATTLE
ガタッ
GRAK
ガ
Ow.
Ow!
Ow!
Stop it.
RAMM
ドスッ

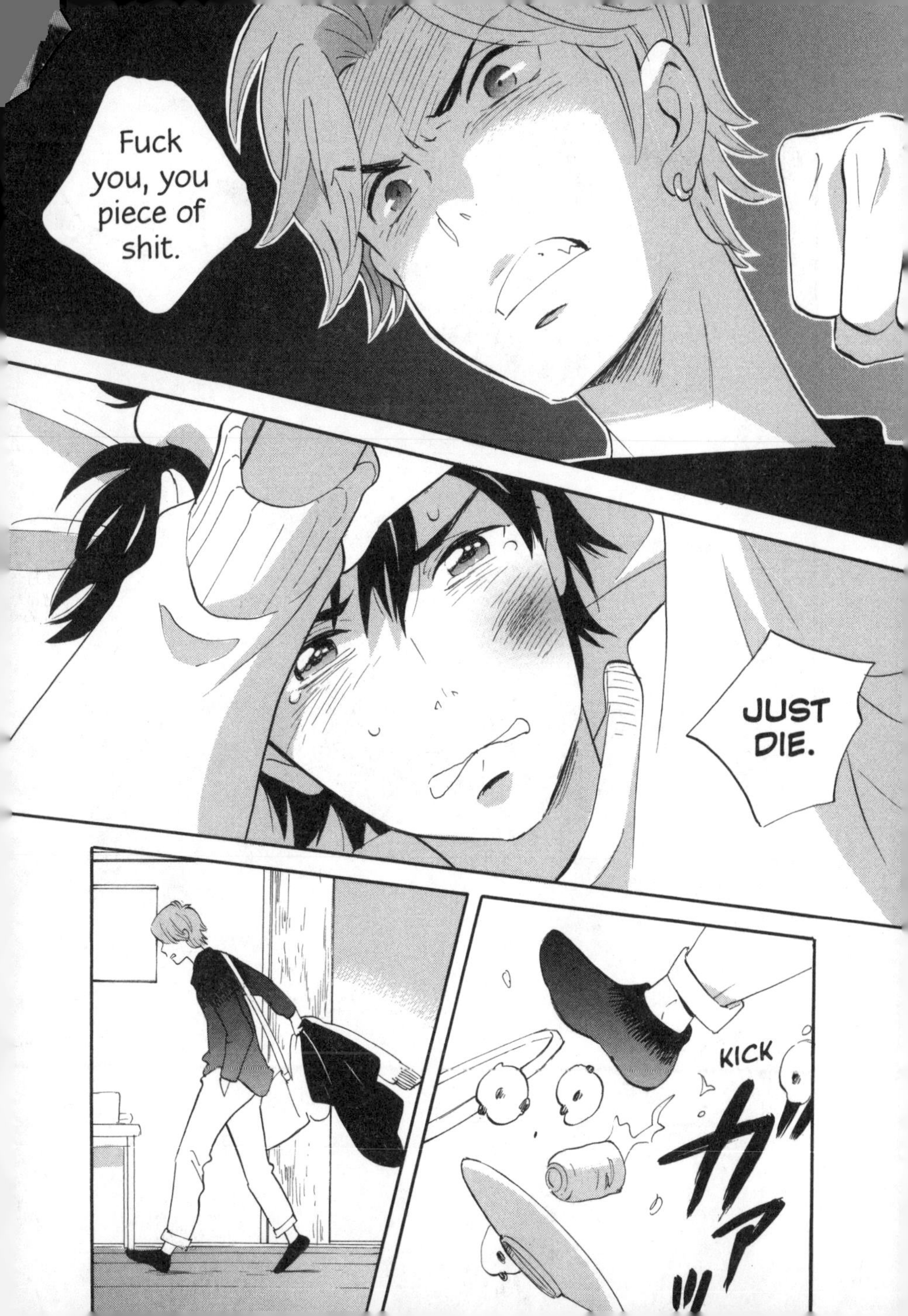
Fuck you, you piece of shit.
JUST DIE.
KICK

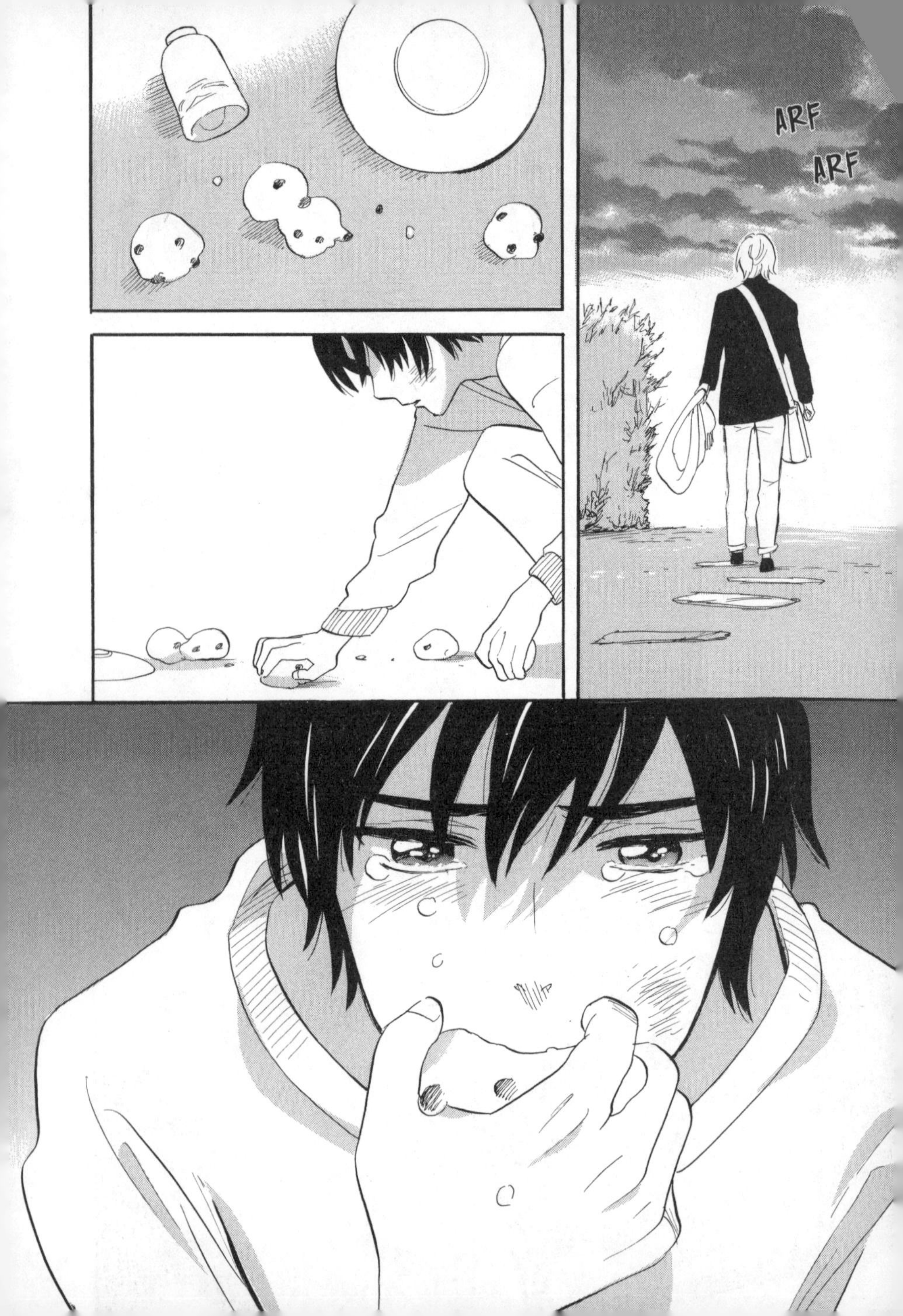
ARF
ARF

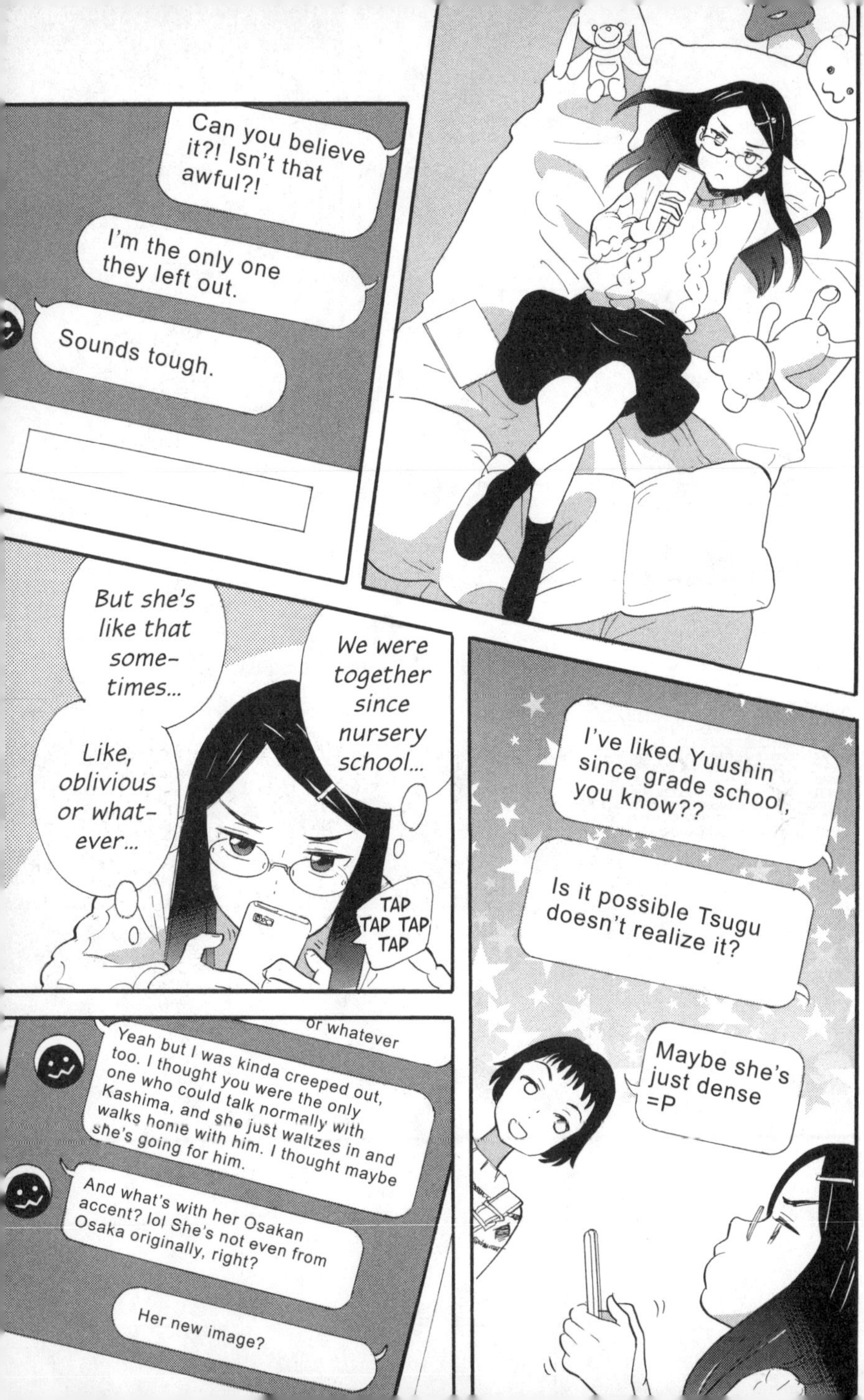
Can you believe it?! Isn't that awful?!
I'm the only one they left out.
Sounds tough.
I've liked Yuushin since grade school, you know??
Is it possible Tsugu doesn't realize it?
Maybe she's just dense =P
We were together since nursery school...
But she's like that some-times...
Like, oblivious or what-ever...
TAP TAP TAP TAP
or whatever
Yeah but I was kinda creeped out, too. I thought you were the only one who could talk normally with Kashima, and she just waltzes in and walks home with him. I thought maybe she's going for him.
And what's with her Osakan accent? lol She's not even from Osaka originally, right?
Her new image?

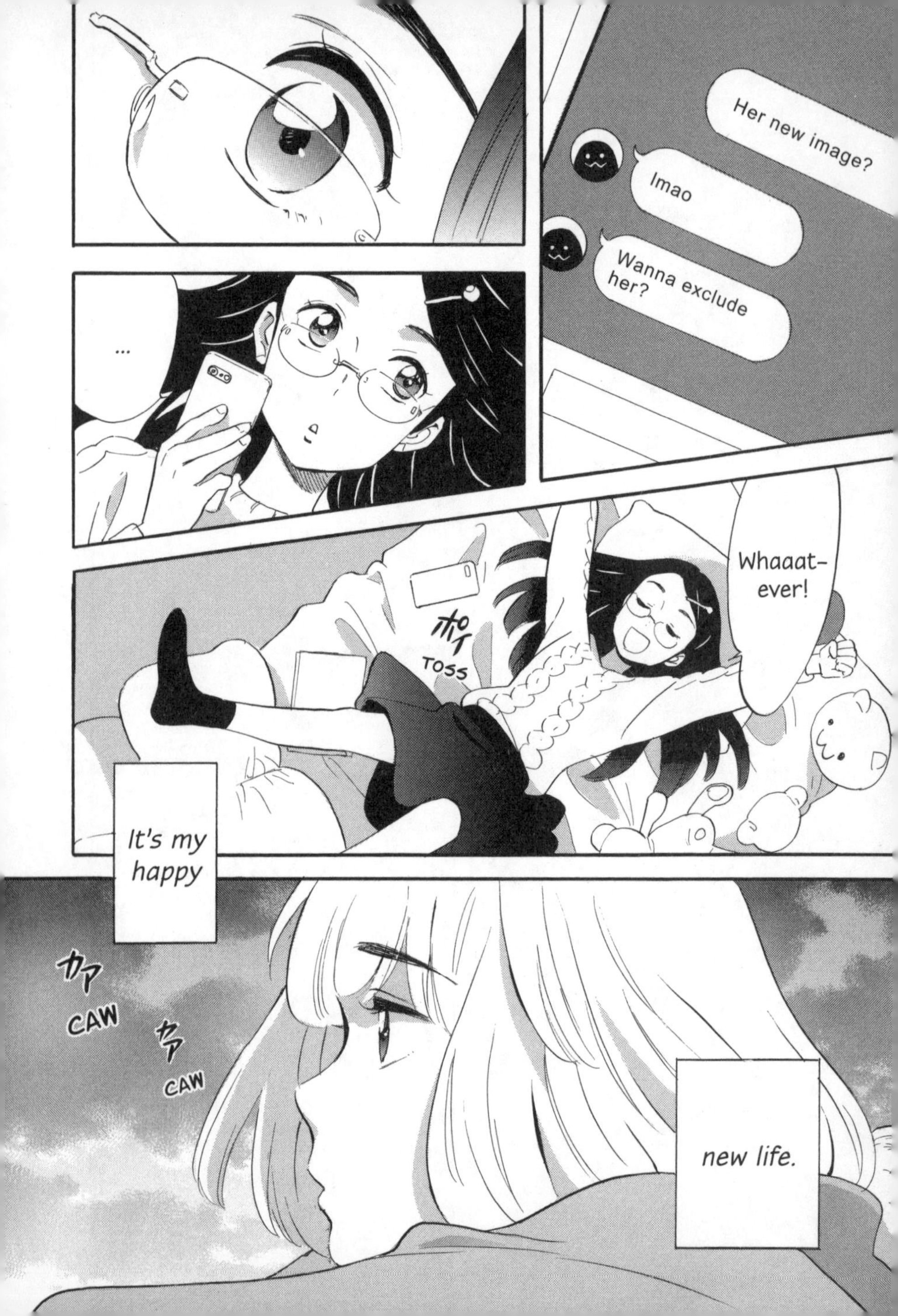
Her new image?
lmao
Wanna exclude her?
...
Whaaat-ever!
ポイ
TOSS
It's my happy
カァ
CAW
カァ
CAW
new life.

THE GOLDEN SHEEP

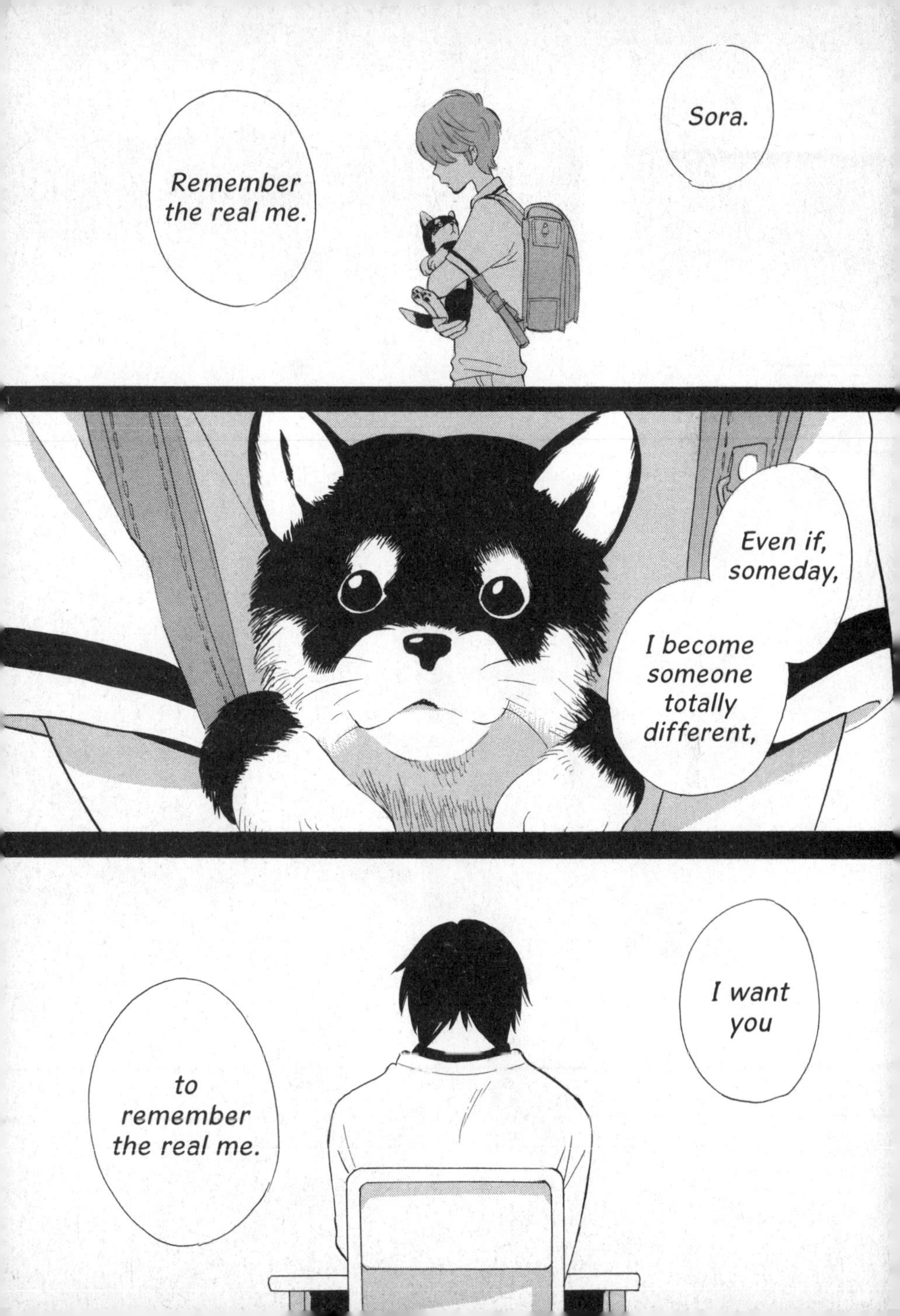
Sora.
Remember the real me.
Even if, someday,
I become someone totally different,
I want you
to remember the real me.

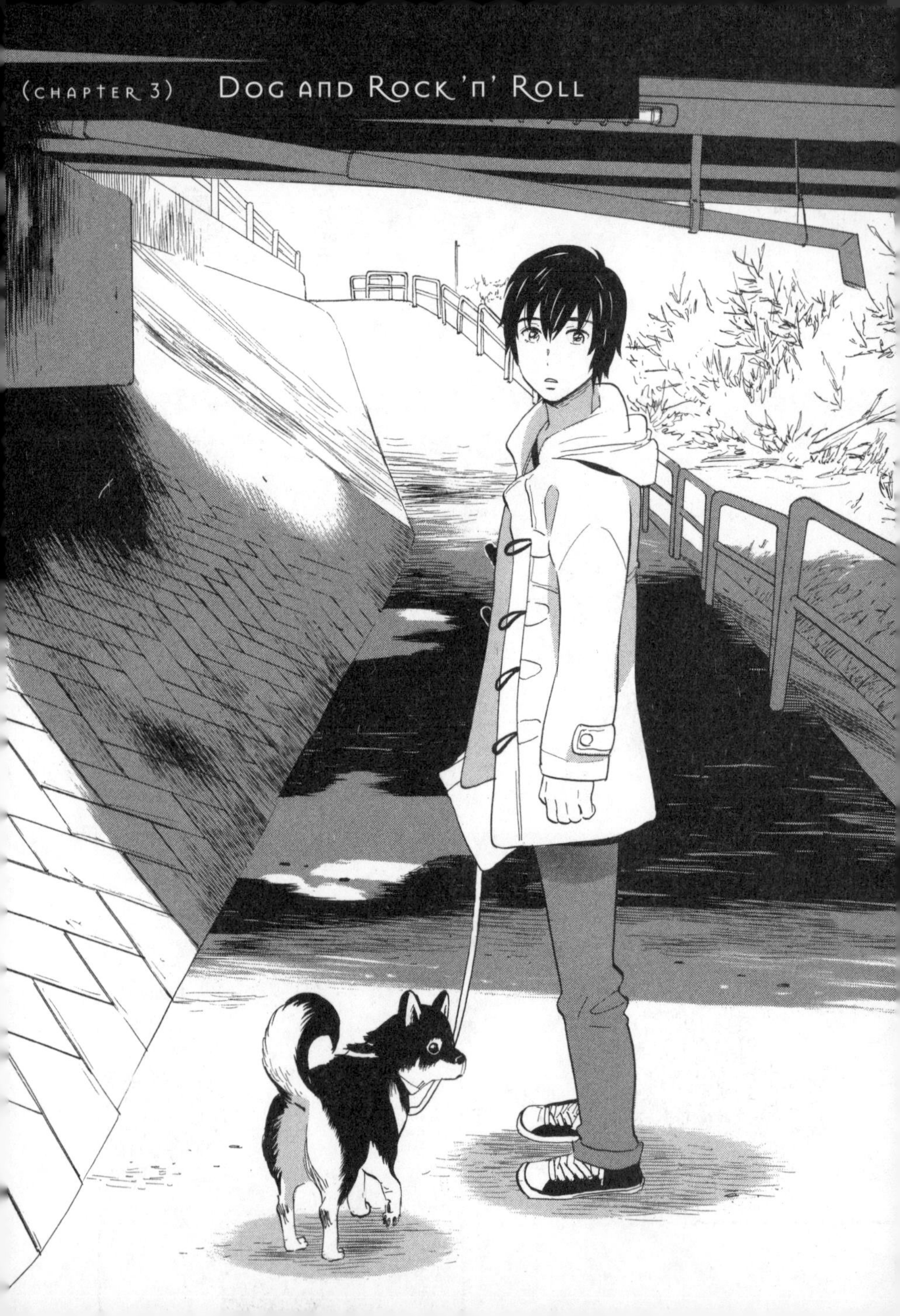
(CHAPTER 3) DOG AND ROCK 'N' ROLL

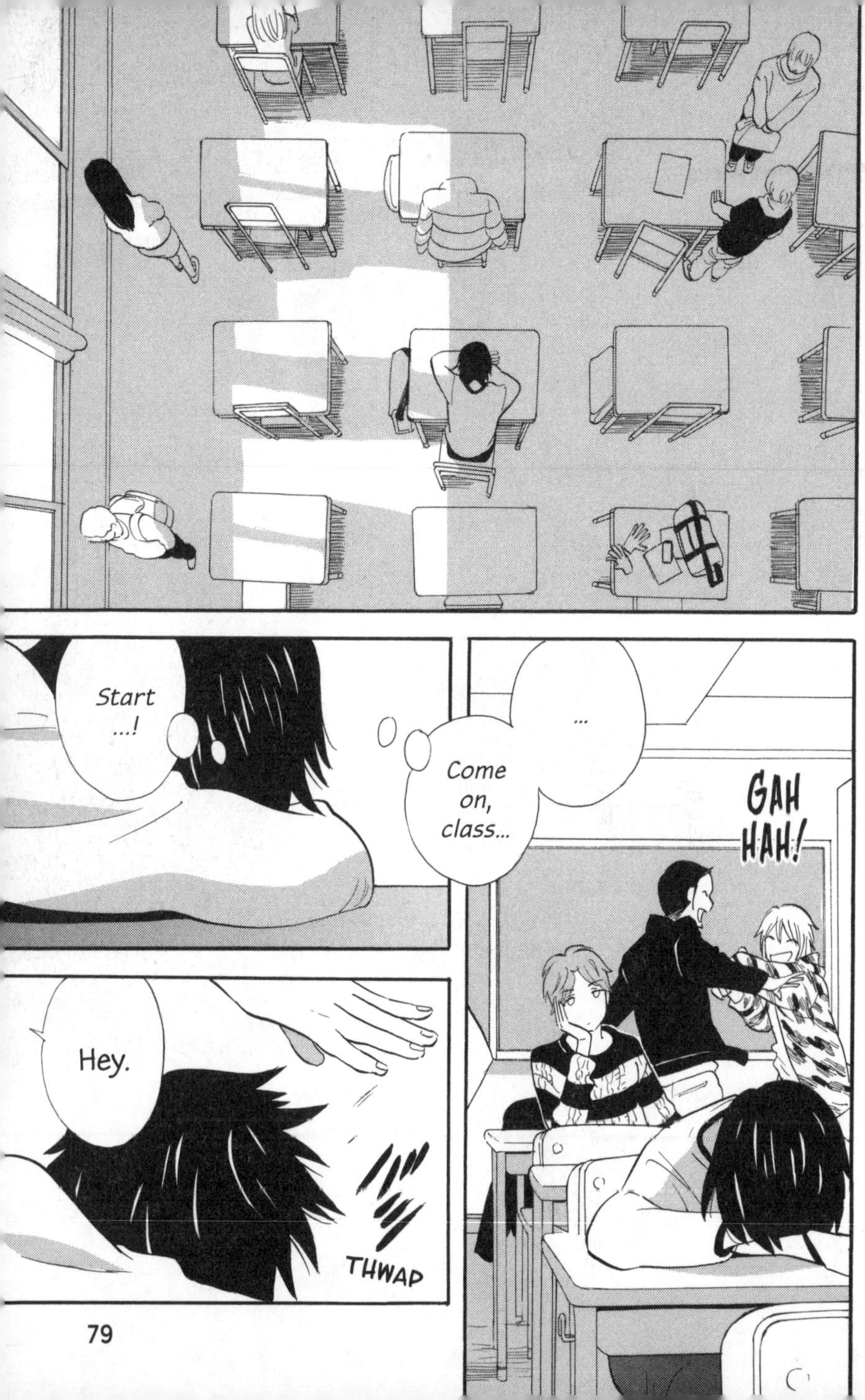
...
Come on, class...
GAH HAH!
Start ...!
Hey.
THWAP

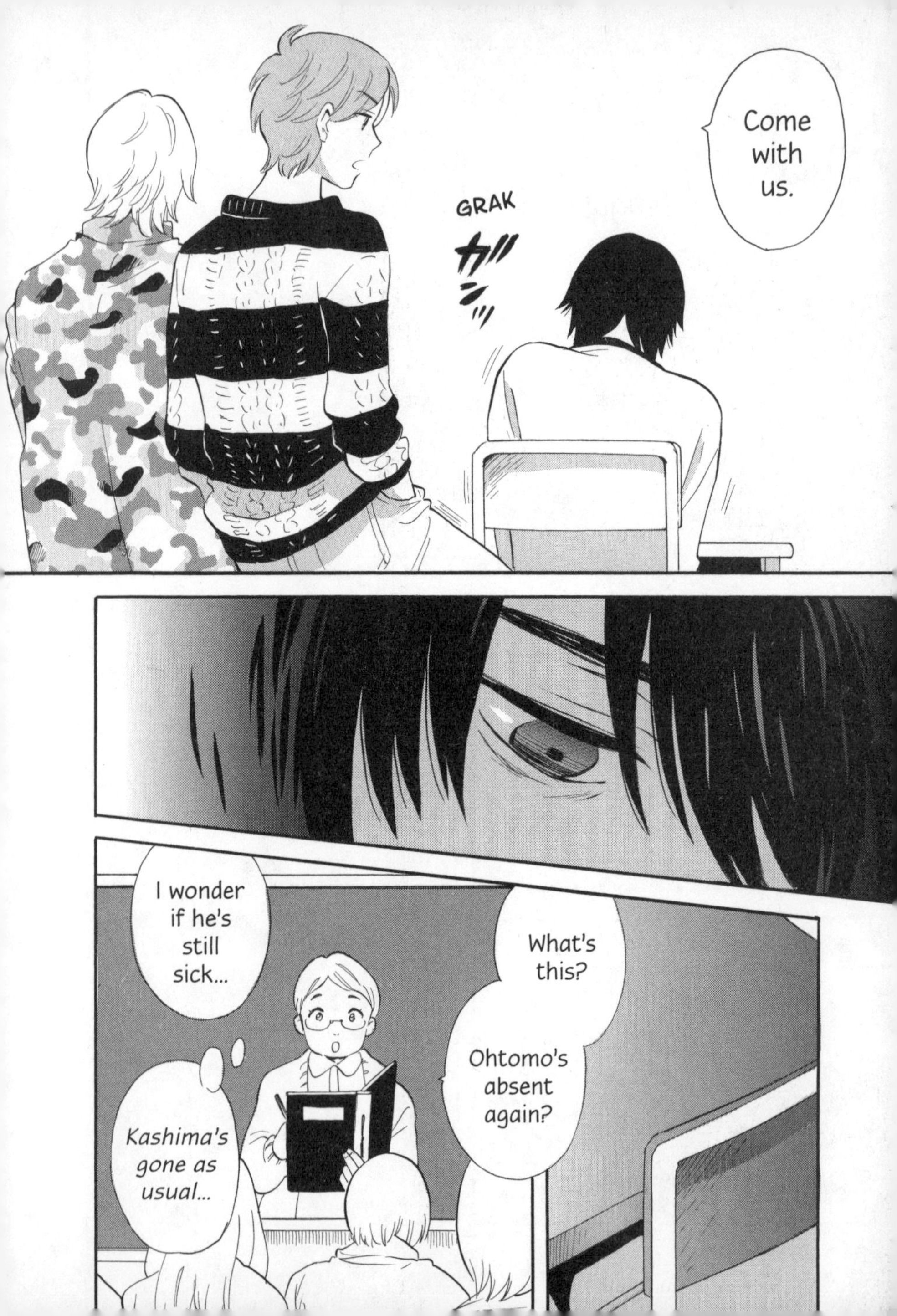
Come with us.
GRAK
What's this?
Ohtomo's absent again?
I wonder if he's still sick...
Kashima's gone as usual...

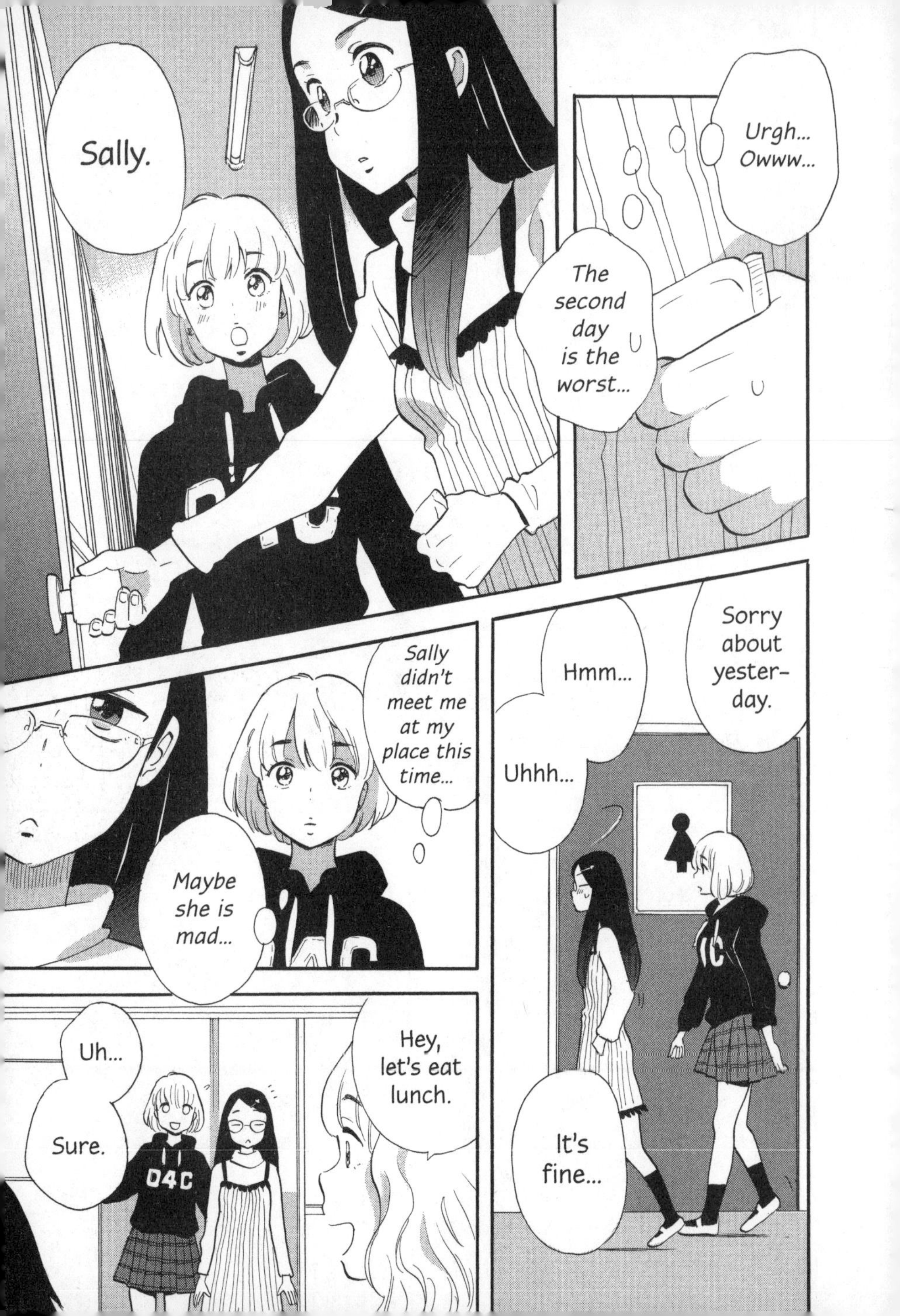
Urgh... Owww...
The second day is the worst...
Sally.
Sorry about yester-day.
Hmm...
Uhhh...
It's fine...
Sally didn't meet me at my place this time...
Maybe she is mad...
Hey, let's eat lunch.
Uh...
Sure.

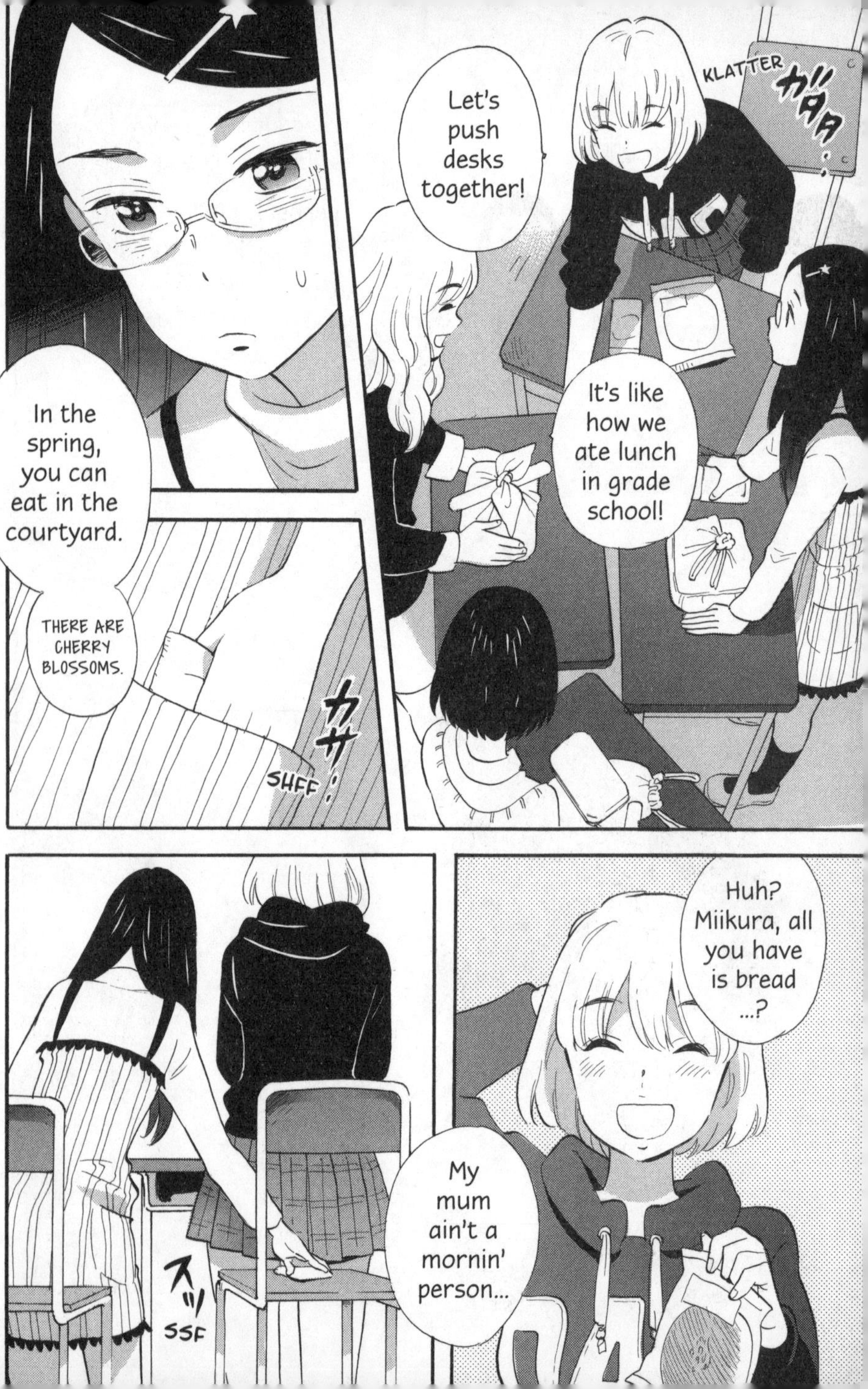
Let's push desks together!
KLATTER
カタタ
It's like how we ate lunch in grade school!
In the spring, you can eat in the courtyard.
THERE ARE CHERRY BLOSSOMS.
カサ
SHFF
Huh? Miikura, all you have is bread ...?
My mum ain't a mornin' person...
スッ
SSF

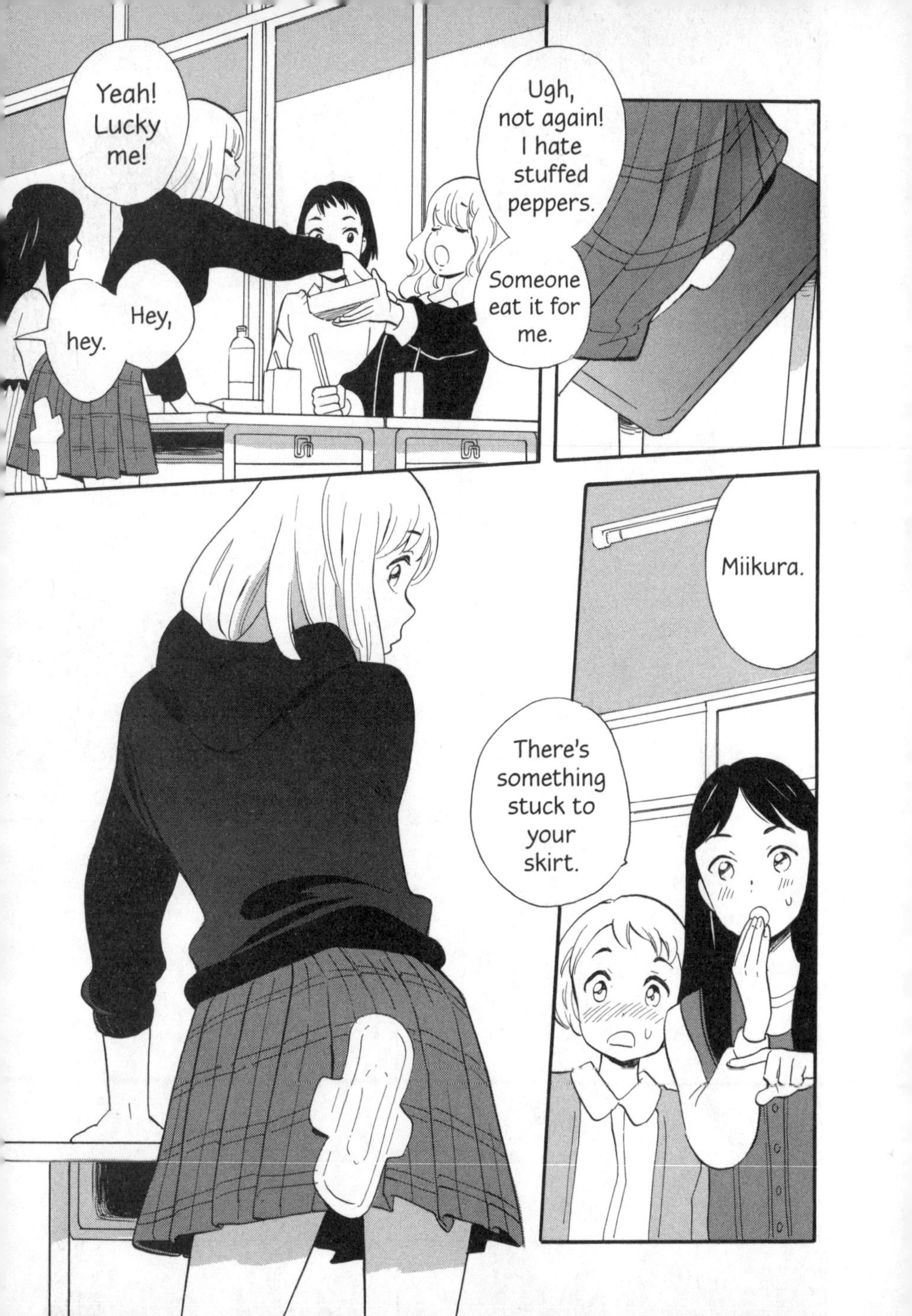
Ugh, not again! I hate stuffed peppers.
Someone eat it for me.
Yeah! Lucky me!
Hey, hey.
Miikura.
There's something stuck to your skirt.

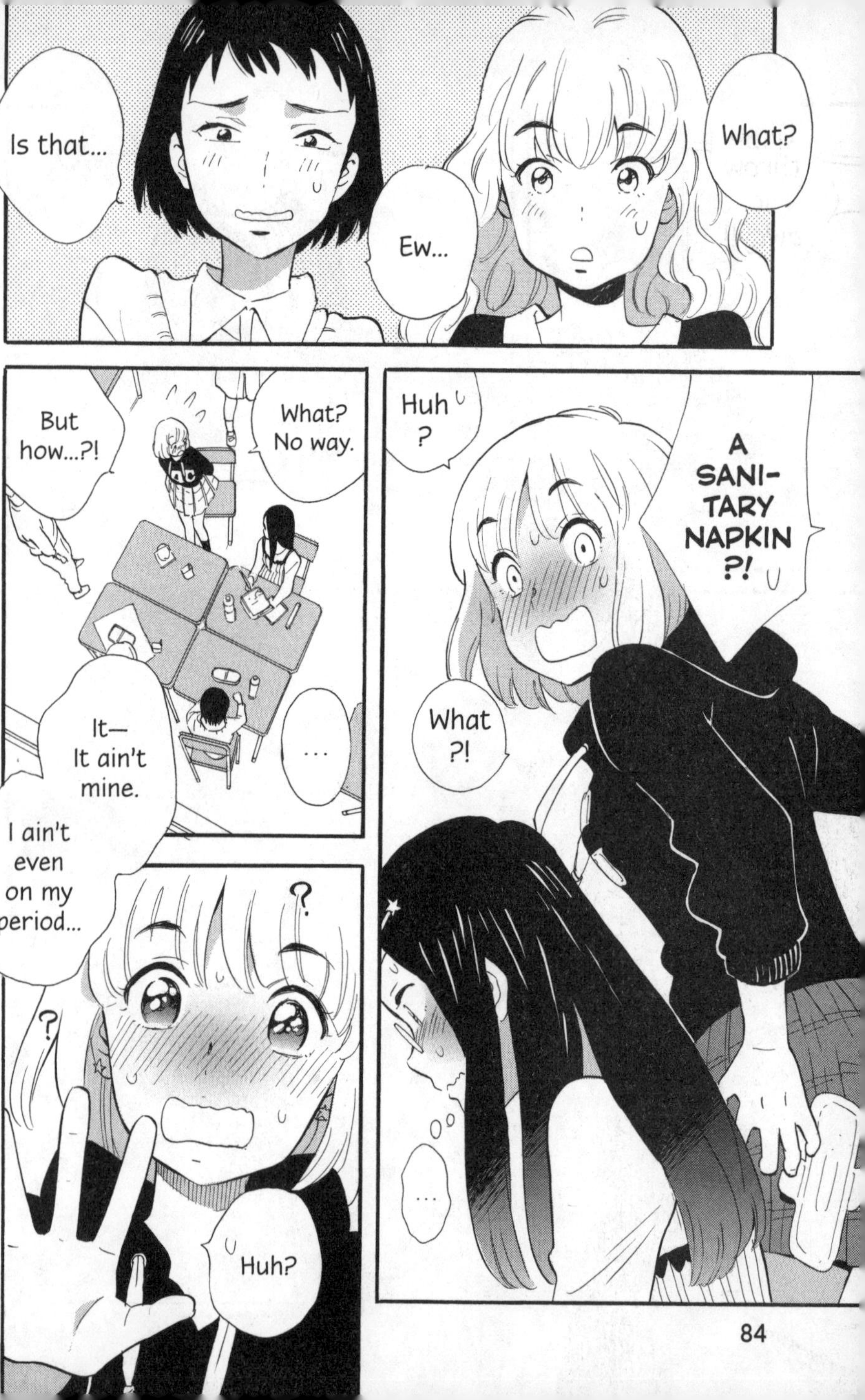
What?
Ew...
Is that...
A SANITARY NAPKIN?!
Huh?
What?!
...
What? No way.
But how...?!
...
It— It ain't mine.
I ain't even on my period...
Huh?

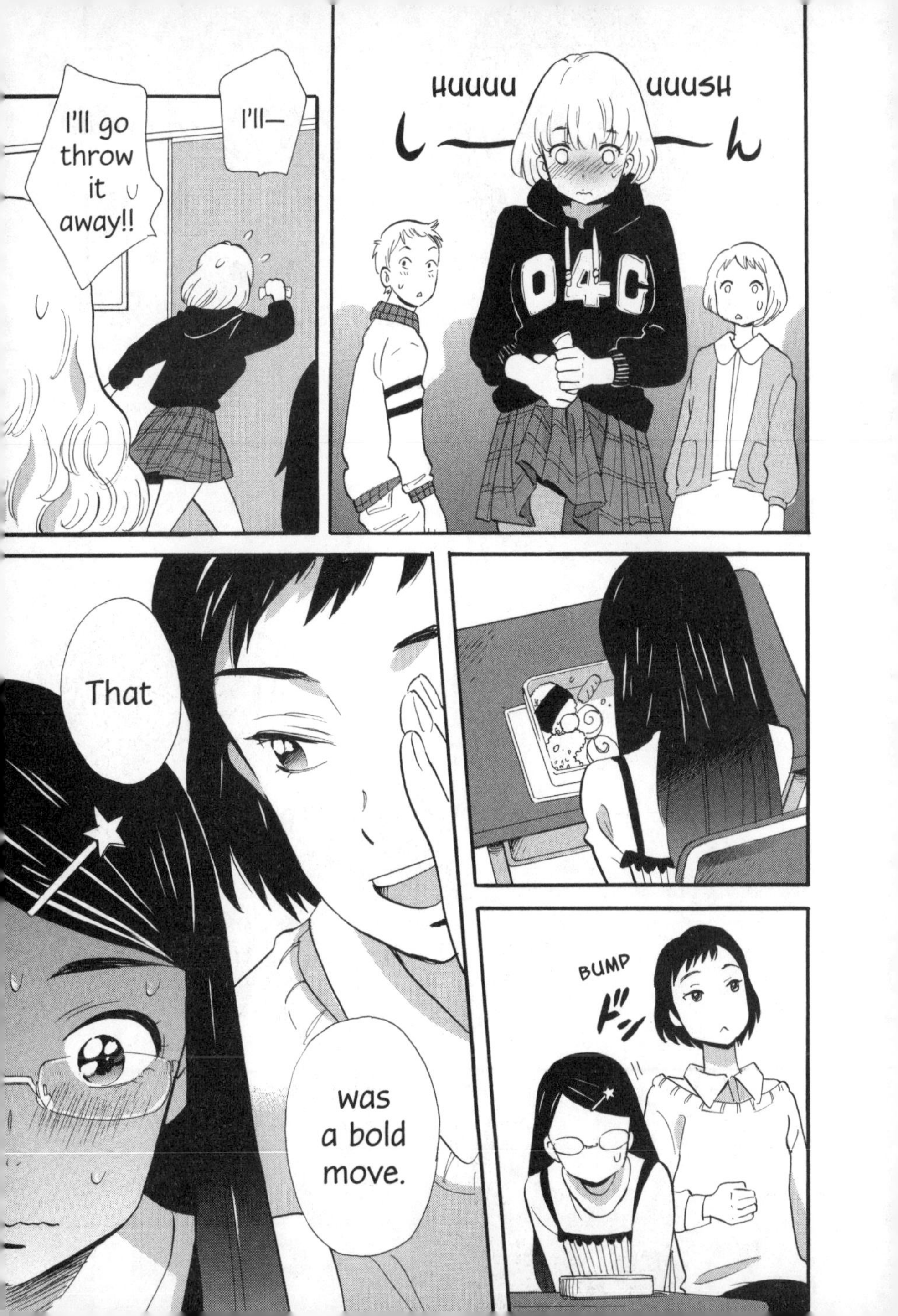
HUUUU UUUSH
しーーん
I'll—
I'll go throw it away!!
BUMP
ドッ
That
was a bold move.

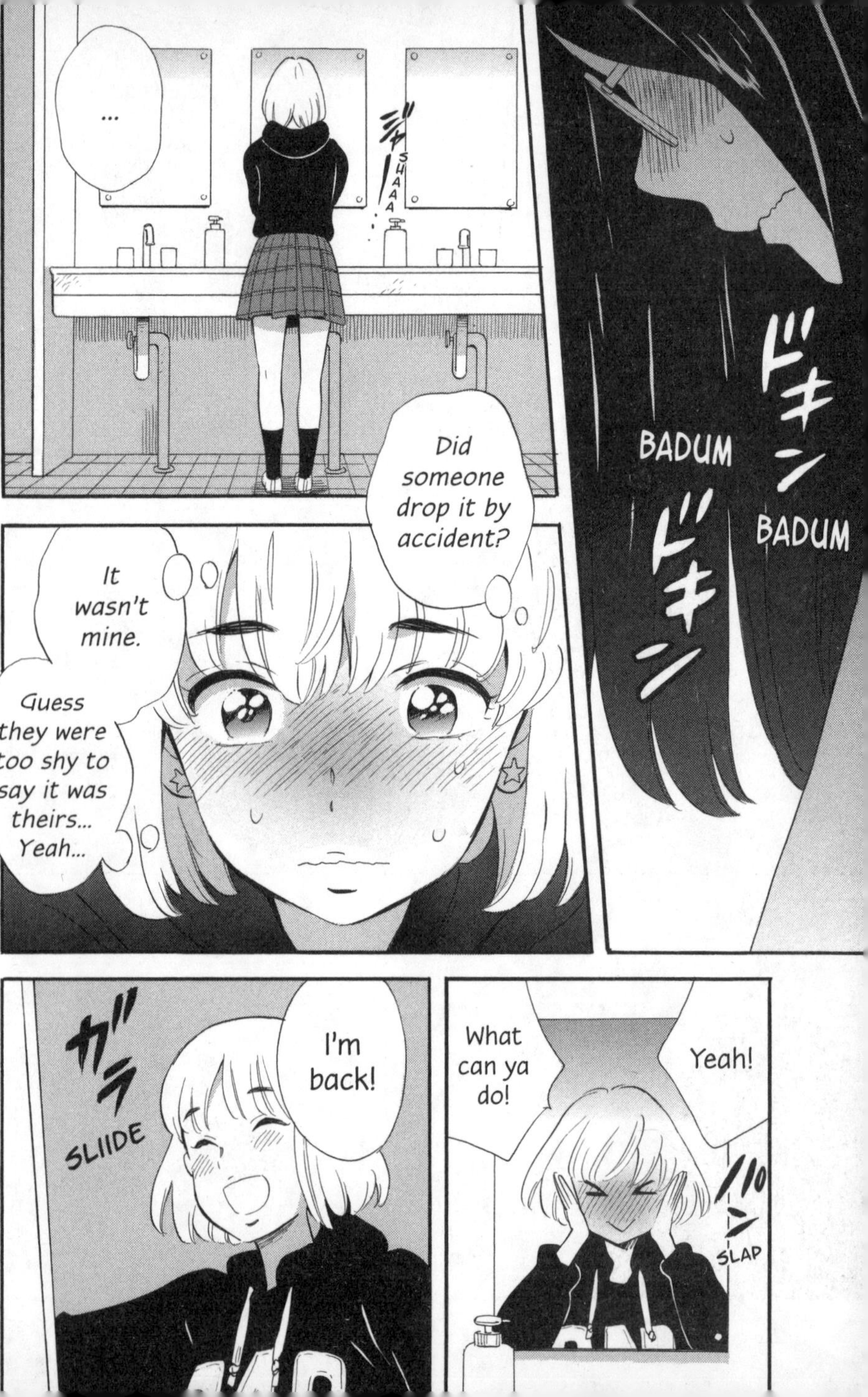
ドキン
BADUM
ドキン
BADUM
...
ジャー
SHAAA
Did someone drop it by accident?
It wasn't mine.
Guess they were too shy to say it was theirs... Yeah...
What can ya do!
Yeah!
パン
SLAP
ガラ
SLIIDE
I'm back!

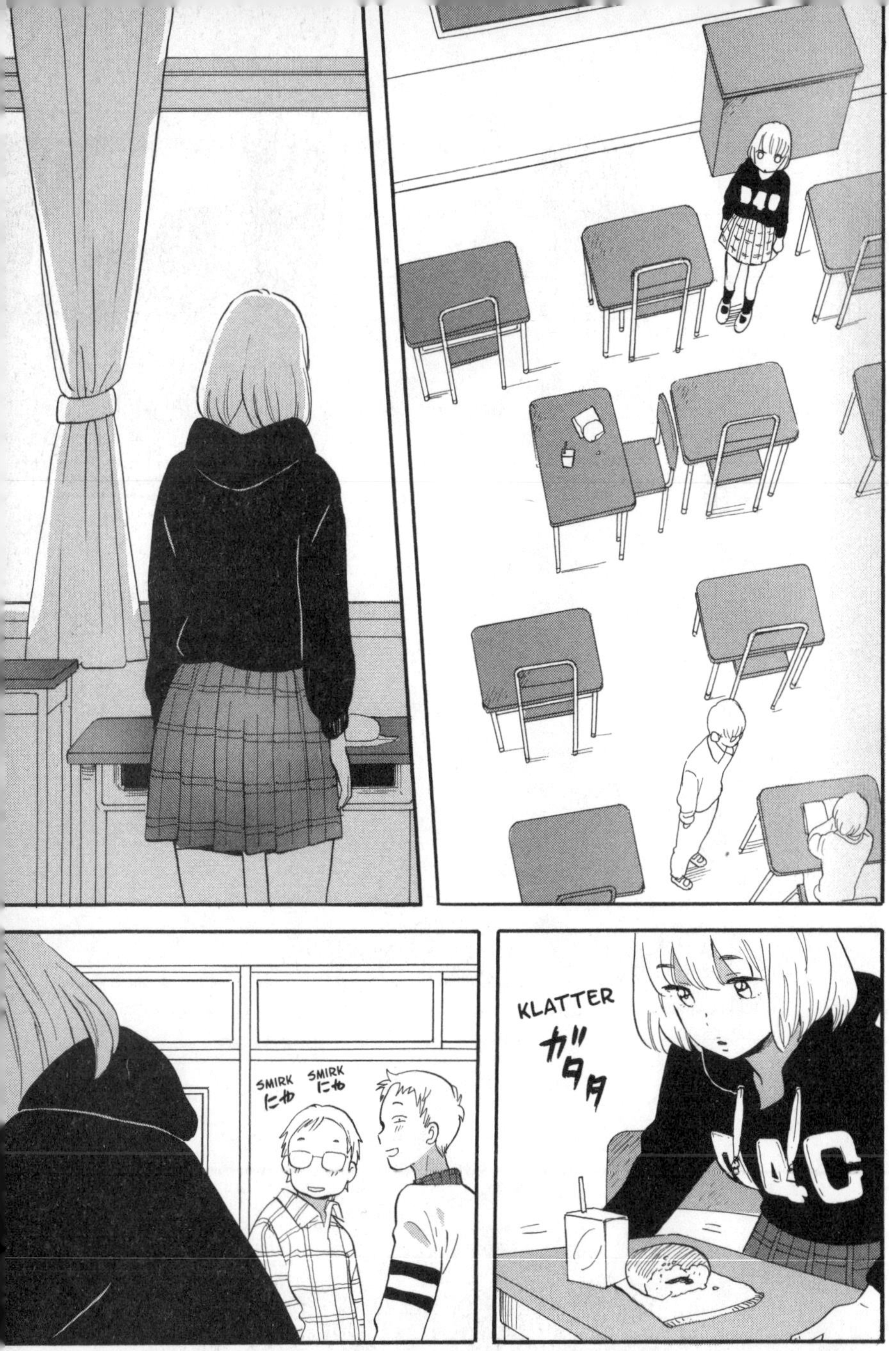
KLATTER
ガタタ
SMIRK
にゃ
SMIRK
にゃ

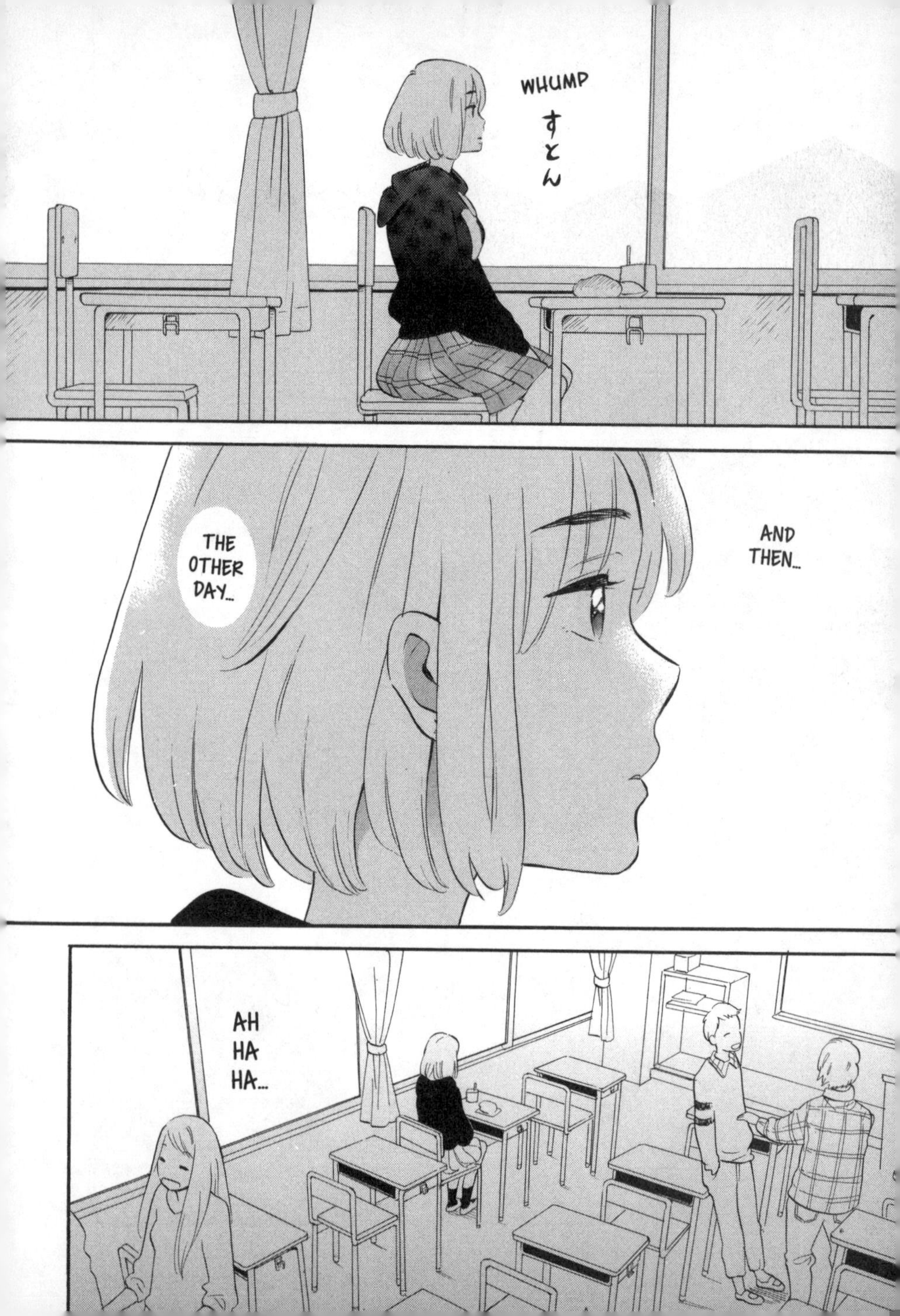
WHUMP
すとん
AND THEN...
THE OTHER DAY...
AH HA HA...

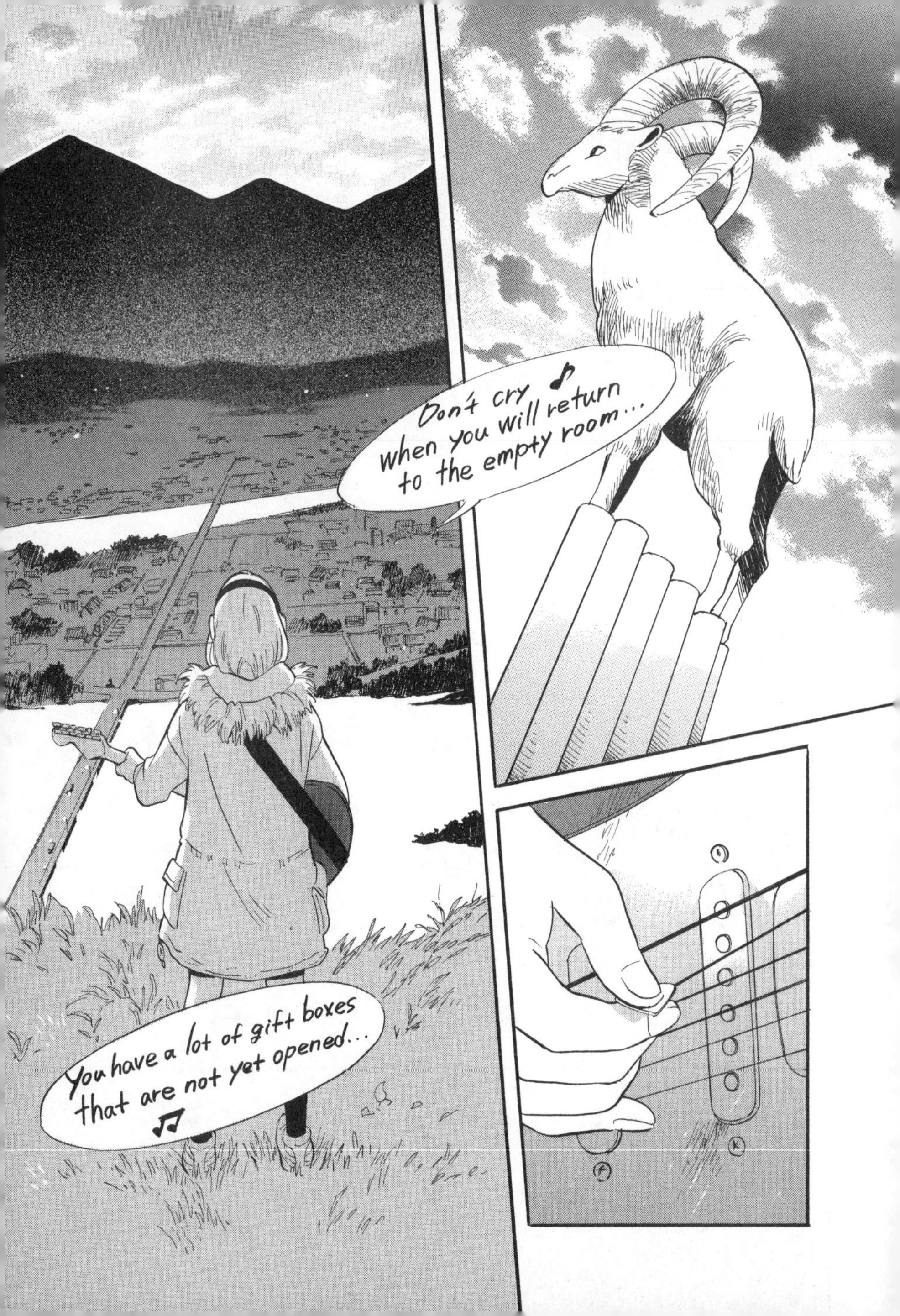
Don't cry ♪ when you will return to the empty room...
You have a lot of gift boxes that are not yet opened... ♫

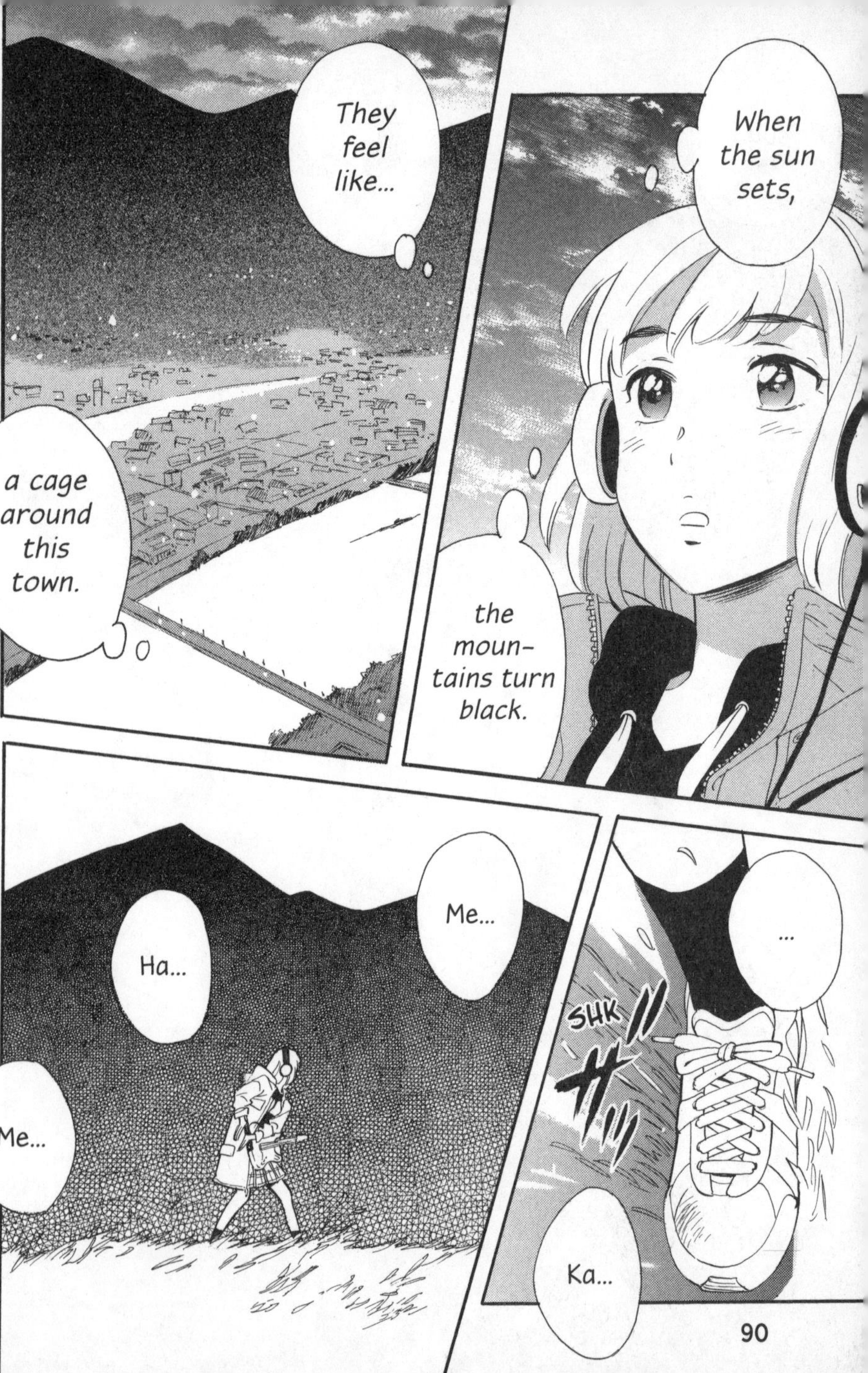
When the sun sets,
the mountains turn black.
They feel like...
a cage around this town.
...
SHK
Ka...
Me...
Ha...
Me...

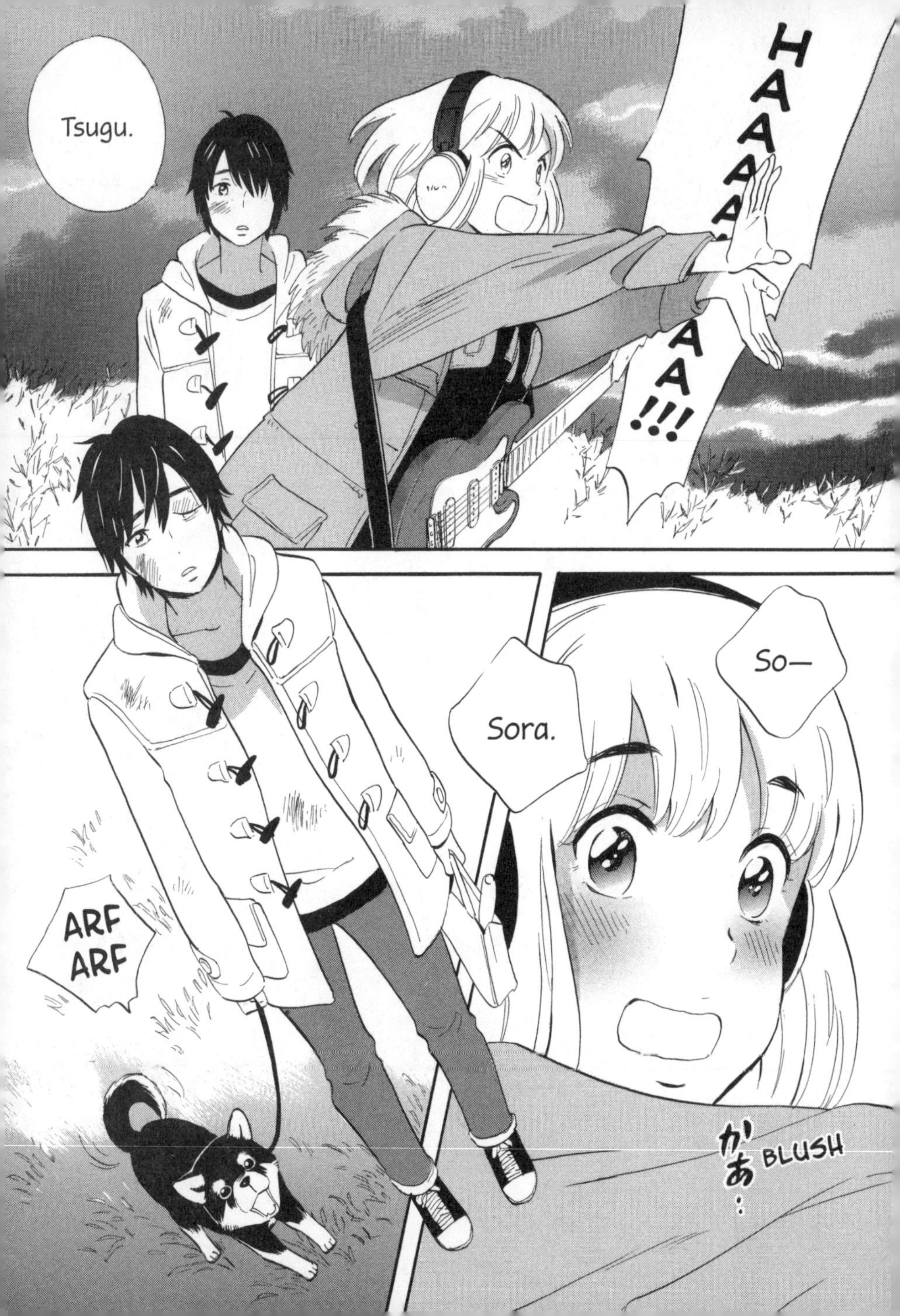
HAAAAAAA!!!
Tsugu.
So—
Sora.
かぁ BLUSH
ARF ARF

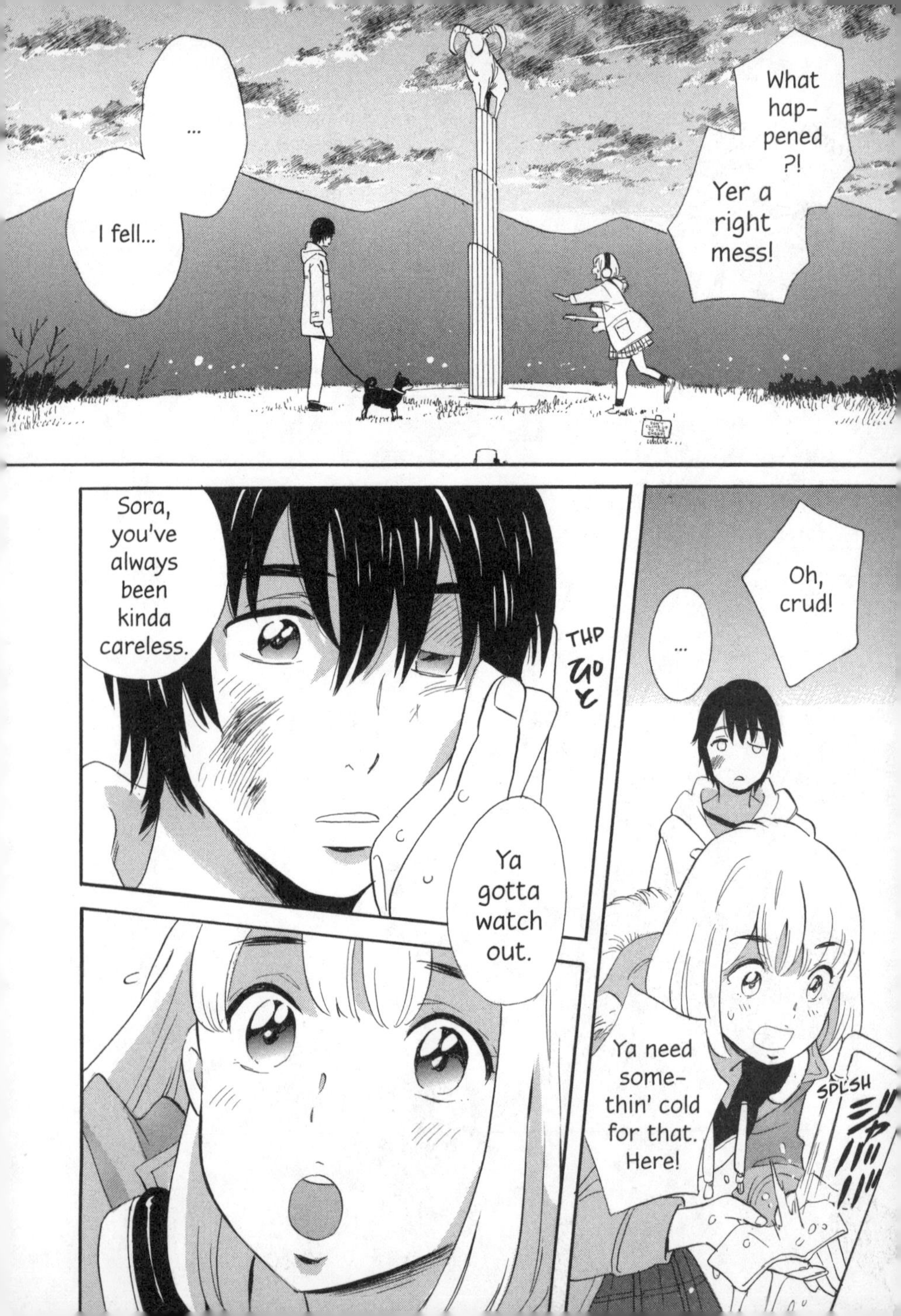
What hap-pened?!
Yer a right mess!
...
I fell...
Oh, crud!
...
Ya need some-thin' cold for that. Here!
SPLSH
Sora, you've always been kinda careless.
THP
Ya gotta watch out.

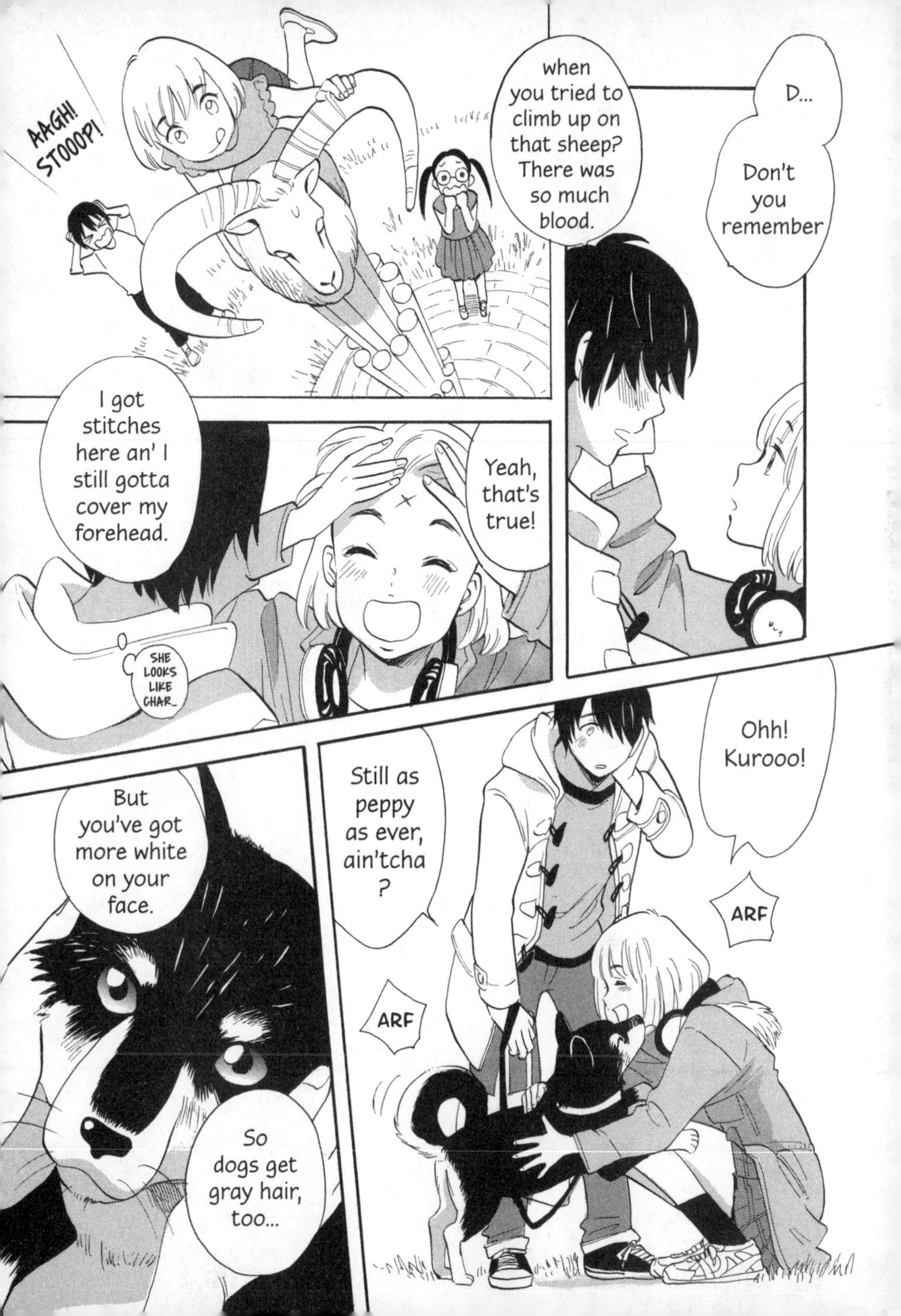
D...
Don't you remember
when you tried to climb up on that sheep? There was so much blood.
AAGH! STOOOP!
Yeah, that's true!
I got stitches here an' I still gotta cover my forehead.
SHE LOOKS LIKE CHAR_
Ohh! Kurooo!
ARF
Still as peppy as ever, ain'tcha ?
ARF
But you've got more white on your face.
So dogs get gray hair, too...

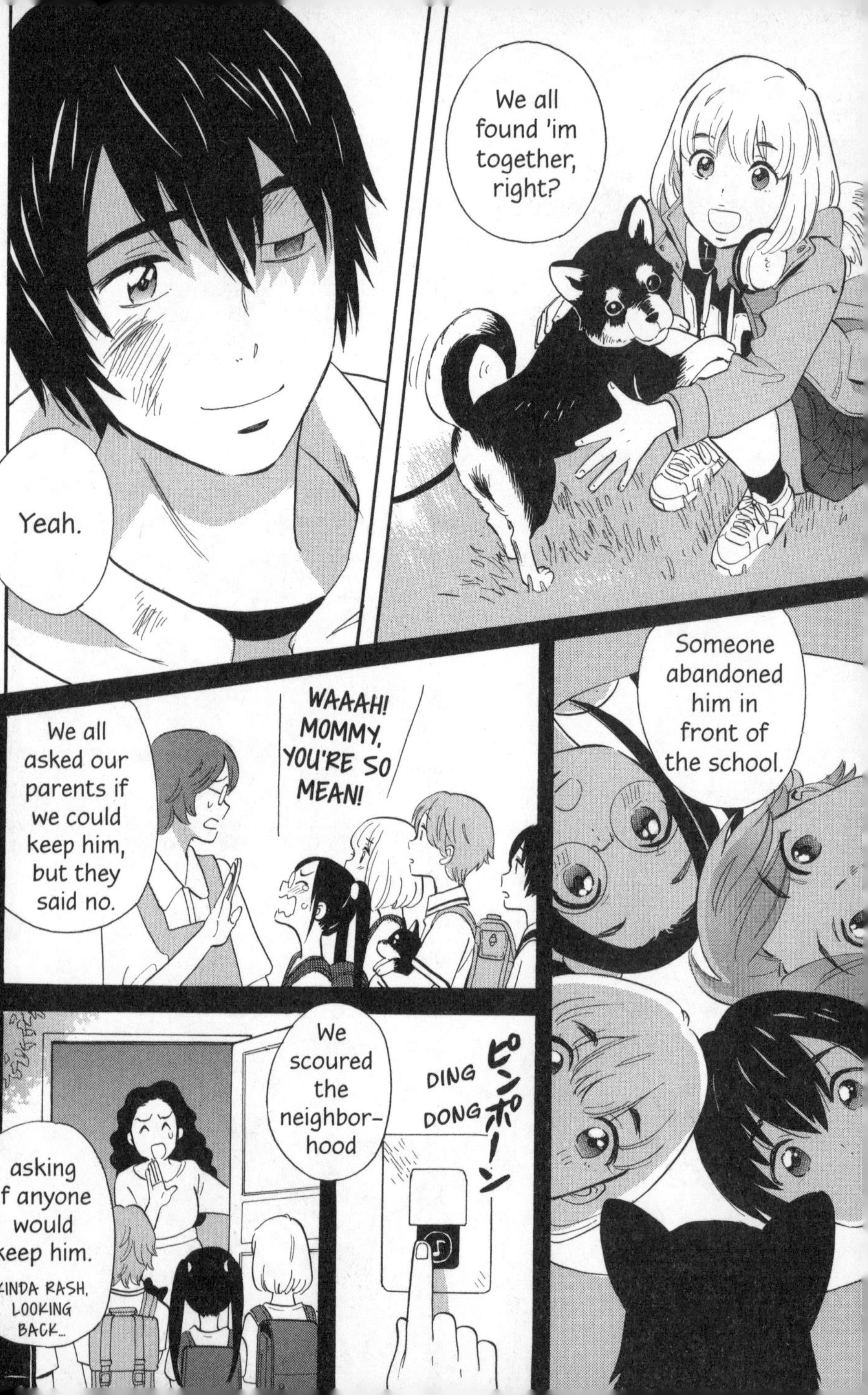
We all found 'im together, right?
Yeah.
Someone abandoned him in front of the school.
WAAAH! MOMMY, YOU'RE SO MEAN!
We all asked our parents if we could keep him, but they said no.
We scoured the neighbor-hood
ピンポーン
DING DONG
asking if anyone would keep him.
KINDA RASH, LOOKING BACK...

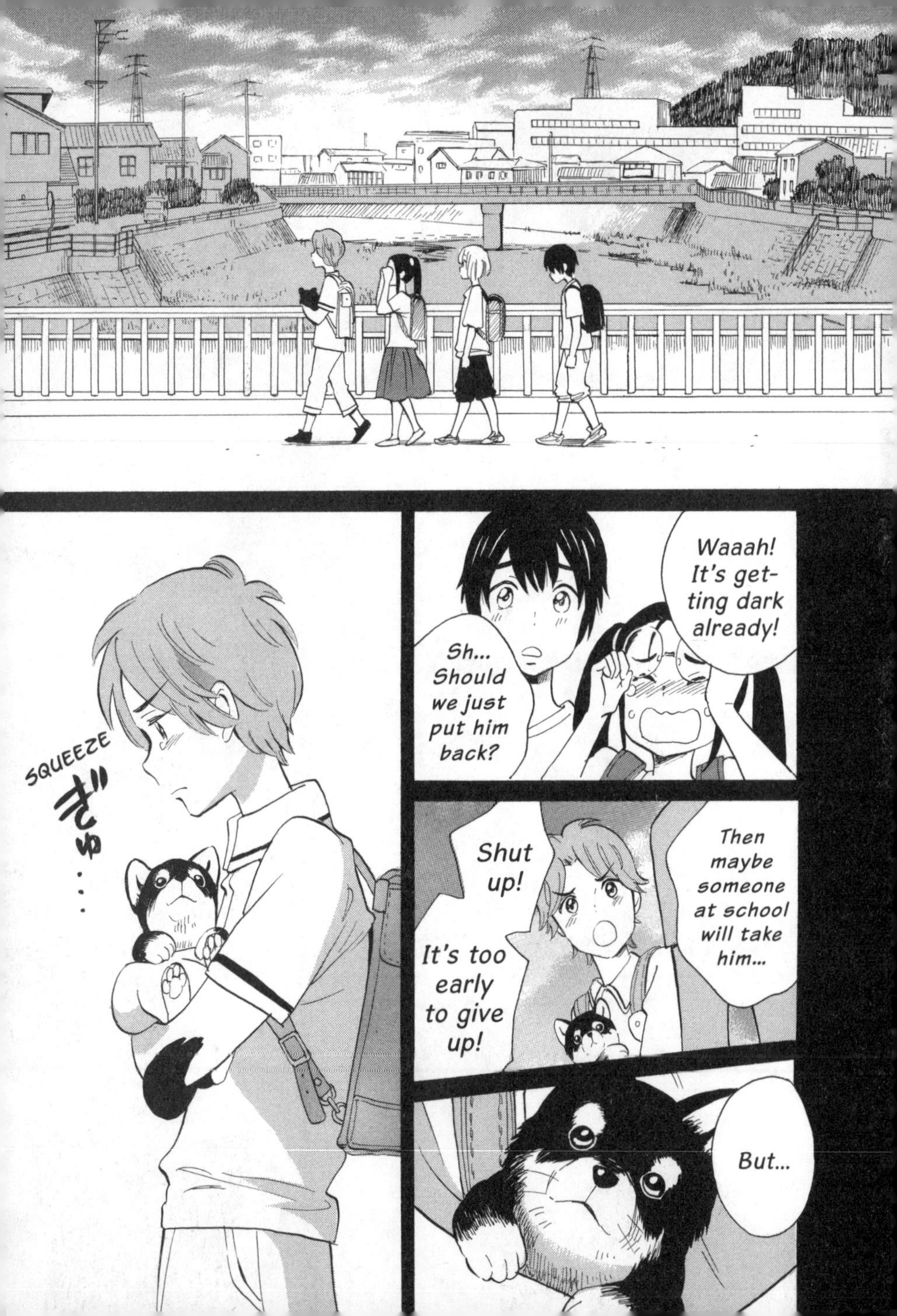
Waaah! It's getting dark already!
Sh... Should we just put him back?
Then maybe someone at school will take him...
Shut up!
It's too early to give up!
But...
SQUEEZE
ぎゅ...

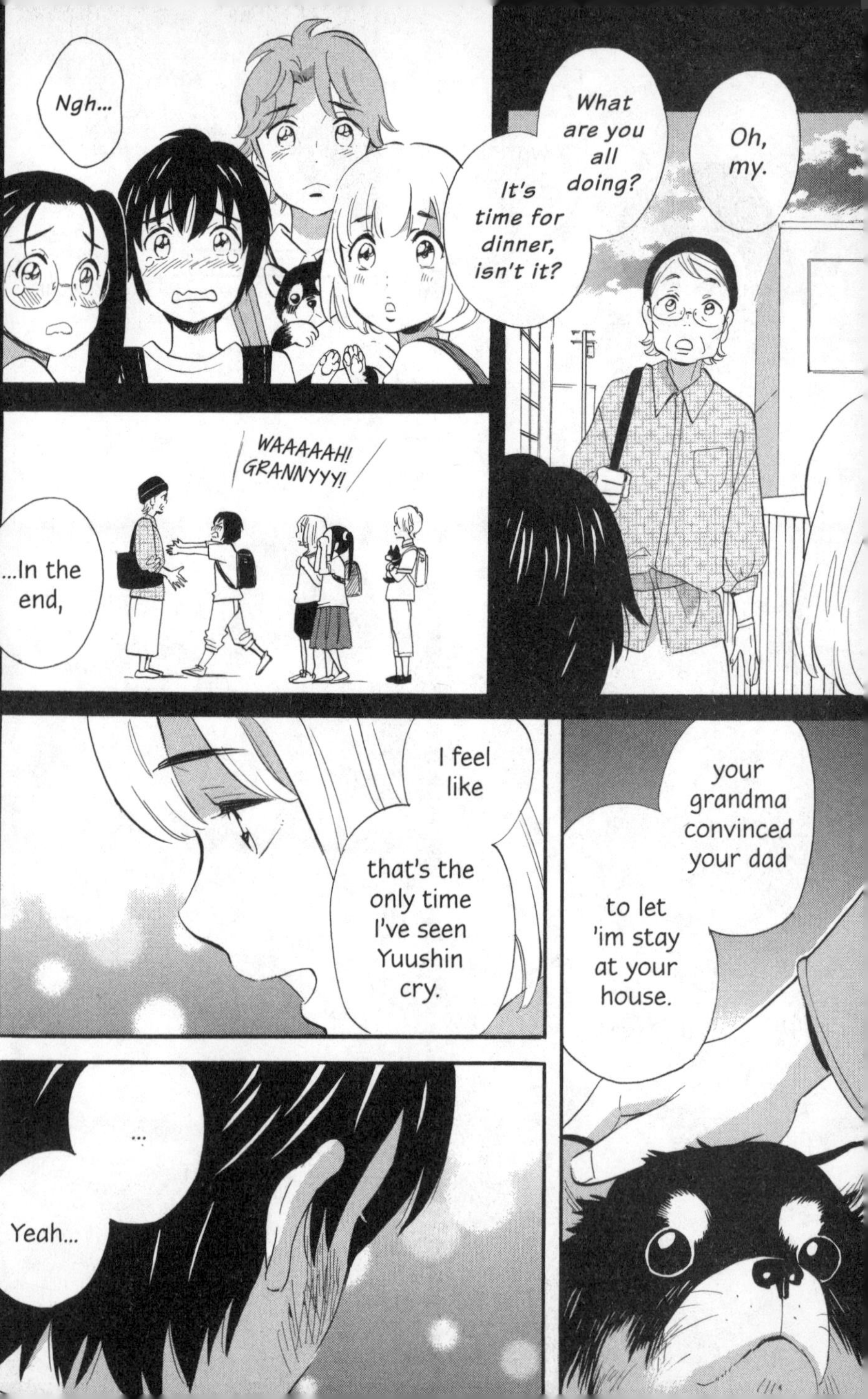
Oh, my.
What are you all doing?
It's time for dinner, isn't it?
Ngh...
WAAAAAH! GRANNYYY!
...In the end,
your grandma convinced your dad
to let 'im stay at your house.
I feel like
that's the only time I've seen Yuushin cry.
...
Yeah...

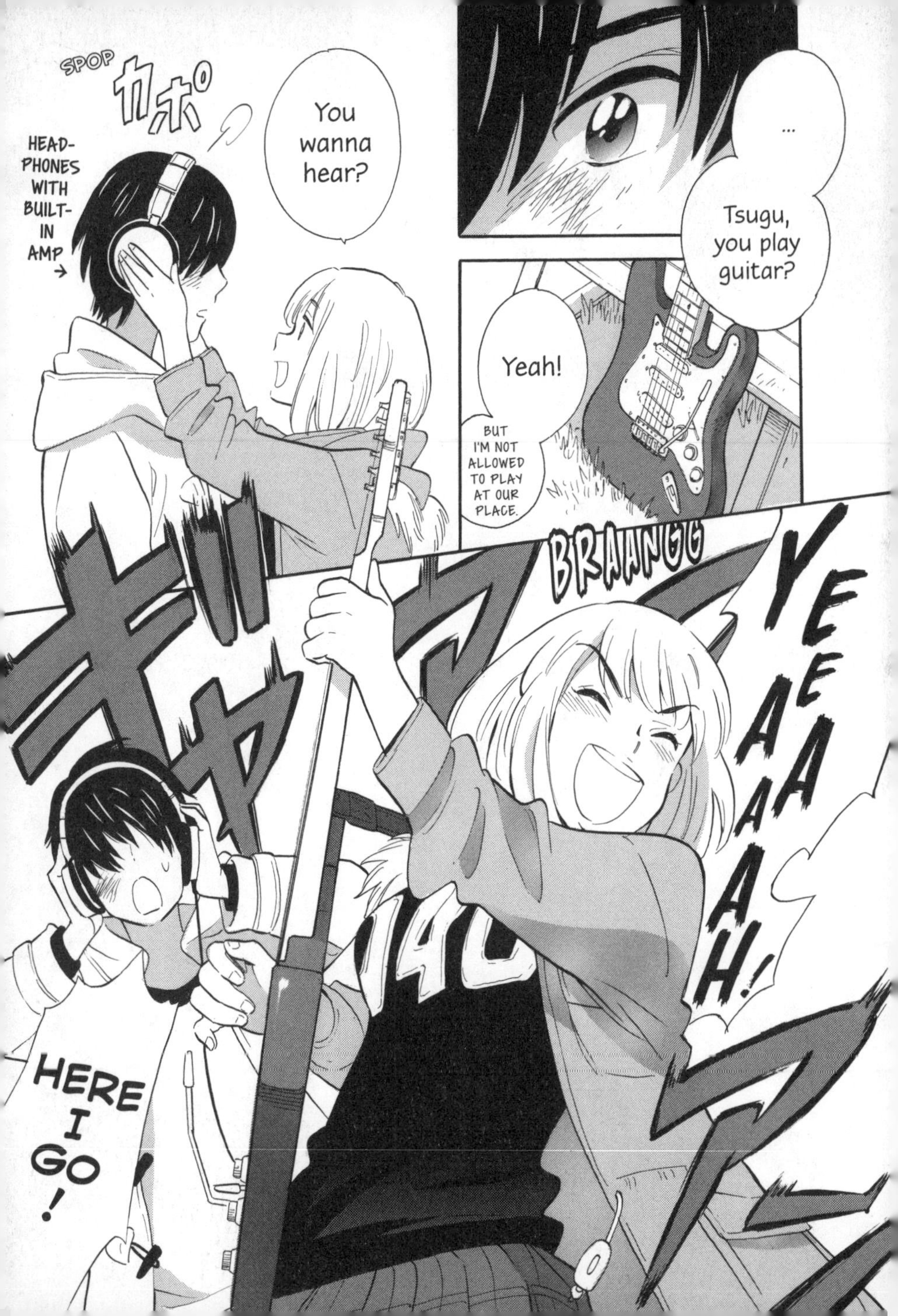
...
Tsugu, you play guitar?
Yeah!
BUT I'M NOT ALLOWED TO PLAY AT OUR PLACE.
SPOP
カポ
HEAD-PHONES WITH BUILT-IN AMP →
You wanna hear?
BRAANGG
YEEAAAAAH!
HERE I GO!

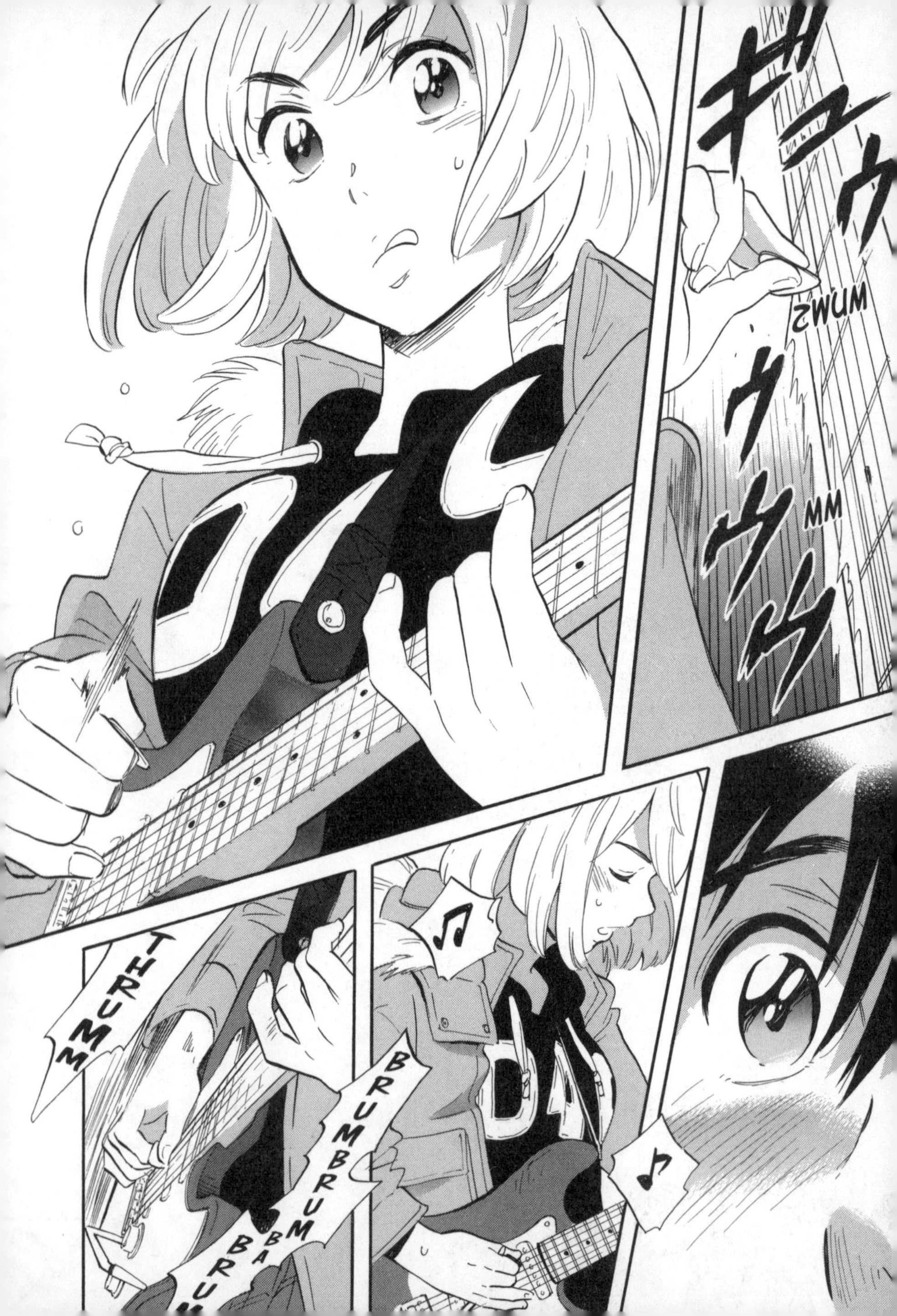
ZWUM
MM
THRUMM
BRUMBRUM
BA BA BRUM

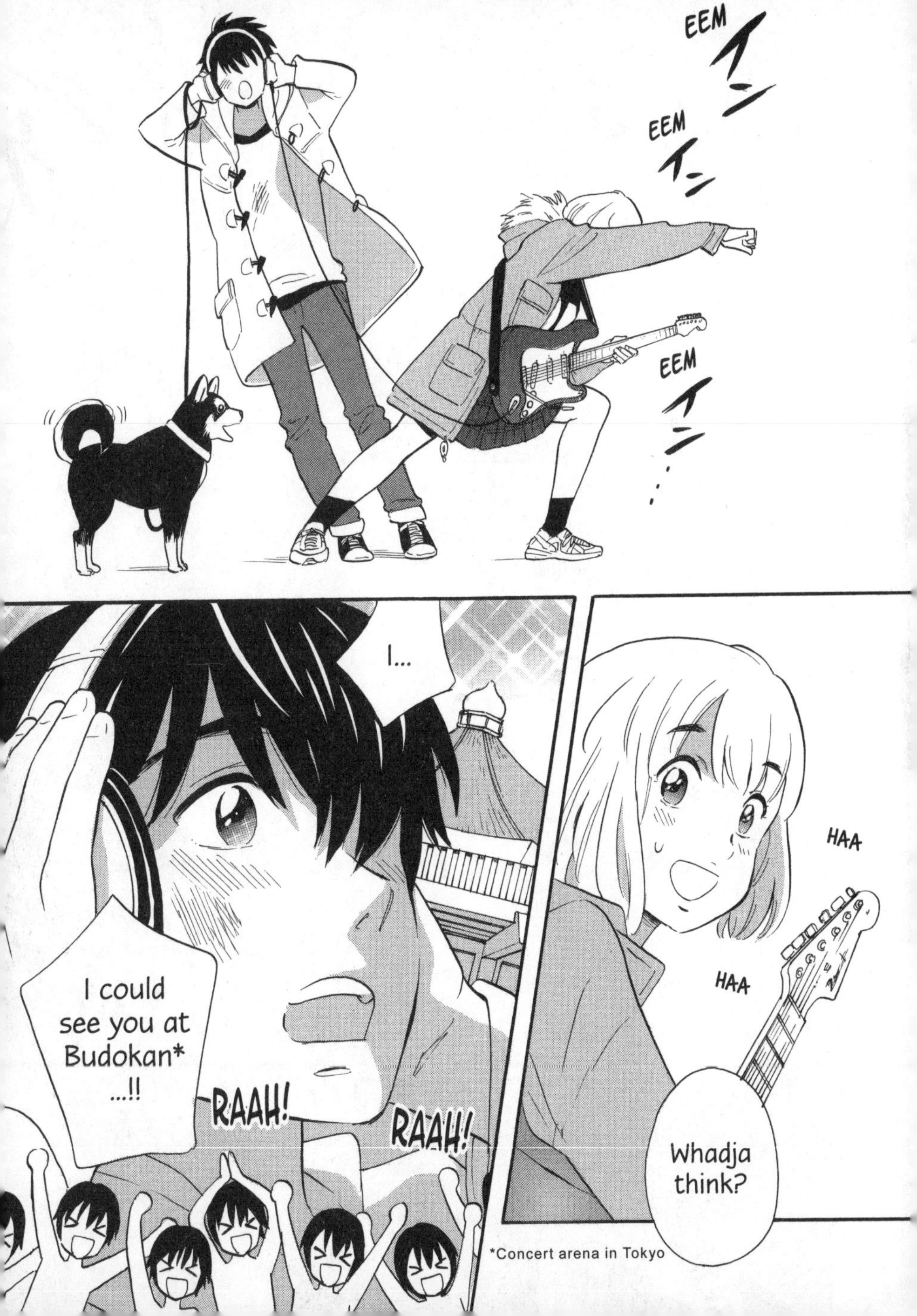
EEM
EEM
EEM
HAA
HAA
Whadja think?
I...
I could see you at Budokan* ...!!
RAAH!
RAAH!
*Concert arena in Tokyo

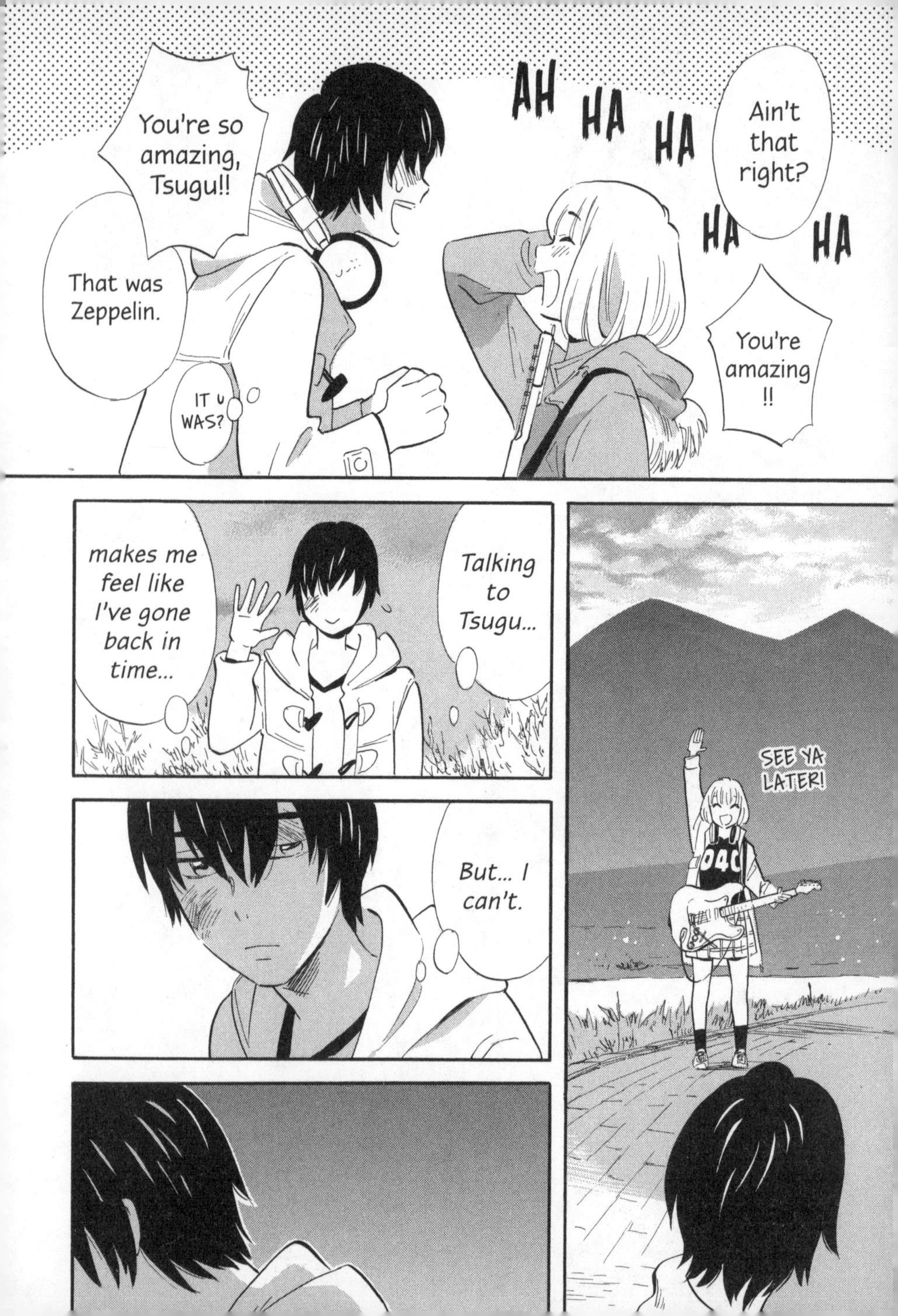
AH HA HA HA HA
Ain't that right?
You're amazing !!
You're so amazing, Tsugu!!
That was Zeppelin.
IT WAS?
SEE YA LATER!
Talking to Tsugu...
makes me feel like I've gone back in time...
But... I can't.

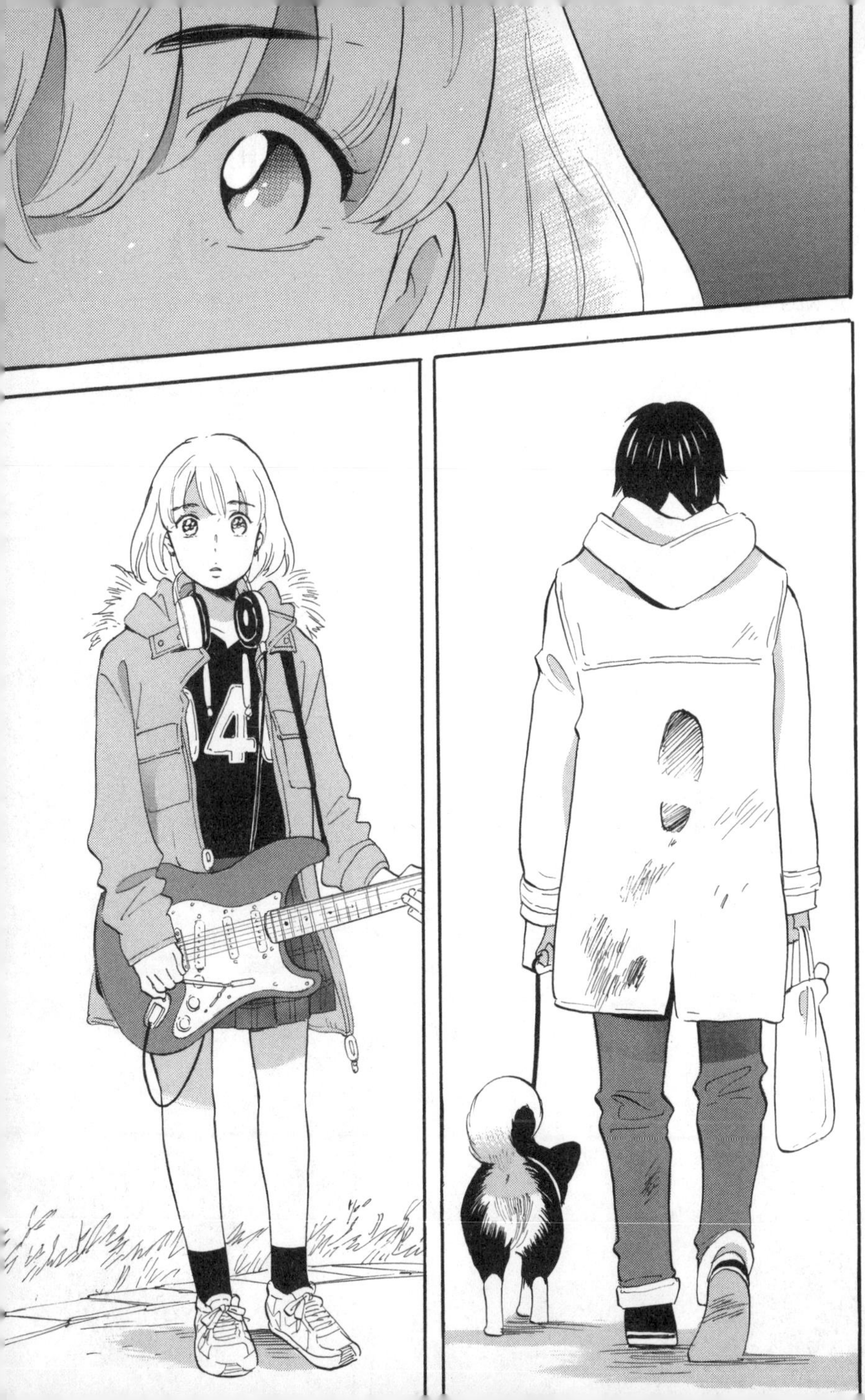

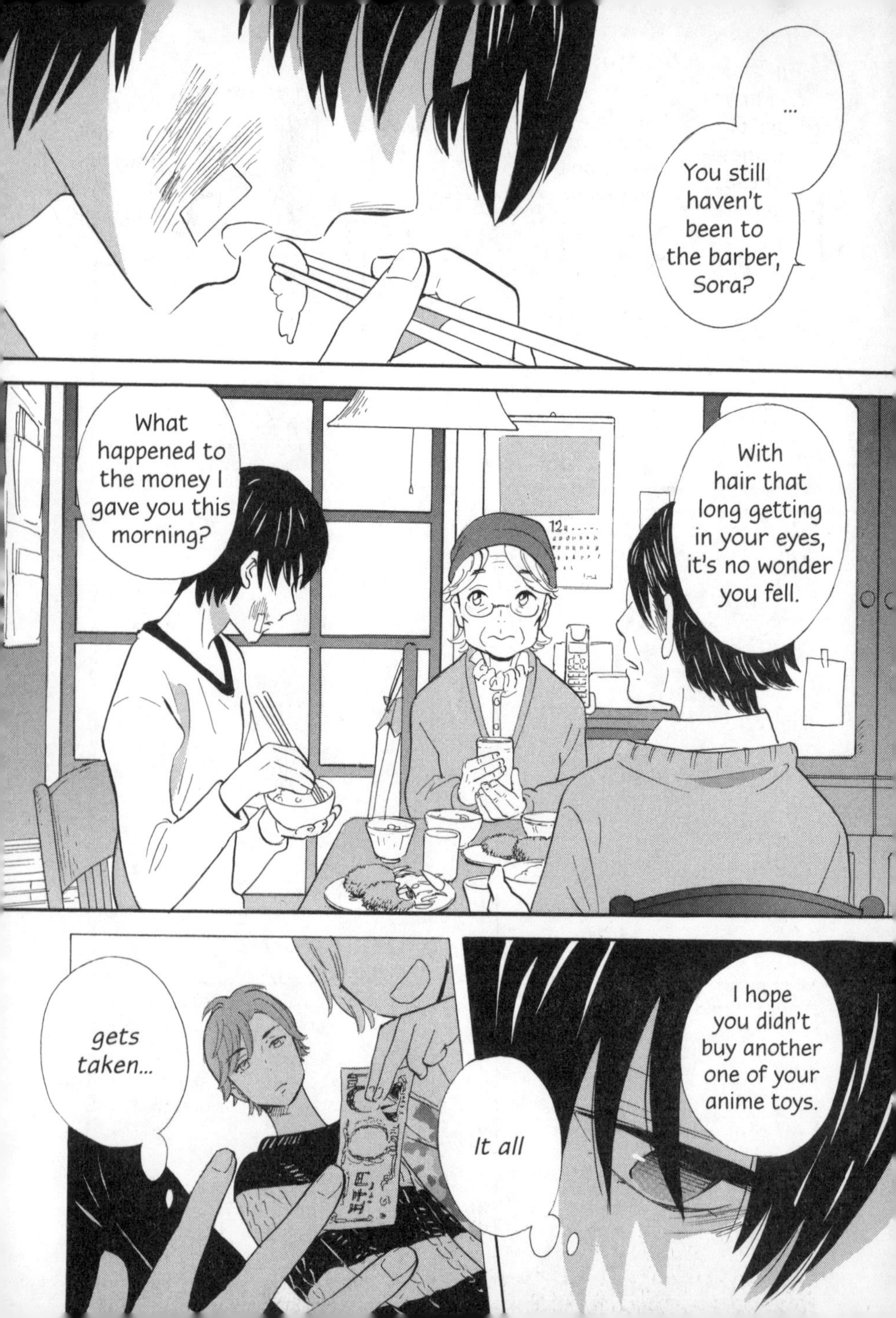
...
You still haven't been to the barber, Sora?
With hair that long getting in your eyes, it's no wonder you fell.
What happened to the money I gave you this morning?
I hope you didn't buy another one of your anime toys.
It all
gets taken...

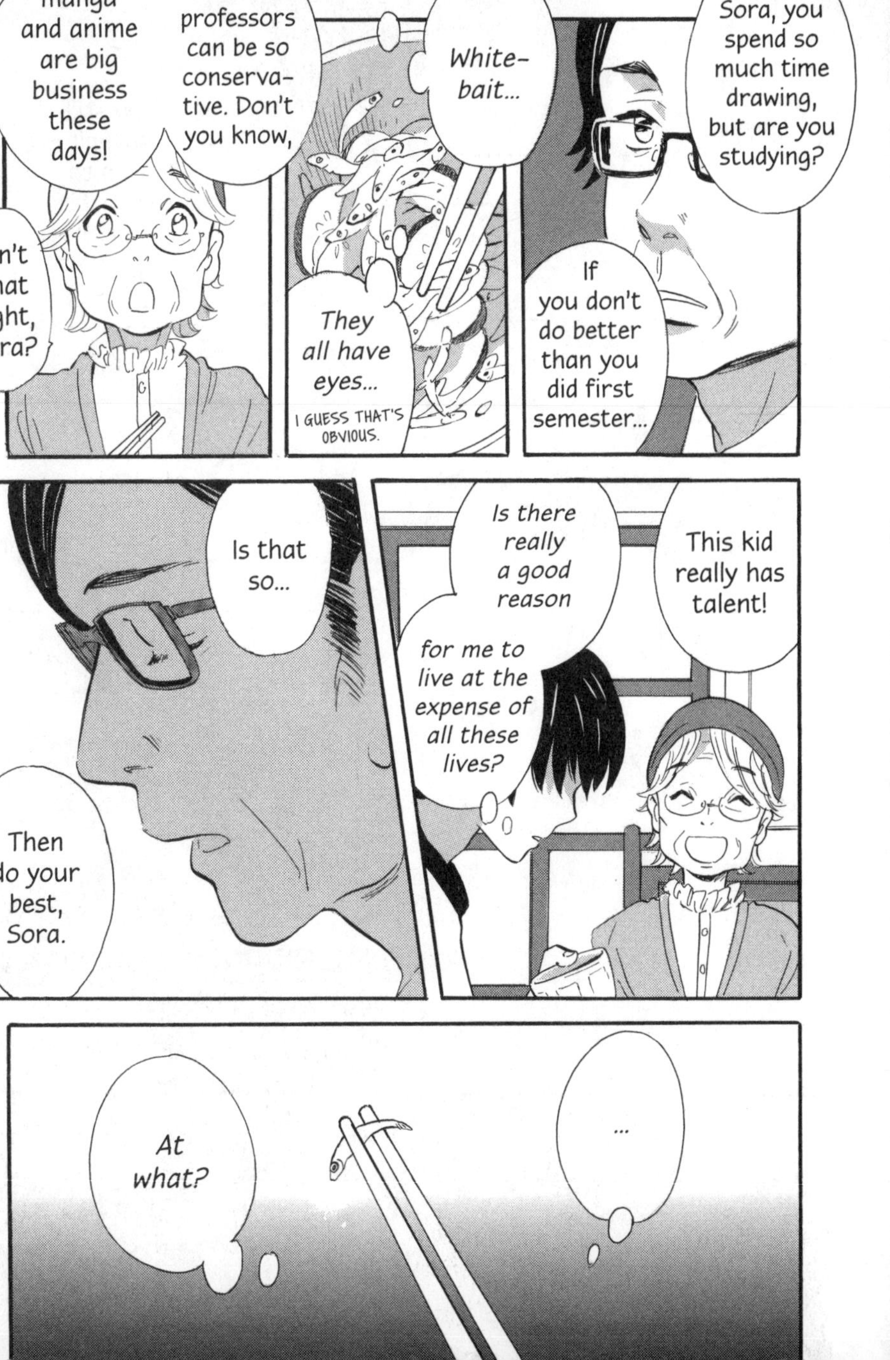
Sora, you spend so much time drawing, but are you studying?
If you don't do better than you did first semester...
White-bait...
They all have eyes...
I GUESS THAT'S OBVIOUS.
You professors can be so conserva-tive. Don't you know,
manga and anime are big business these days!
Isn't that right, Sora?
This kid really has talent!
Is there really a good reason
for me to live at the expense of all these lives?
Is that so...
Then do your best, Sora.
...
At what?

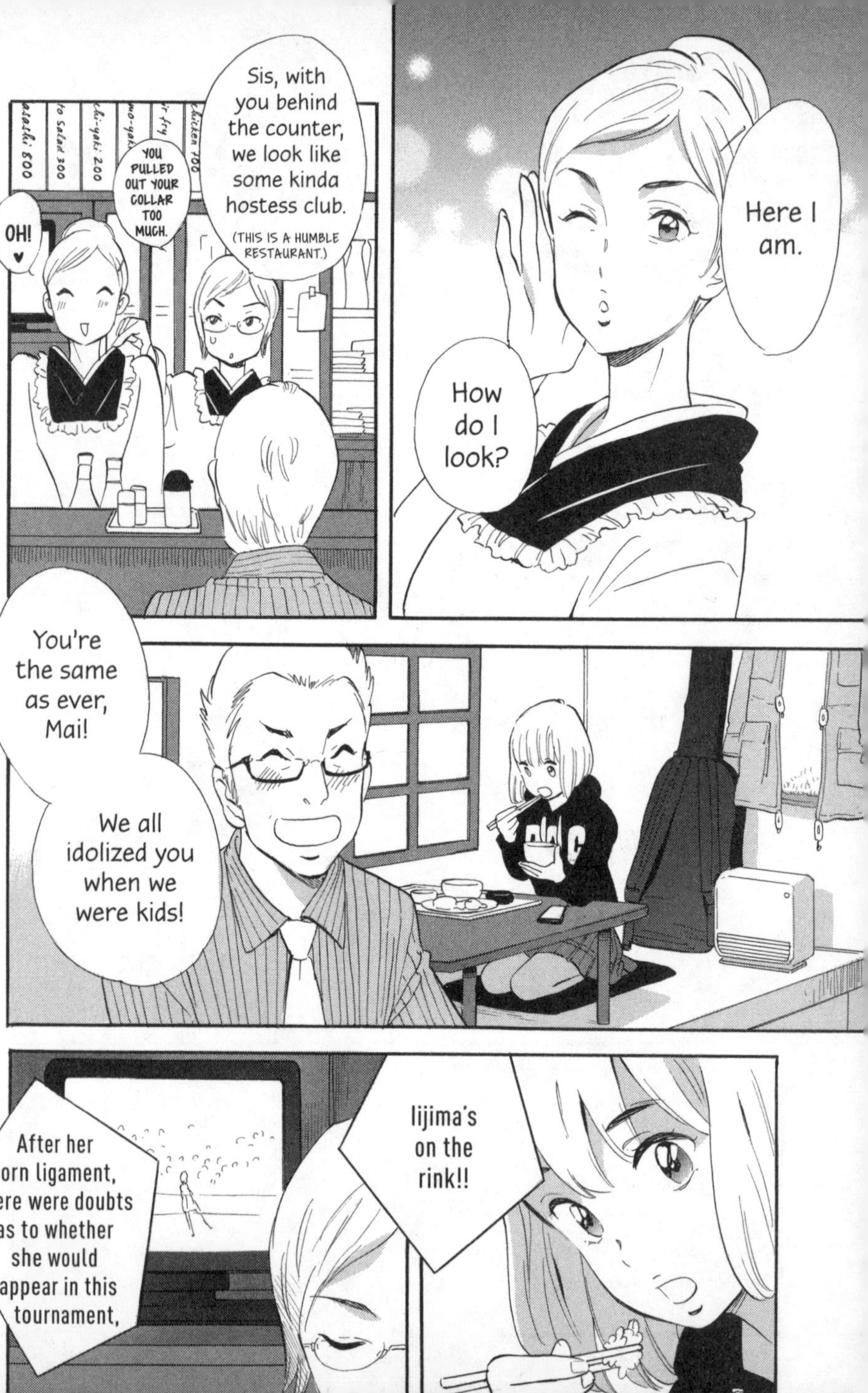
Here I am.
How do I look?
Sis, with you behind the counter, we look like some kinda hostess club.
(THIS IS A HUMBLE RESTAURANT.)
YOU PULLED OUT YOUR COLLAR TOO MUCH.
OH! ♥
You're the same as ever, Mai!
We all idolized you when we were kids!
Iijima's on the rink!!
After her torn ligament, there were doubts as to whether she would appear in this tournament,

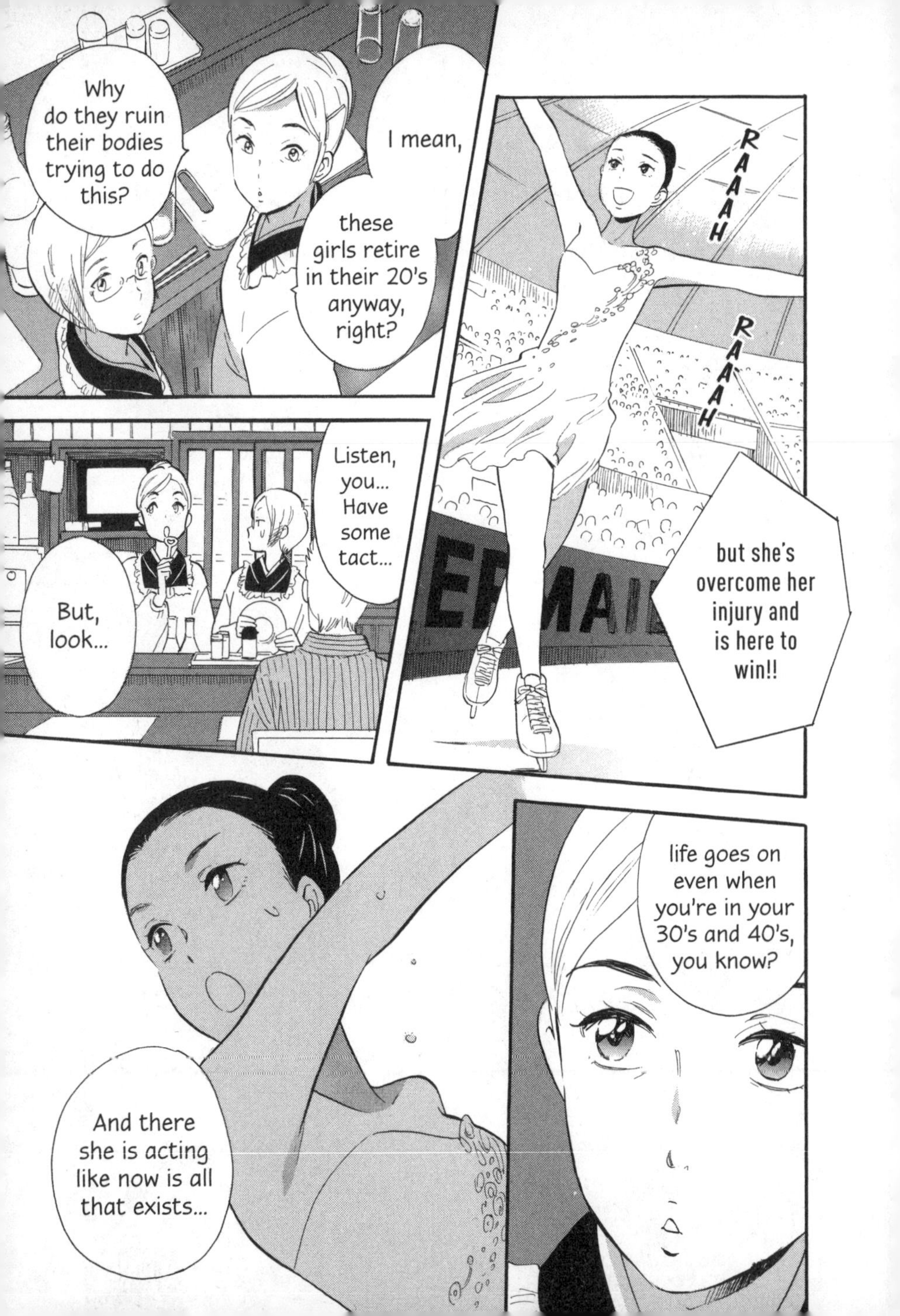
RAAAH
RAAAH
but she's overcome her injury and is here to win!!
Why do they ruin their bodies trying to do this?
I mean,
these girls retire in their 20's anyway, right?
Listen, you... Have some tact...
But, look...
life goes on even when you're in your 30's and 40's, you know?
And there she is acting like now is all that exists...

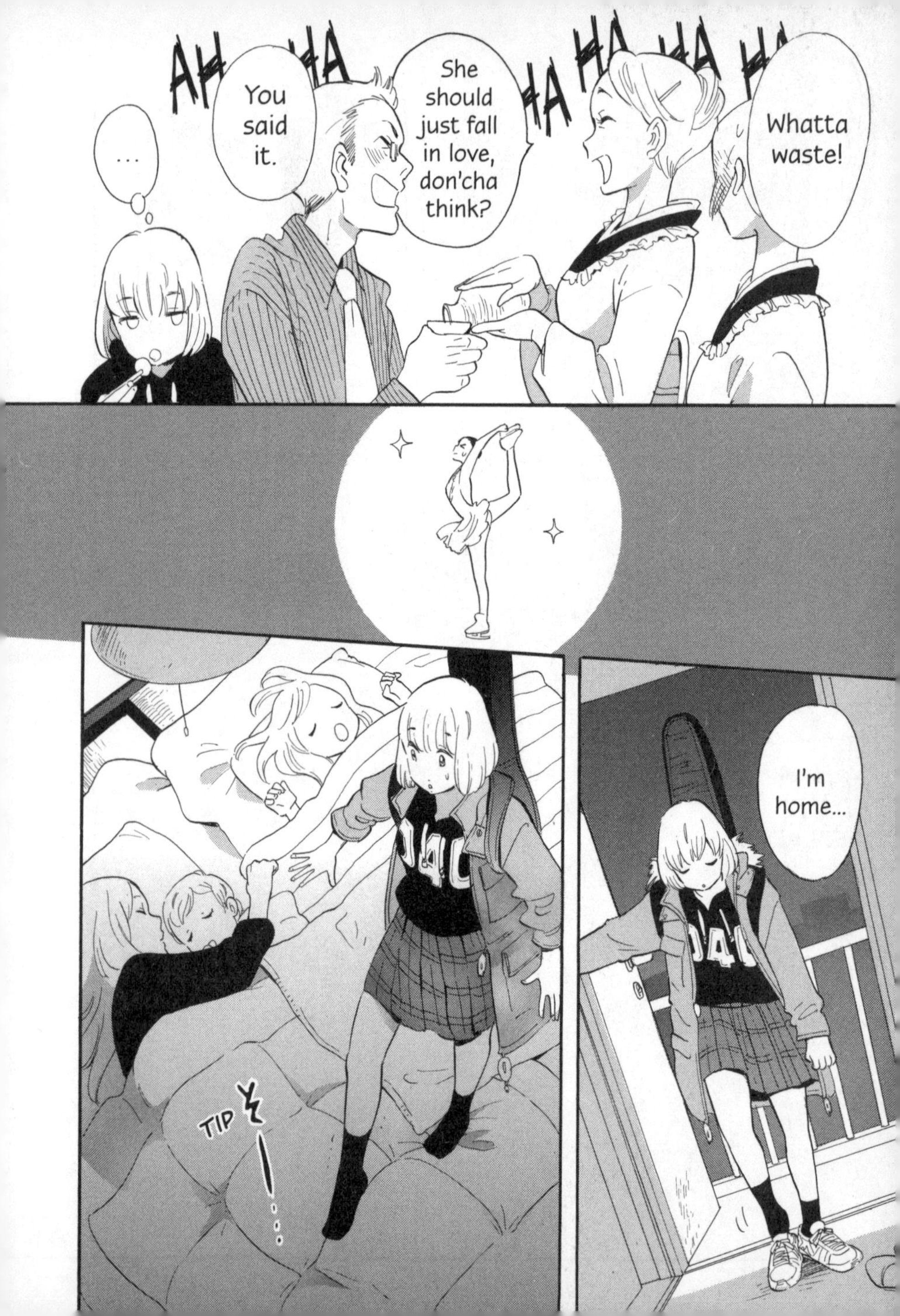
AH HA HA HA HA HA
Whatta waste!
She should just fall in love, don'cha think?
You said it.
...
I'm home...
TIP

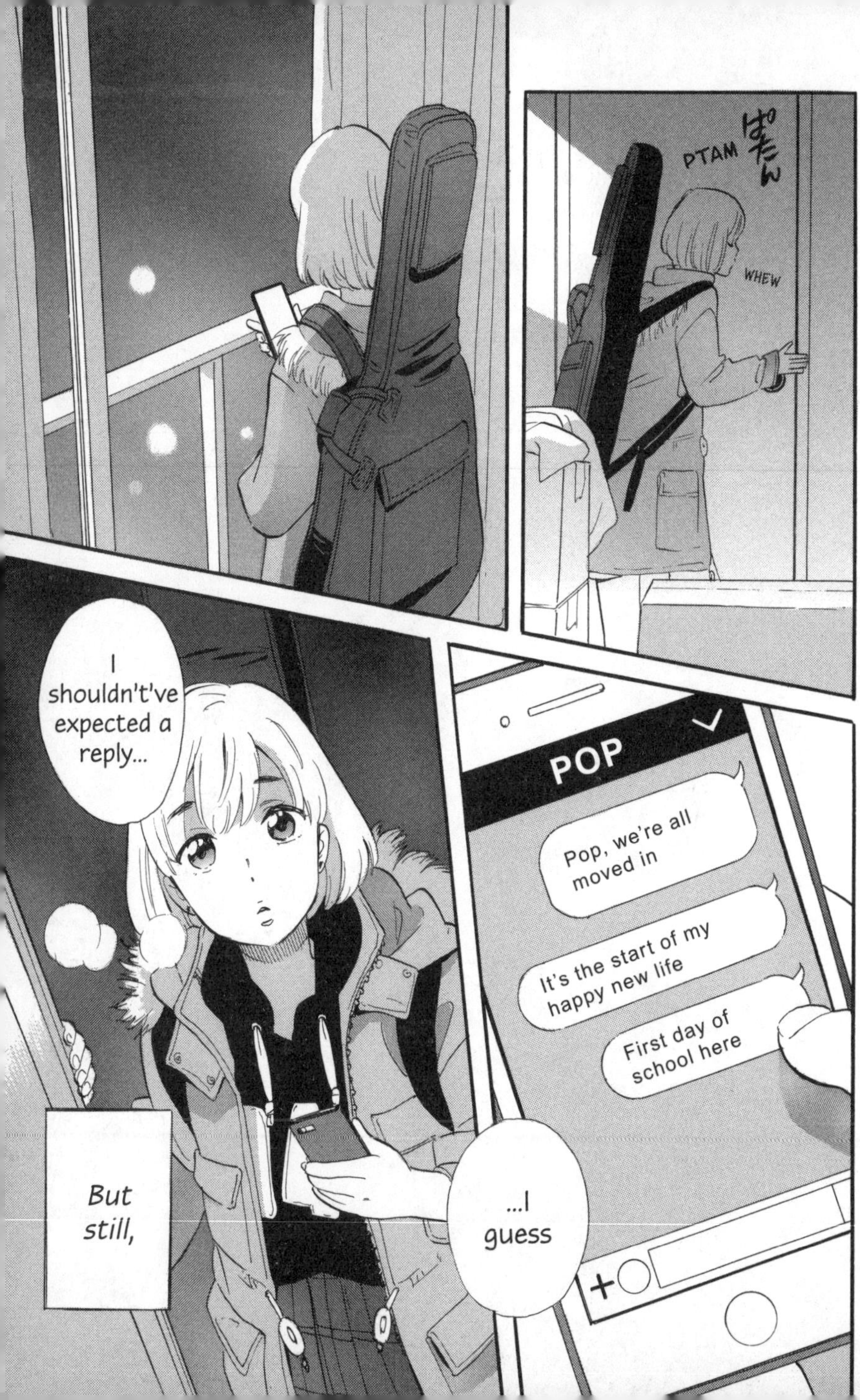
PTAM
ぱたん
WHEW
POP
Pop, we're all moved in
It's the start of my happy new life
First day of school here
I shouldn't've expected a reply...
But still,
...I guess

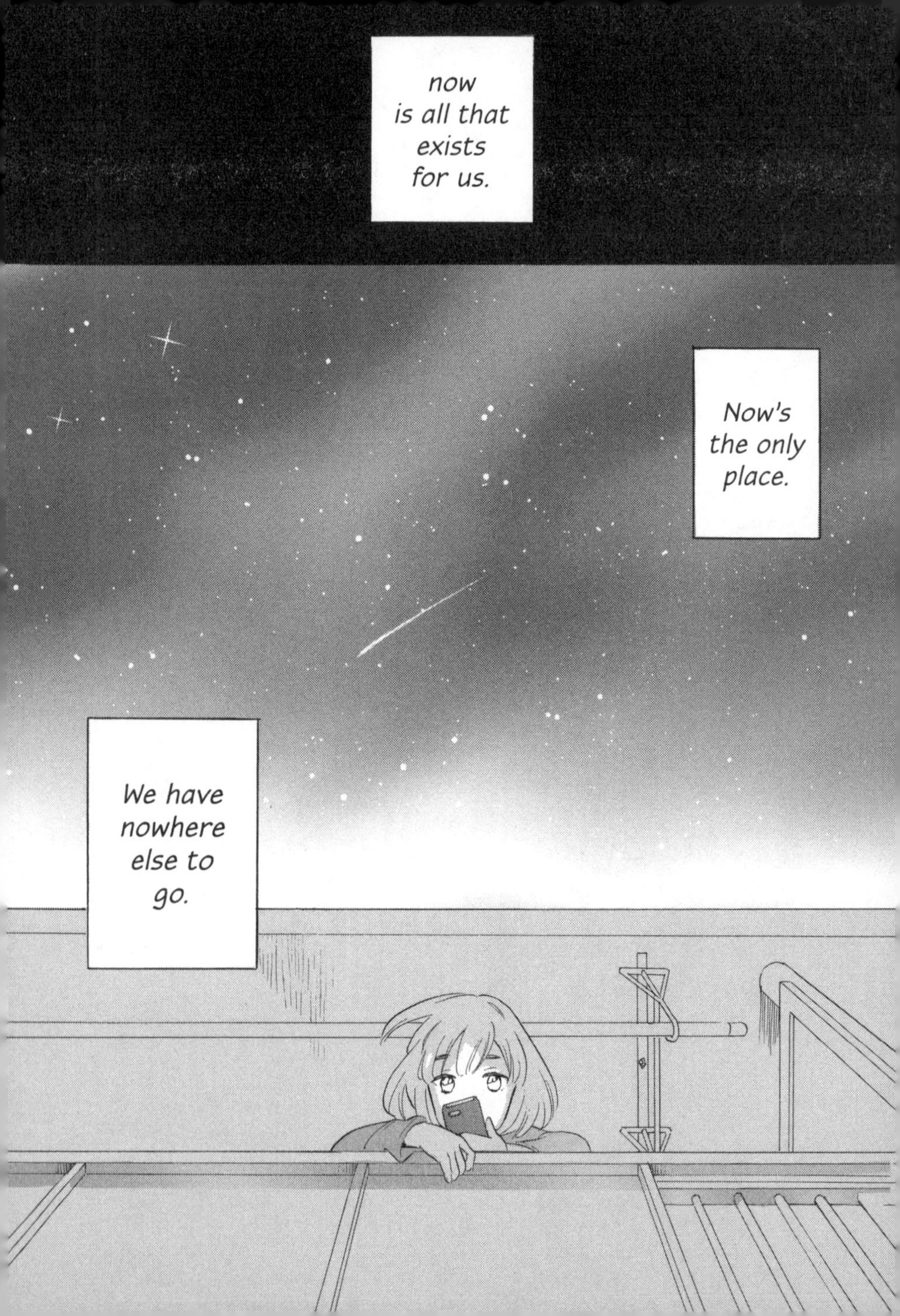
now is all that exists for us.
Now's the only place.
We have nowhere else to go.

THE GOLDEN SHEEP

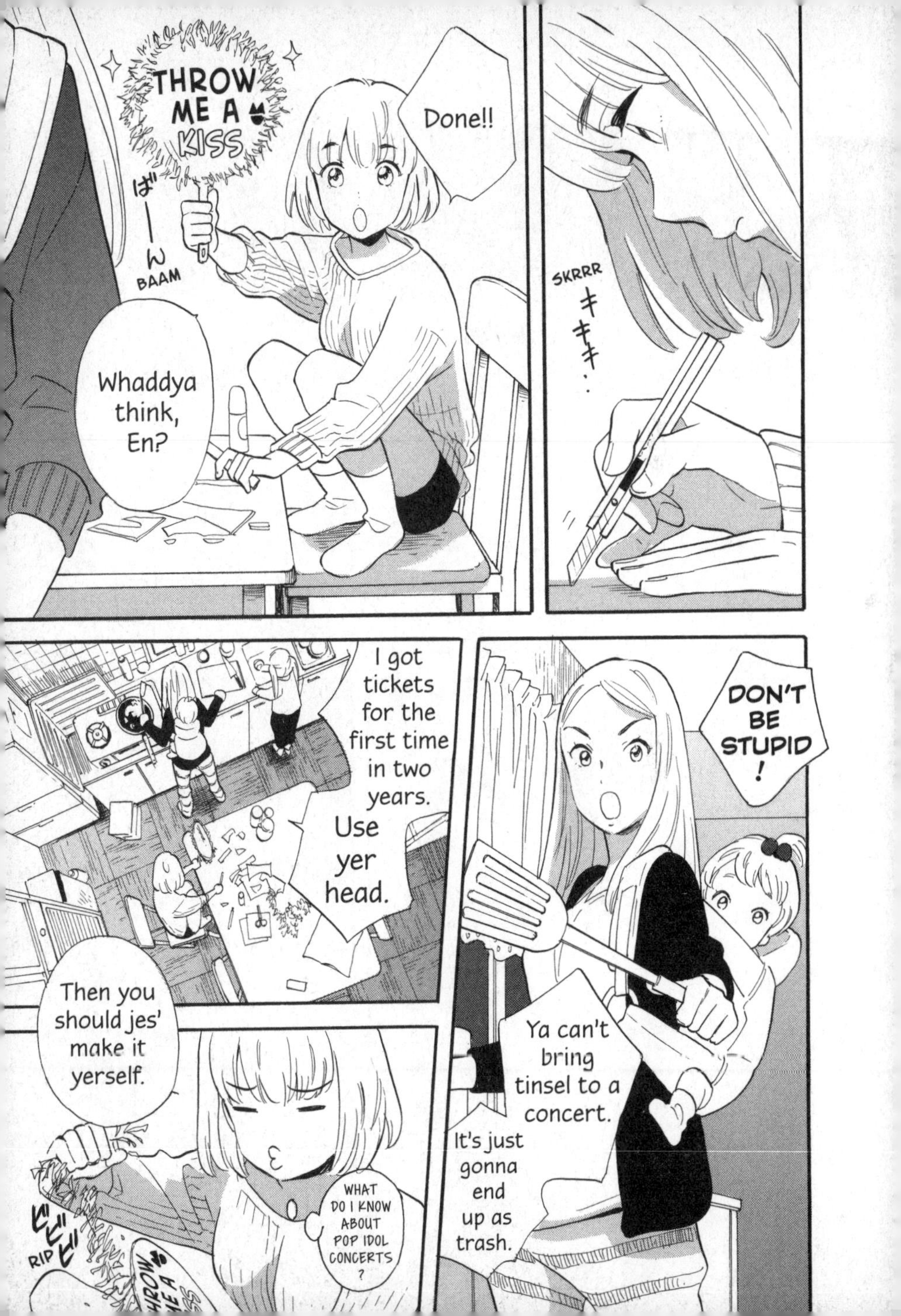

SKRRR
キキキ…
Done!!
THROW ME A KISS
ばーん
BAAM
Whaddya think, En?
DON'T BE STUPID!
Ya can't bring tinsel to a concert.
It's just gonna end up as trash.
I got tickets for the first time in two years.
Use yer head.
Then you should jes' make it yerself.
WHAT DO I KNOW ABOUT POP IDOL CONCERTS?
ビビビ
RIP

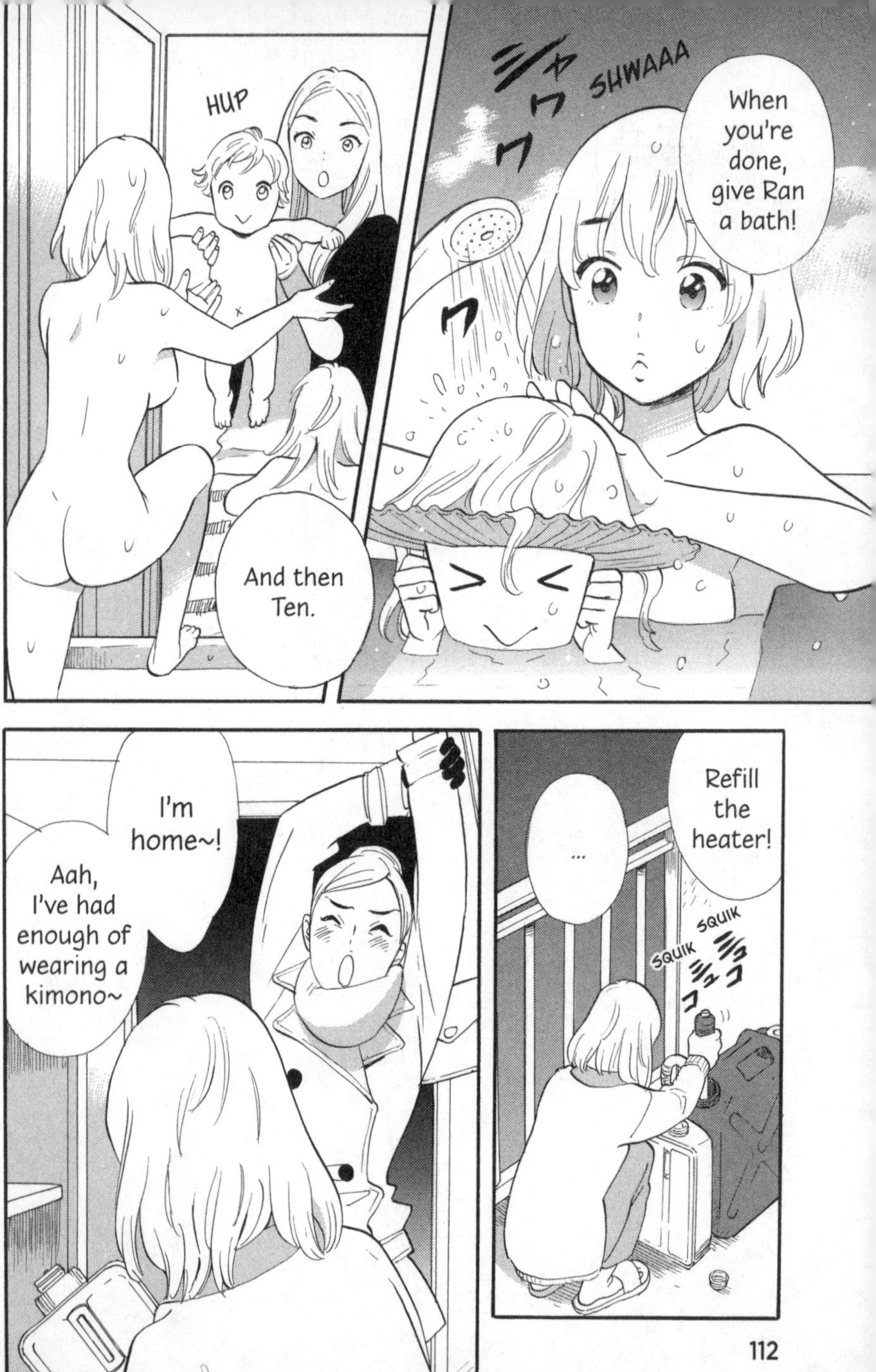
SHWAAA
When you're done, give Ran a bath!
HUP
And then Ten.
Refill the heater!
...
SQUIK
SQUIK
I'm home~!
Aah, I've had enough of wearing a kimono~

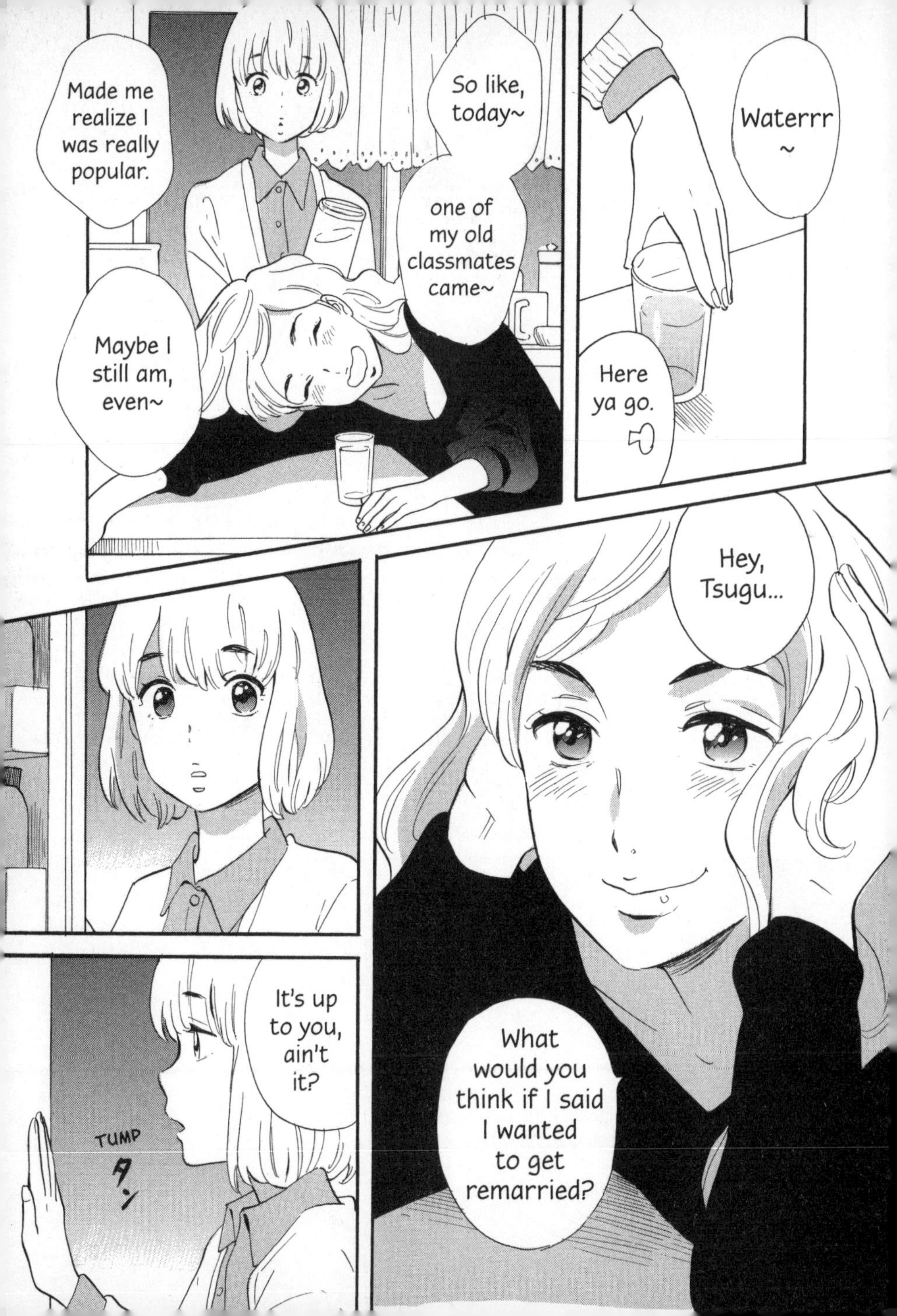
Waterrr ~
Here ya go.
So like, today~
one of my old classmates came~
Made me realize I was really popular.
Maybe I still am, even~
Hey, Tsugu...
What would you think if I said I wanted to get remarried?
It's up to you, ain't it?
TUMP
タン

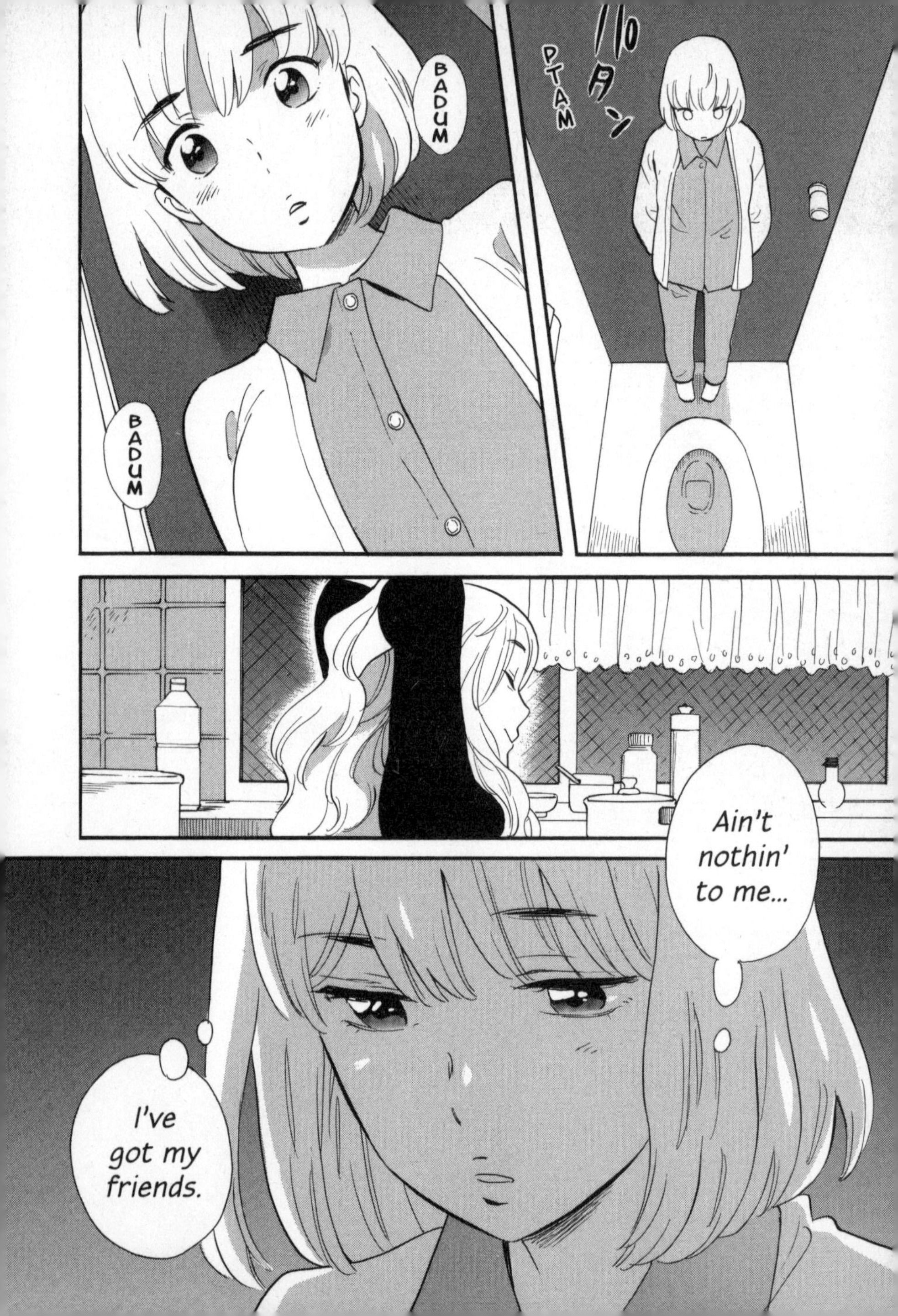
バタン
PTAM
BADUM
BADUM
Ain't nothin' to me...
I've got my friends.

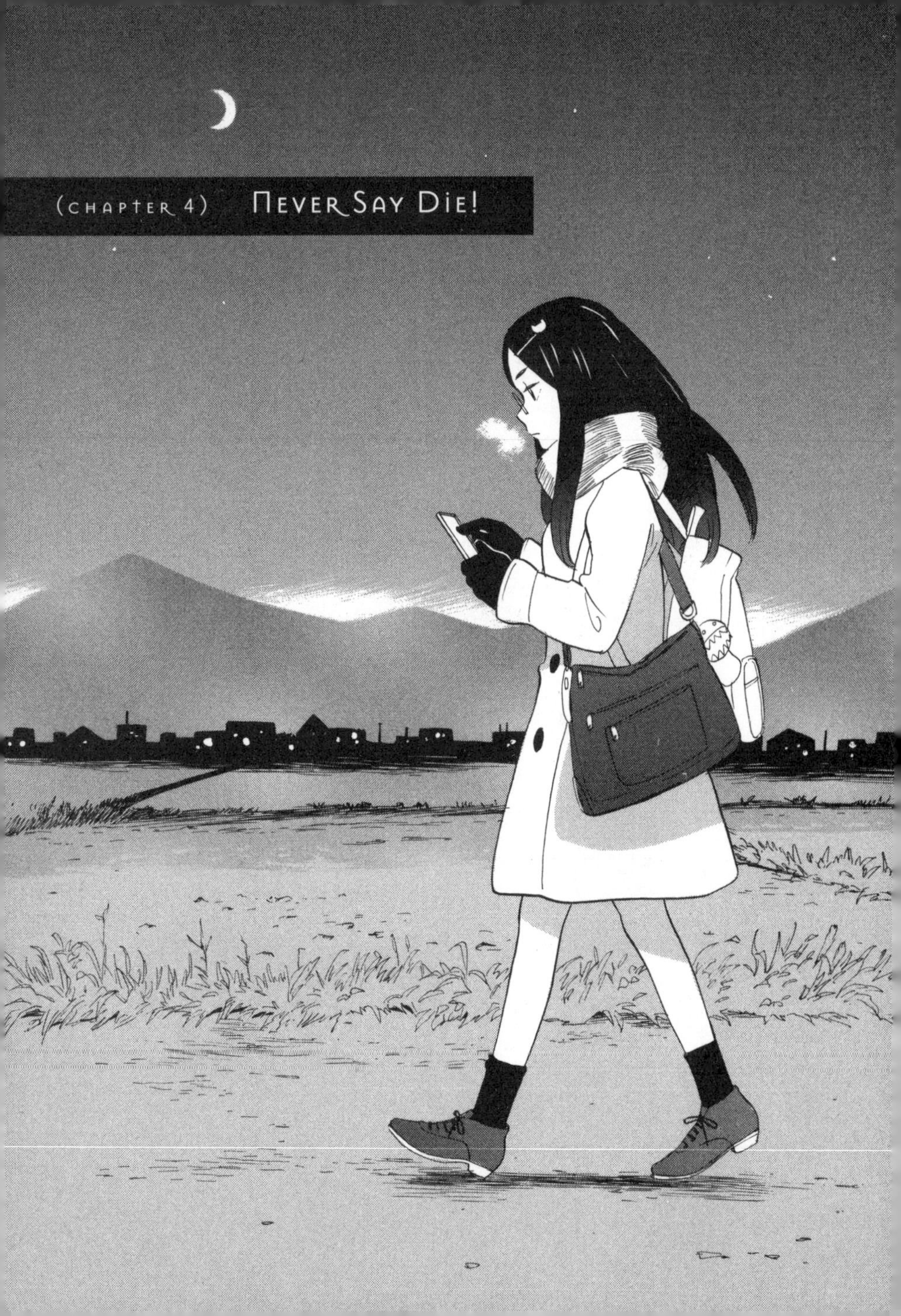
(CHAPTER 4) NEVER SAY DIE!

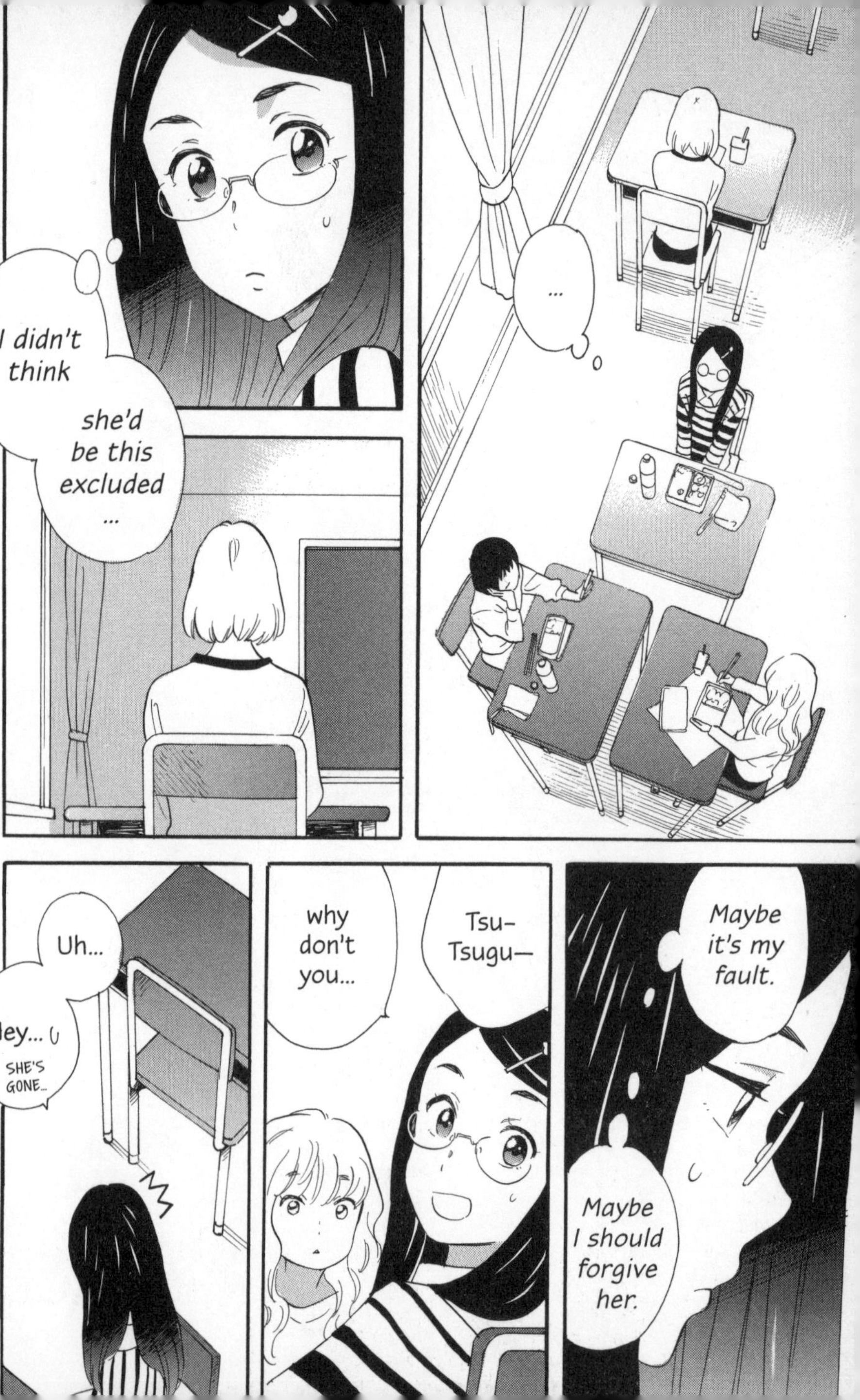
...
I didn't think
she'd be this excluded ...
Maybe it's my fault.
Maybe I should forgive her.
Tsu-Tsugu—
why don't you...
Uh...
Hey...
SHE'S GONE...

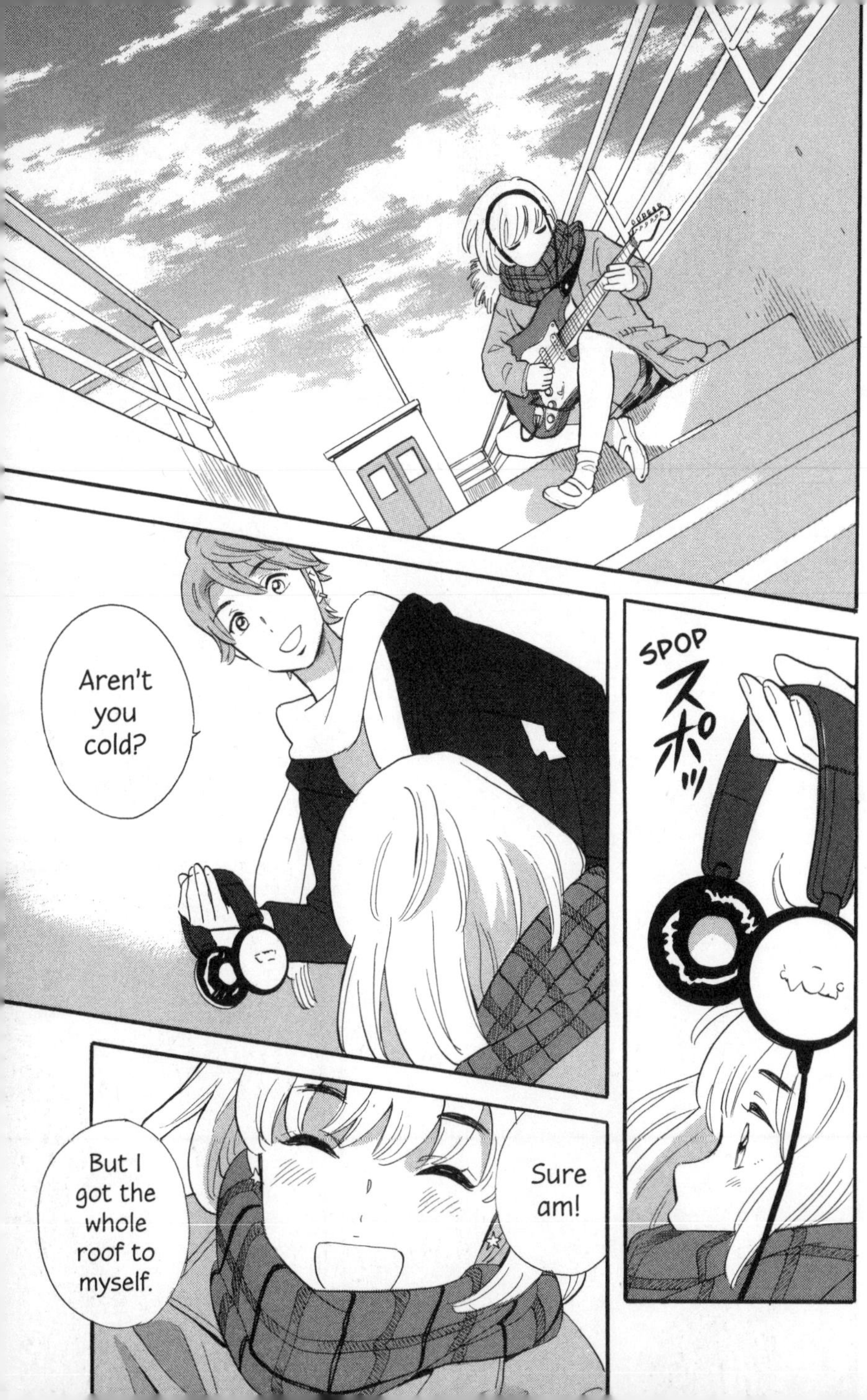
SPOP
スポッ
Aren't you cold?
Sure am!
But I got the whole roof to myself.

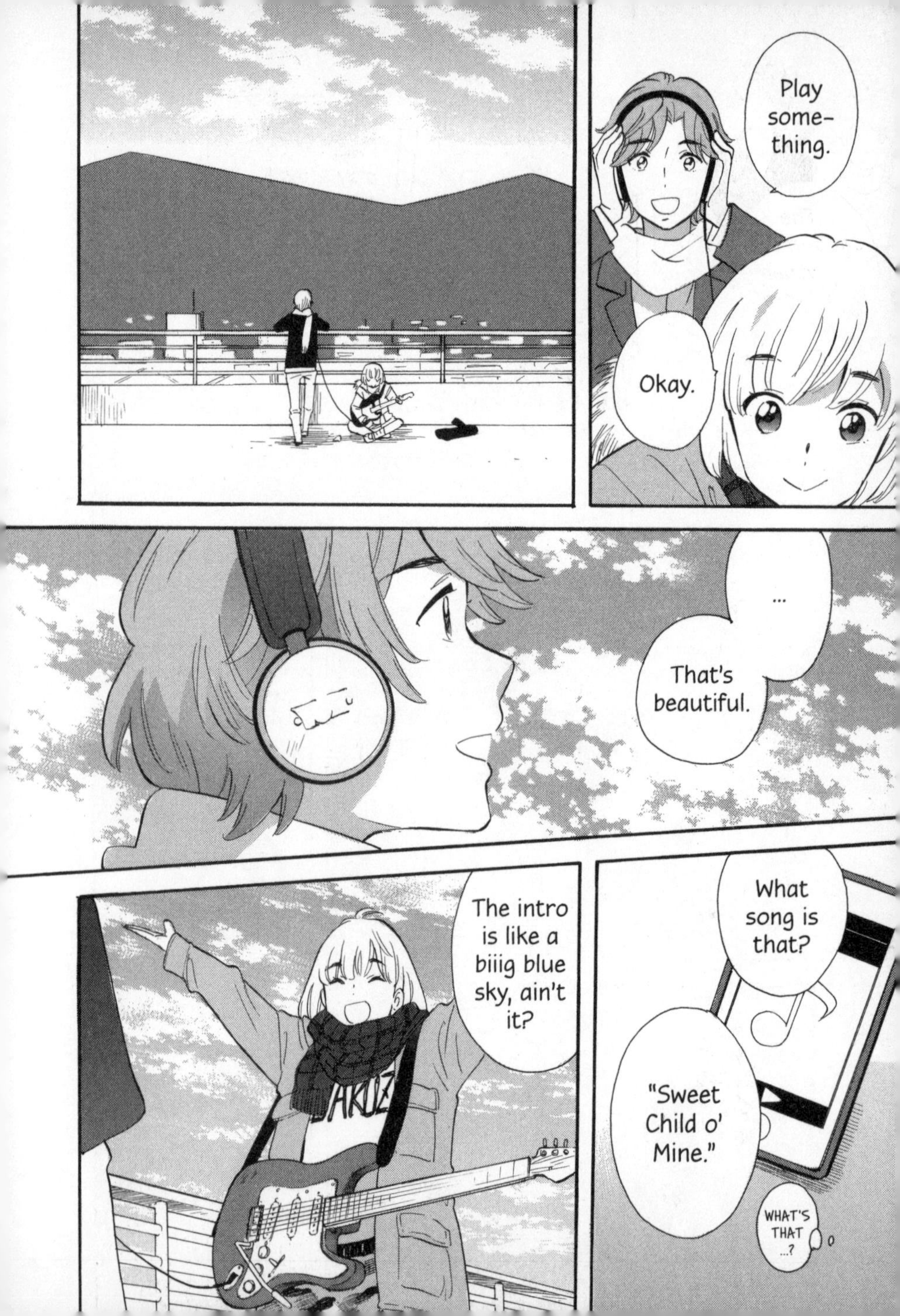
Play something.
Okay.
...
That's beautiful.
What song is that?
"Sweet Child o' Mine."
WHAT'S THAT ...?
The intro is like a biiig blue sky, ain't it?

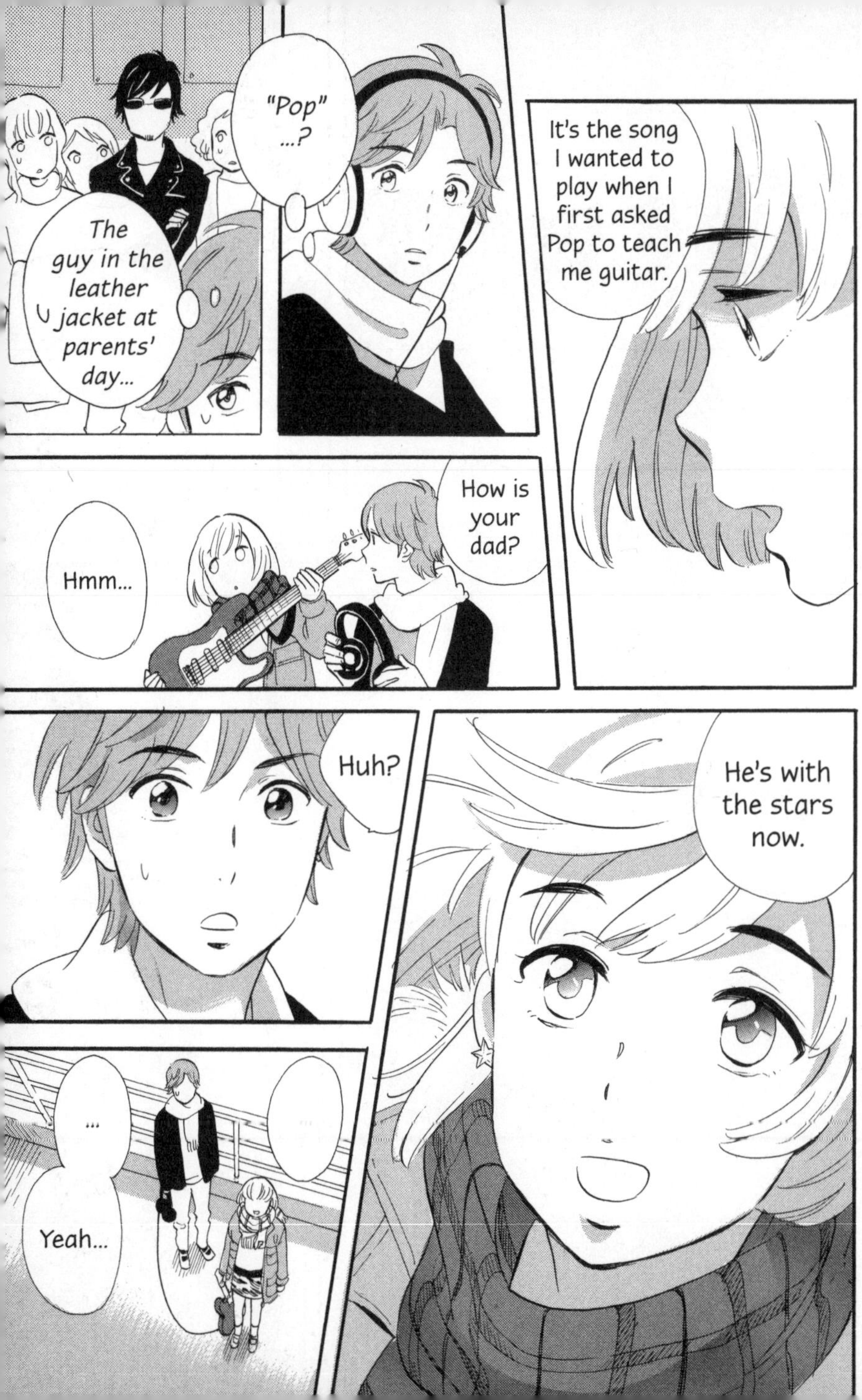
It's the song I wanted to play when I first asked Pop to teach me guitar.
"Pop" ...?
The guy in the leather jacket at parents' day...
How is your dad?
Hmm...
He's with the stars now.
Huh?
...
...
Yeah...

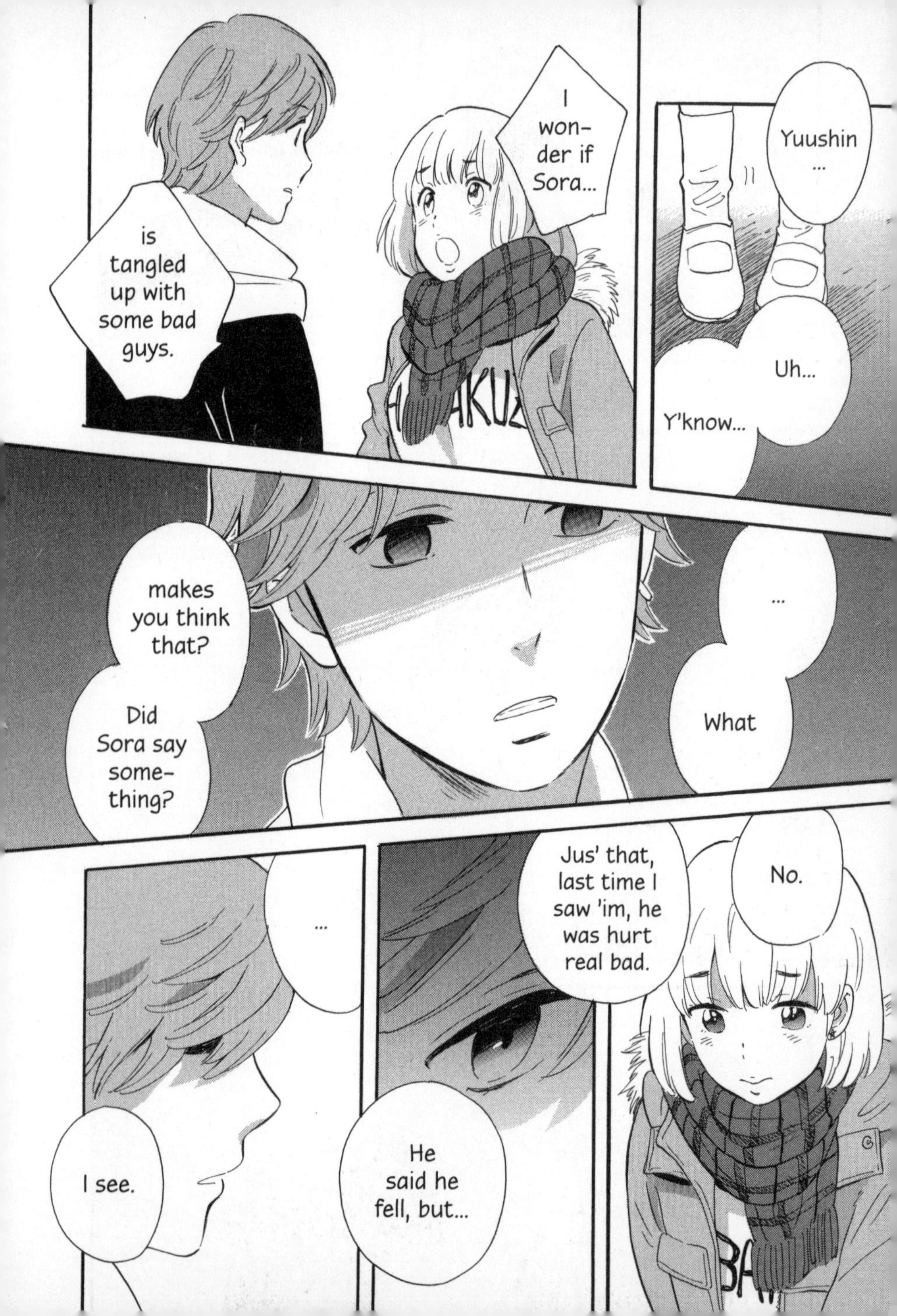
Yuushin ...
Uh...
Y'know...
I wonder if Sora...
is tangled up with some bad guys.
...
What
makes you think that?
Did Sora say something?
No.
Jus' that, last time I saw 'im, he was hurt real bad.
He said he fell, but...
...
I see.

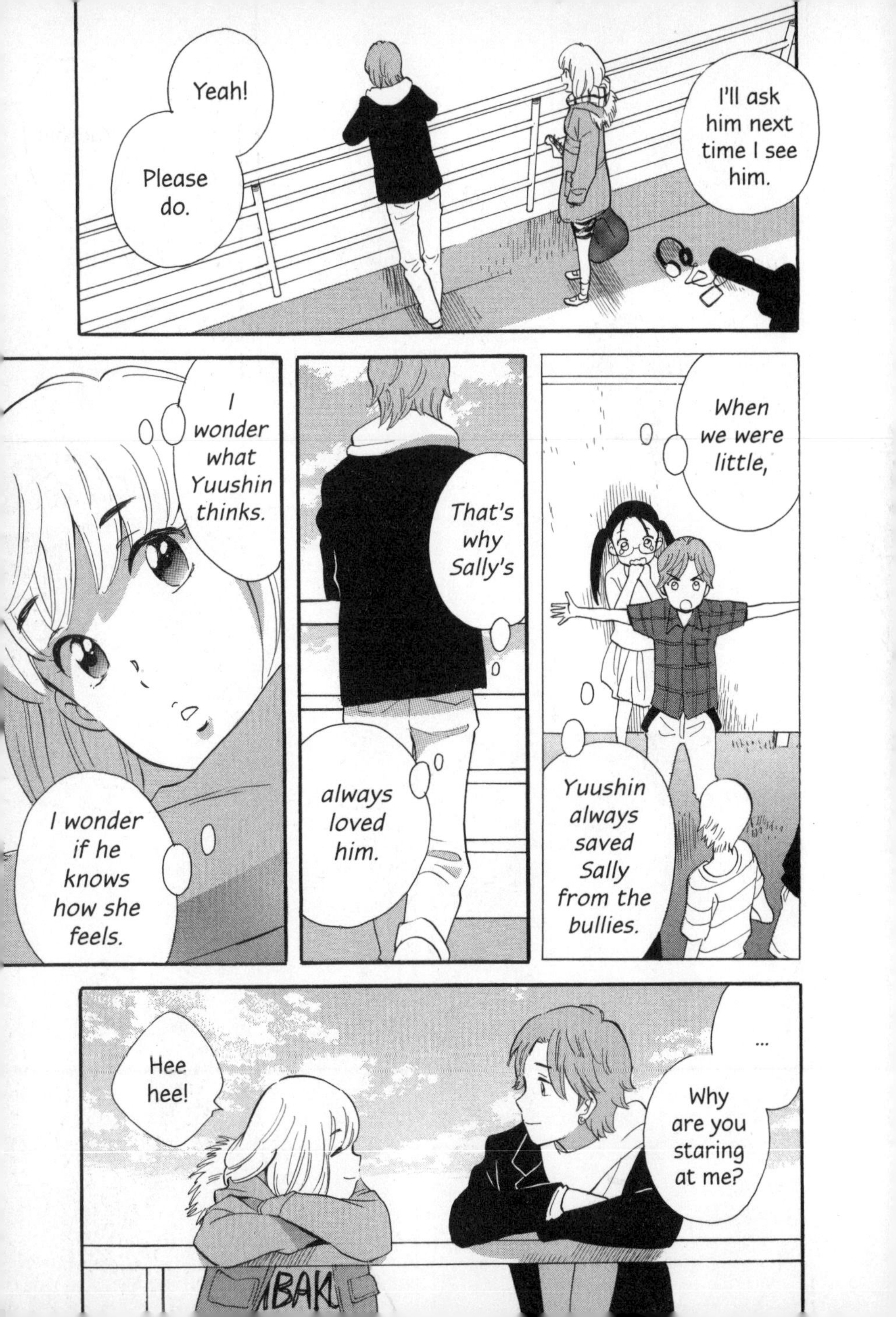

I'll ask him next time I see him.
Yeah!
Please do.
When we were little,
Yuushin always saved Sally from the bullies.
That's why Sally's
always loved him.
I wonder what Yuushin thinks.
I wonder if he knows how she feels.
...
Why are you staring at me?
Hee hee!
BAK

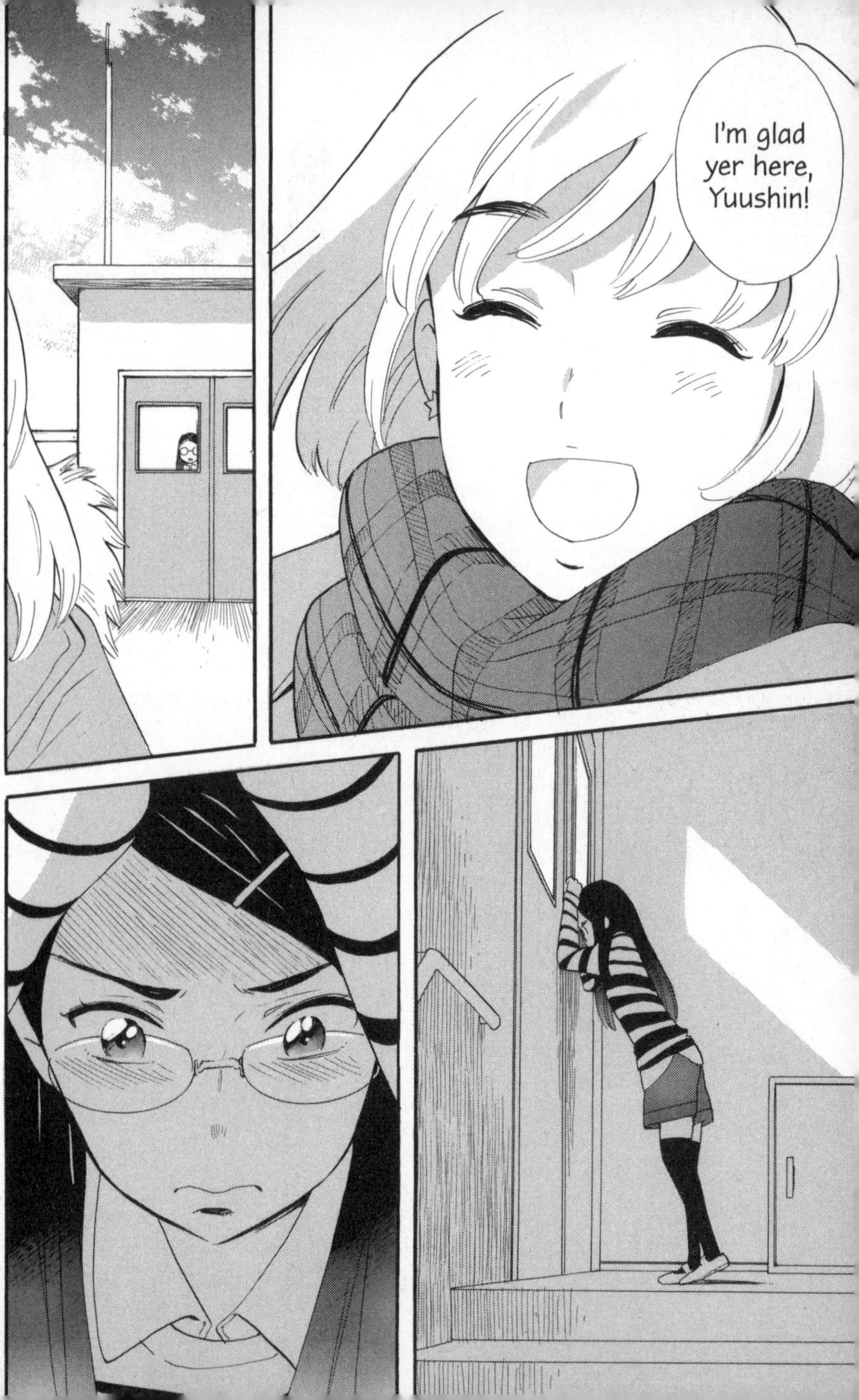
I'm glad yer here, Yuushin!

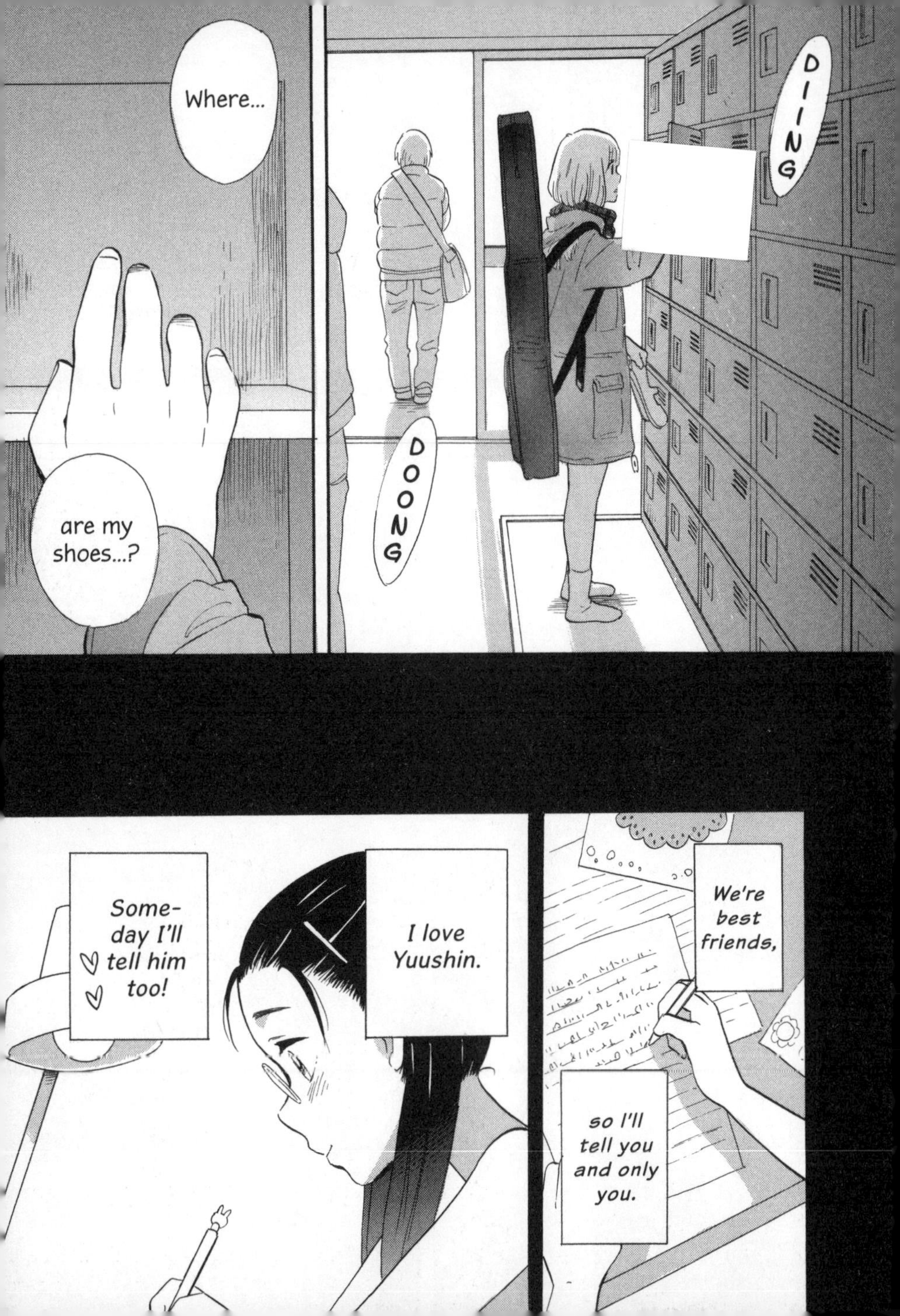
DIING
DOONG
Where...
are my shoes...?
We're best friends,
so I'll tell you and only you.
I love Yuushin.
Some-day I'll tell him too!

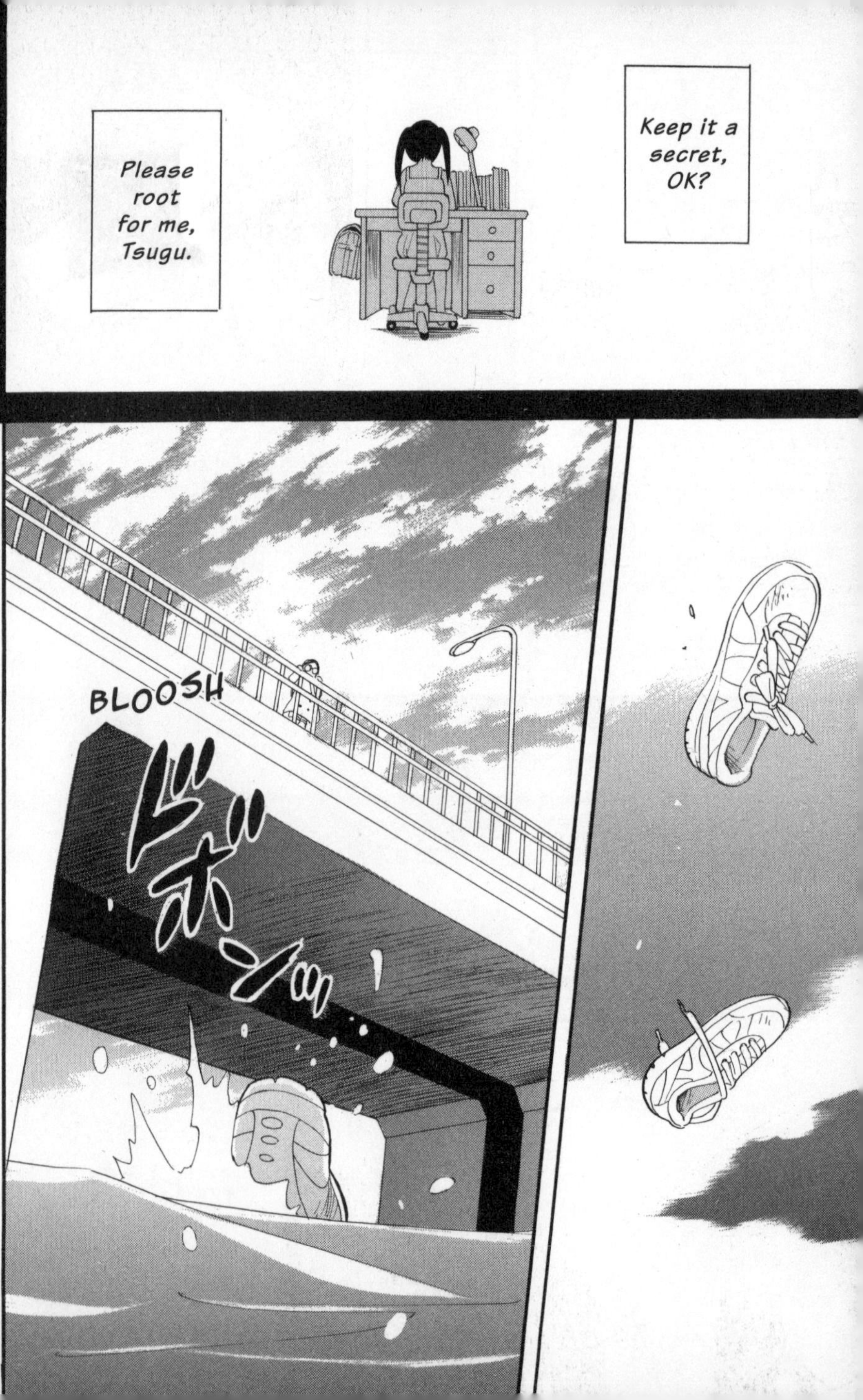
Keep it a secret, OK?
Please root for me, Tsugu.
BLOOSH
ドボーン

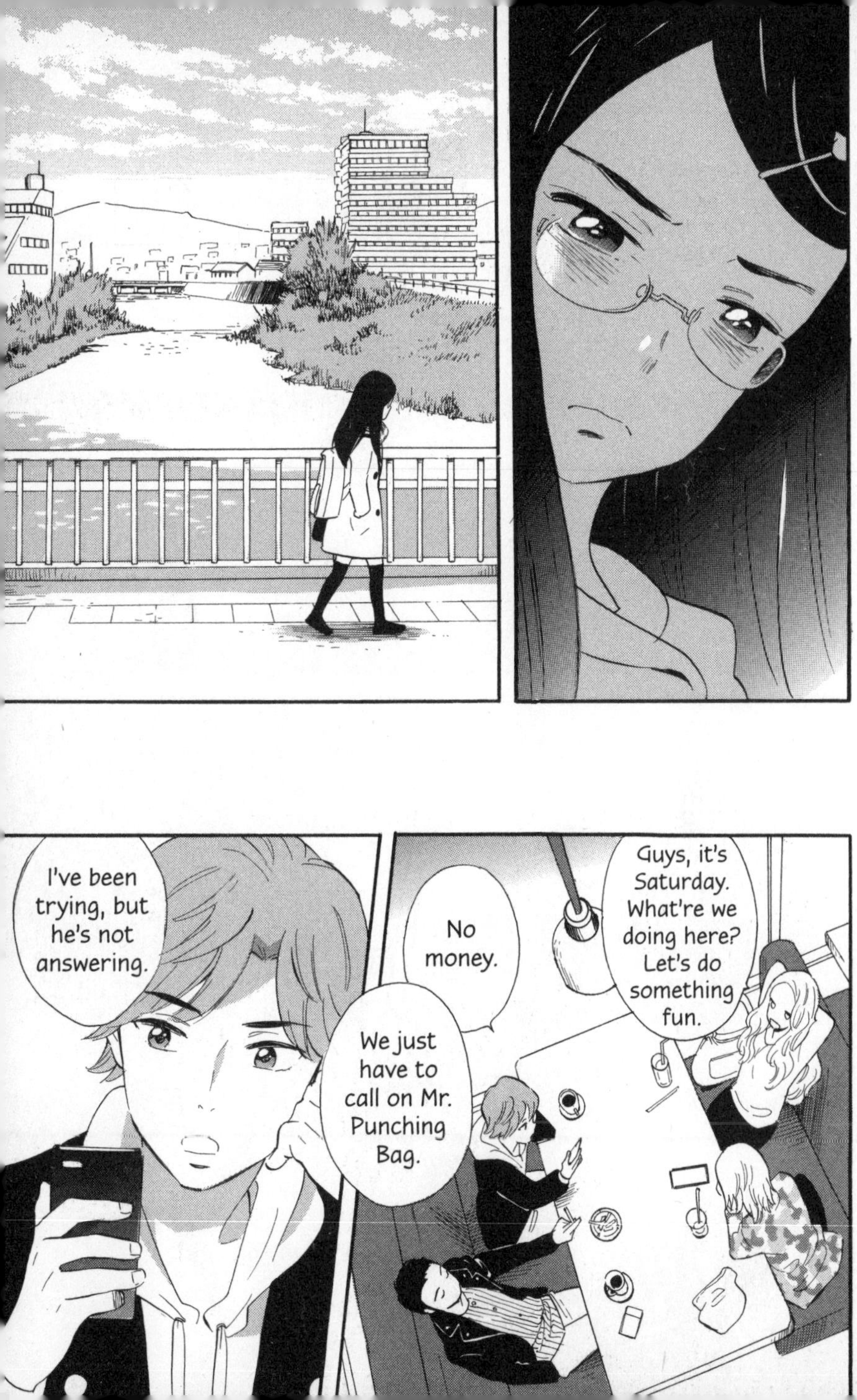
Guys, it's Saturday. What're we doing here? Let's do something fun.
No money.
We just have to call on Mr. Punching Bag.
I've been trying, but he's not answering.

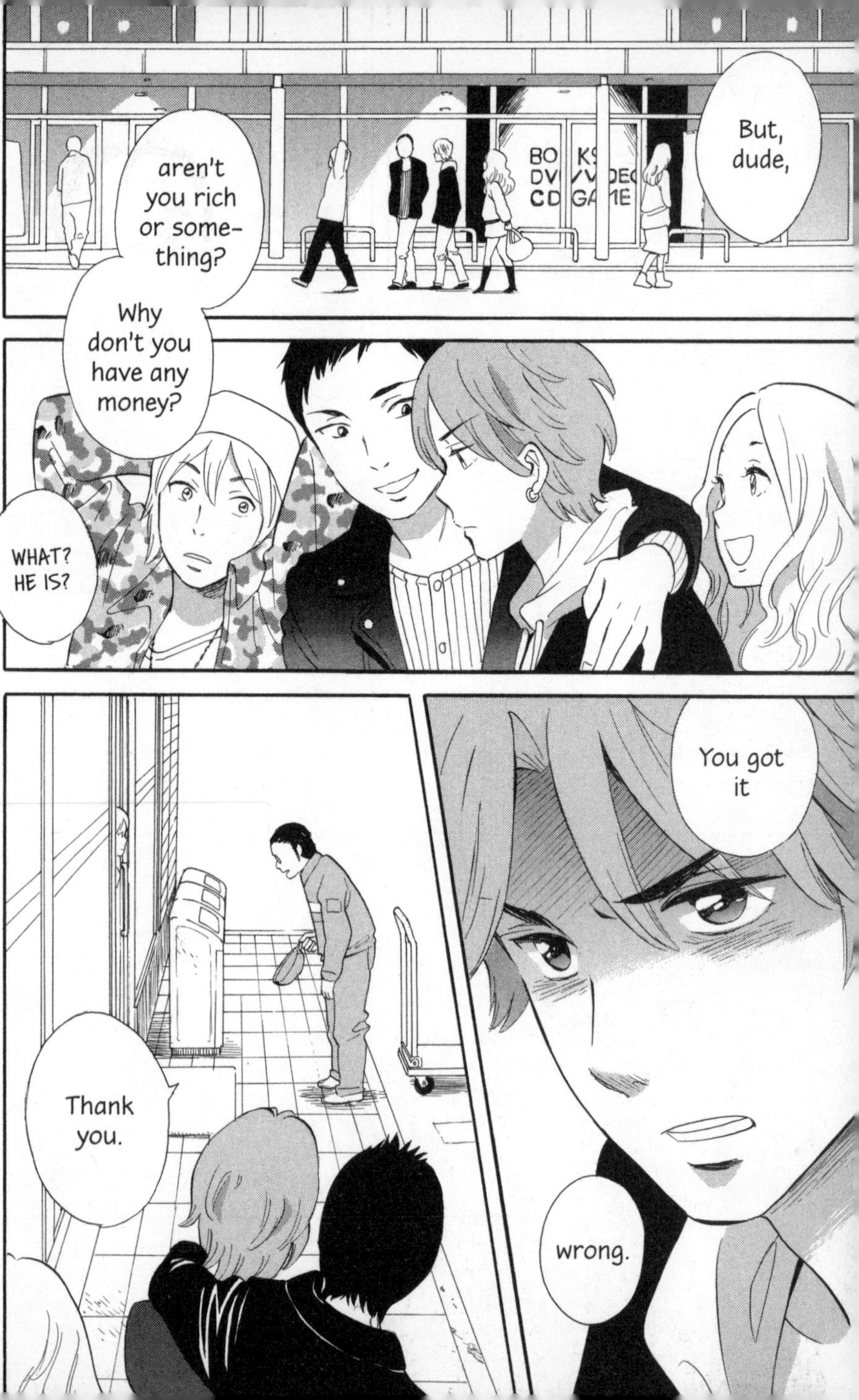
But, dude,
aren't you rich or some-thing?
Why don't you have any money?
WHAT? HE IS?
You got it
wrong.
Thank you.

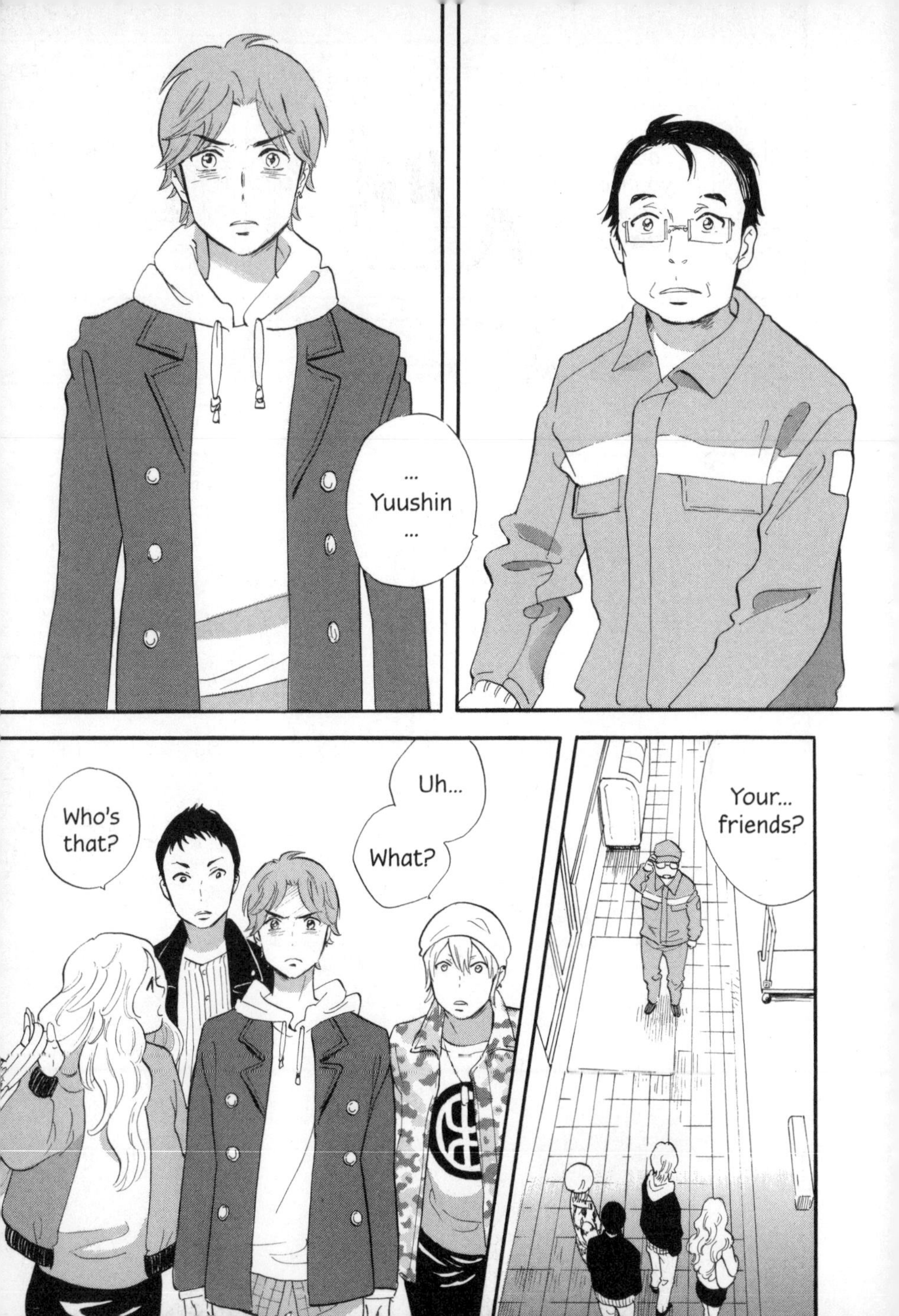
... Yuushin ...
Your... friends?
Uh...
What?
Who's that?

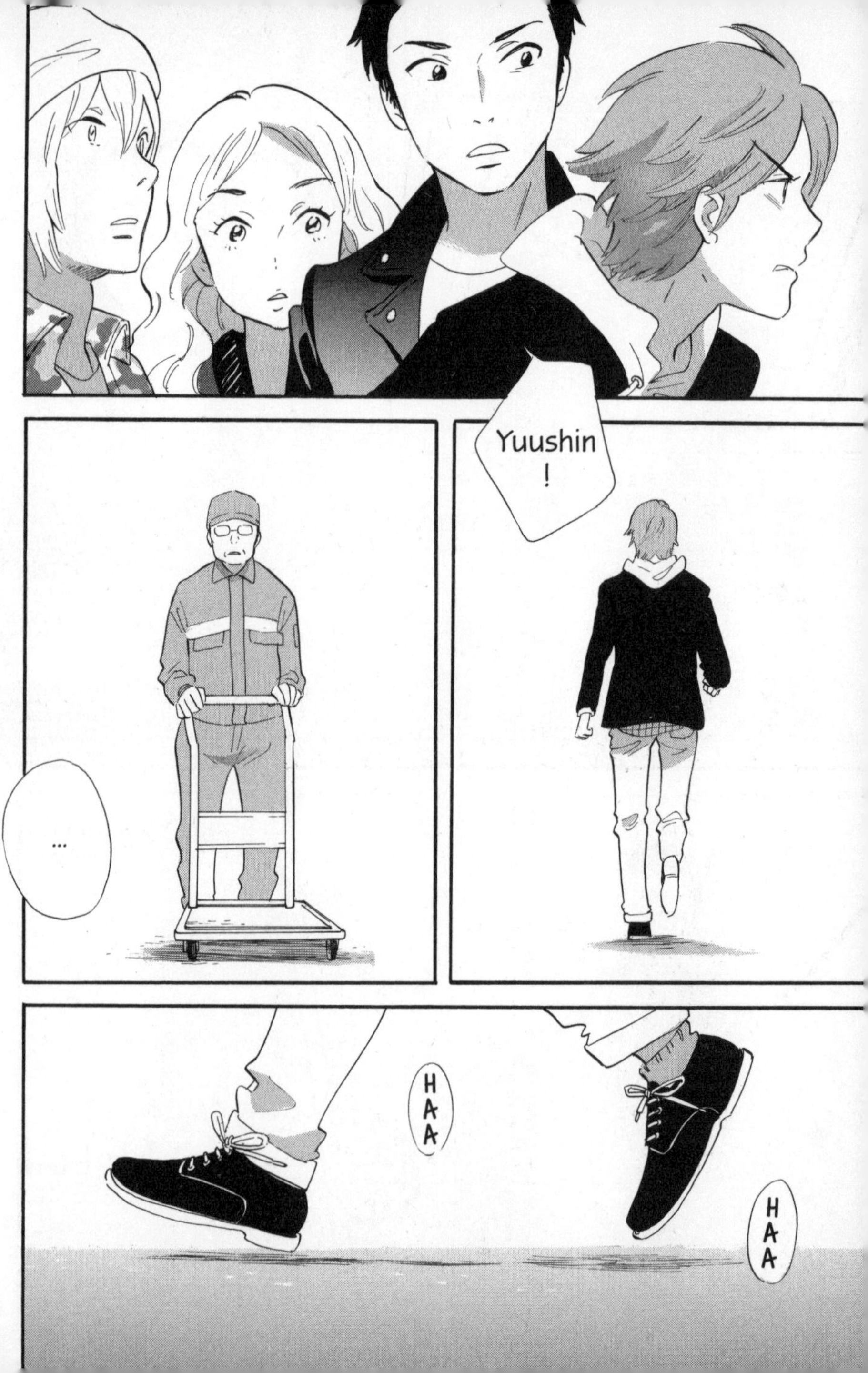
Yuushin !
...
HAA
HAA

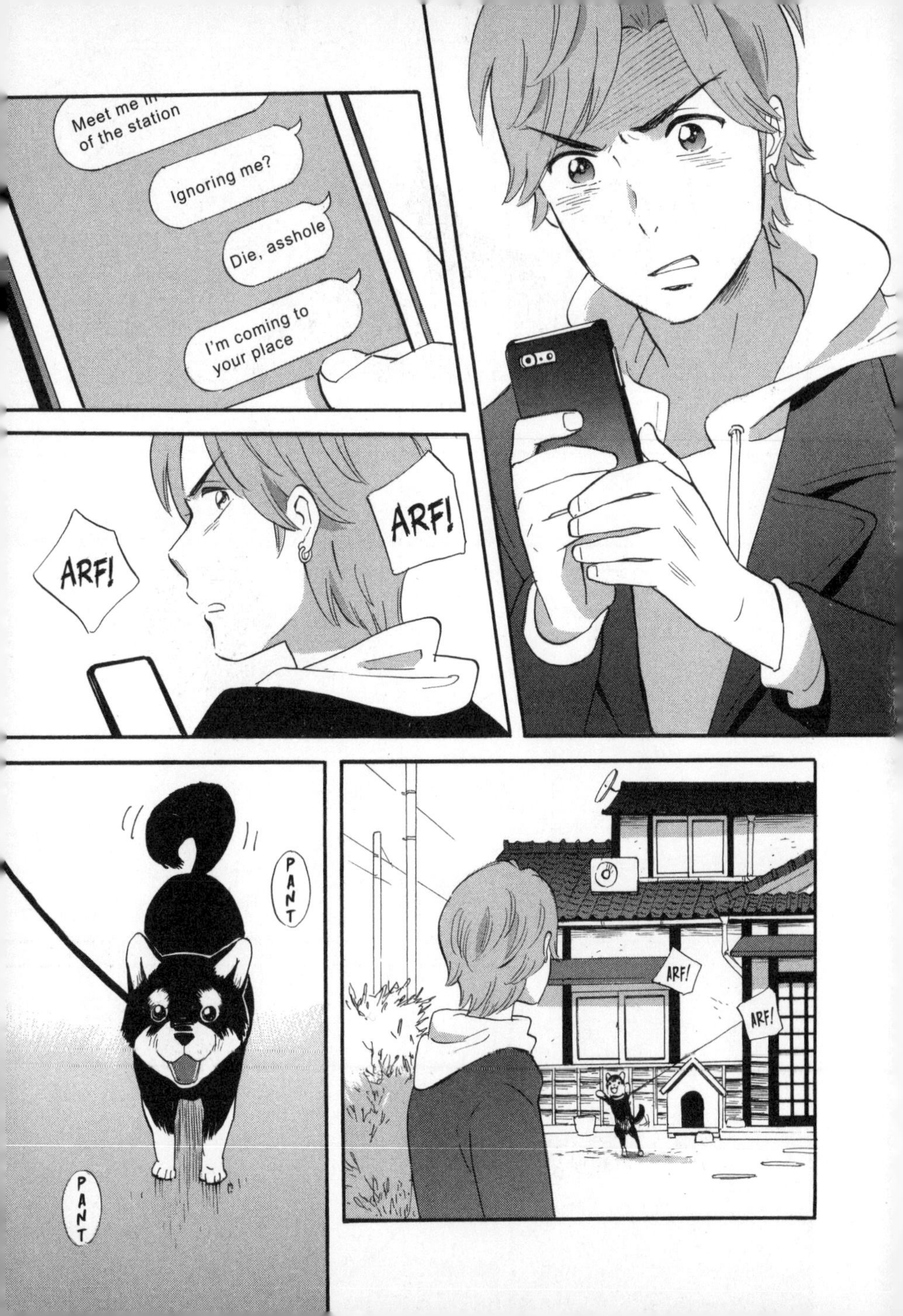
Meet me of the station
Ignoring me?
Die, asshole
I'm coming to your place
ARF!
ARF!
ARF!
ARF!
PANT
PANT

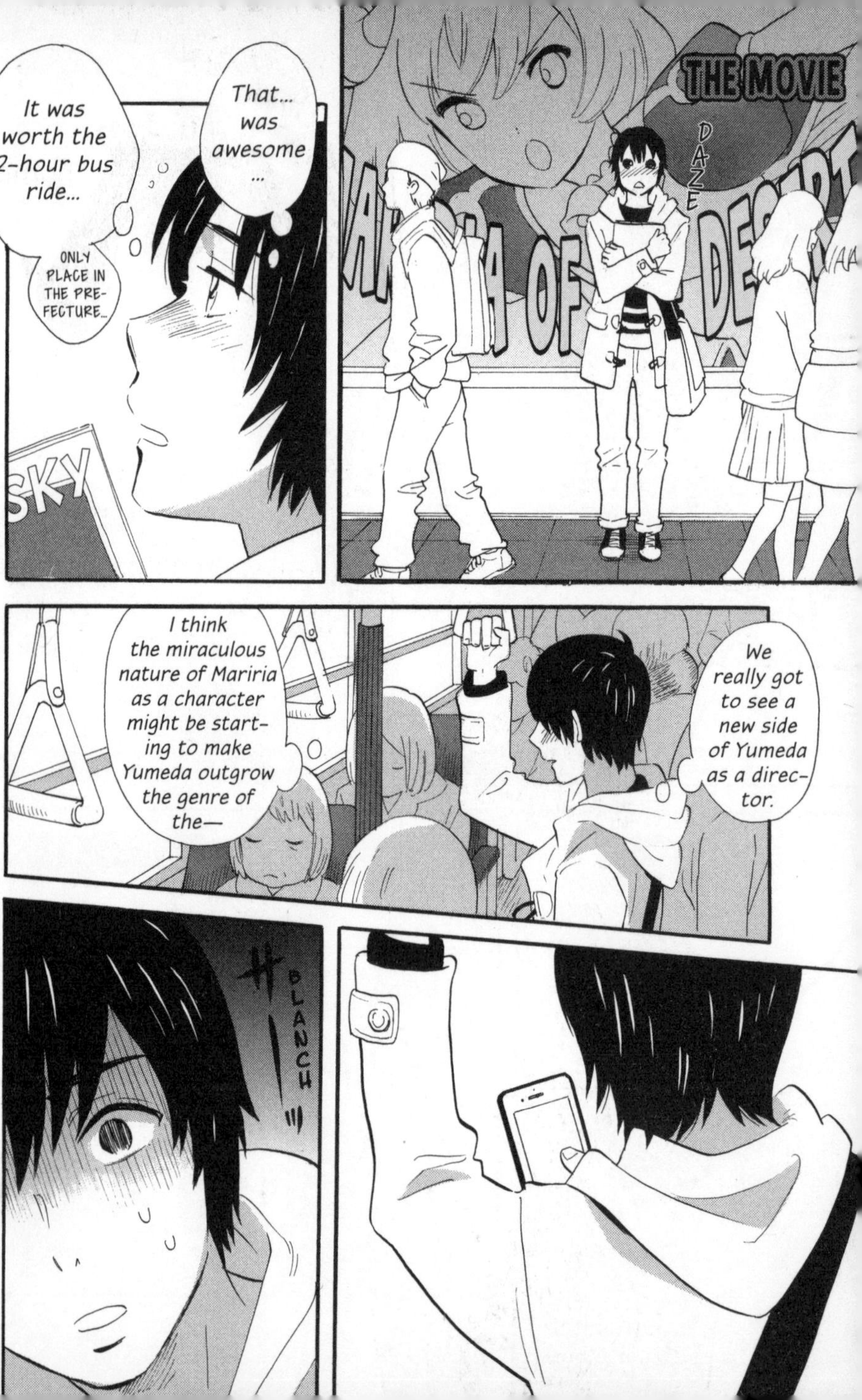
THE MOVIE
DAZE
That... was awesome...
It was worth the 2-hour bus ride...
ONLY PLACE IN THE PRE-FECTURE...
SKY
We really got to see a new side of Yumeda as a director.
I think the miraculous nature of Mariria as a character might be starting to make Yumeda outgrow the genre of the—
BLANCH

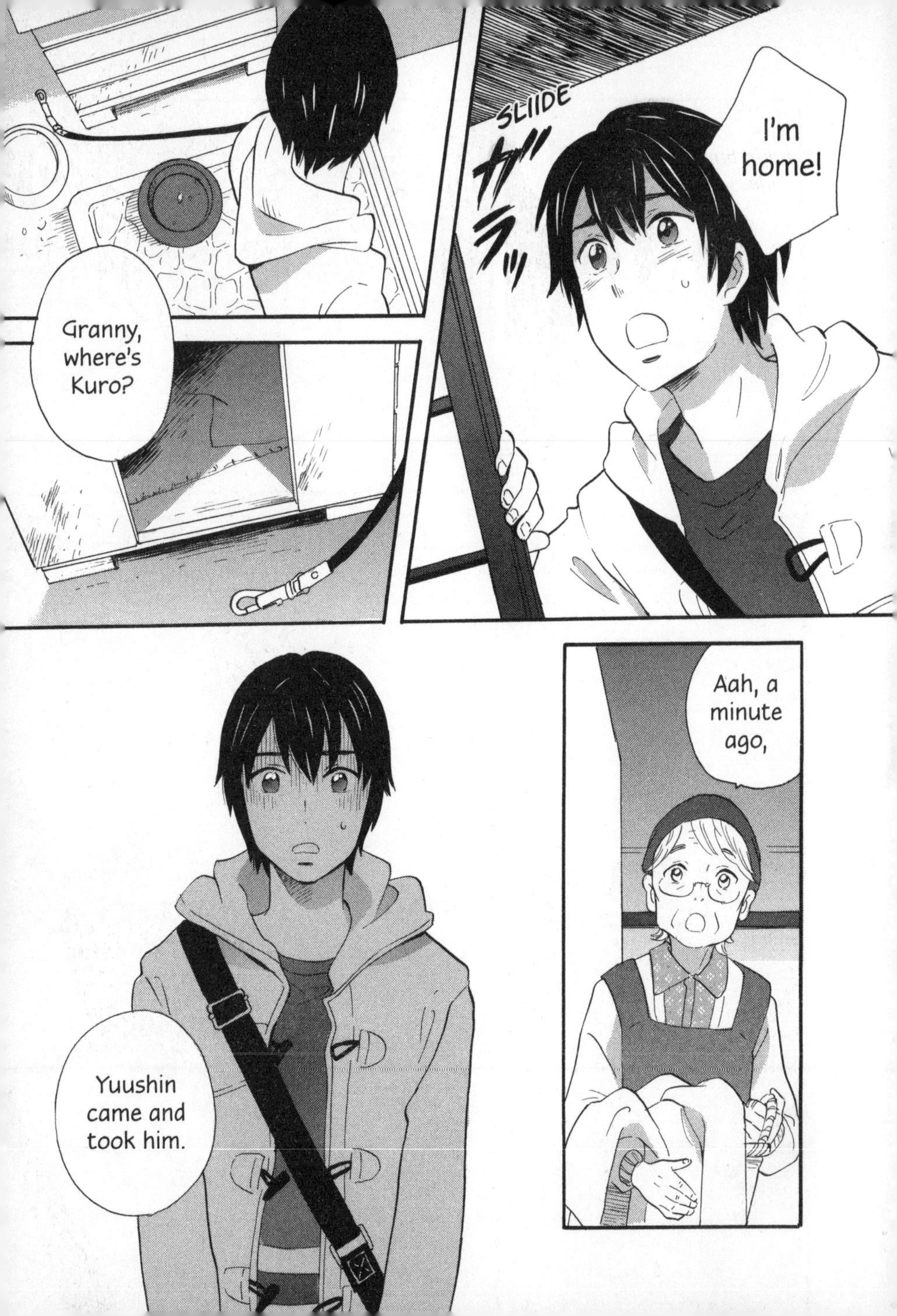
SLIIDE
ガラッ
I'm home!
Granny, where's Kuro?
Aah, a minute ago,
Yuushin came and took him.

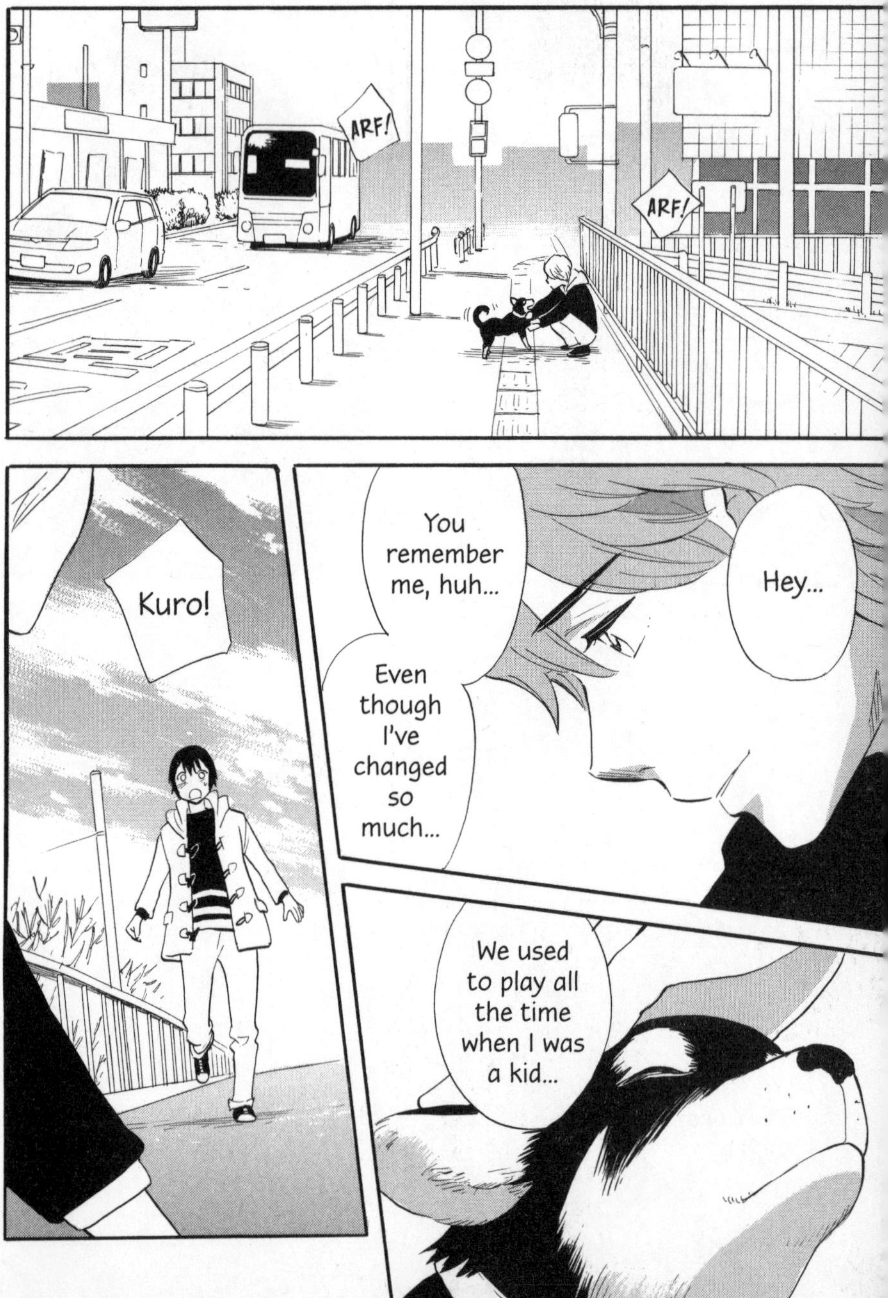
ARF!
ARF!
Hey...
You remember me, huh...
Even though I've changed so much...
We used to play all the time when I was a kid...
Kuro!

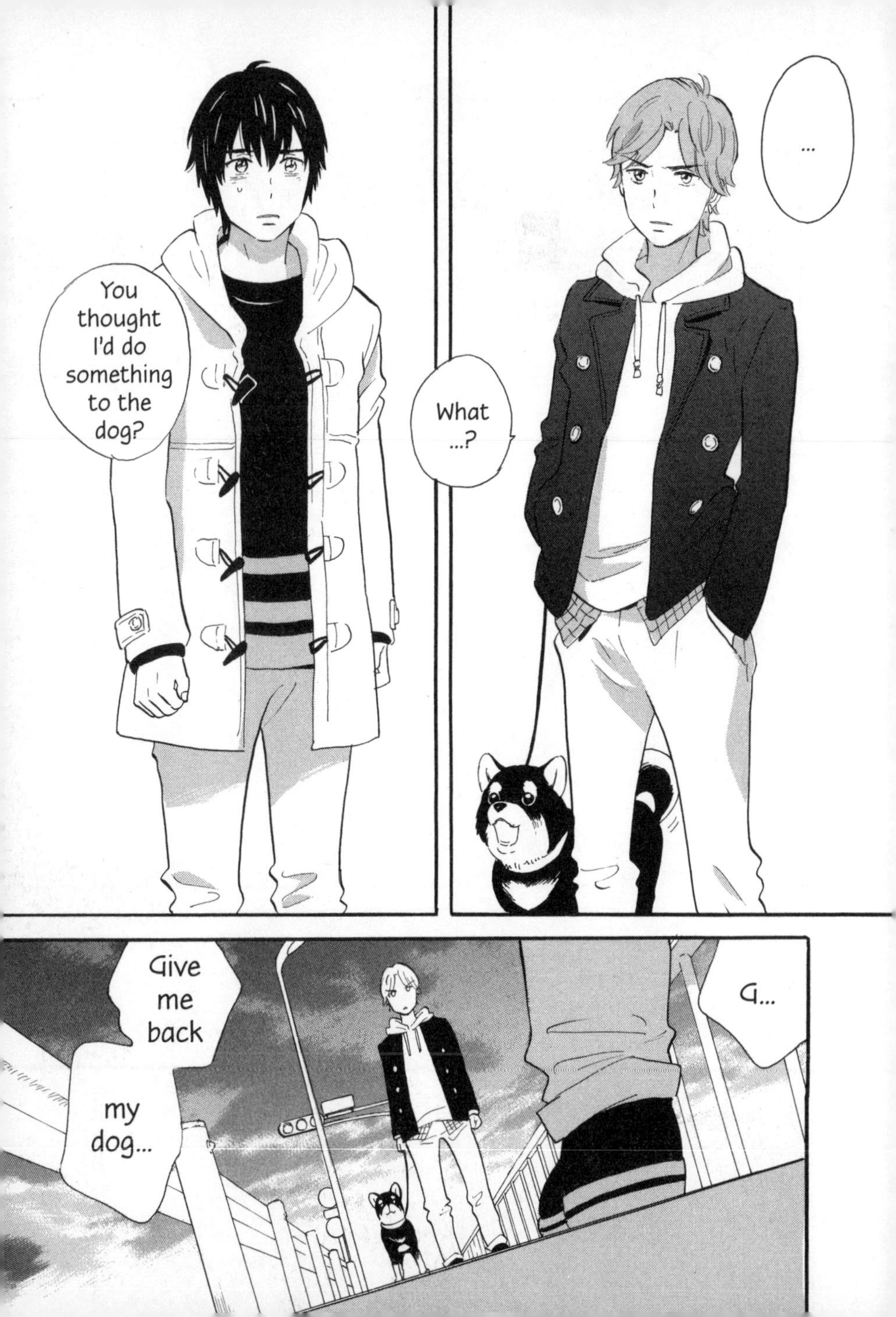
...
What ...?
You thought I'd do something to the dog?
G...
Give me back
my dog...

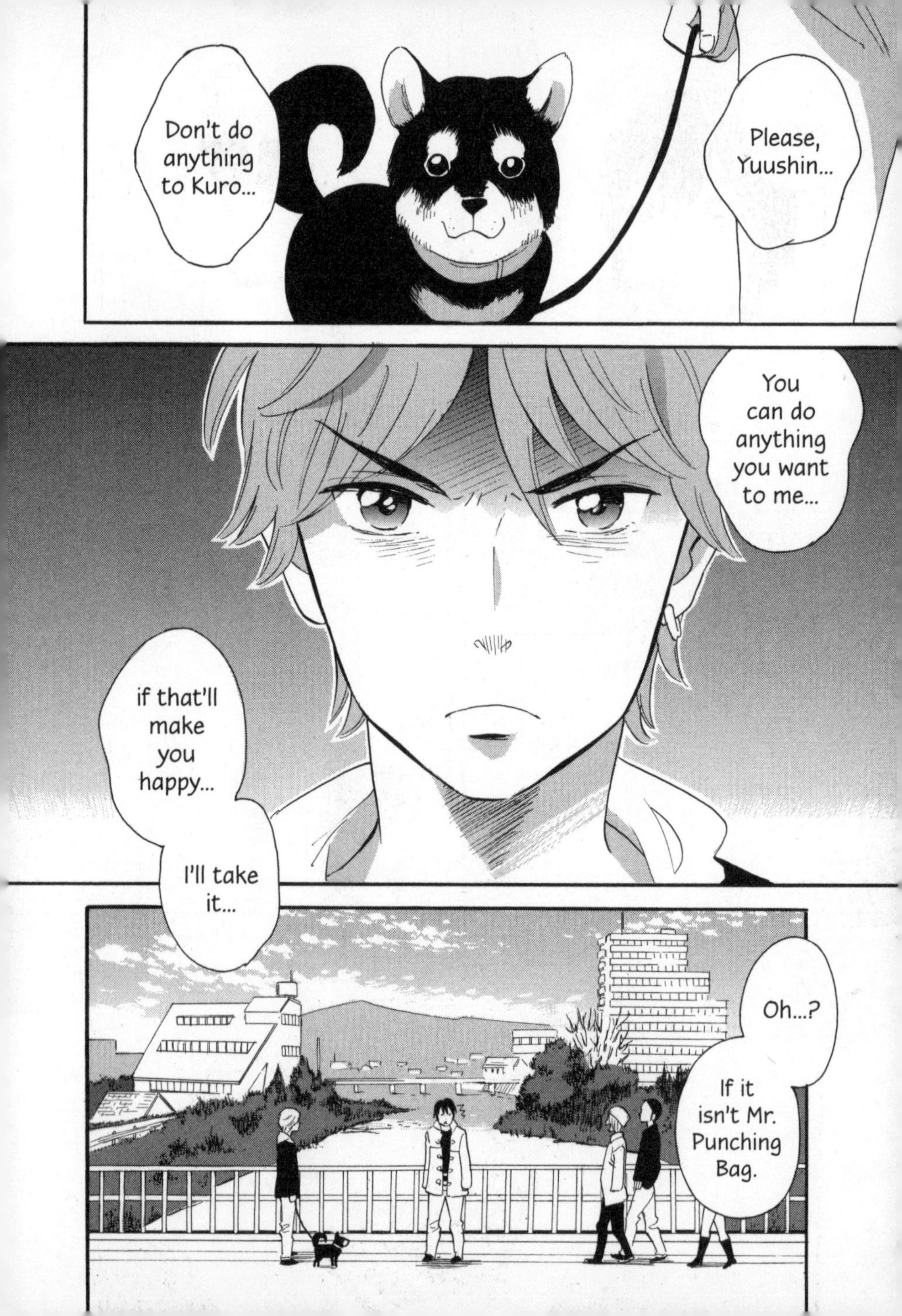
Please, Yuushin...
Don't do anything to Kuro...
You can do anything you want to me...
if that'll make you happy...
I'll take it...
Oh...?
If it isn't Mr. Punching Bag.

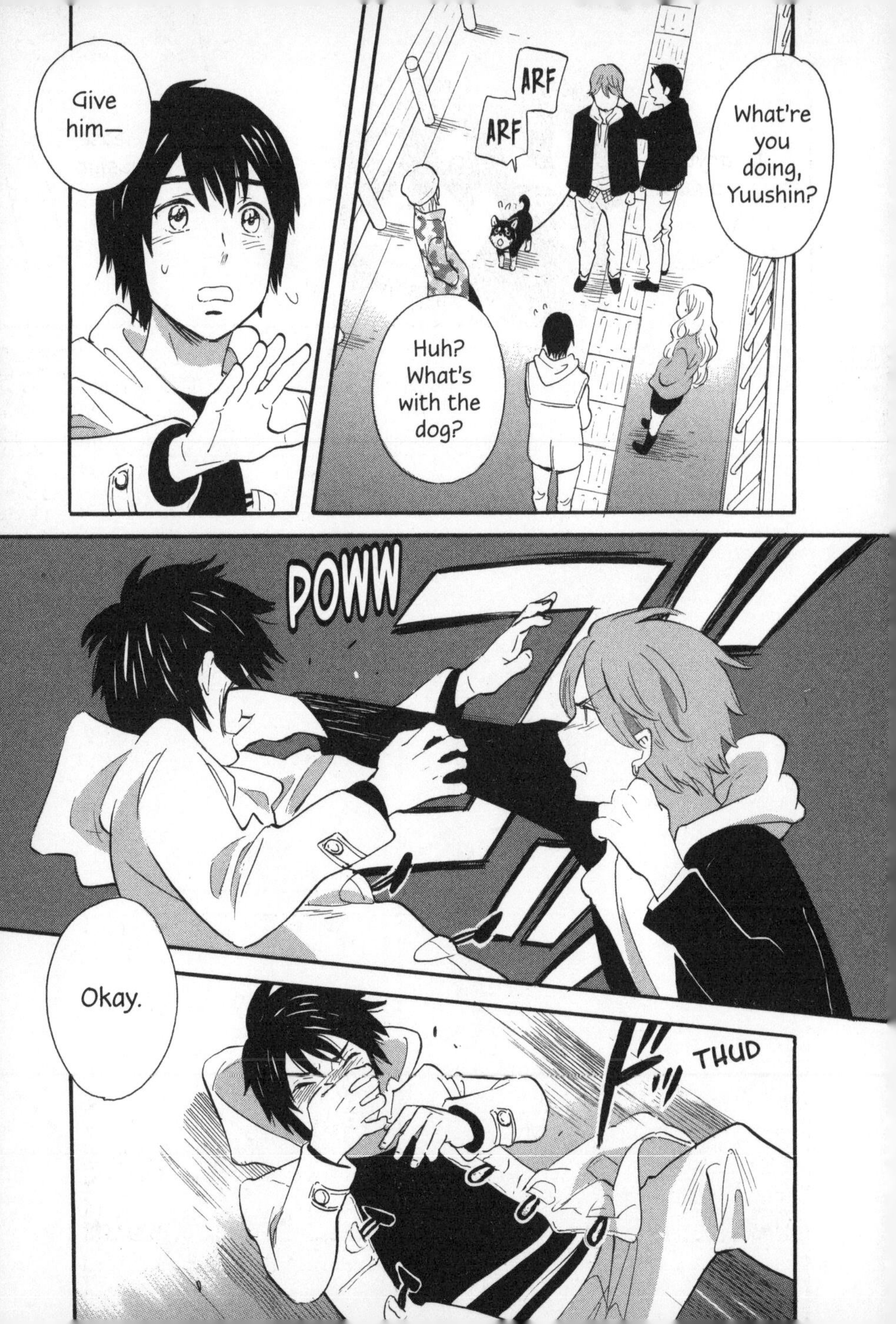
What're you doing, Yuushin?
ARF
ARF
Huh? What's with the dog?
Give him—
POWW
Okay.
THUD

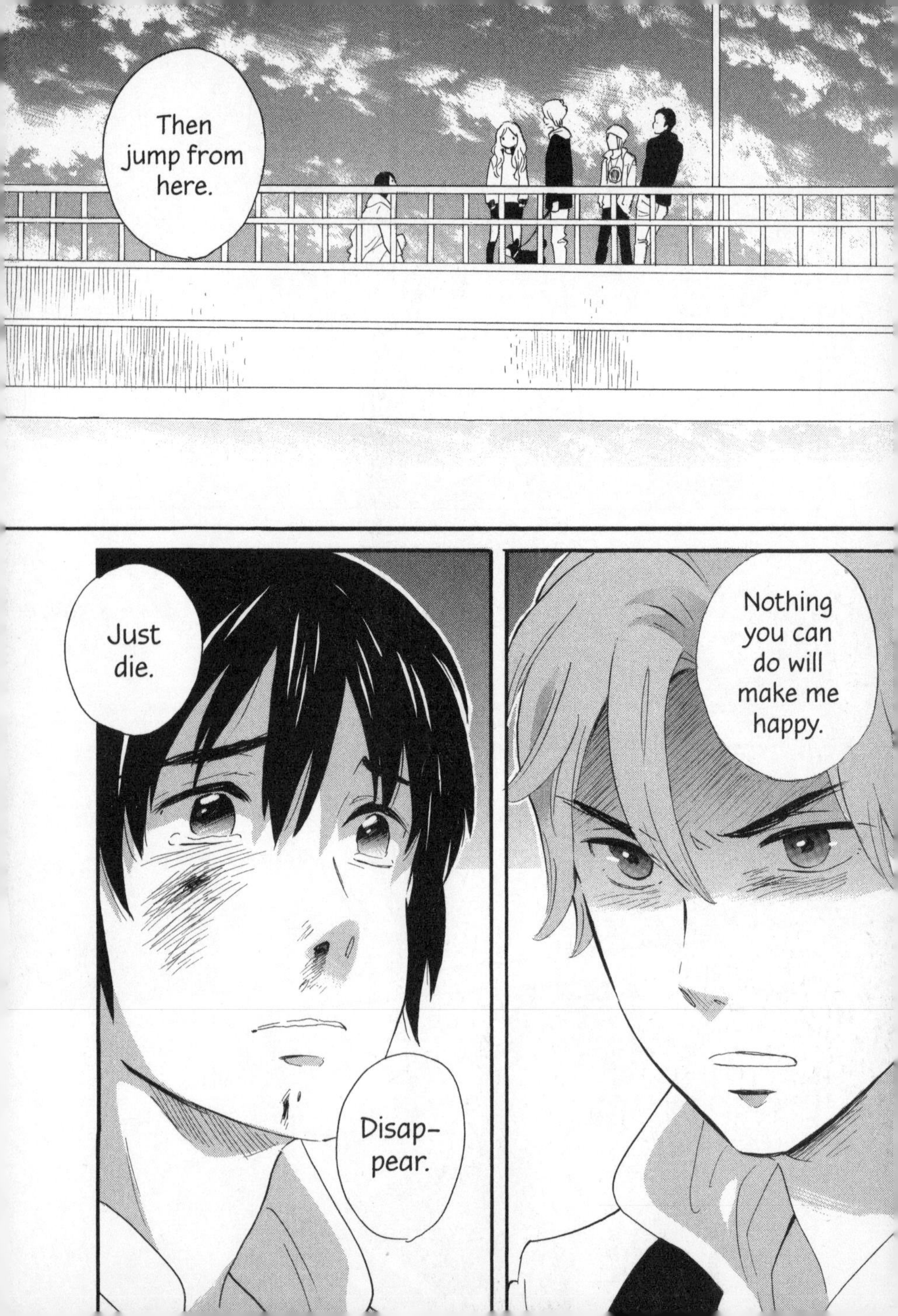
Then jump from here.
Nothing you can do will make me happy.
Just die.
Disap-pear.

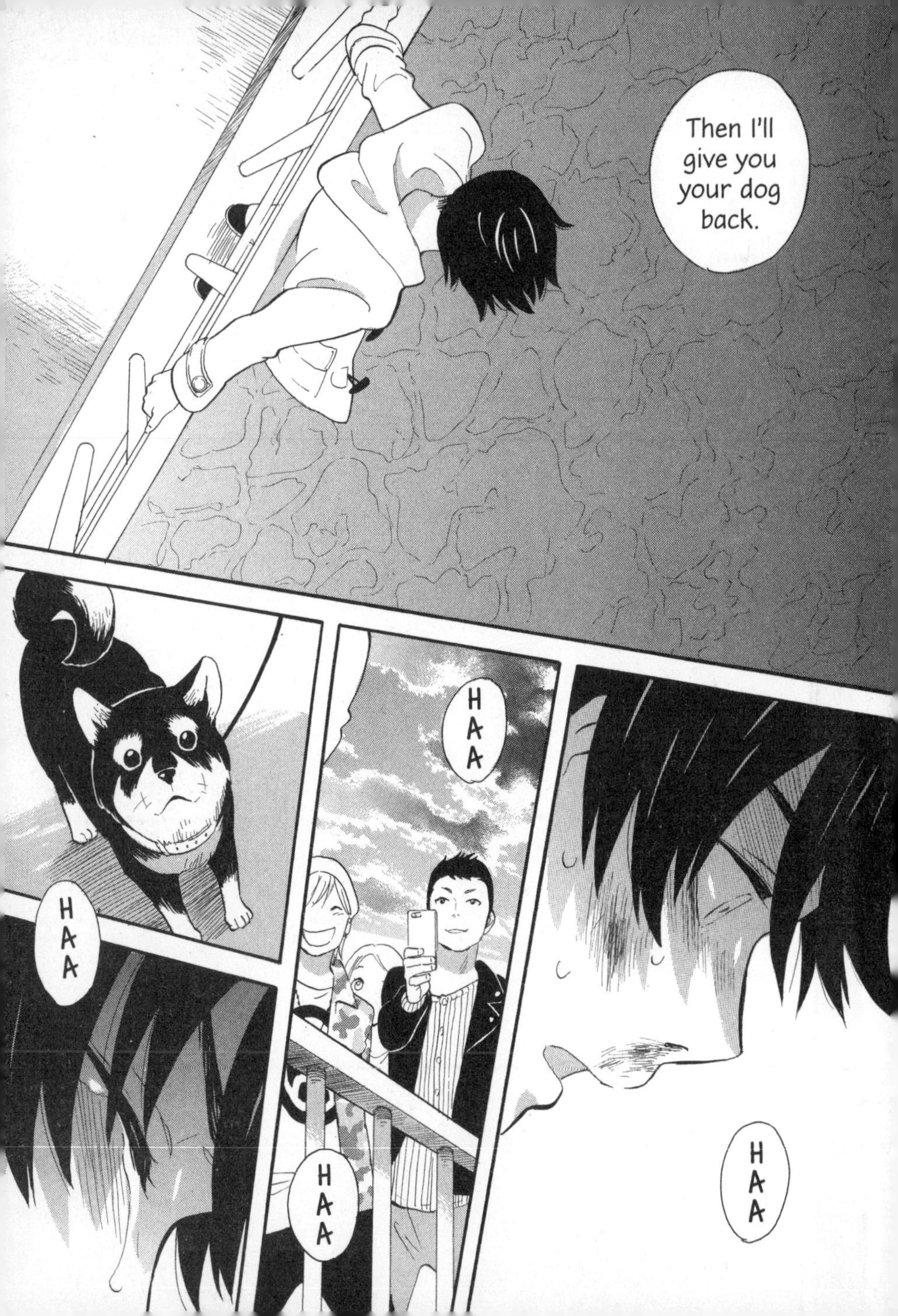
Then I'll give you your dog back.
HAA
HAA
HAA
HAA

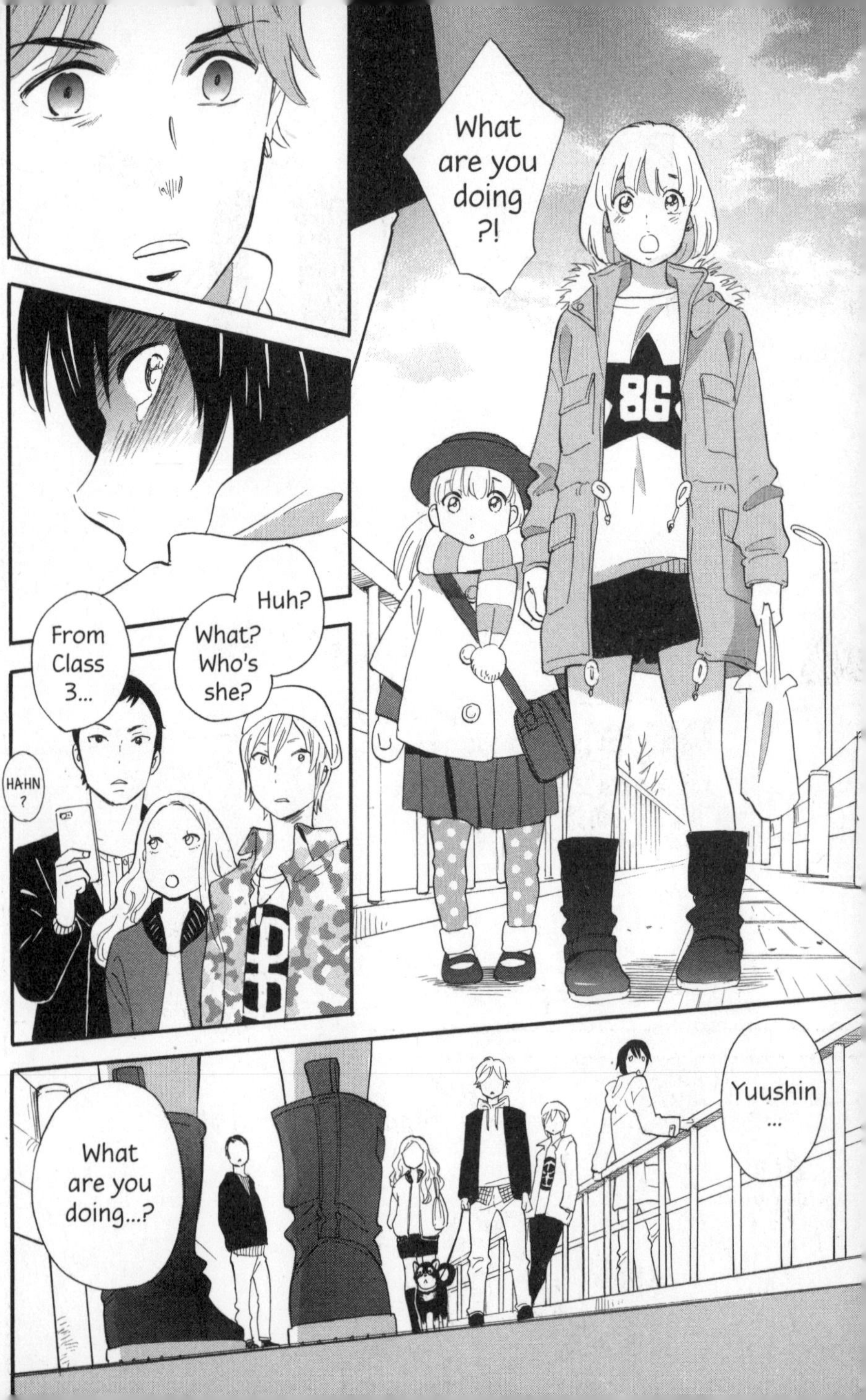
What are you doing ?!
Huh?
What? Who's she?
From Class 3...
HAHN ?
Yuushin ...
What are you doing...?

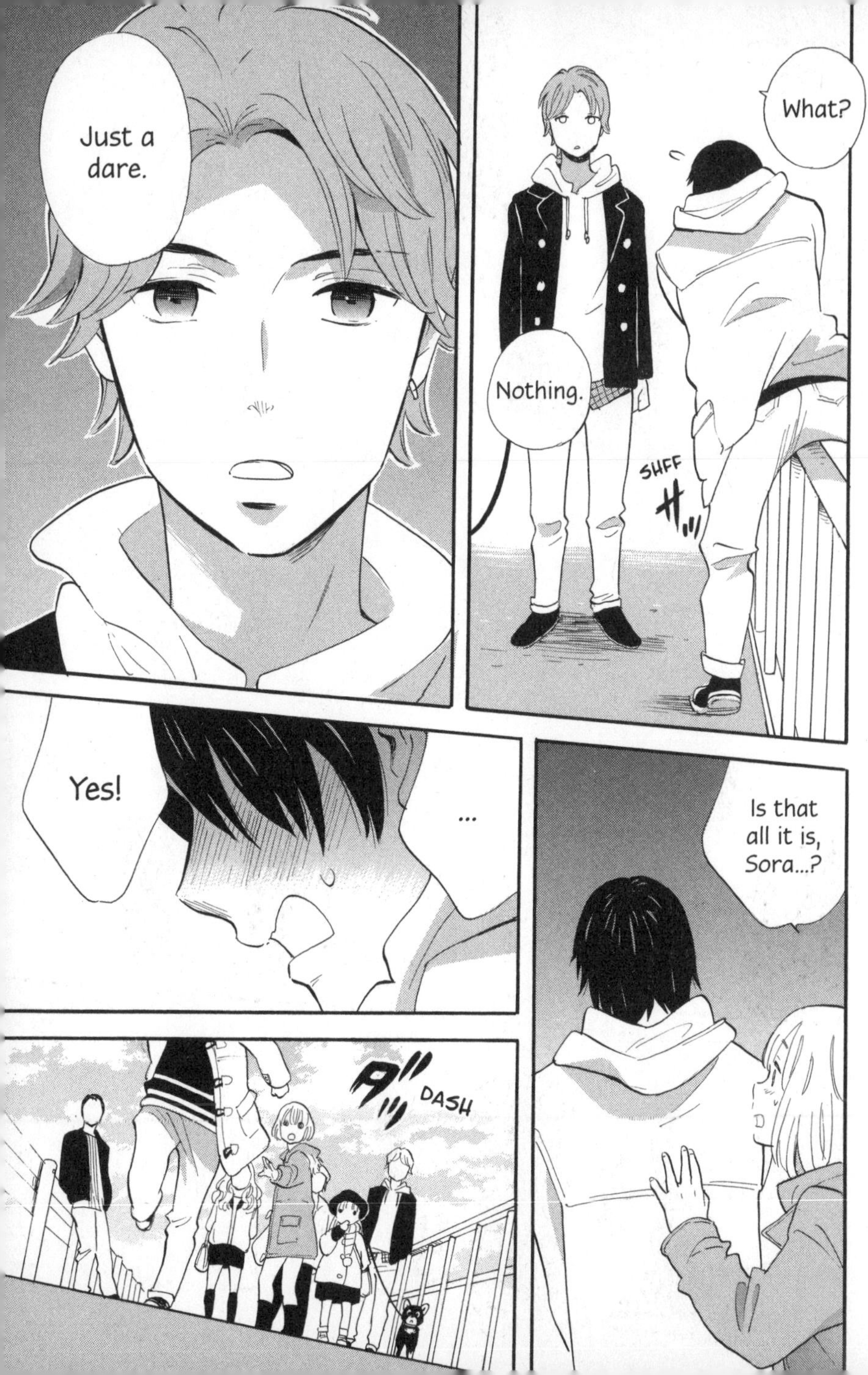
What?
Nothing.
SHFF
Just a dare.
Is that all it is, Sora...?
...
Yes!
DASH

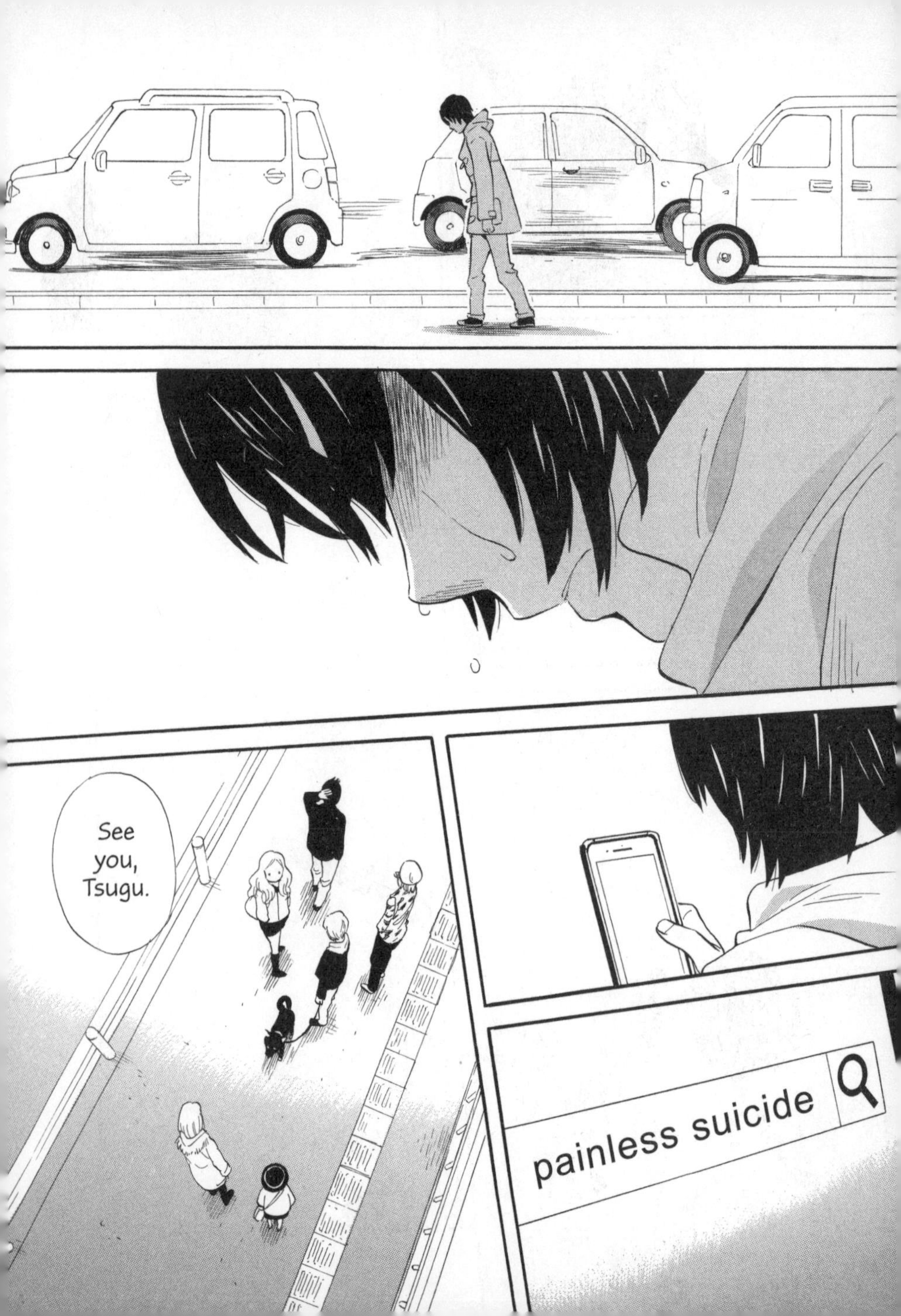
painless suicide
See you, Tsugu.

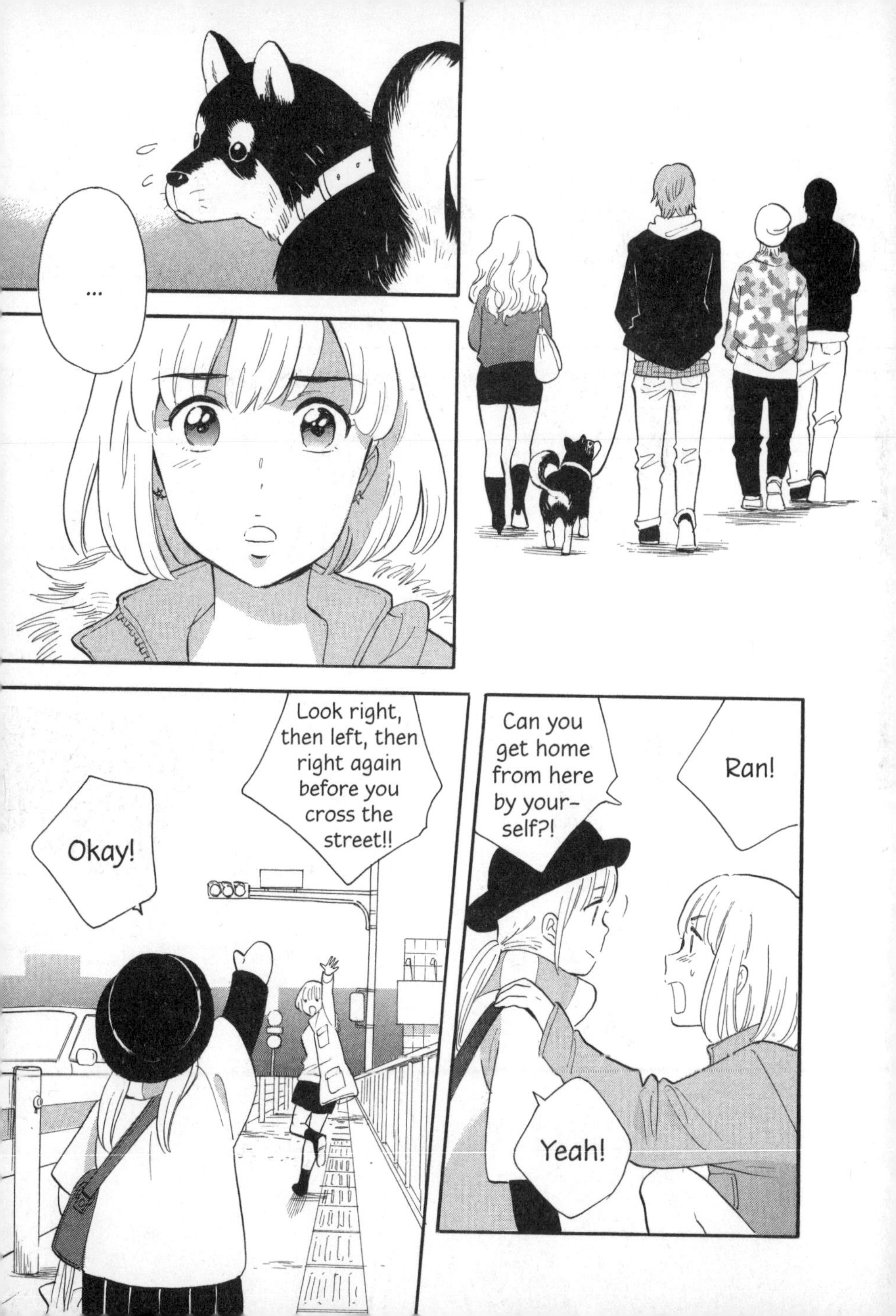
...
Ran!
Can you get home from here by your-self?!
Yeah!
Look right, then left, then right again before you cross the street!!
Okay!

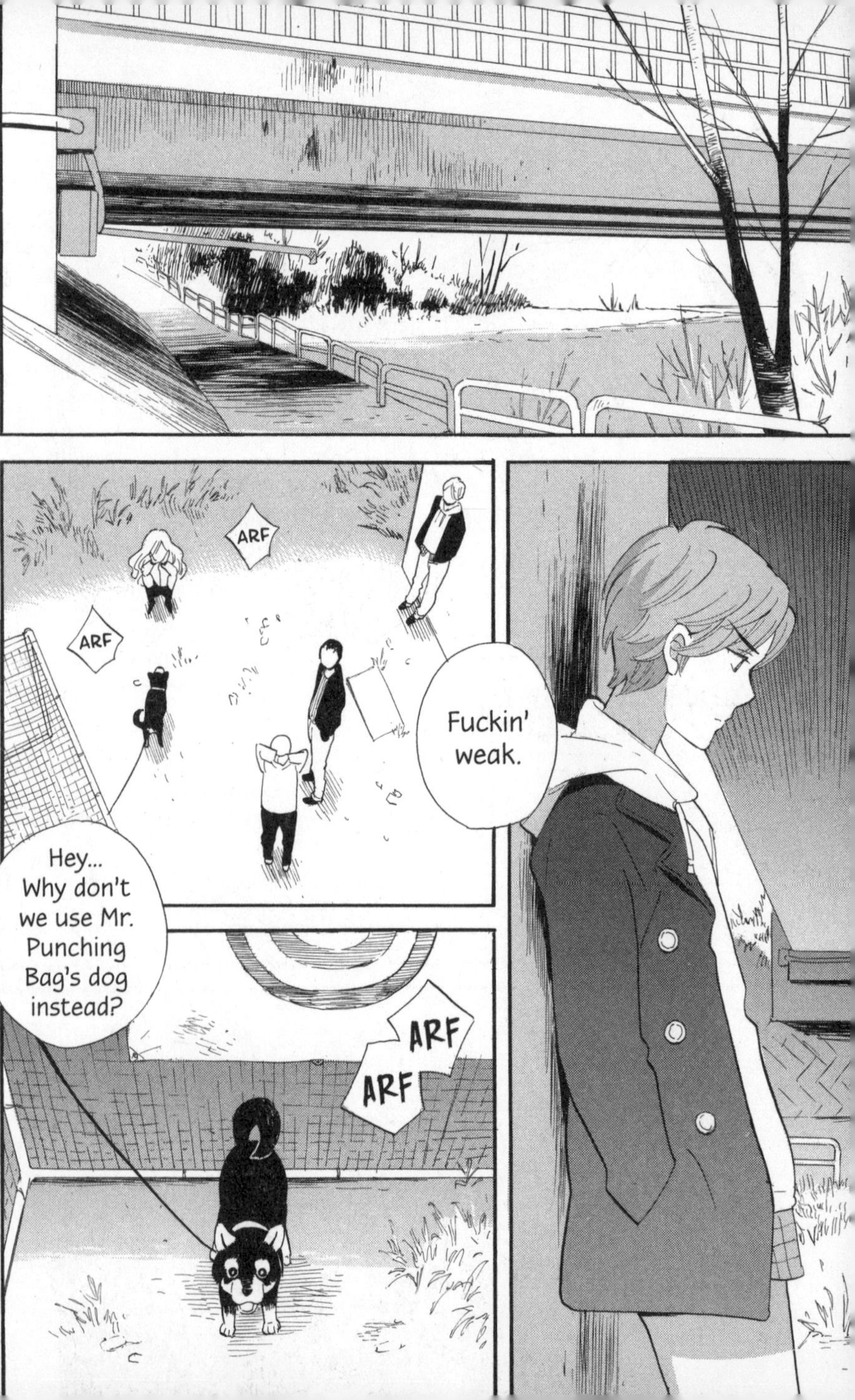
Fuckin' weak.
ARF
ARF
Hey... Why don't we use Mr. Punching Bag's dog instead?
ARF
ARF

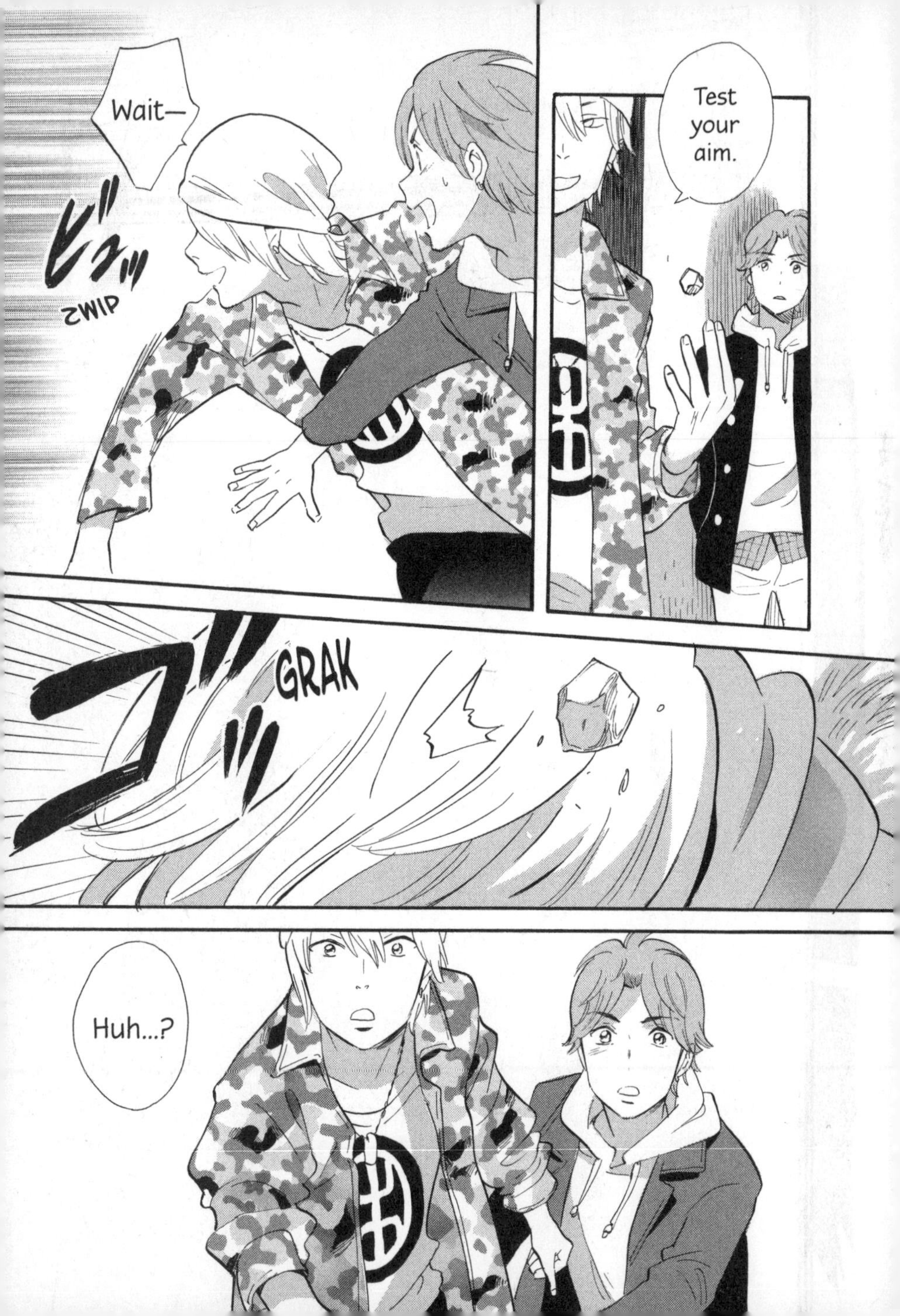
Test your aim.
Wait—
ZWIP
GRAK
Huh...?

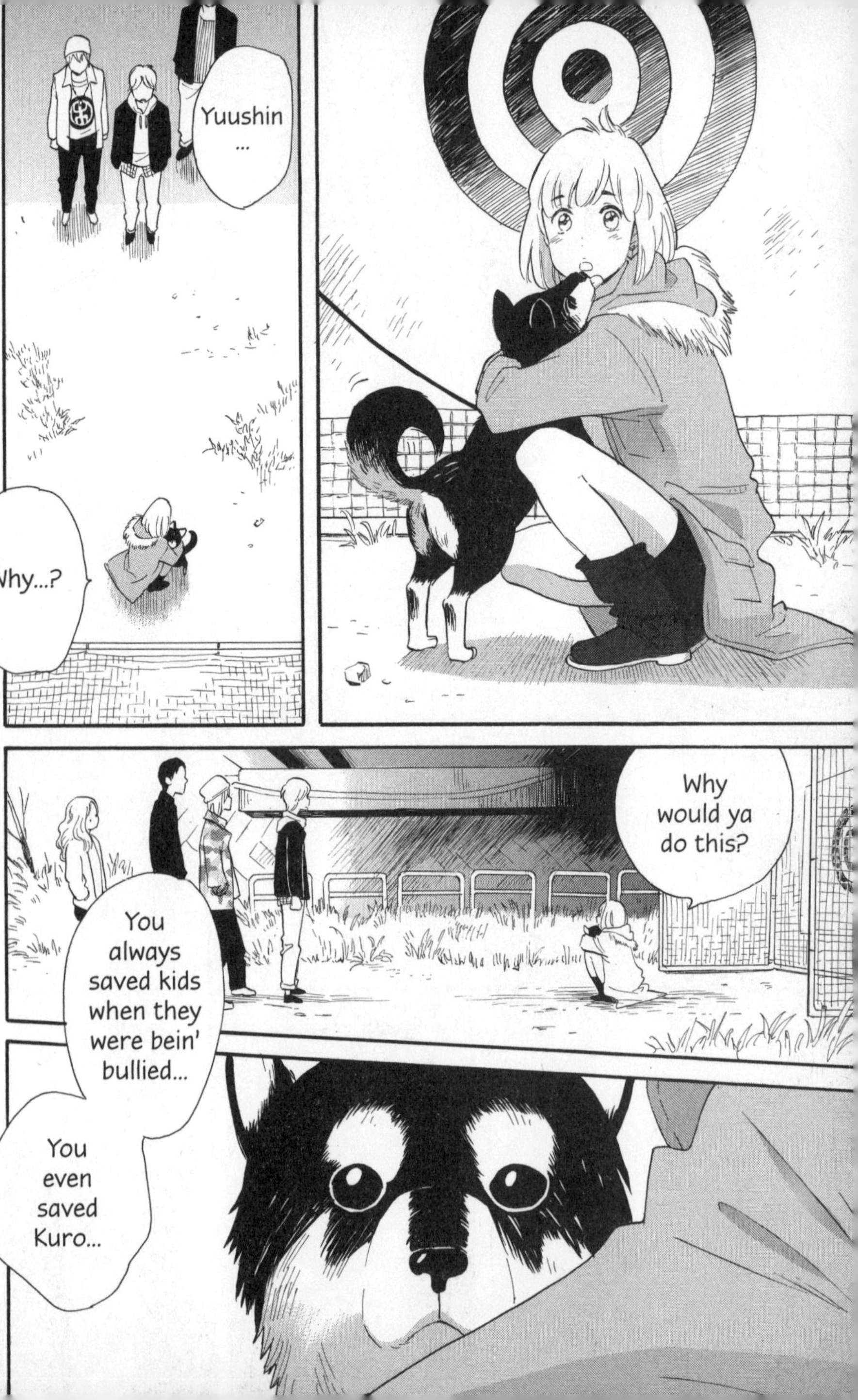
Yuushin ...
Why...?
Why would ya do this?
You always saved kids when they were bein' bullied...
You even saved Kuro...

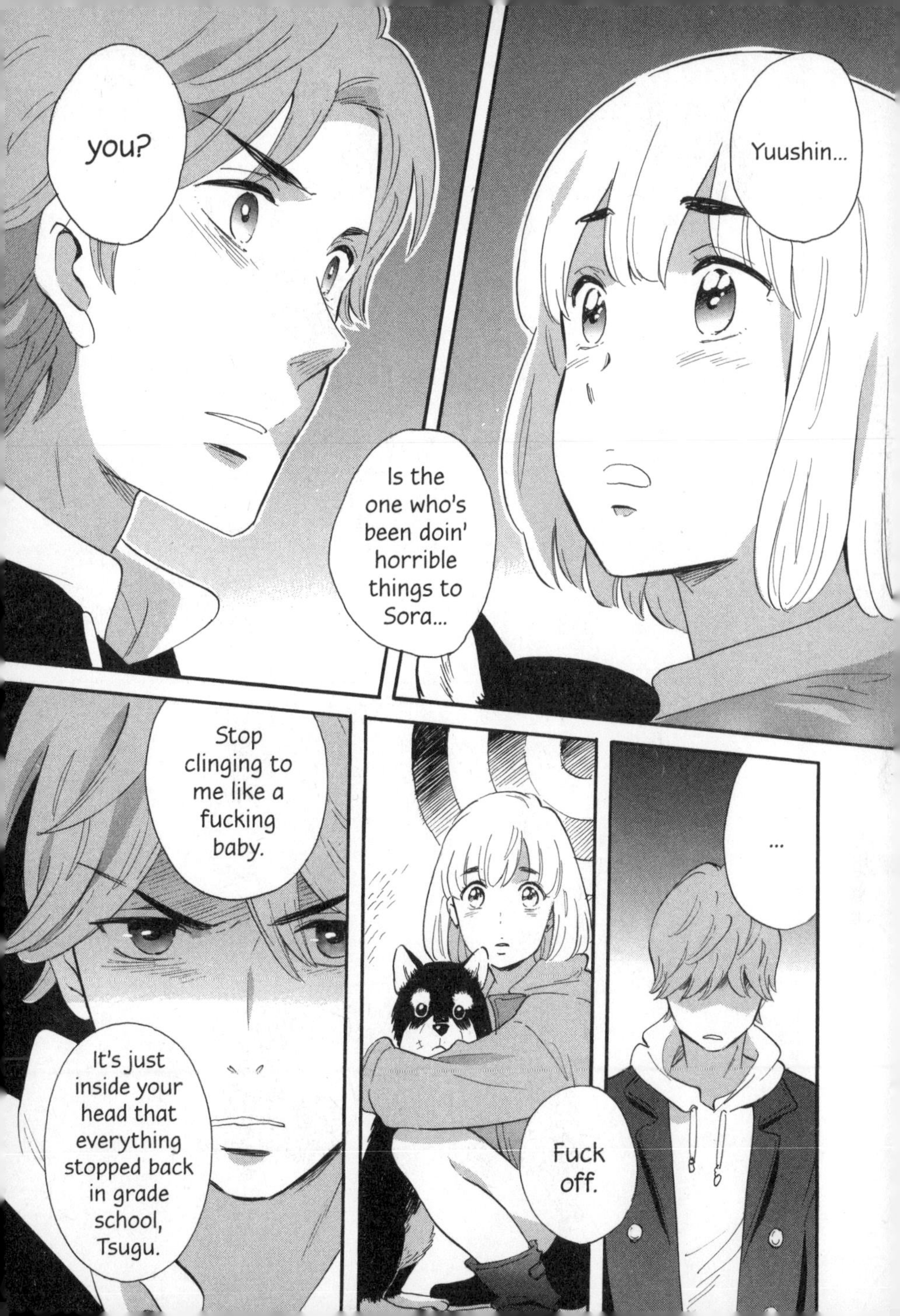
Yuushin...
Is the one who's been doin' horrible things to Sora...
you?
...
Fuck off.
Stop clinging to me like a fucking baby.
It's just inside your head that everything stopped back in grade school, Tsugu.

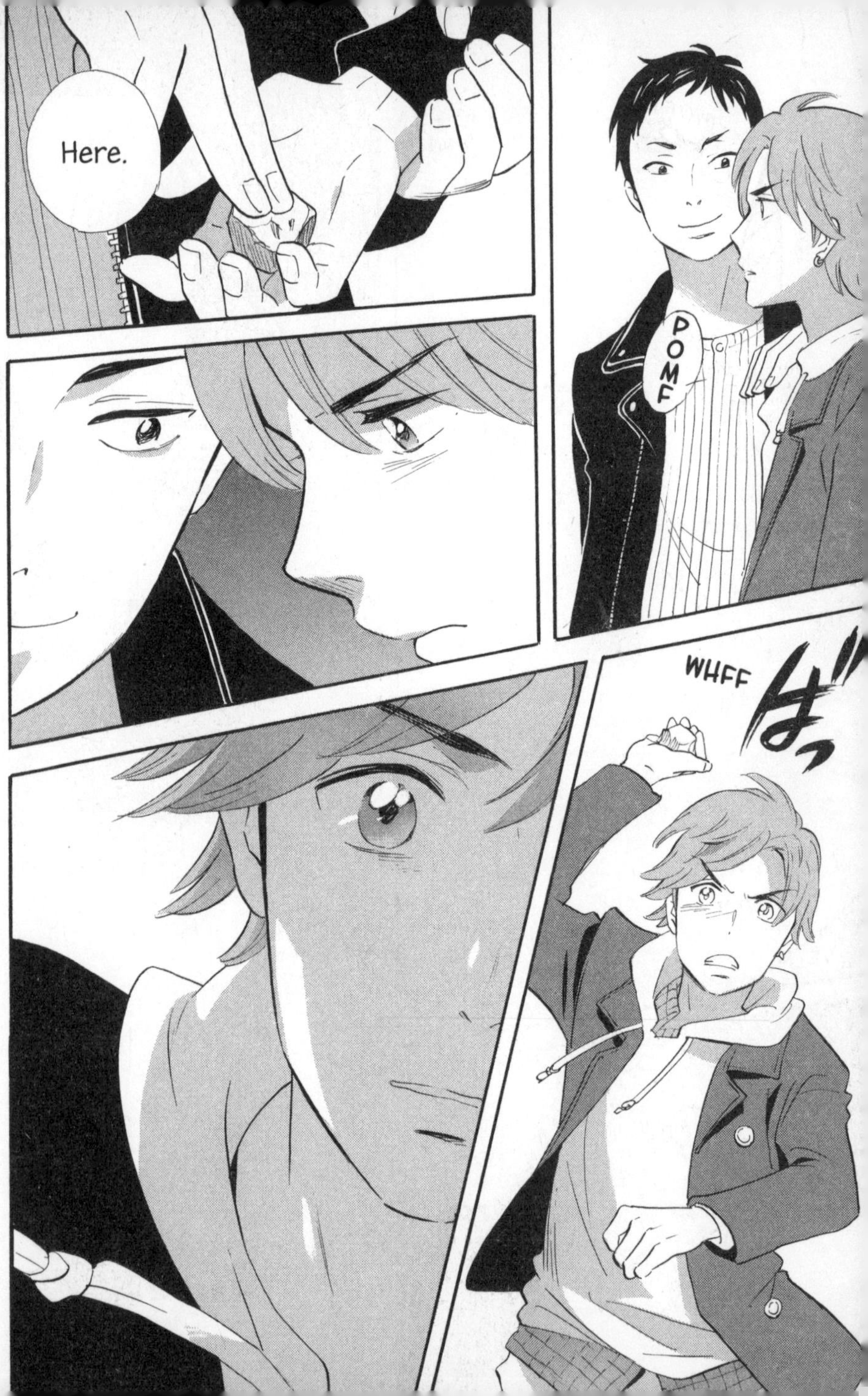
POMF
Here.
WHFF
ばっ

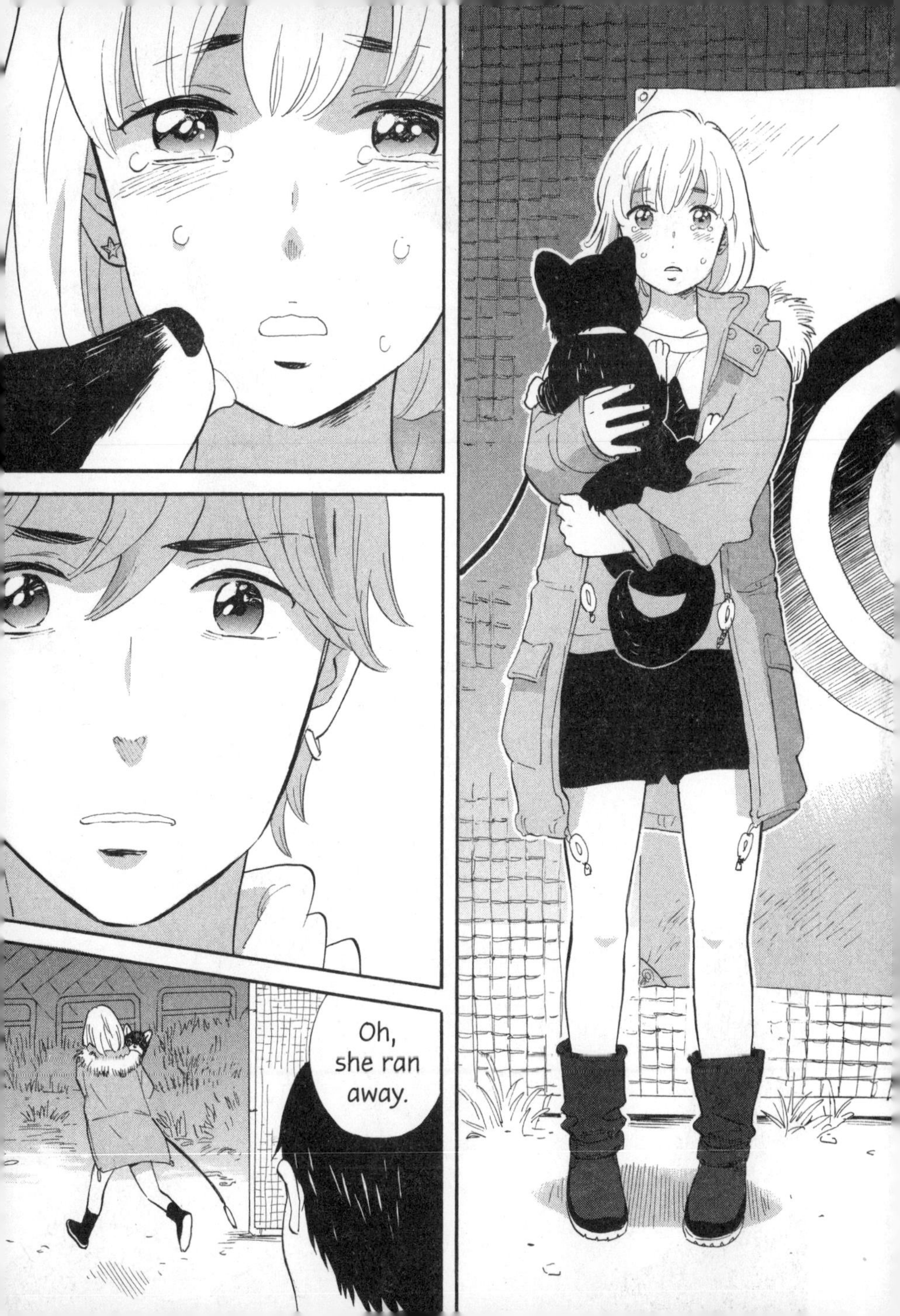
Oh, she ran away.

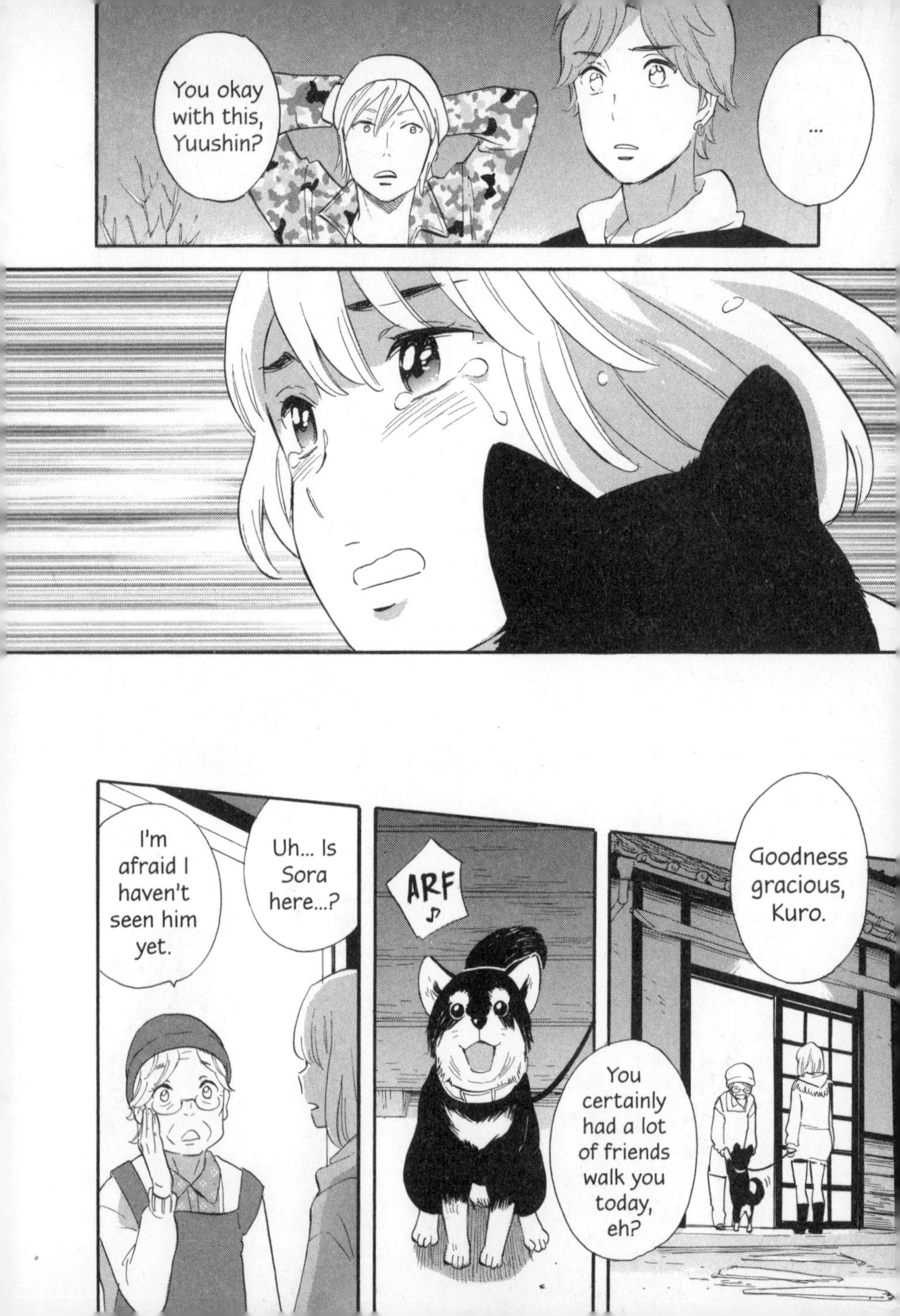
...
You okay with this, Yuushin?
Goodness gracious, Kuro.
You certainly had a lot of friends walk you today, eh?
ARF ♪
Uh... Is Sora here...?
I'm afraid I haven't seen him yet.

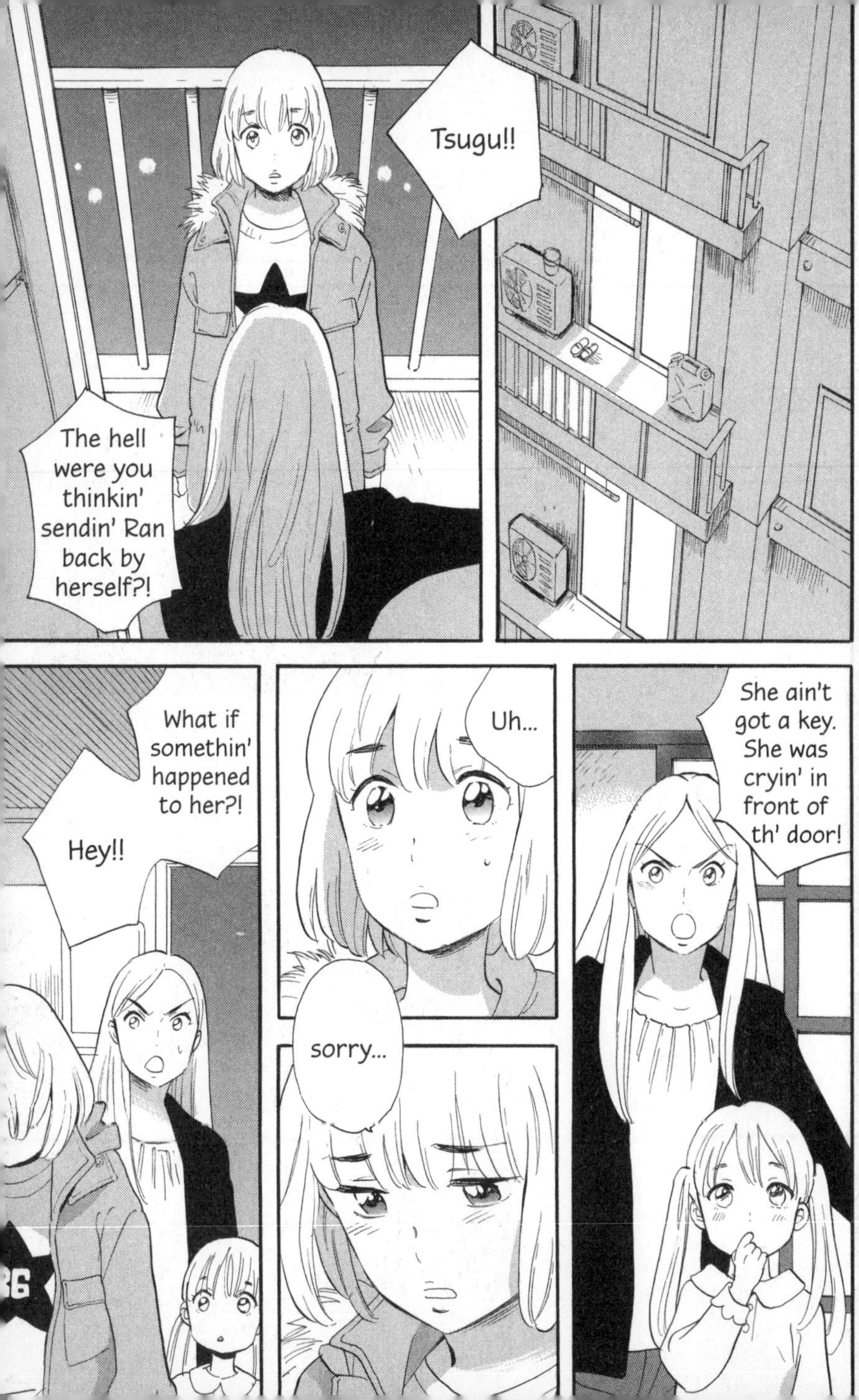
Tsugu!!
The hell were you thinkin' sendin' Ran back by herself?!
She ain't got a key. She was cryin' in front of th' door!
Uh...
sorry...
What if somethin' happened to her?!
Hey!!

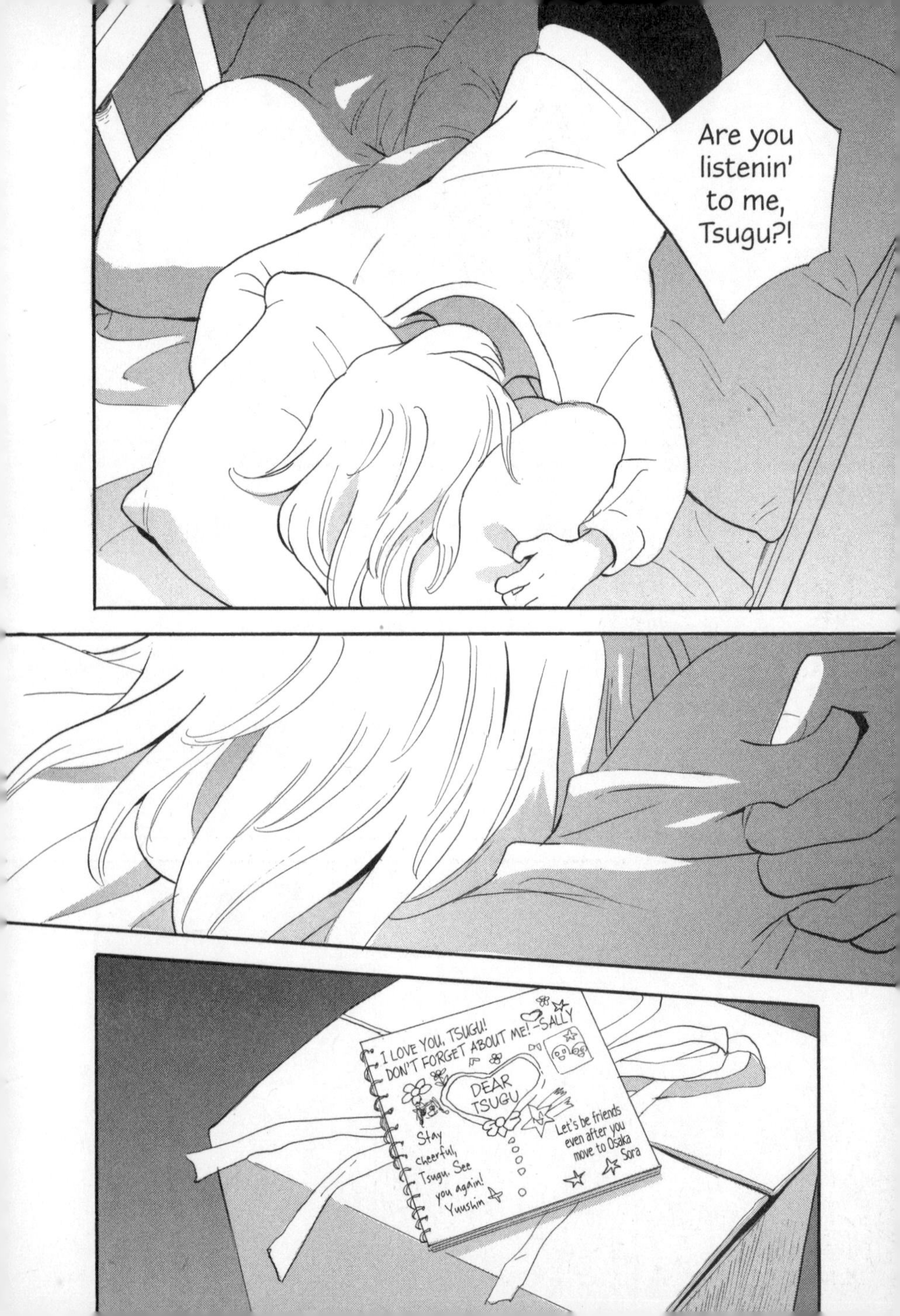
Are you listenin' to me, Tsugu?!
I LOVE YOU, TSUGU! DON'T FORGET ABOUT ME! -SALLY
DEAR TSUGU
Let's be friends even after you move to Osaka Sora
Stay cheerful, Tsugu. See you again! Yuushin

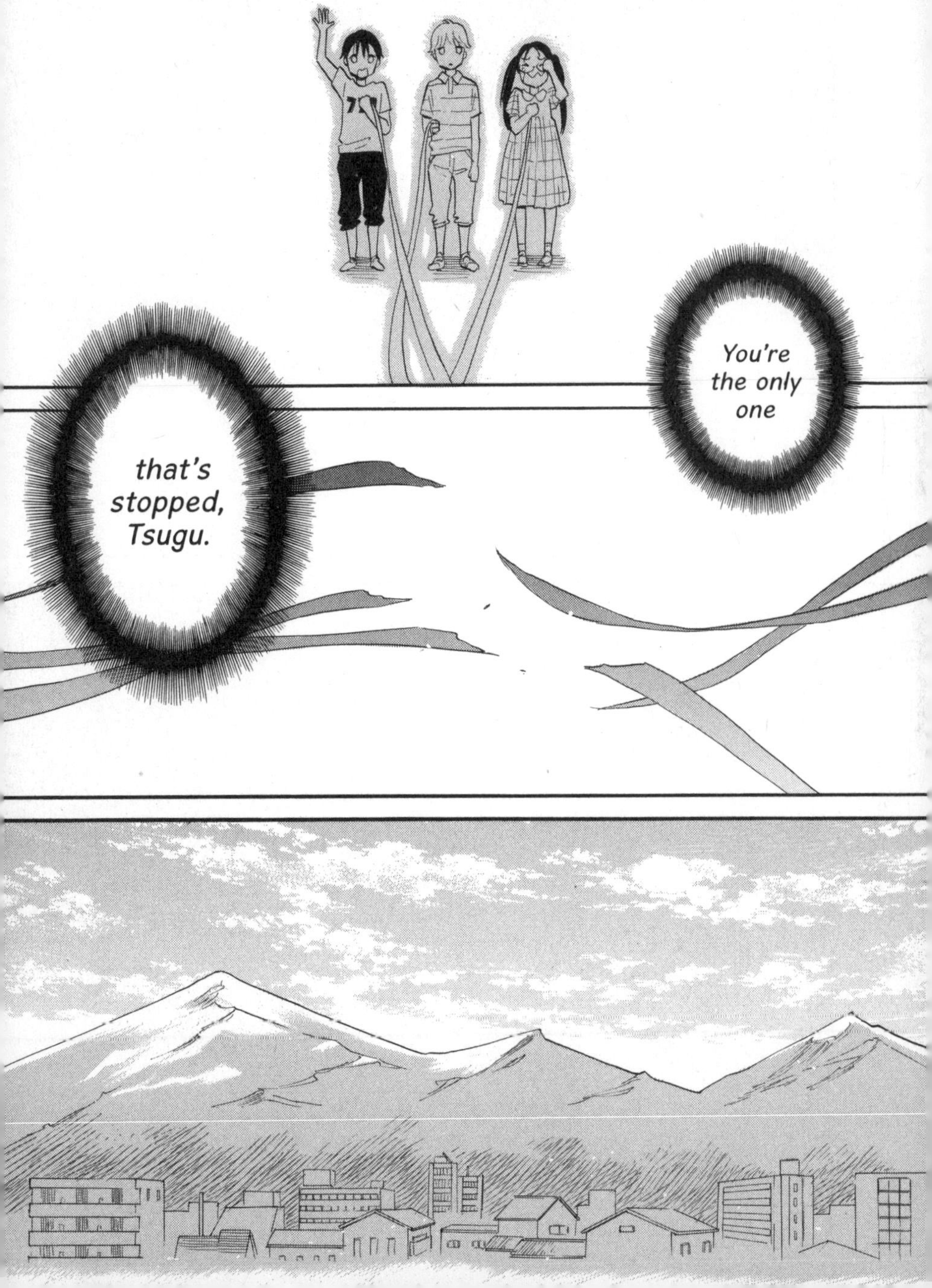
You're the only one
that's stopped, Tsugu.

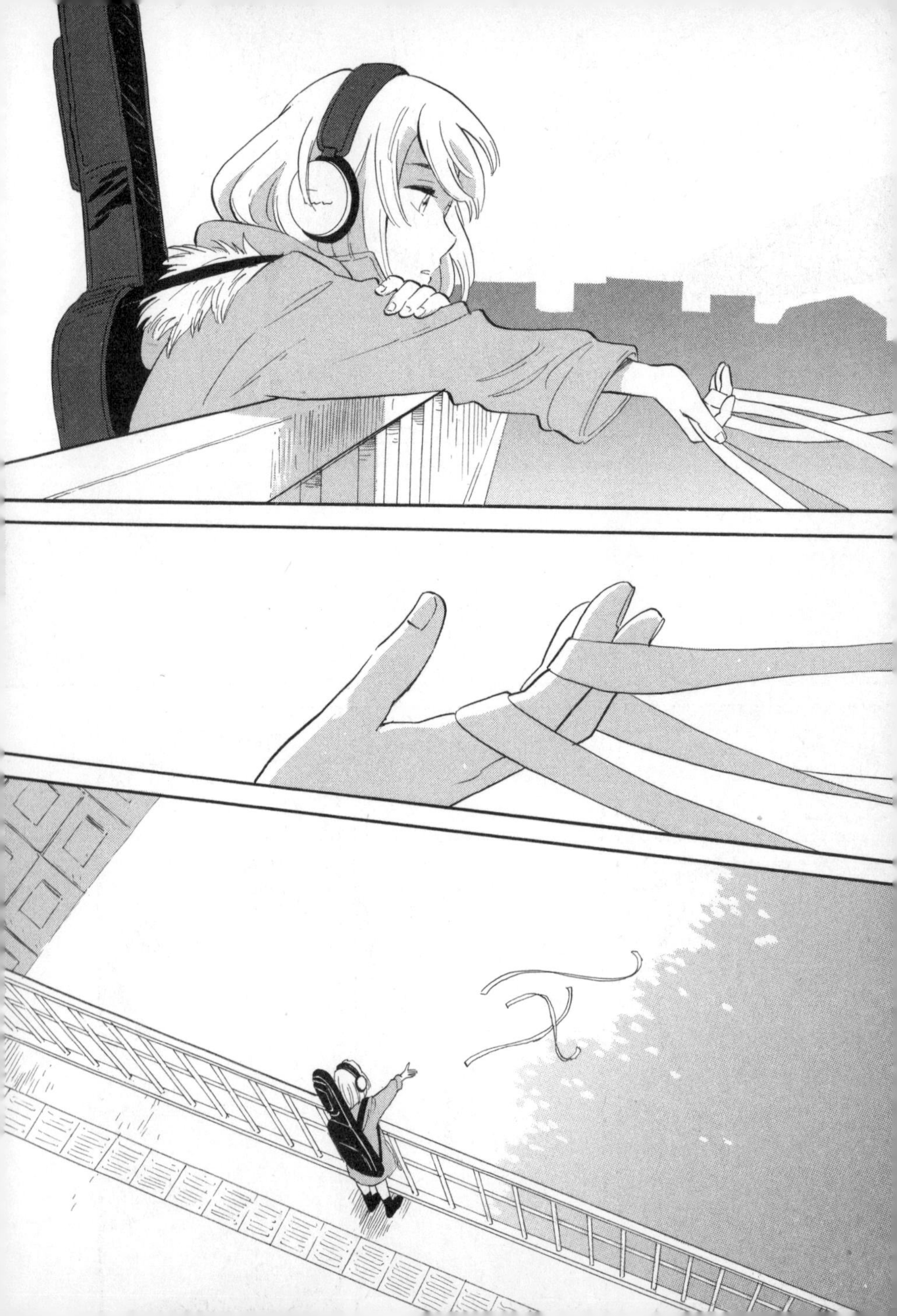

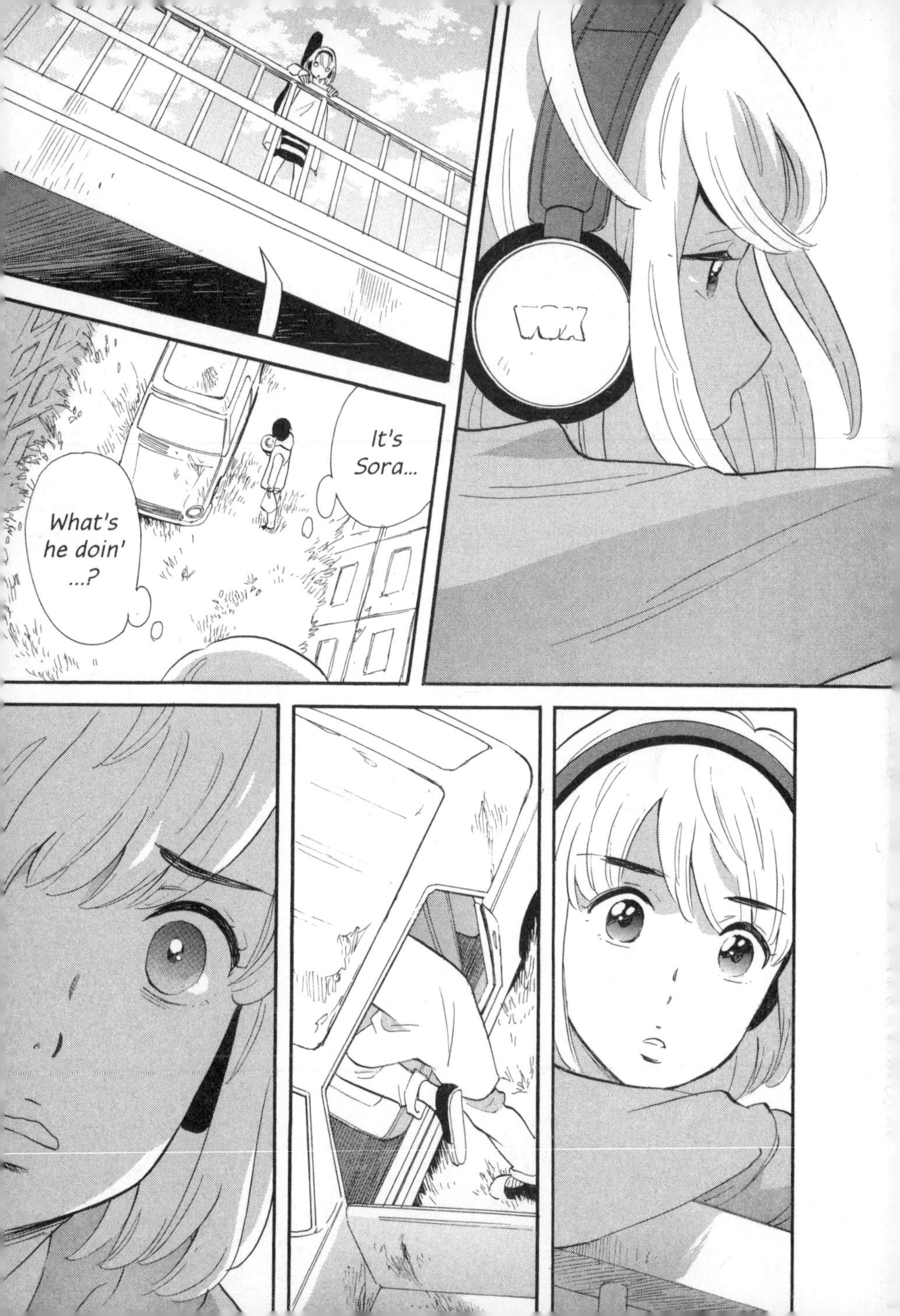
It's Sora...
What's he doin' ...?

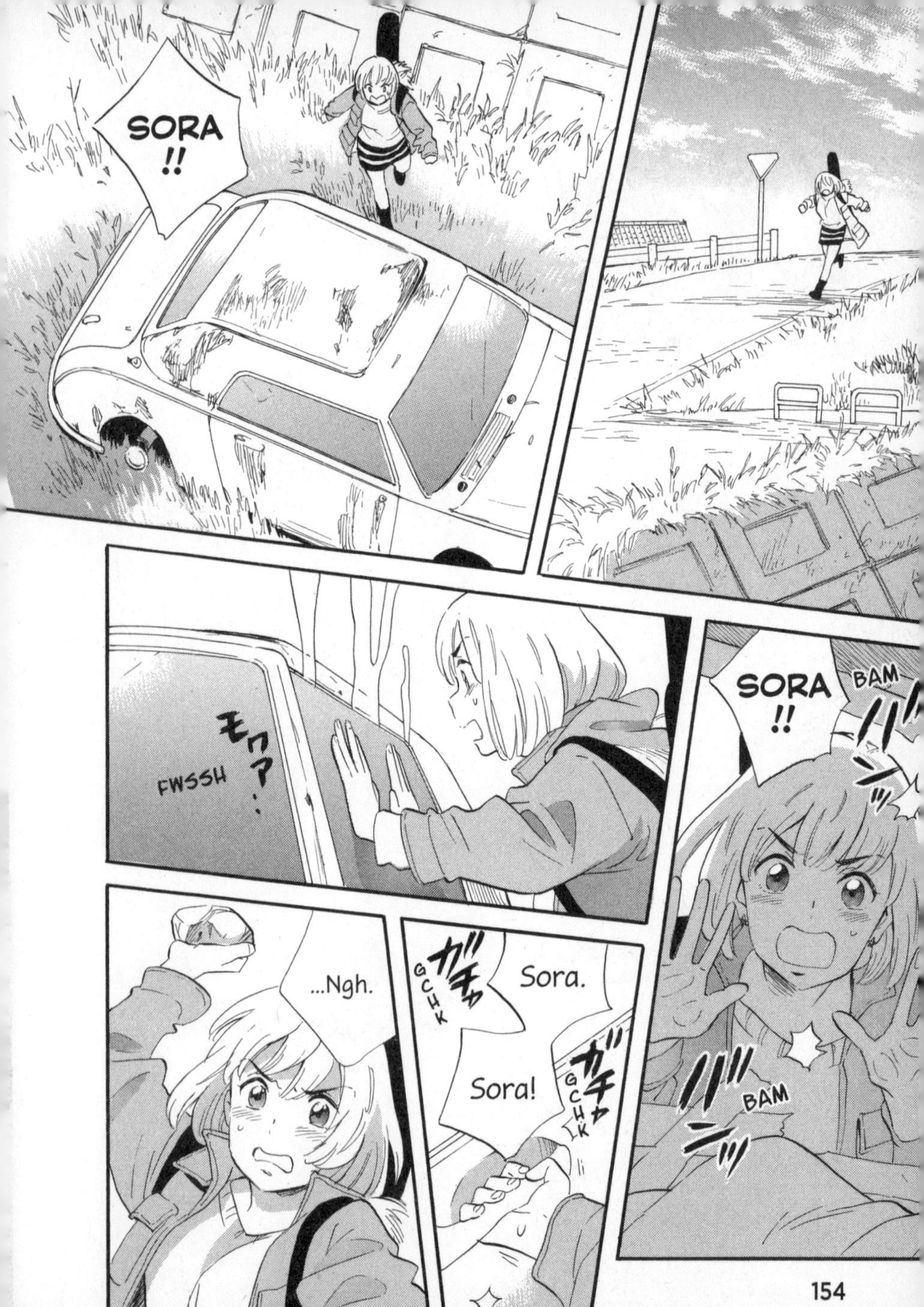
SORA !!
SORA !!
BAM
BAM
モワァ
FWSSH
Sora.
ガチャ
GCHK
Sora!
ガチャ
GCHK
...Ngh.

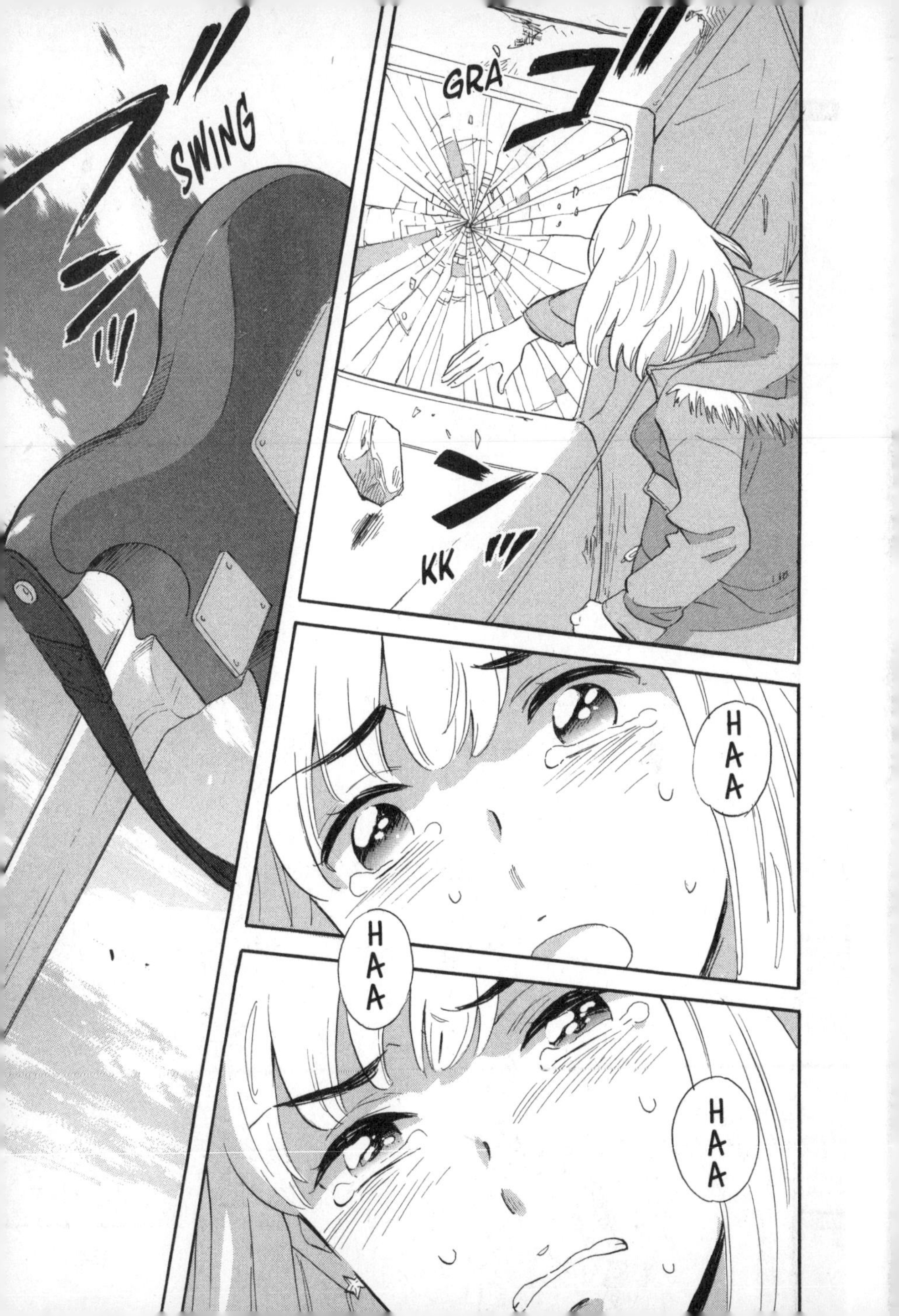
GRA
KK
HAA
HAA
HAA
SWING

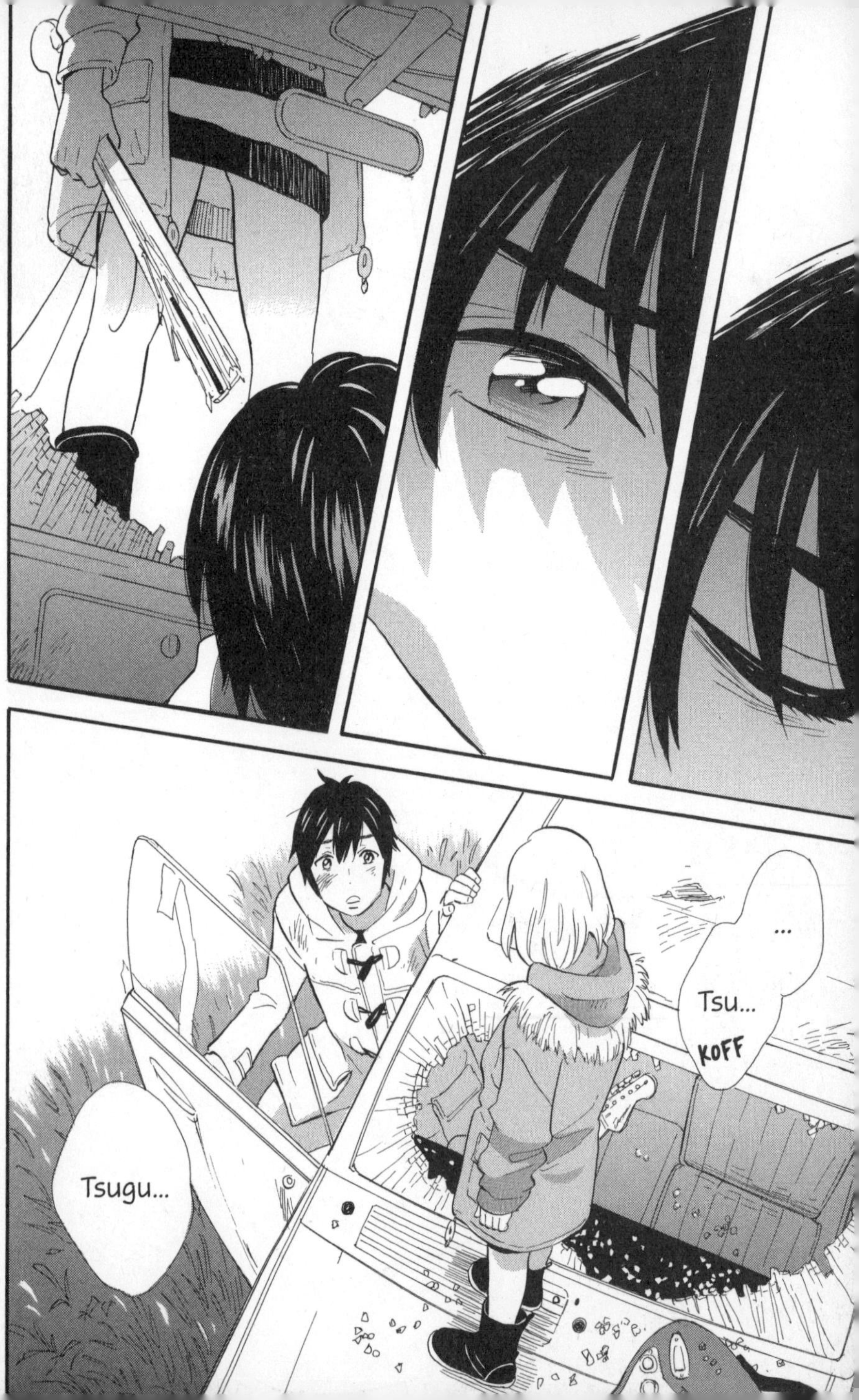
...
Tsu...
KOFF
Tsugu...

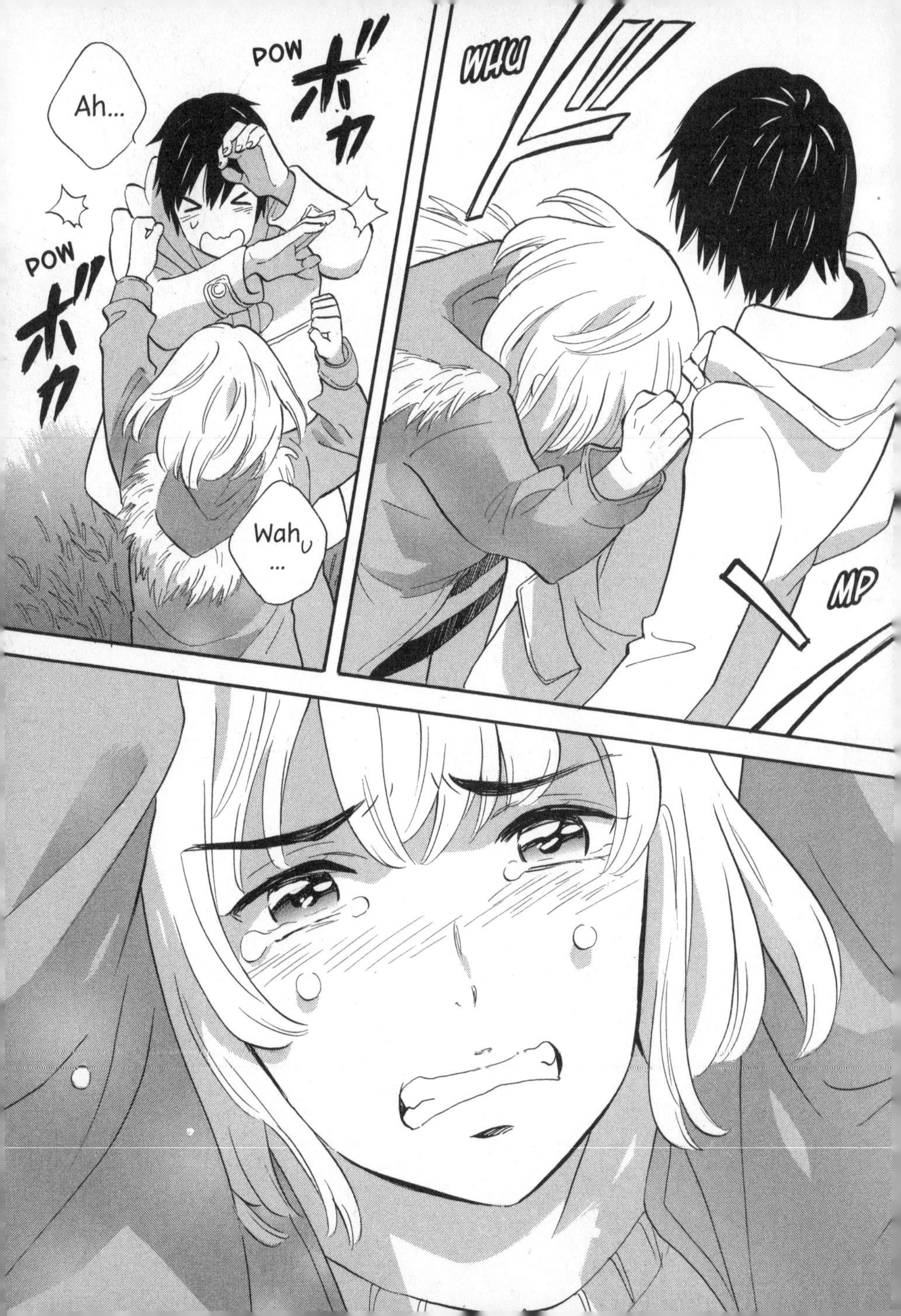
WHU
MP
POW
Ah...
POW
Wah...

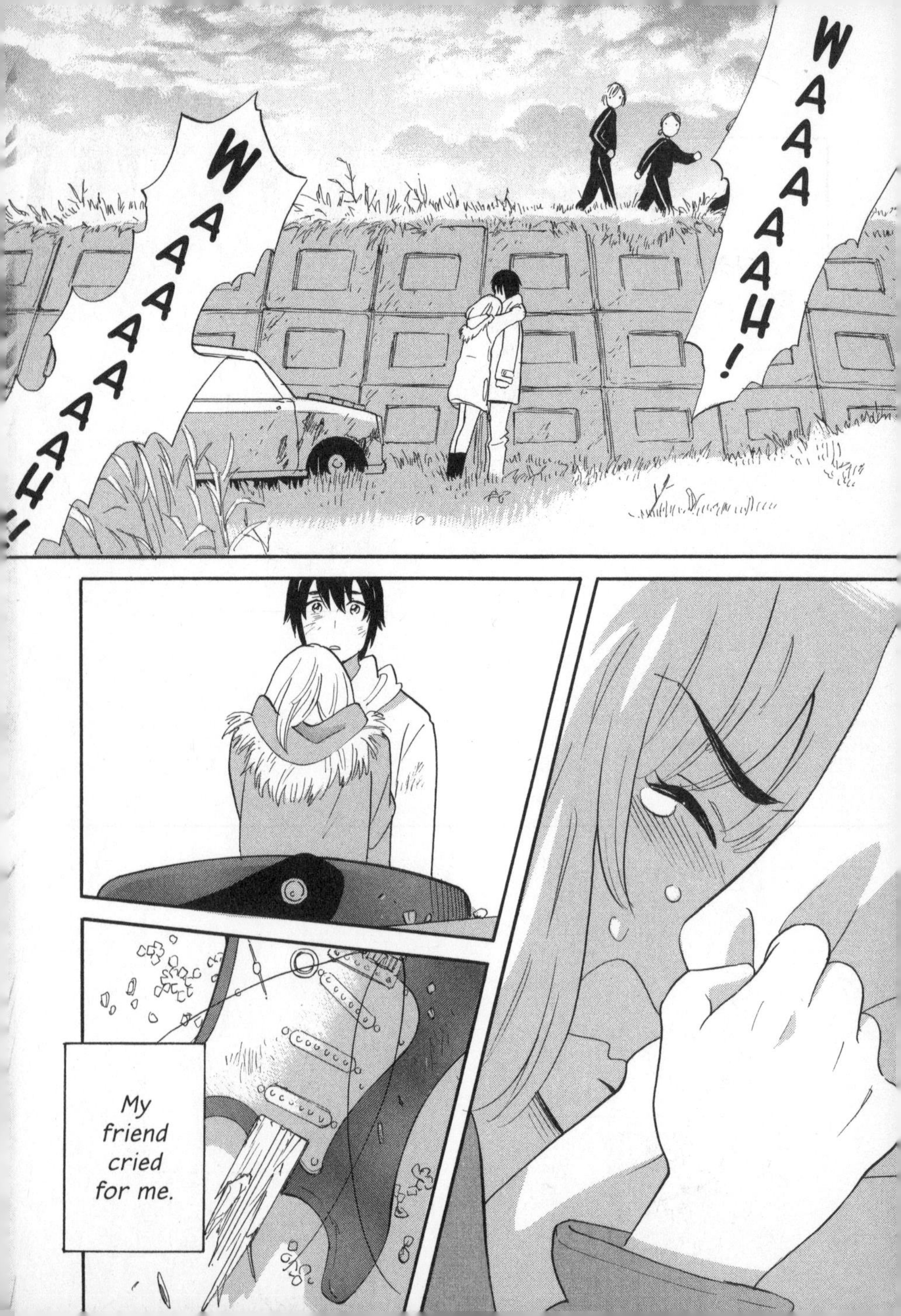
WAAAAAH!
WAAAAAAAH!!
My friend cried for me.

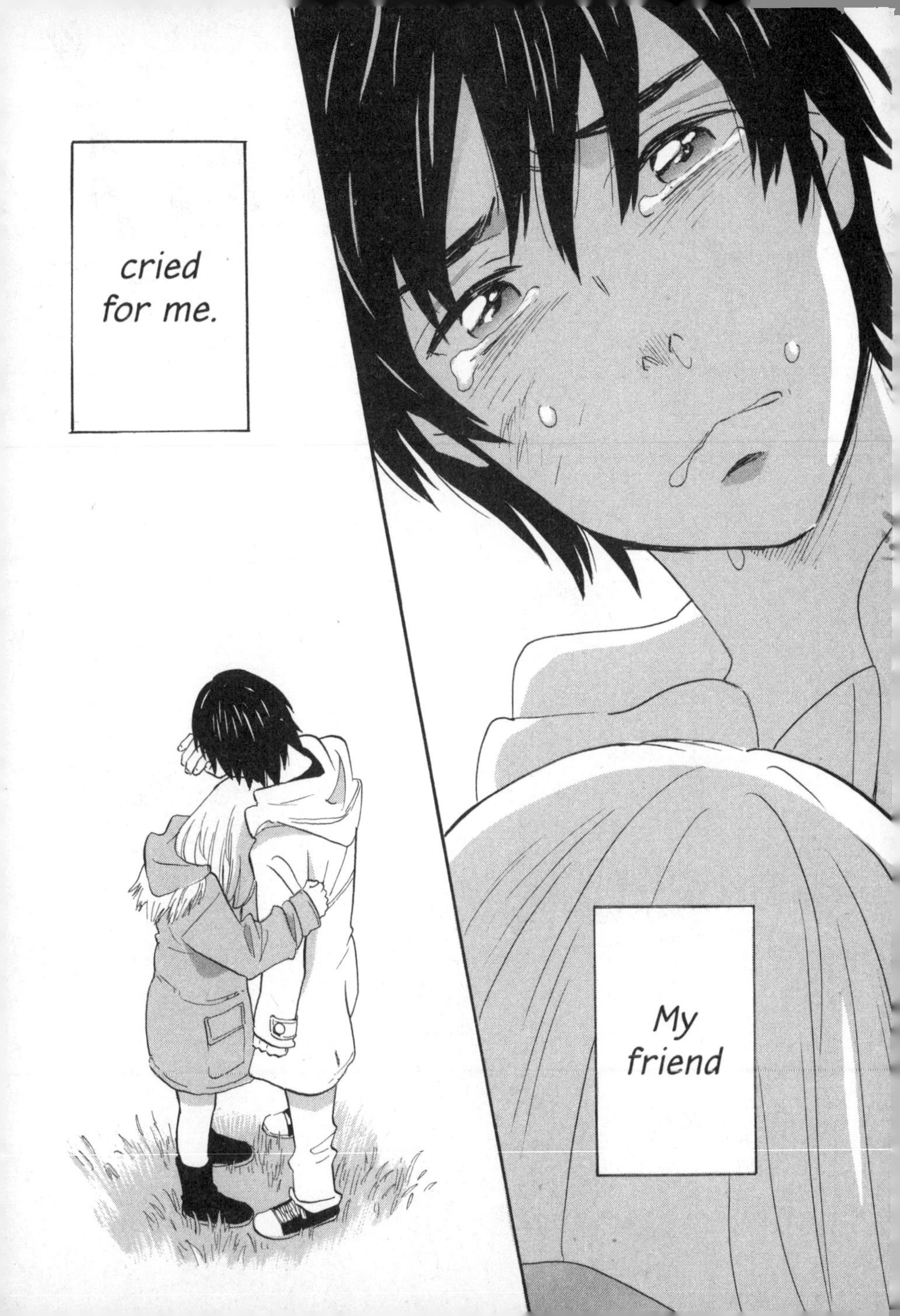
My friend
cried for me.

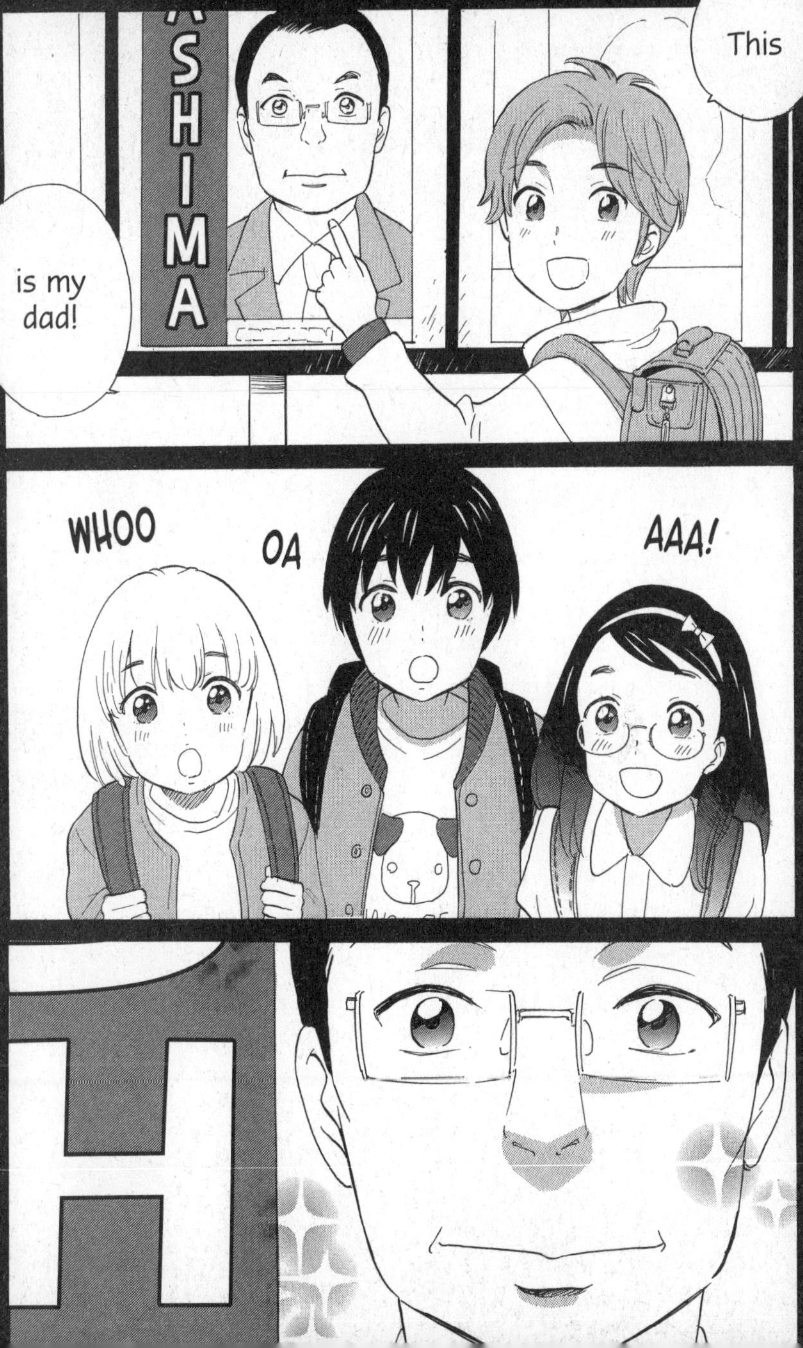
This
is my dad!
WHOO
OA
AAA!

(CHAPTER 5) DAWN RUNAWAYS

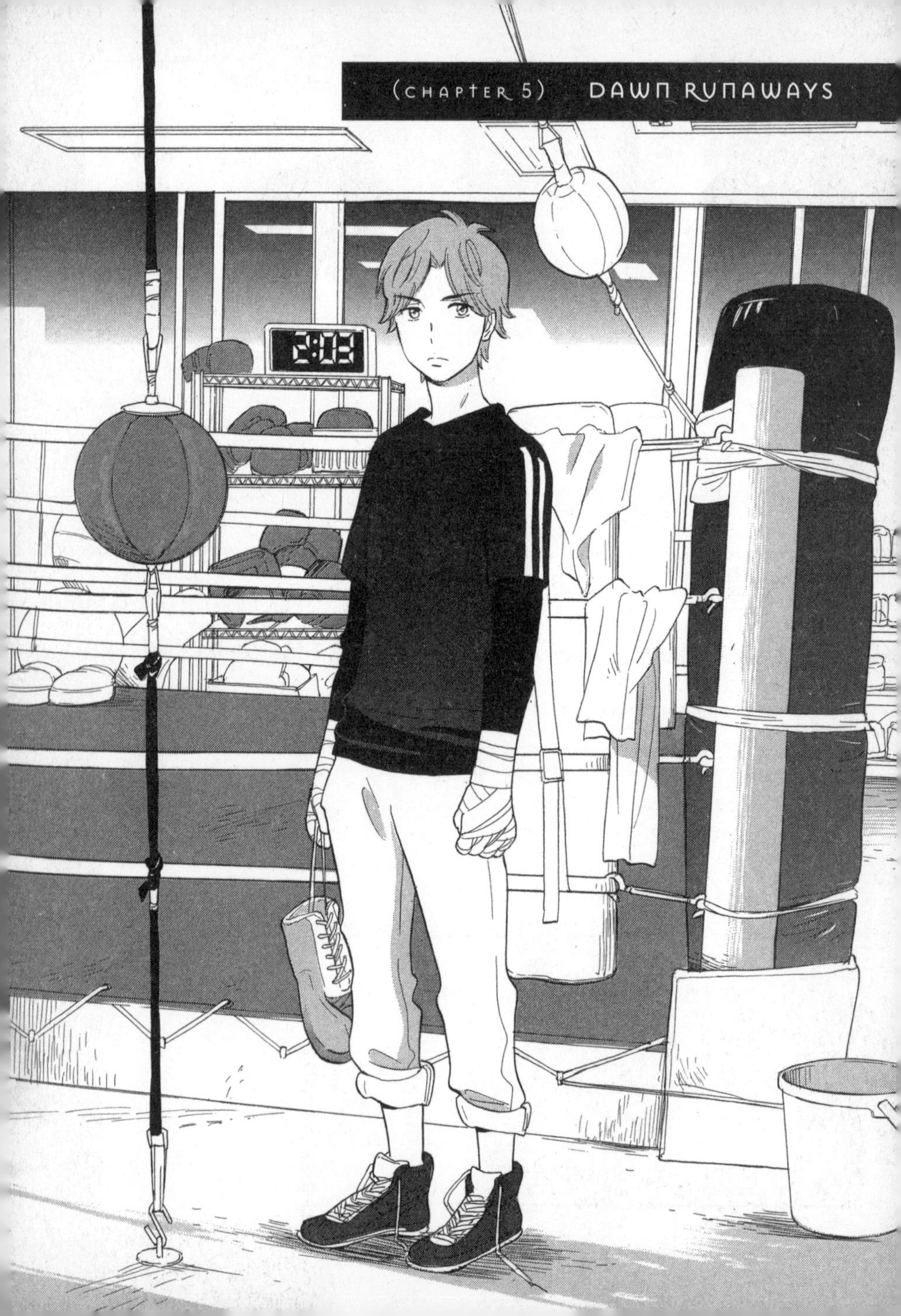

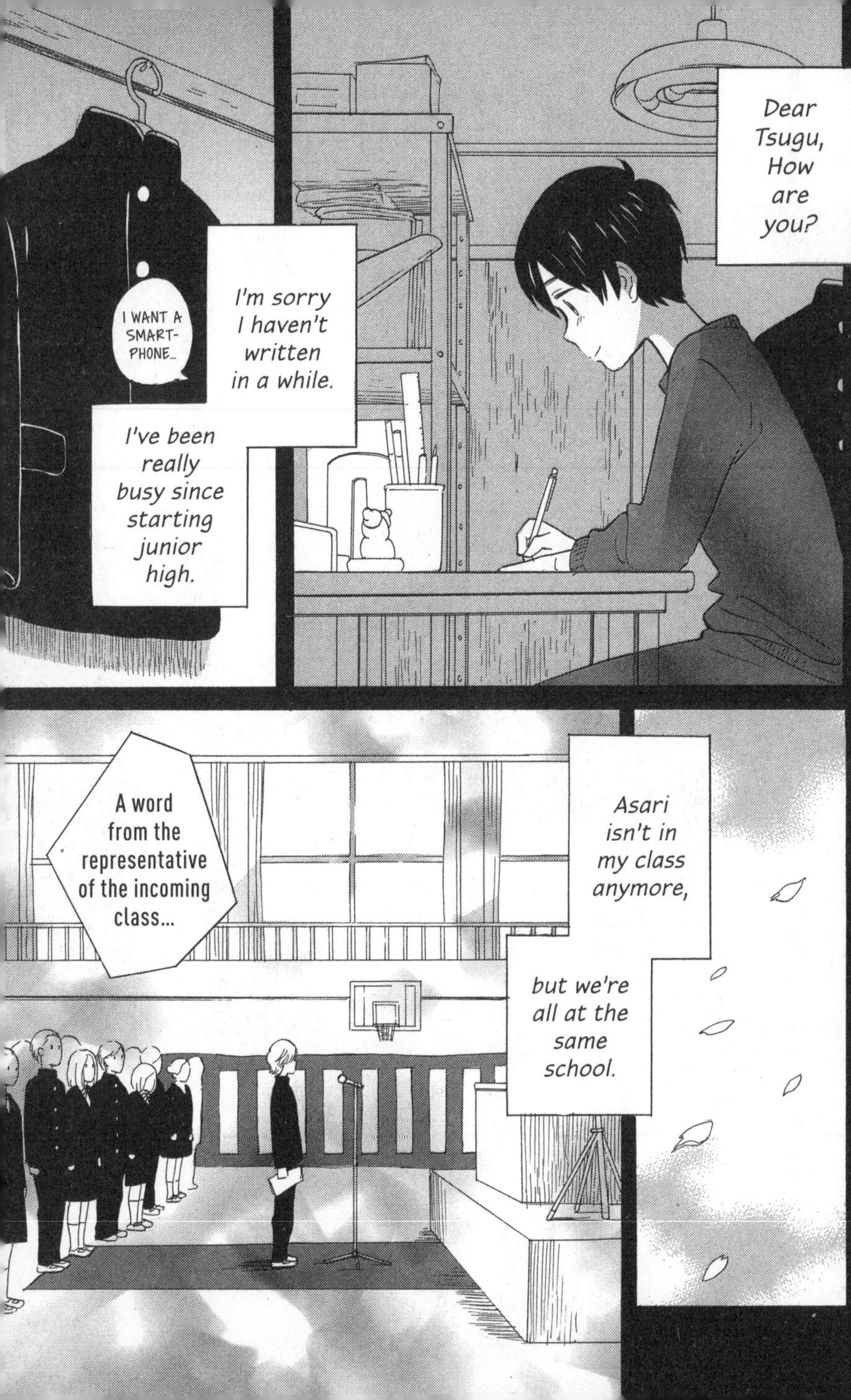
Dear Tsugu, How are you?
I'm sorry I haven't written in a while.
I've been really busy since starting junior high.
I WANT A SMARTPHONE...
Asari isn't in my class anymore,
but we're all at the same school.
A word from the representative of the incoming class...

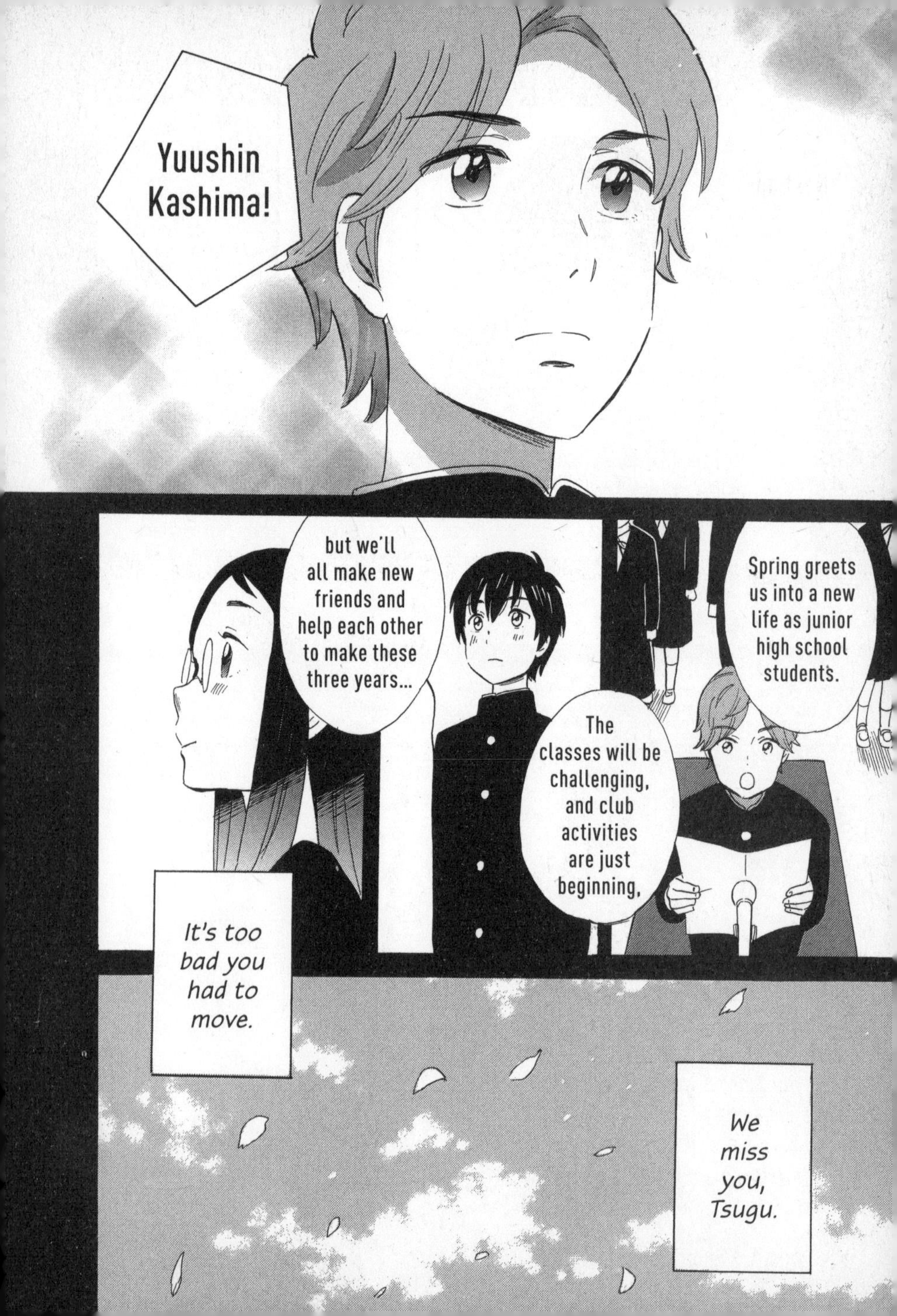

Yuushin Kashima!
Spring greets us into a new life as junior high school students.
The classes will be challenging, and club activities are just beginning,
but we'll all make new friends and help each other to make these three years...
It's too bad you had to move.
We miss you, Tsugu.

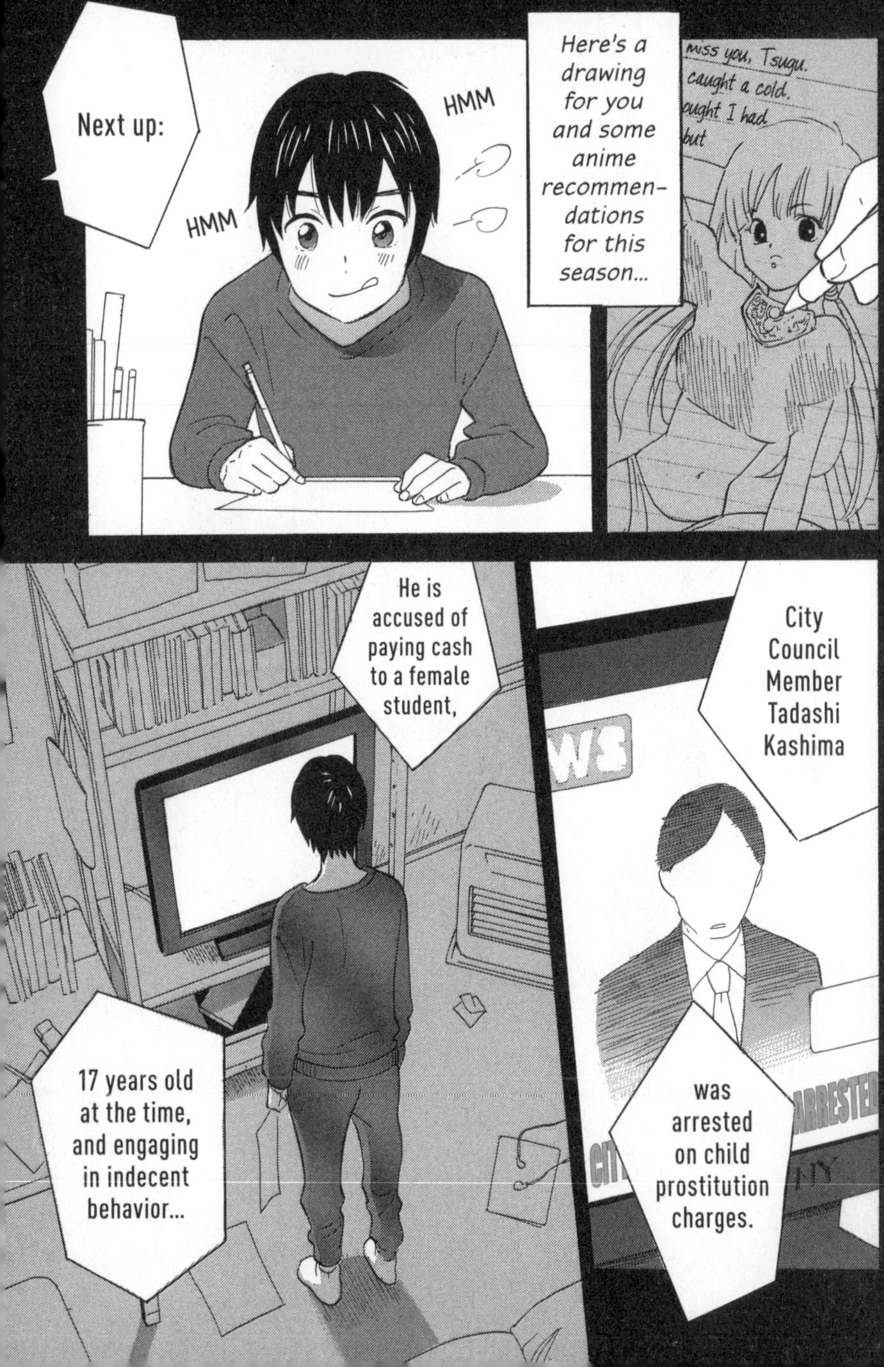
miss you, Tsugu.
caught a cold.
Here's a drawing for you and some anime recommendations for this season...
HMM
HMM
Next up:
City Council Member Tadashi Kashima
was arrested on child prostitution charges.
He is accused of paying cash to a female student,
17 years old at the time, and engaging in indecent behavior...

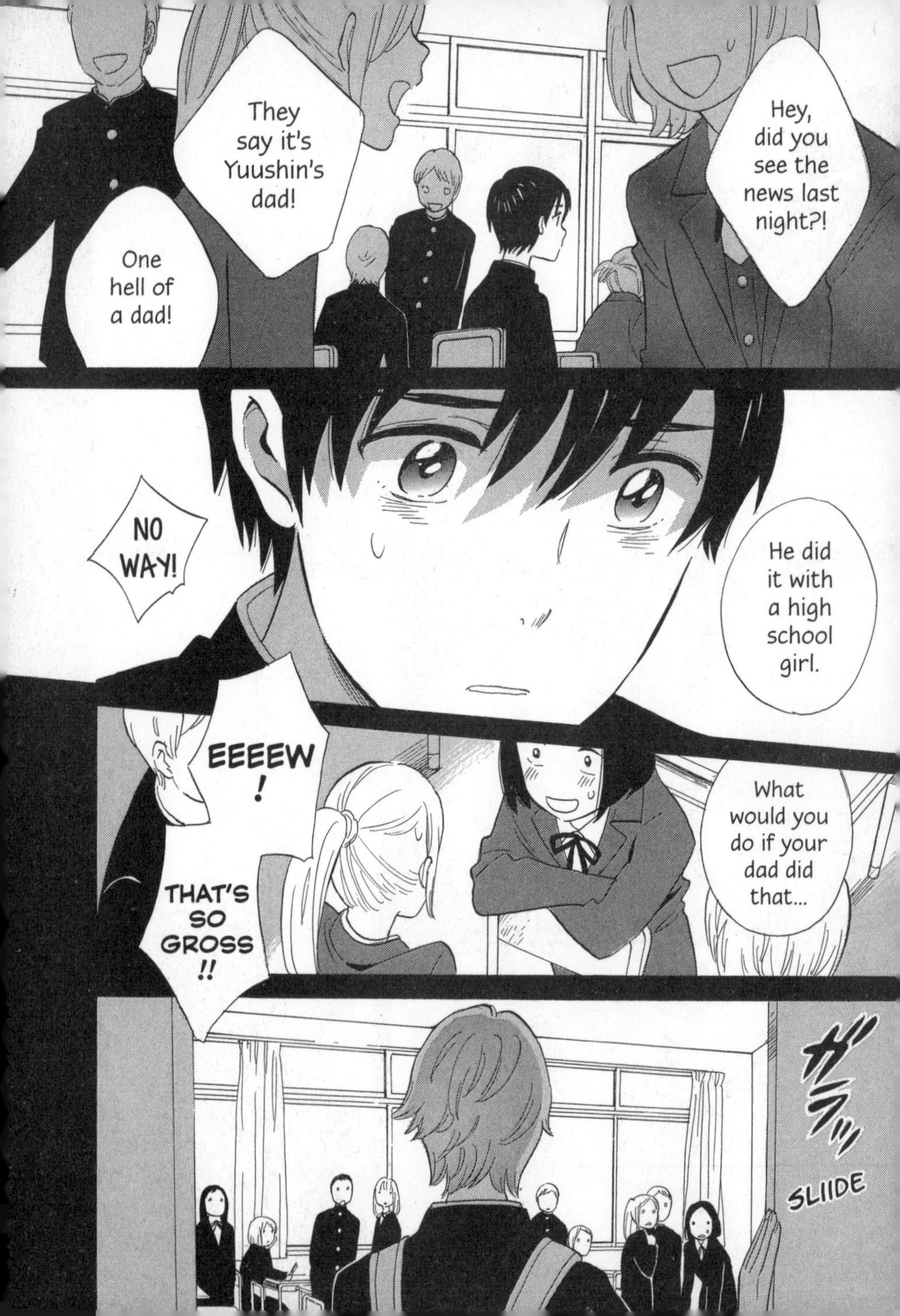
Hey, did you see the news last night?!
They say it's Yuushin's dad!
One hell of a dad!
He did it with a high school girl.
NO WAY!
What would you do if your dad did that...
EEEEW!
THAT'S SO GROSS!!
ガラッ
SLIIDE

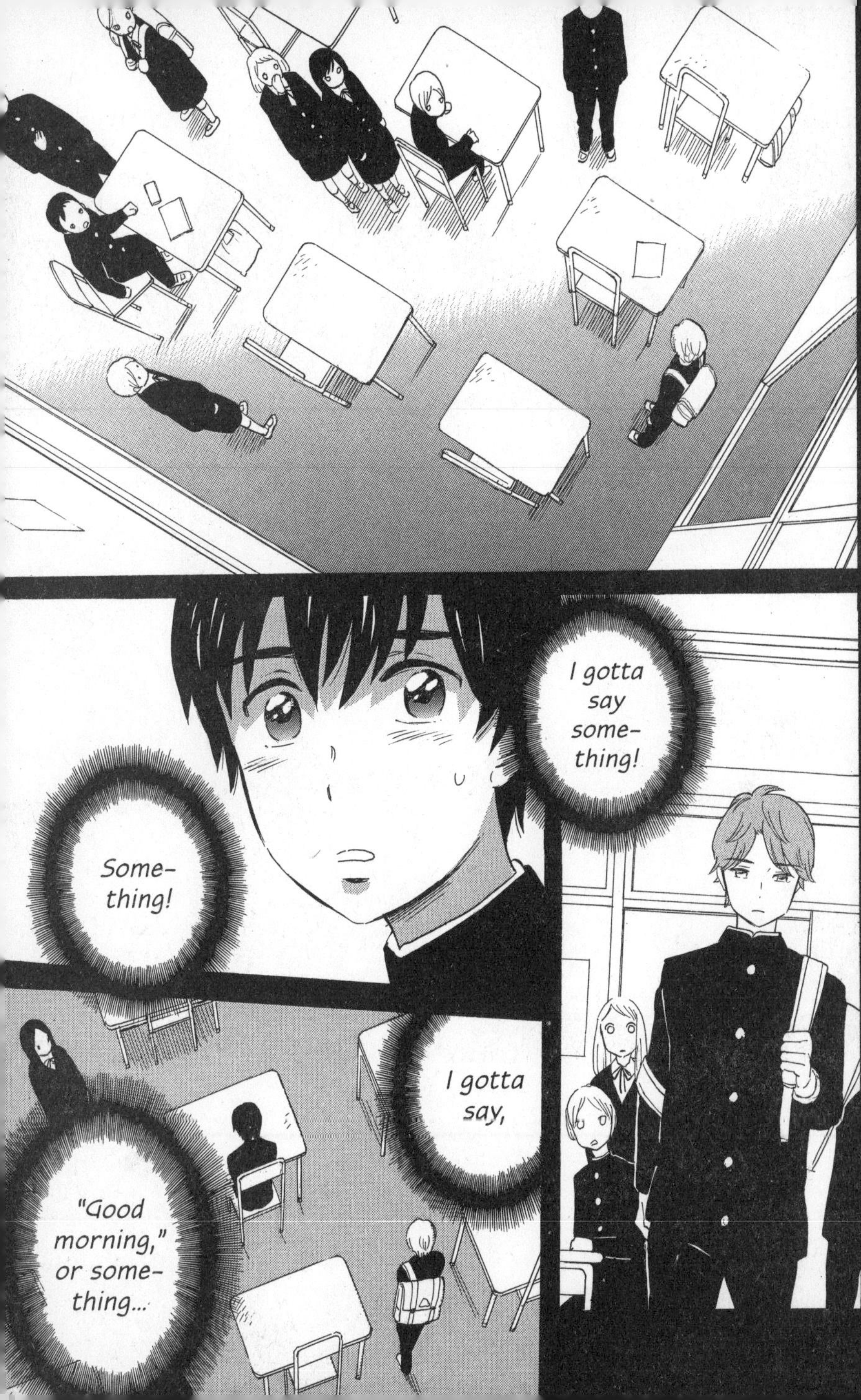
I gotta say some-thing!
Some-thing!
I gotta say,
"Good morning," or some-thing...

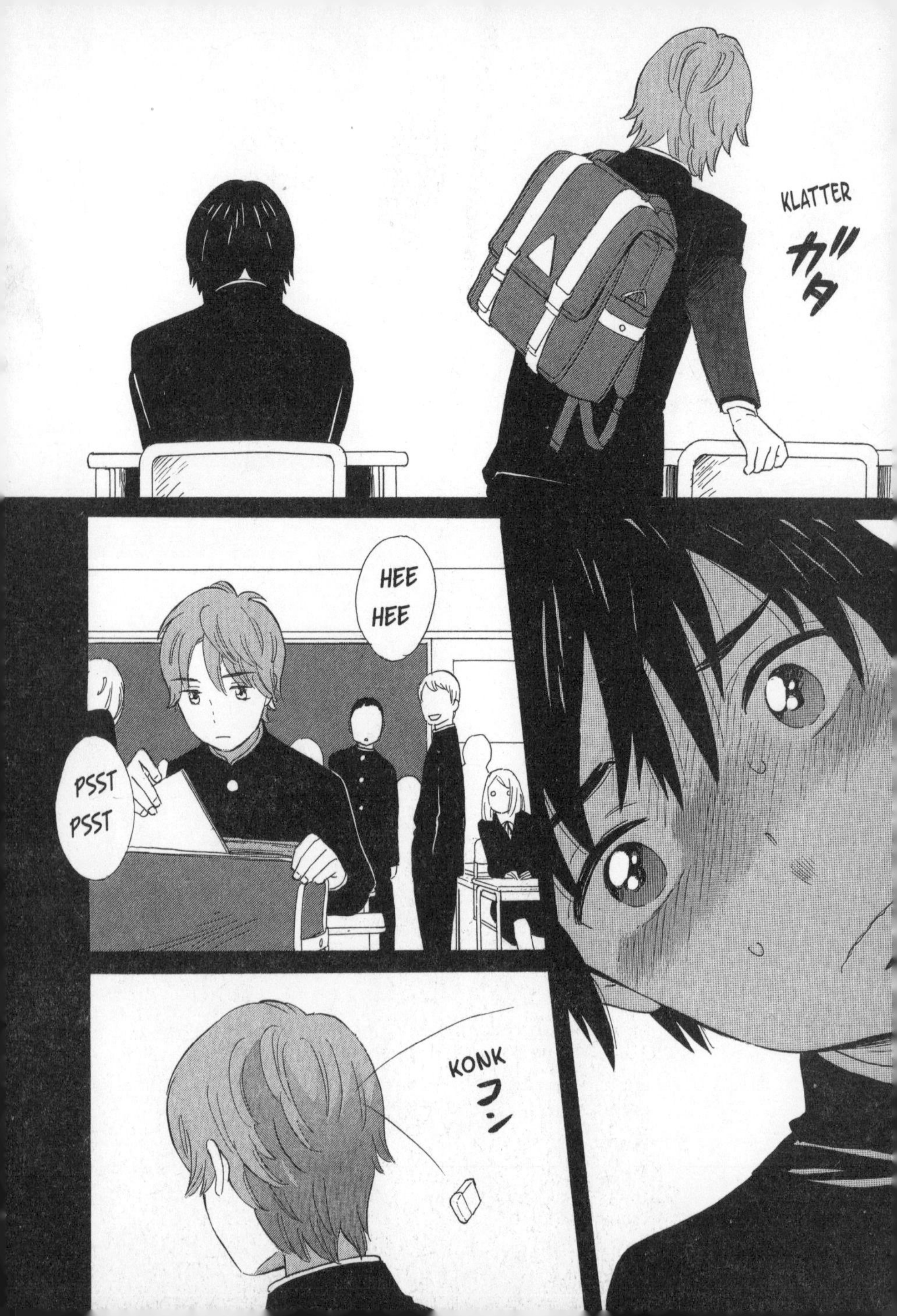
KLATTER
ガタ
HEE HEE
PSST PSST
KONK
フン

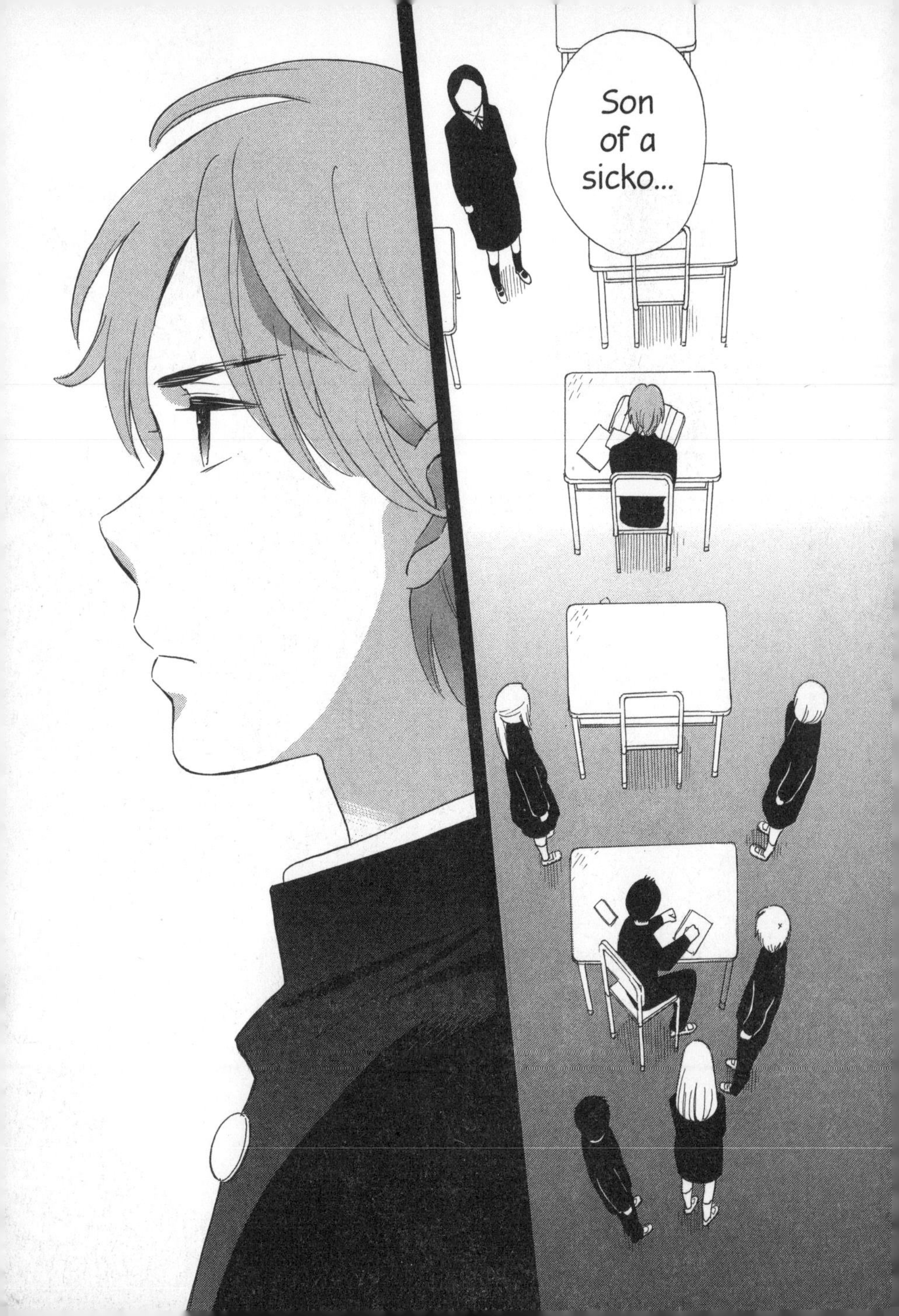
Son of a sicko...

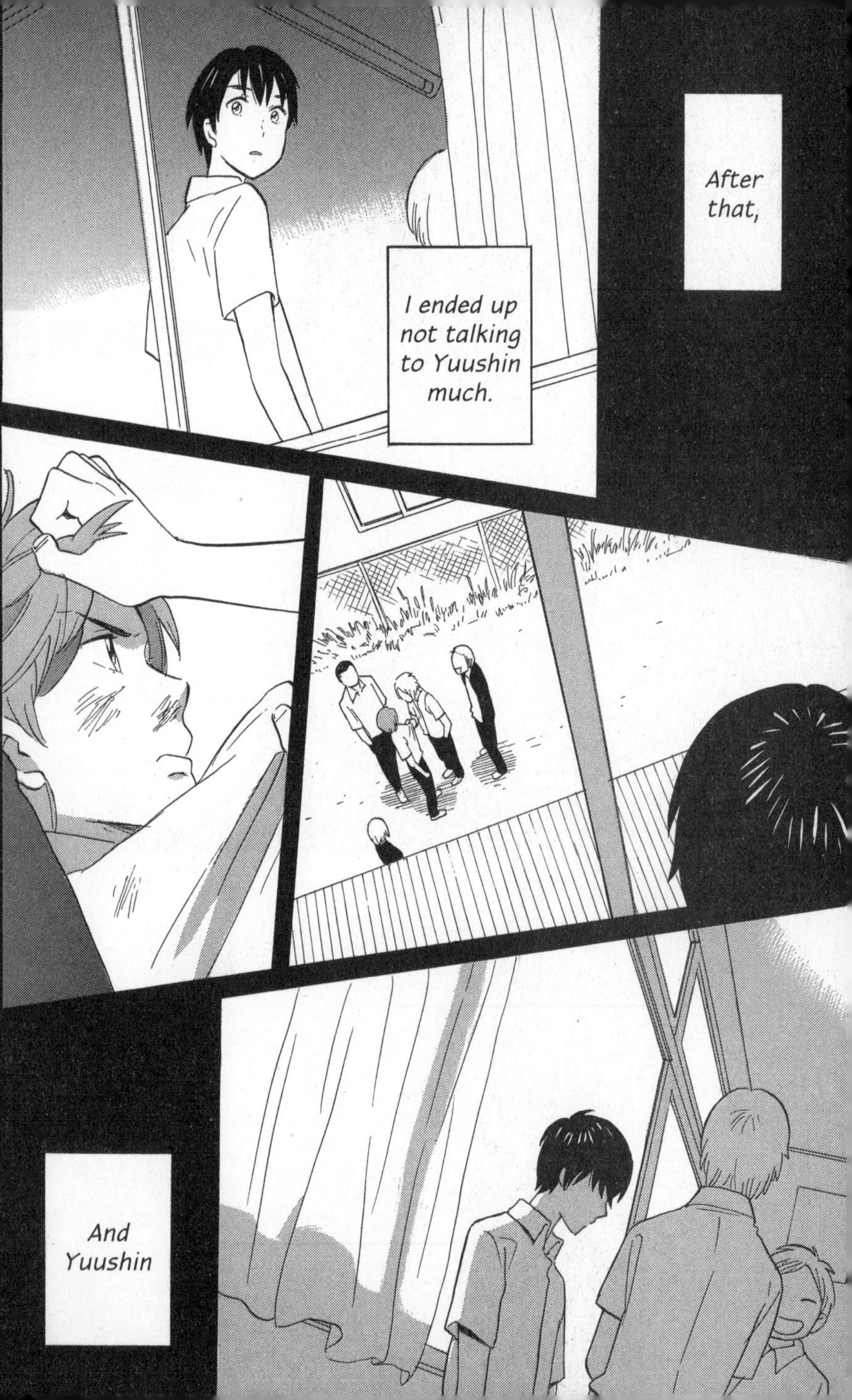
After that,
I ended up not talking to Yuushin much.
And Yuushin

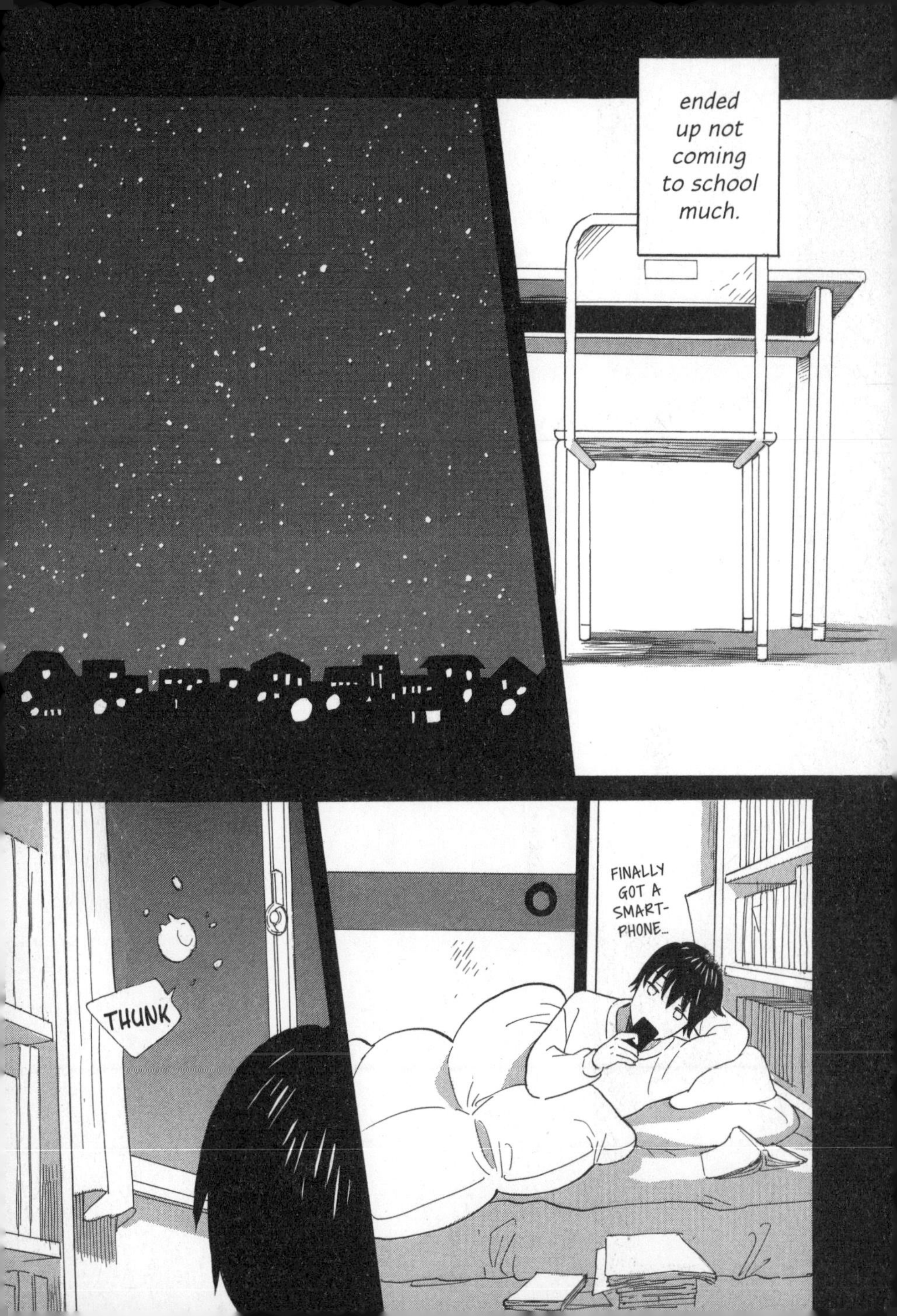
ended up not coming to school much.
FINALLY GOT A SMART-PHONE...
THUNK

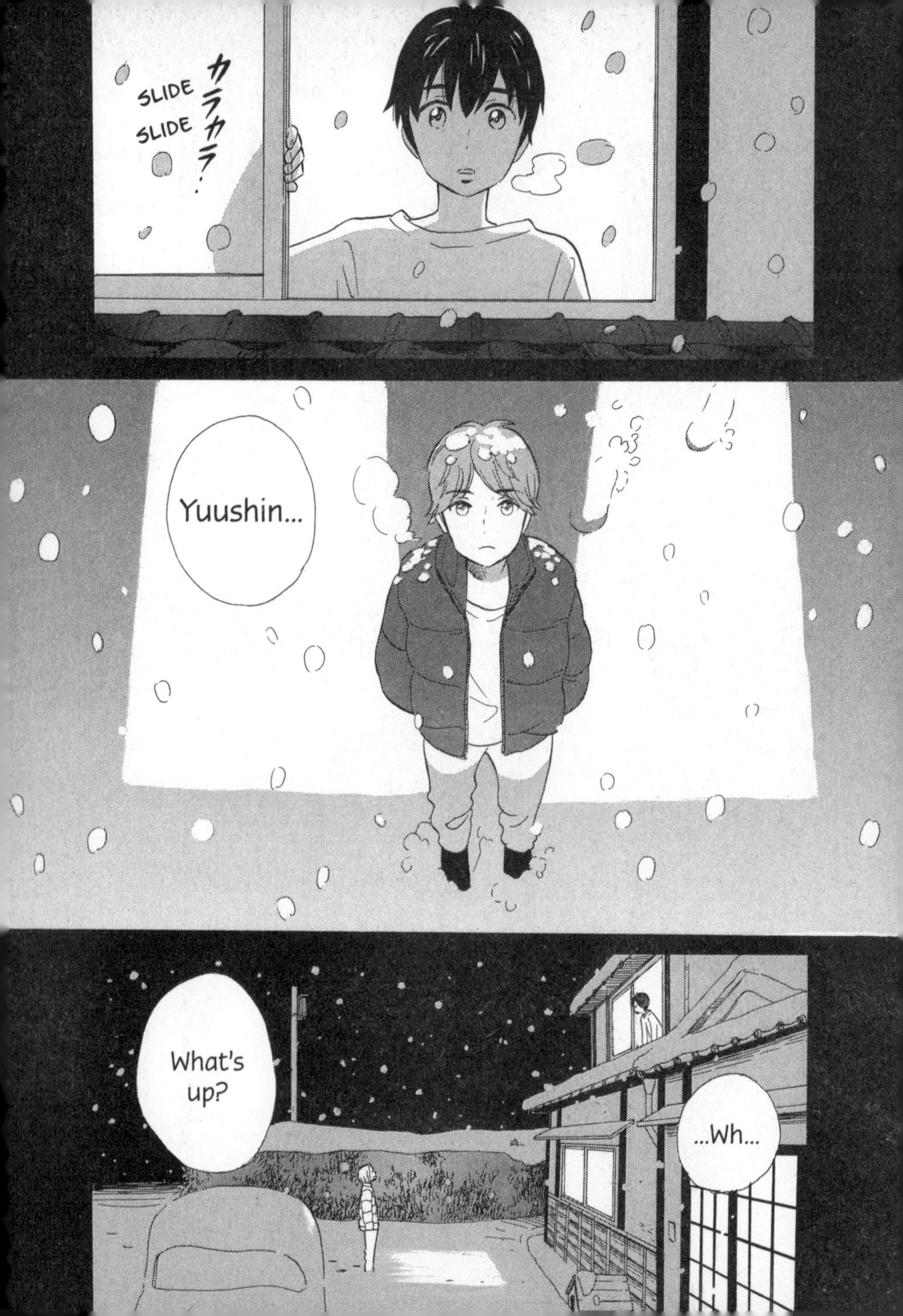
SLIDE SLIDE
カラカラ…
Yuushin...
...Wh...
What's up?

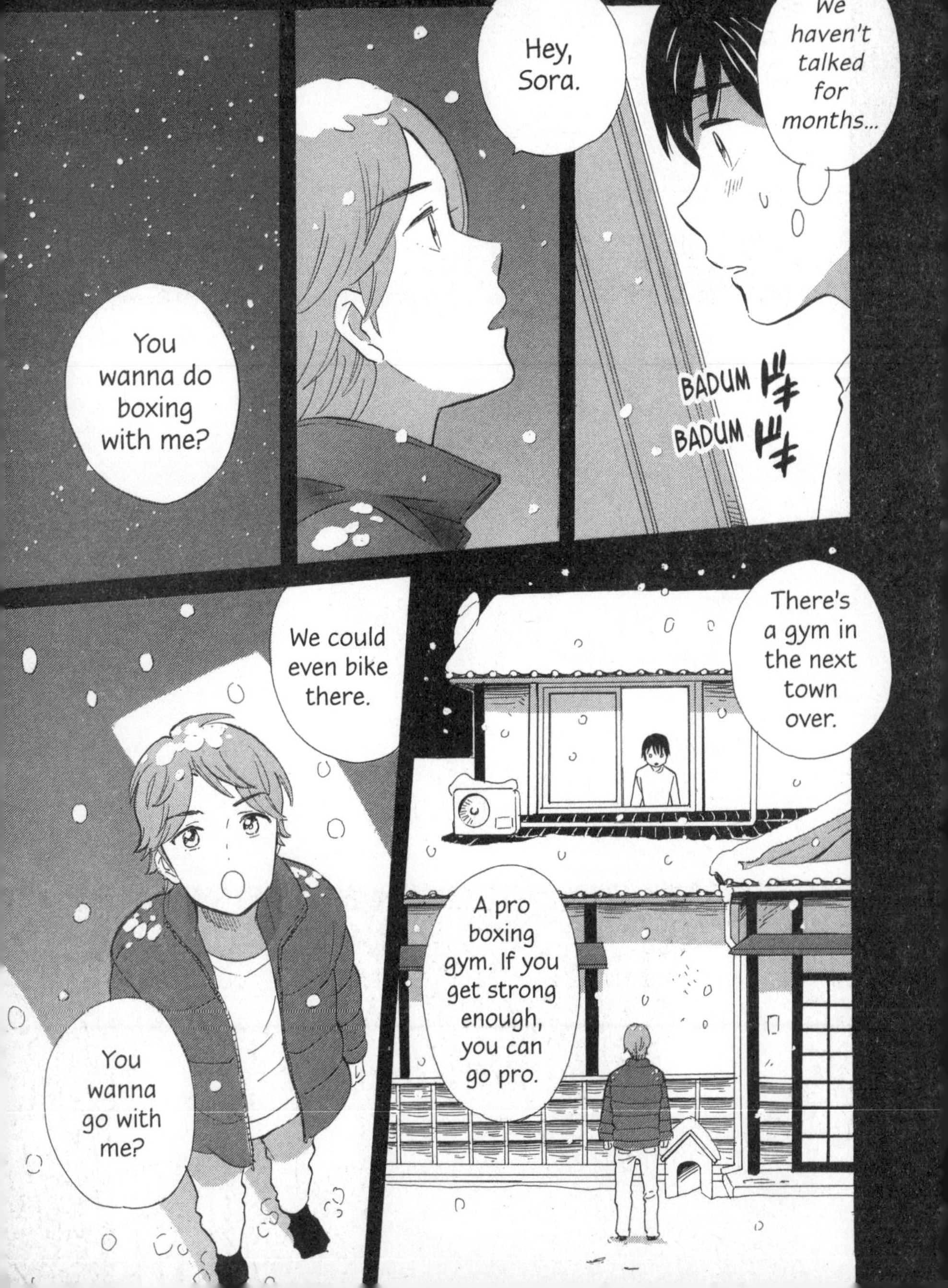
We haven't talked for months...
BADUM
BADUM
Hey, Sora.
You wanna do boxing with me?
There's a gym in the next town over.
A pro boxing gym. If you get strong enough, you can go pro.
We could even bike there.
You wanna go with me?

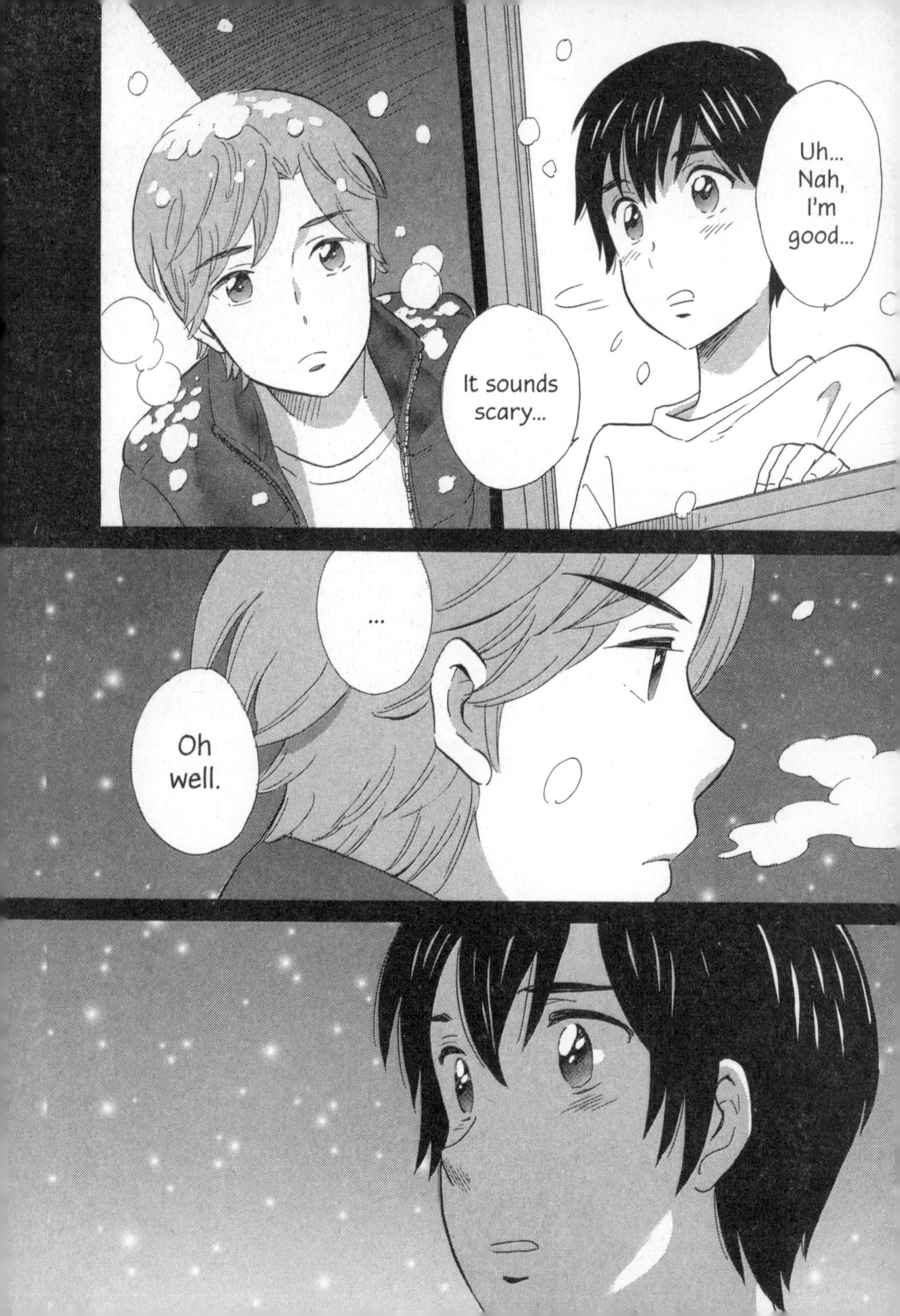
Uh... Nah, I'm good...
It sounds scary...
...
Oh well.

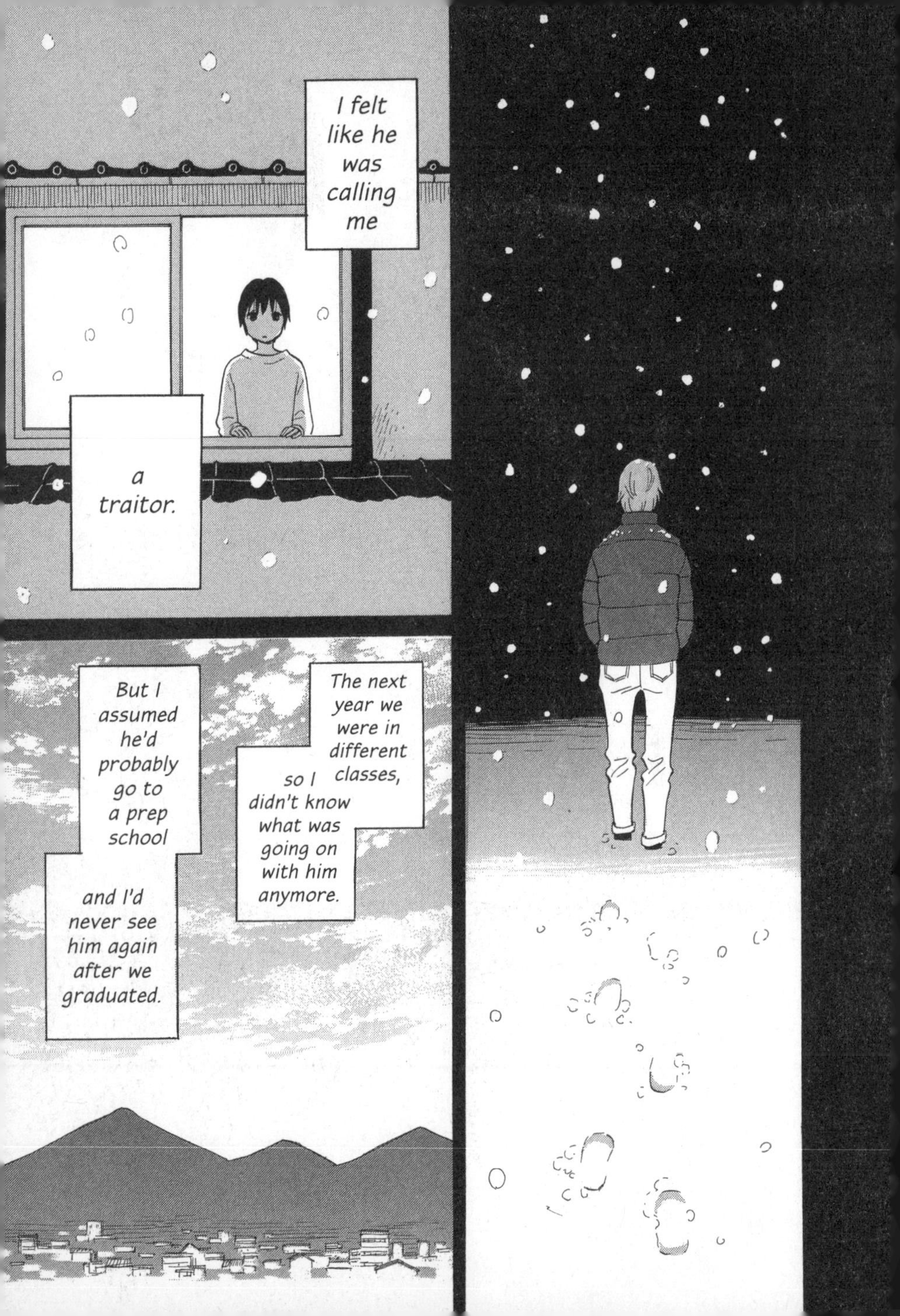
I felt like he was calling me
a traitor.
The next year we were in different classes,
so I didn't know what was going on with him anymore.
But I assumed he'd probably go to a prep school
and I'd never see him again after we graduated.

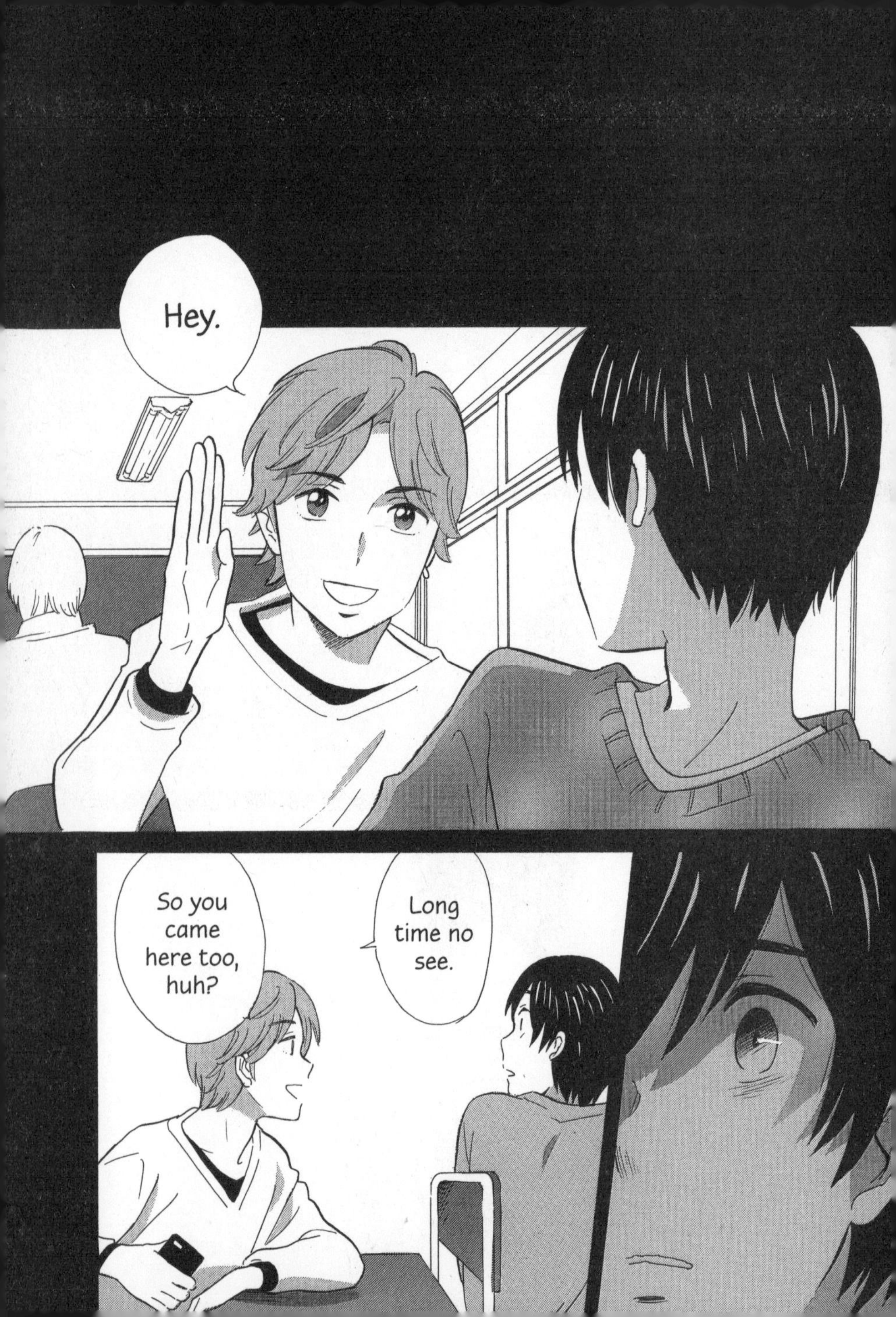
Hey.
Long time no see.
So you came here too, huh?

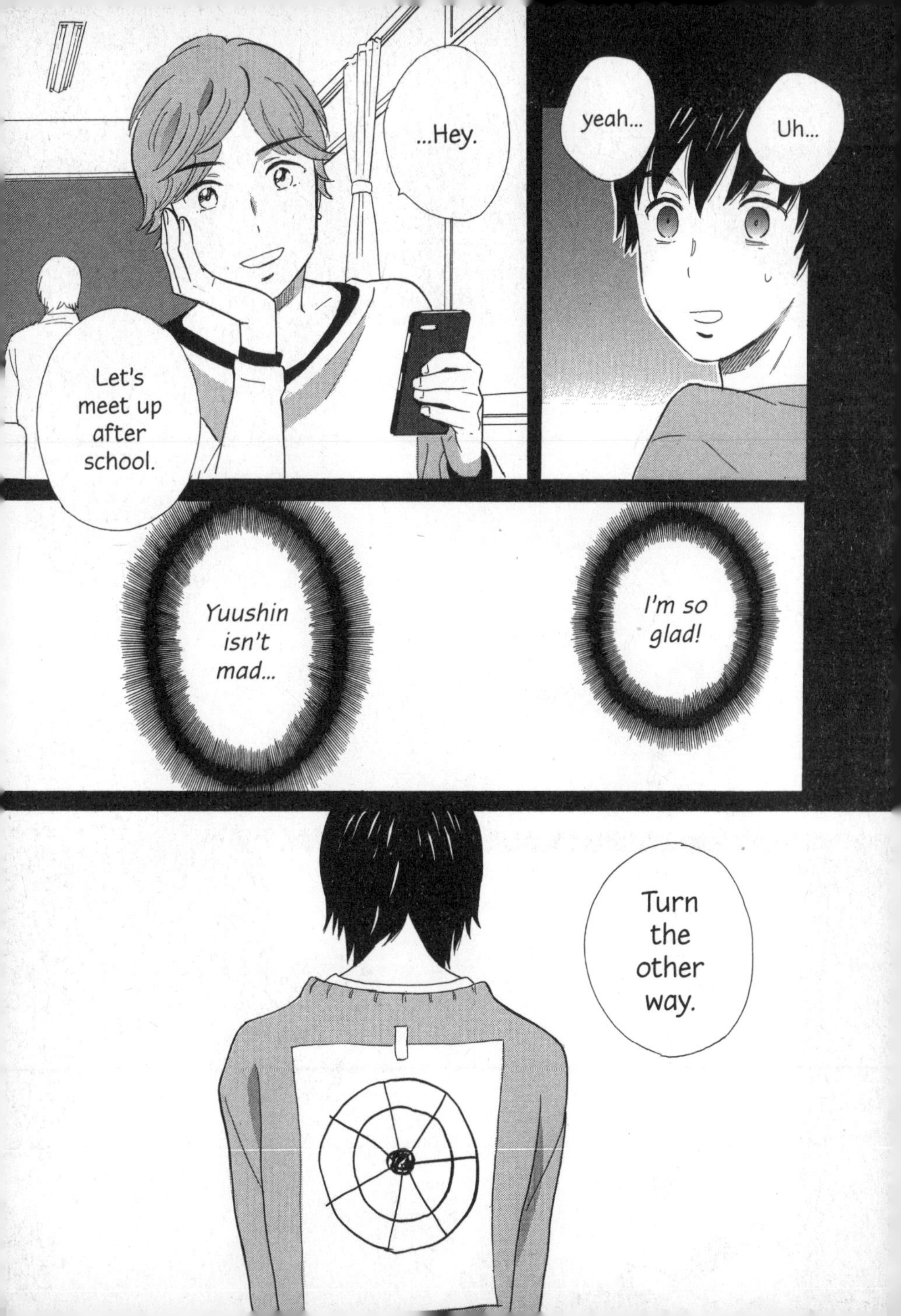

Uh...
yeah...
...Hey.
Let's meet up after school.
I'm so glad!
Yuushin isn't mad...
Turn the other way.

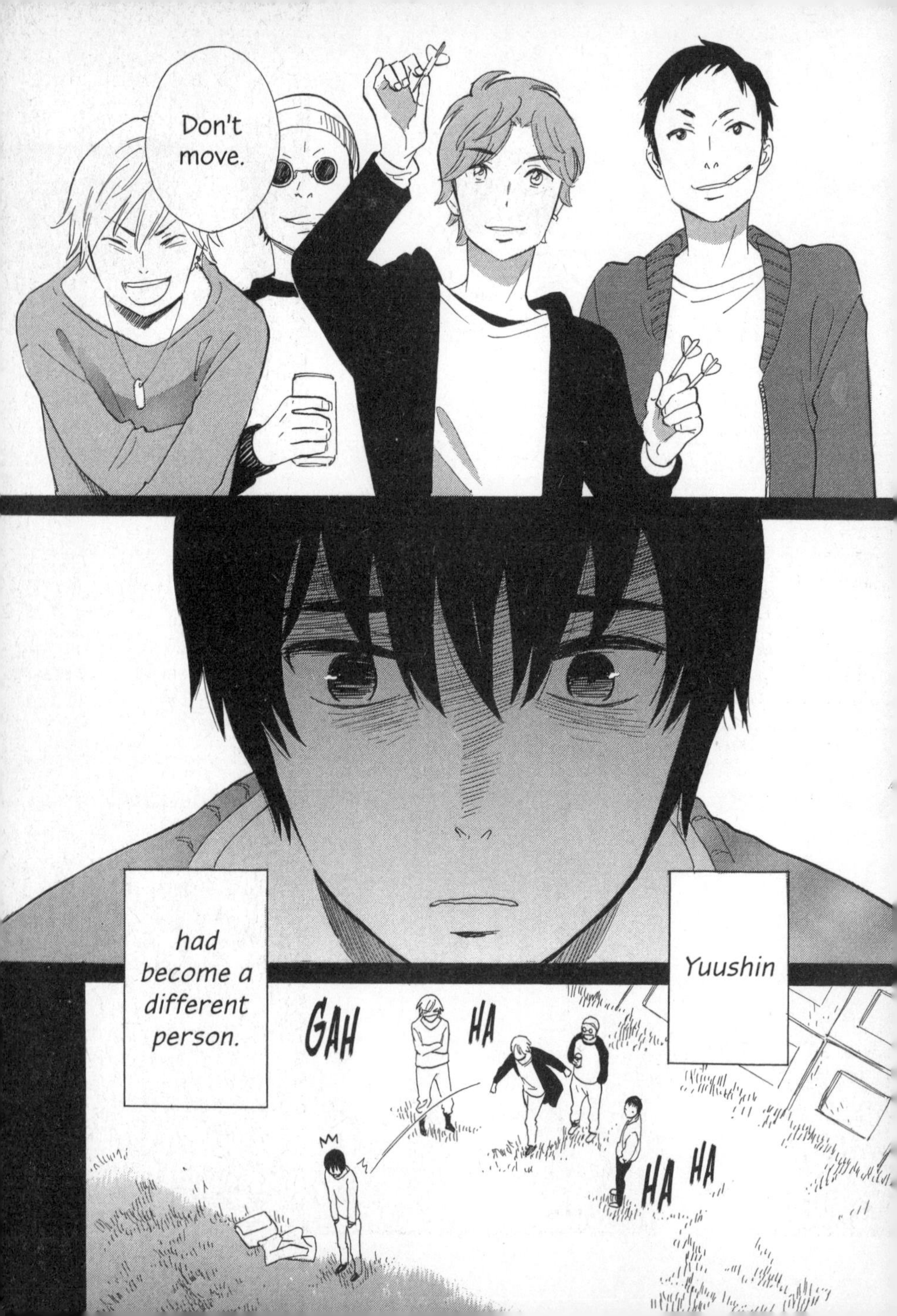
Don't move.
Yuushin
had become a different person.
GAH
HA
HA
HA

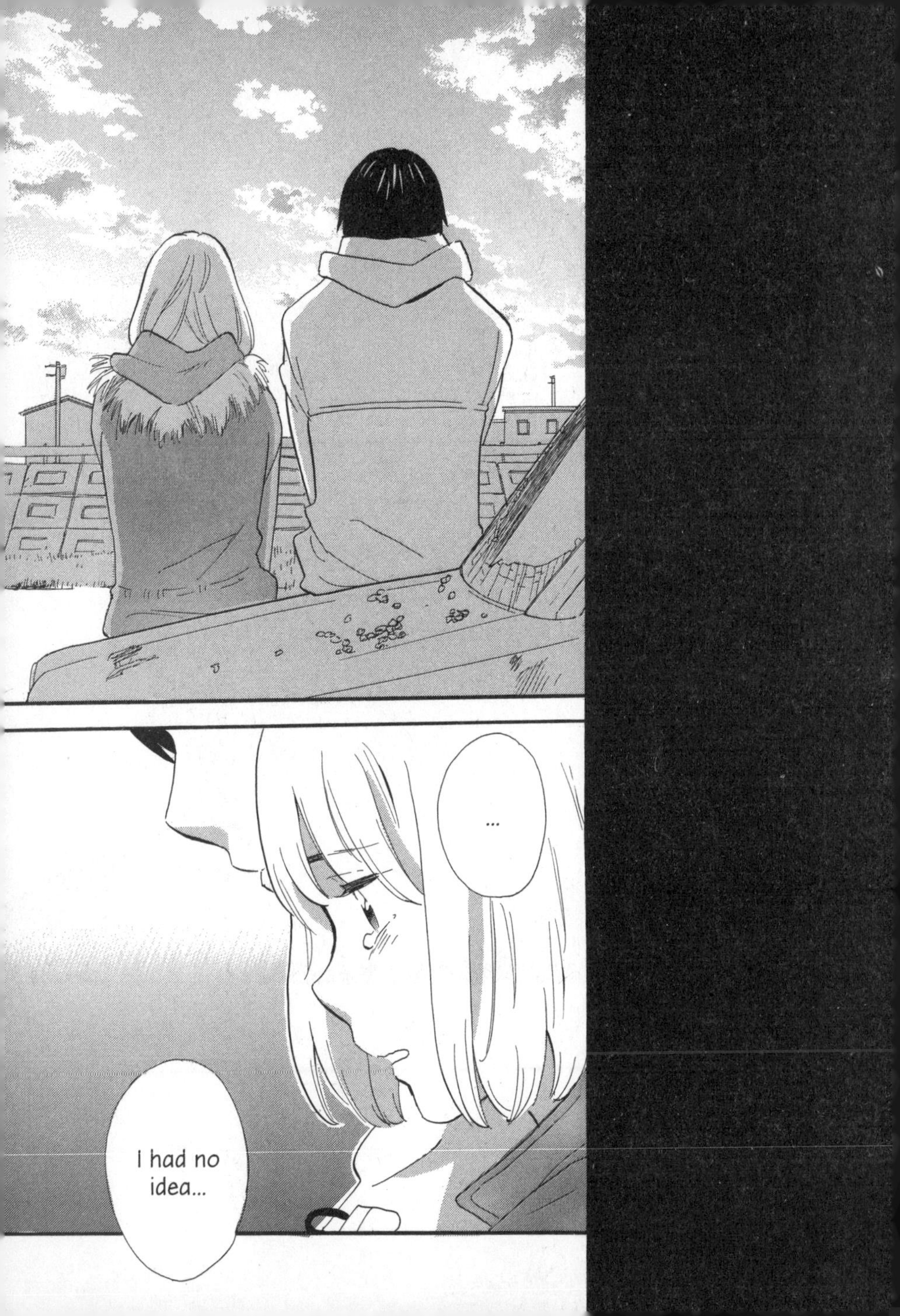
...
I had no idea...

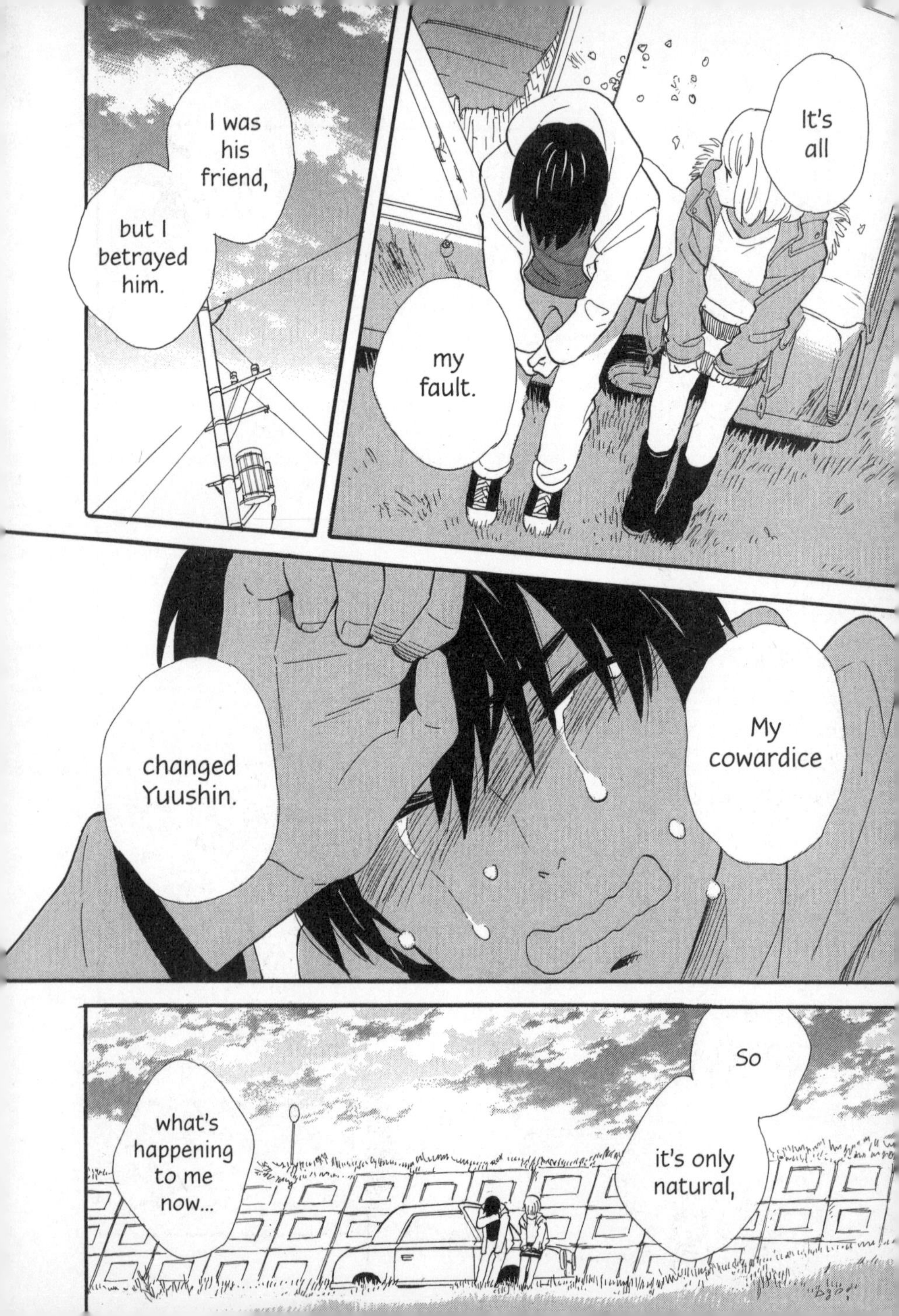
It's all
my fault.
I was his friend,
but I betrayed him.
My cowardice
changed Yuushin.
So
it's only natural,
what's happening to me now...

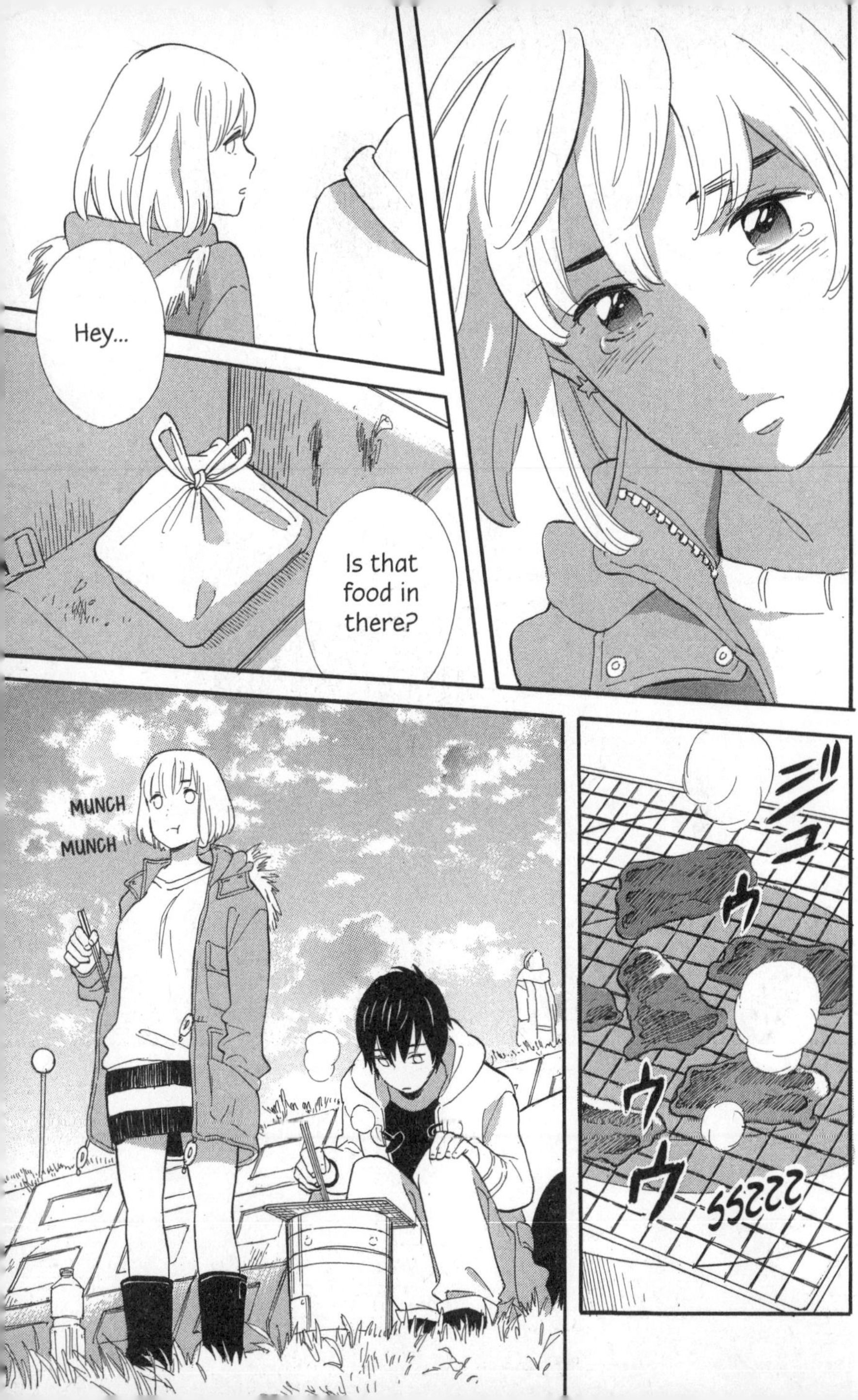
Hey...
Is that food in there?
ジュウウウ
SSZZZ
MUNCH
MUNCH

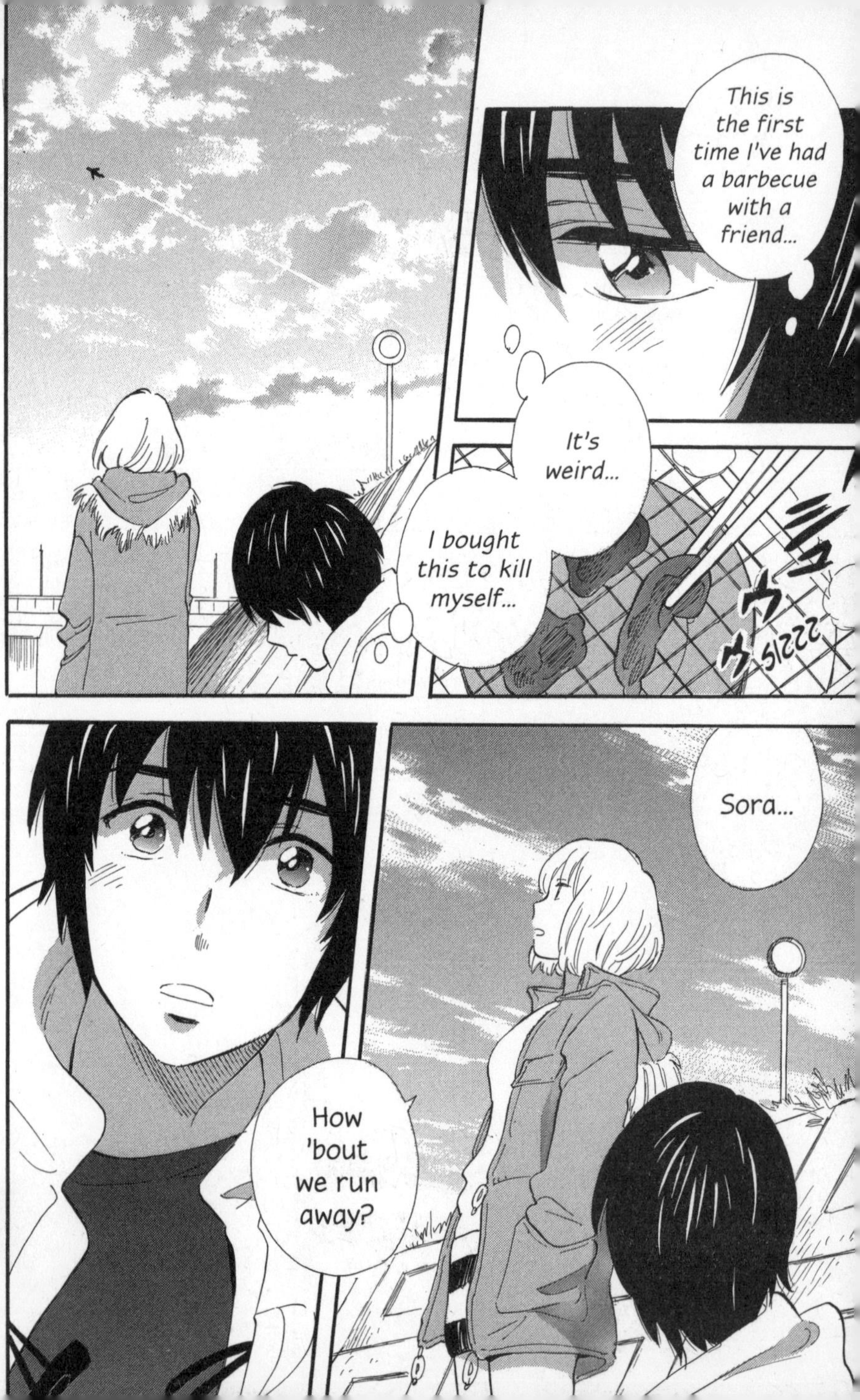
This is the first time I've had a barbecue with a friend...
It's weird...
I bought this to kill myself...
ジュウウ
SIZZZZ
Sora...
How 'bout we run away?

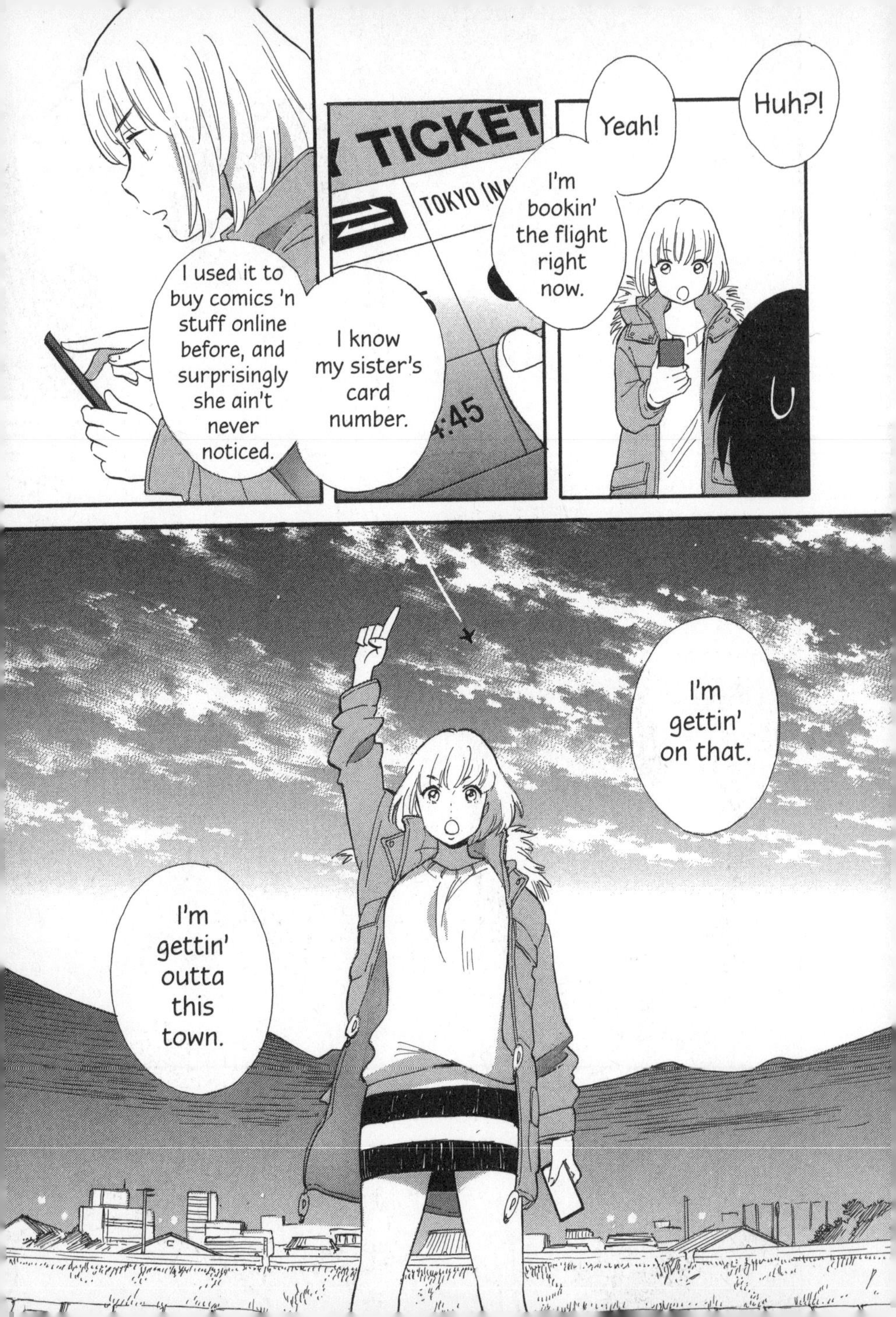
Huh?!
Yeah!
I'm bookin' the flight right now.
TICKET
I know my sister's card number.
I used it to buy comics 'n stuff online before, and surprisingly she ain't never noticed.
I'm gettin' on that.
I'm gettin' outta this town.

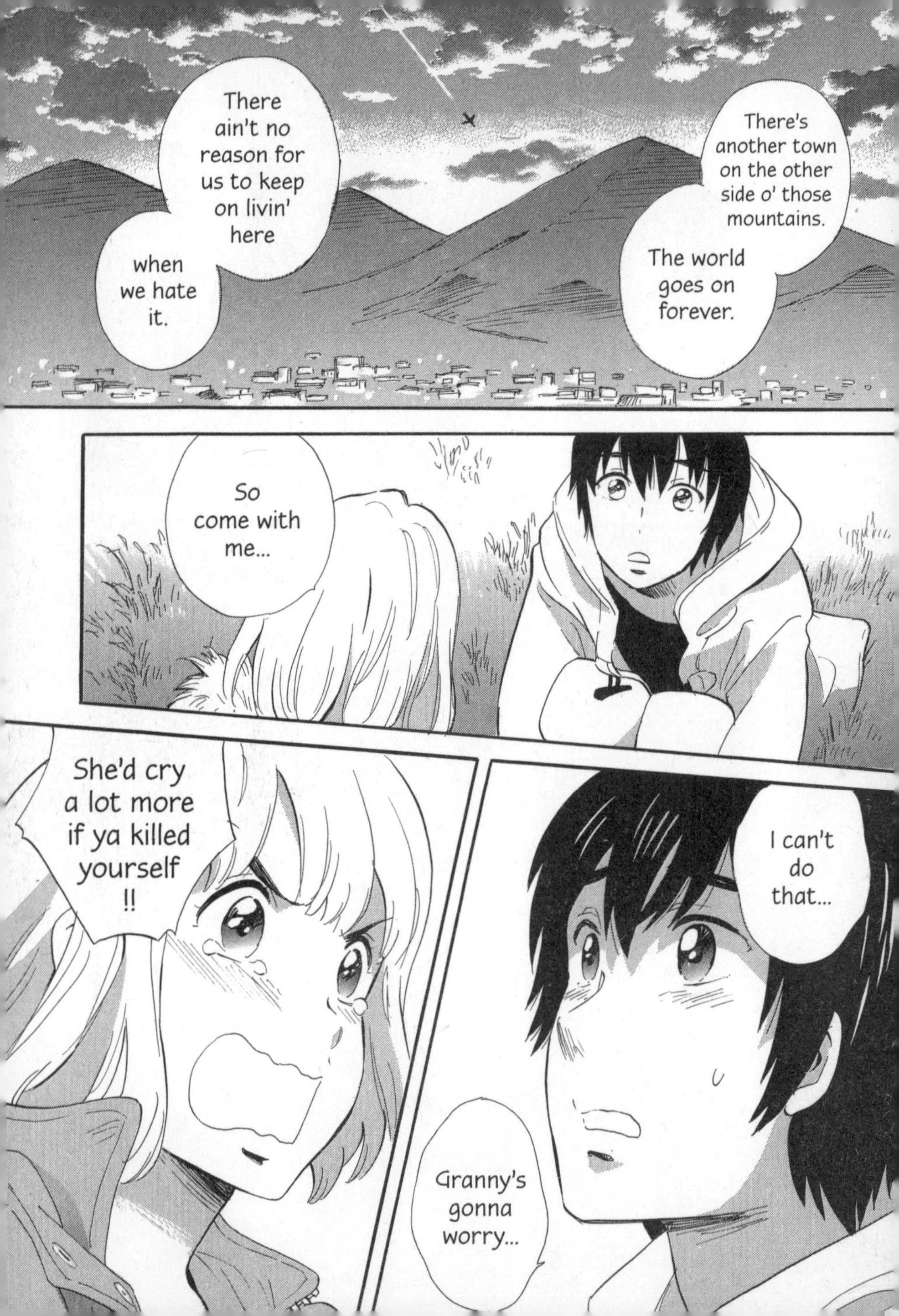
There's another town on the other side o' those mountains.
The world goes on forever.
There ain't no reason for us to keep on livin' here
when we hate it.
So come with me...
I can't do that...
Granny's gonna worry...
She'd cry a lot more if ya killed yourself !!

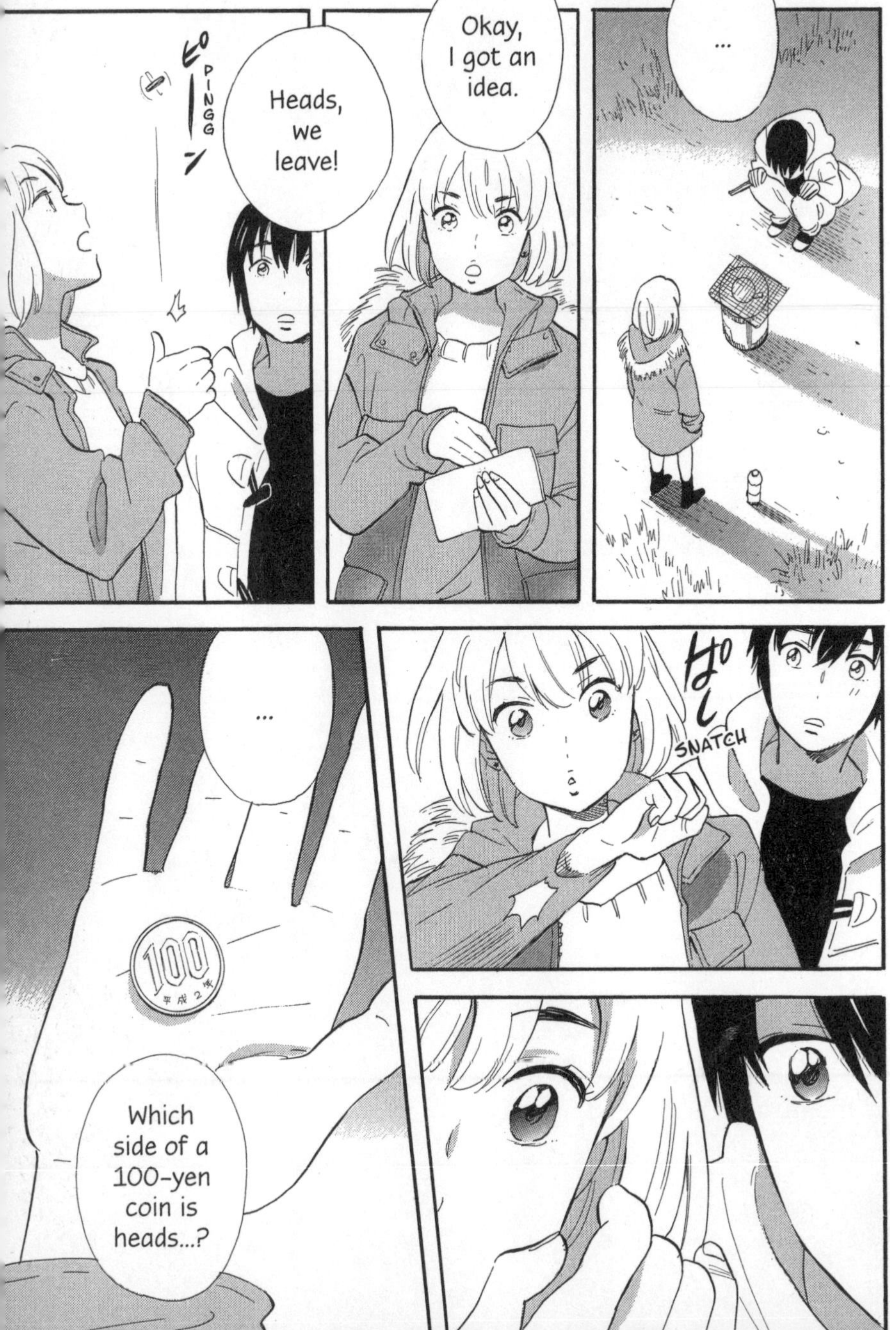
...
Okay, I got an idea.
PINGG
Heads, we leave!
SNATCH
...
100
Which side of a 100-yen coin is heads...?

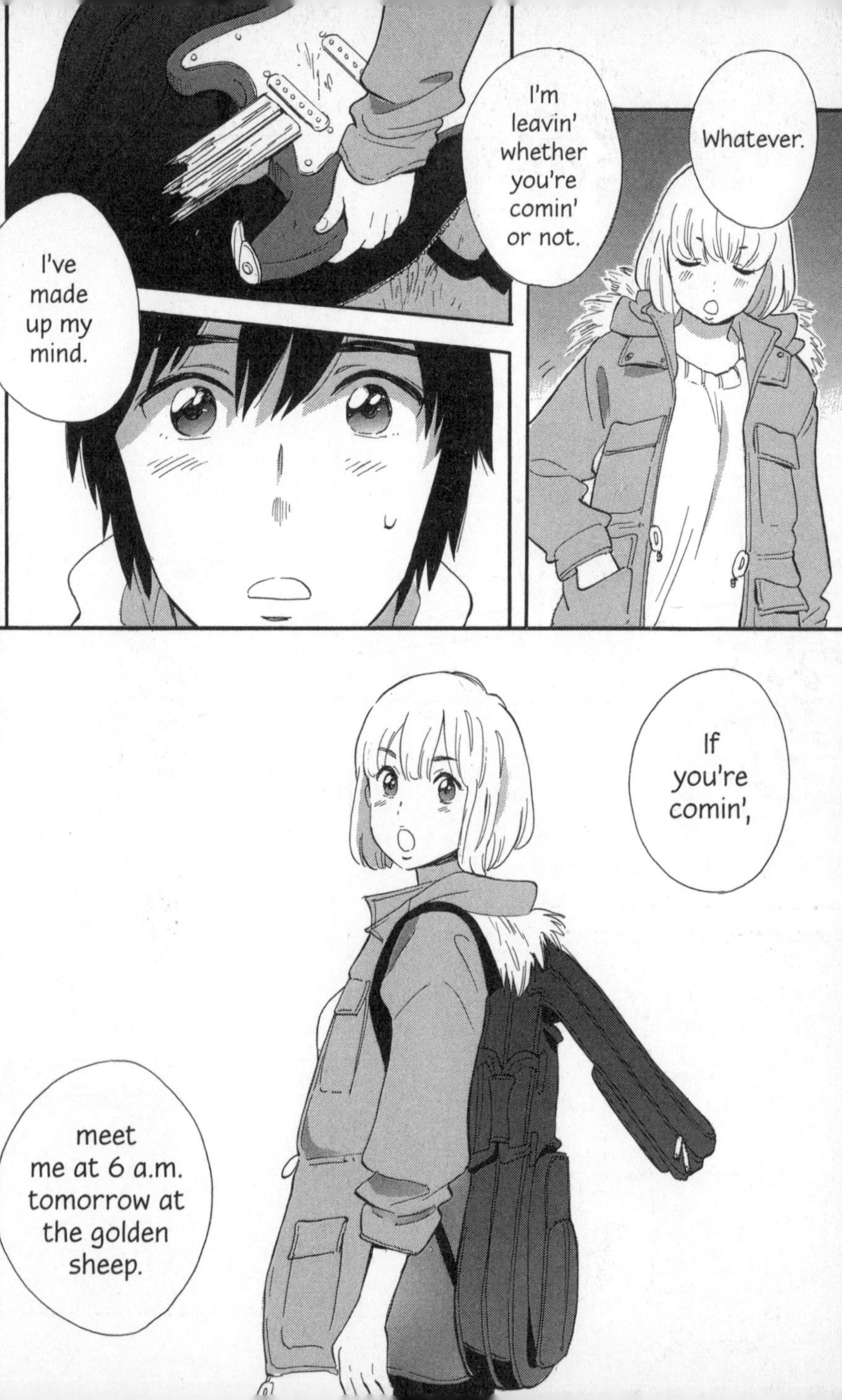
Whatever.
I'm leavin' whether you're comin' or not.
I've made up my mind.
If you're comin',
meet me at 6 a.m. tomorrow at the golden sheep.

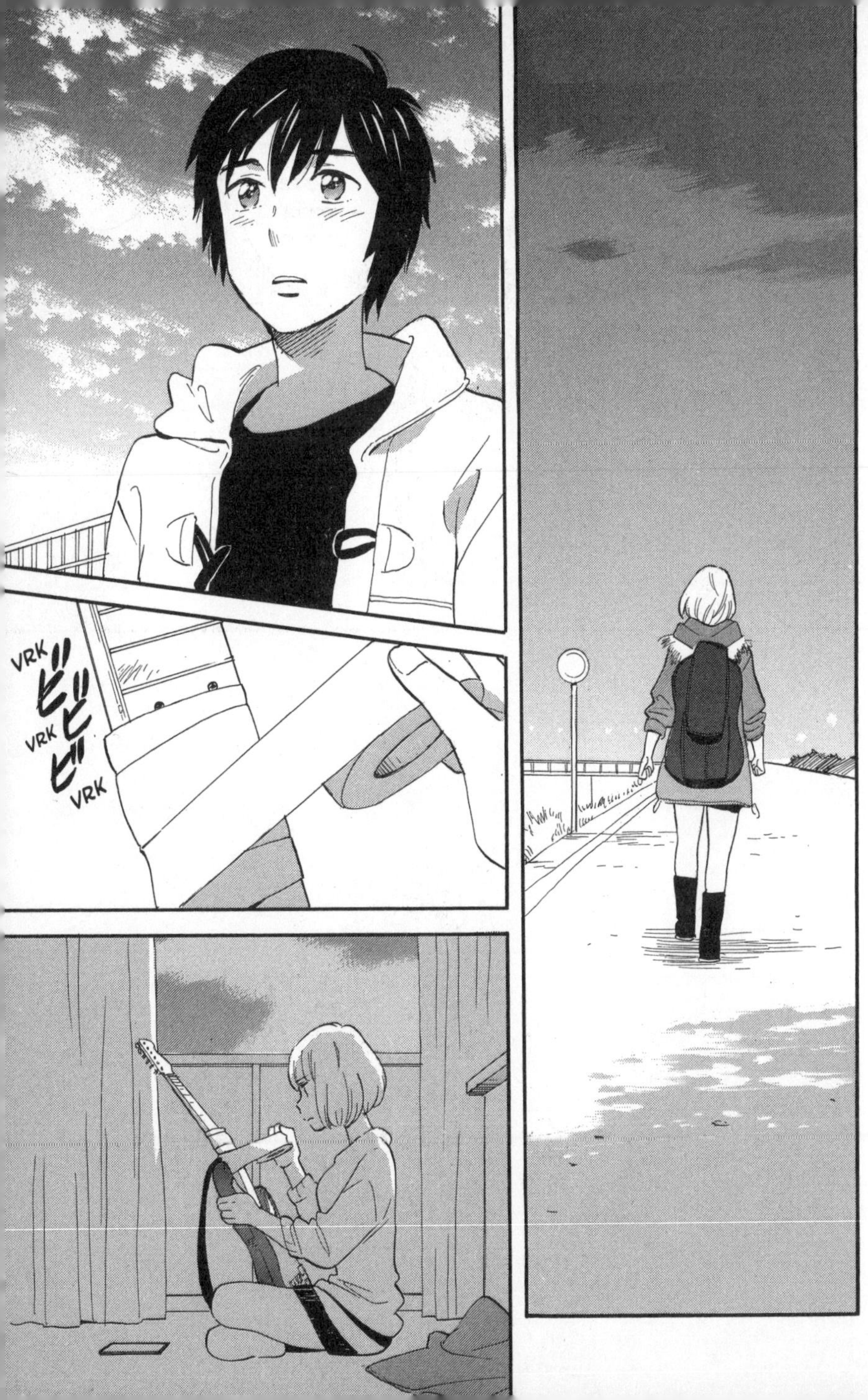
VRK
ビビビ
VRK
VRK

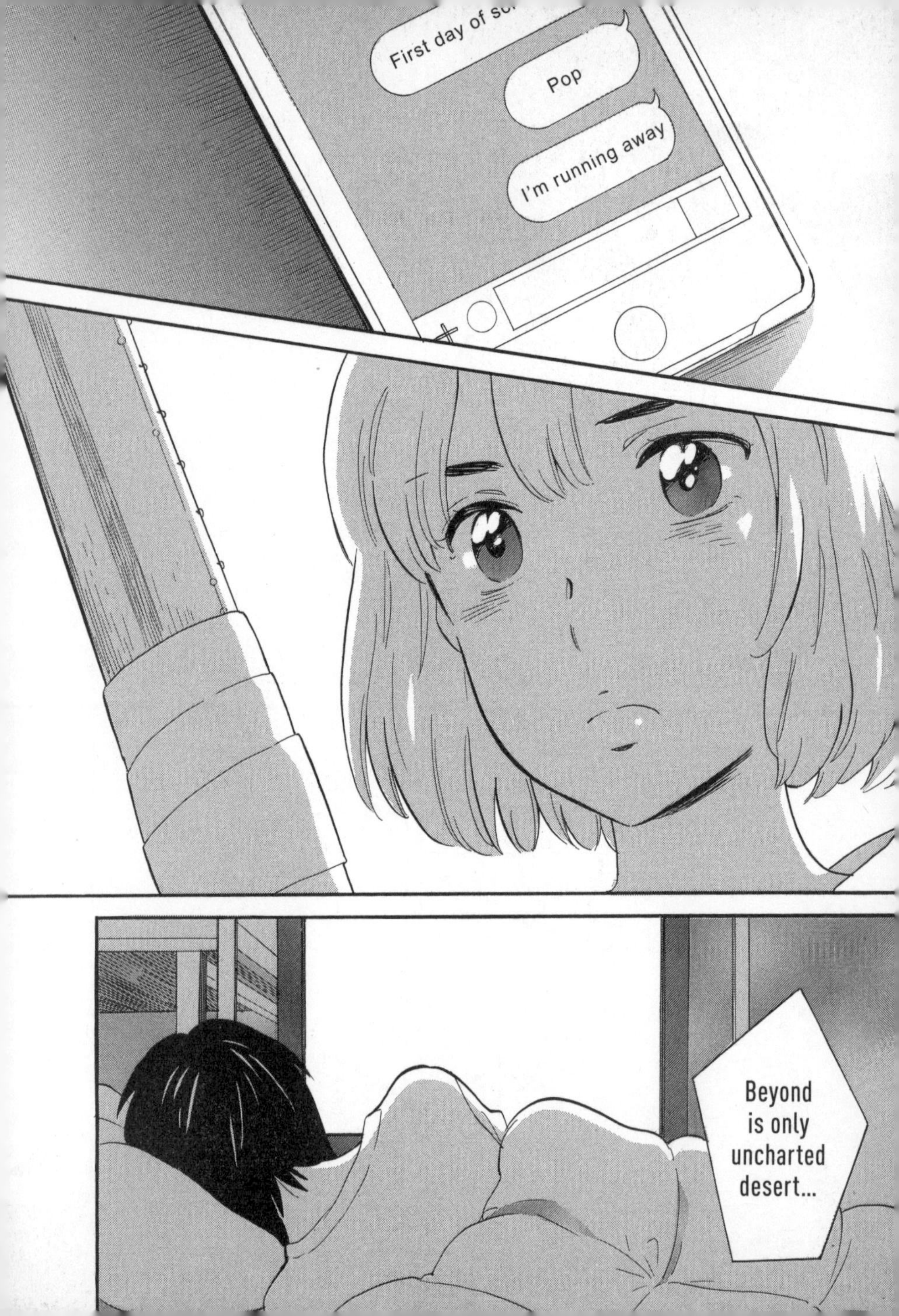
First day of sc
Pop
I'm running away
Beyond is only uncharted desert...

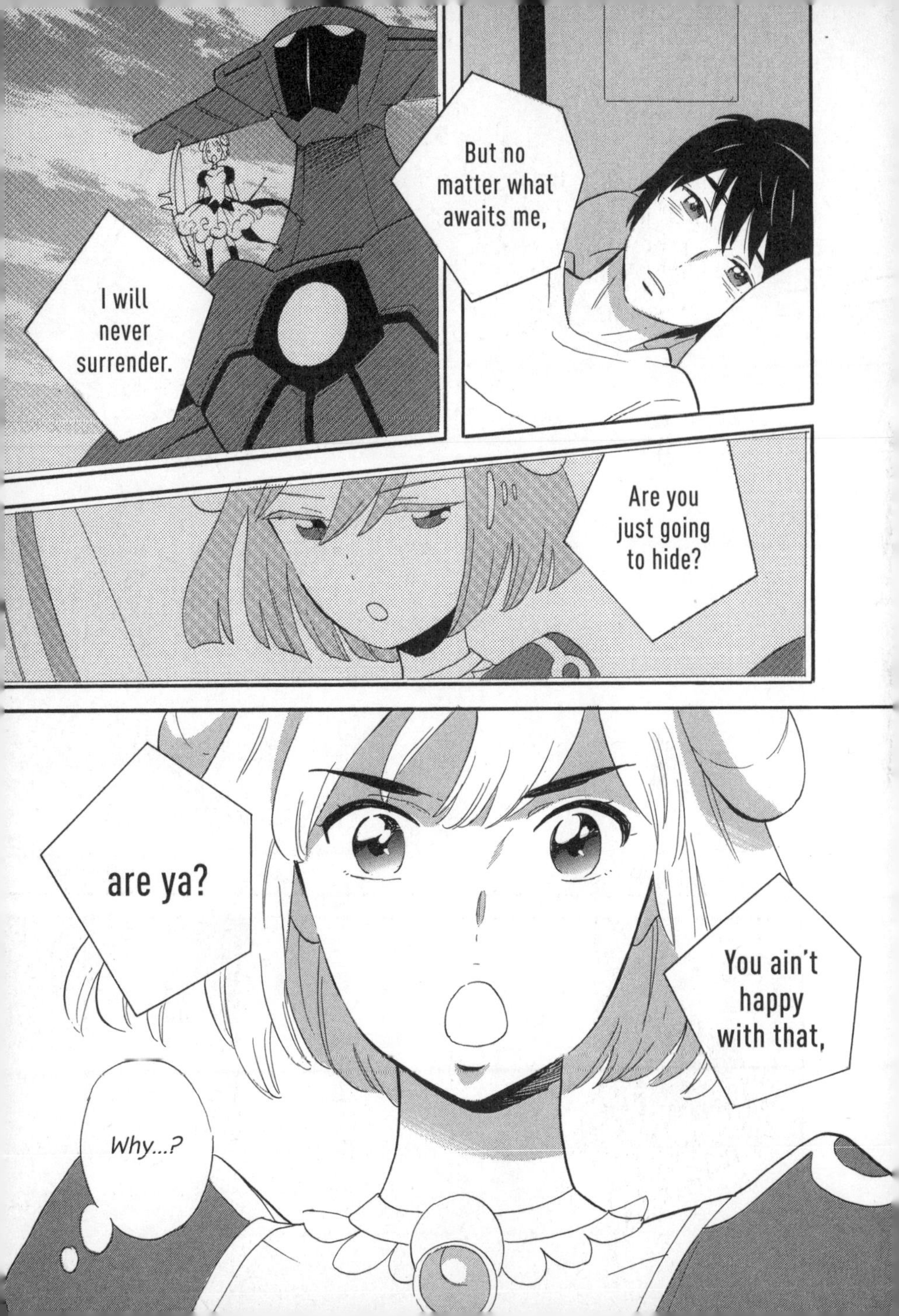
But no matter what awaits me,
I will never surrender.
Are you just going to hide?
You ain't happy with that,
are ya?
Why...?

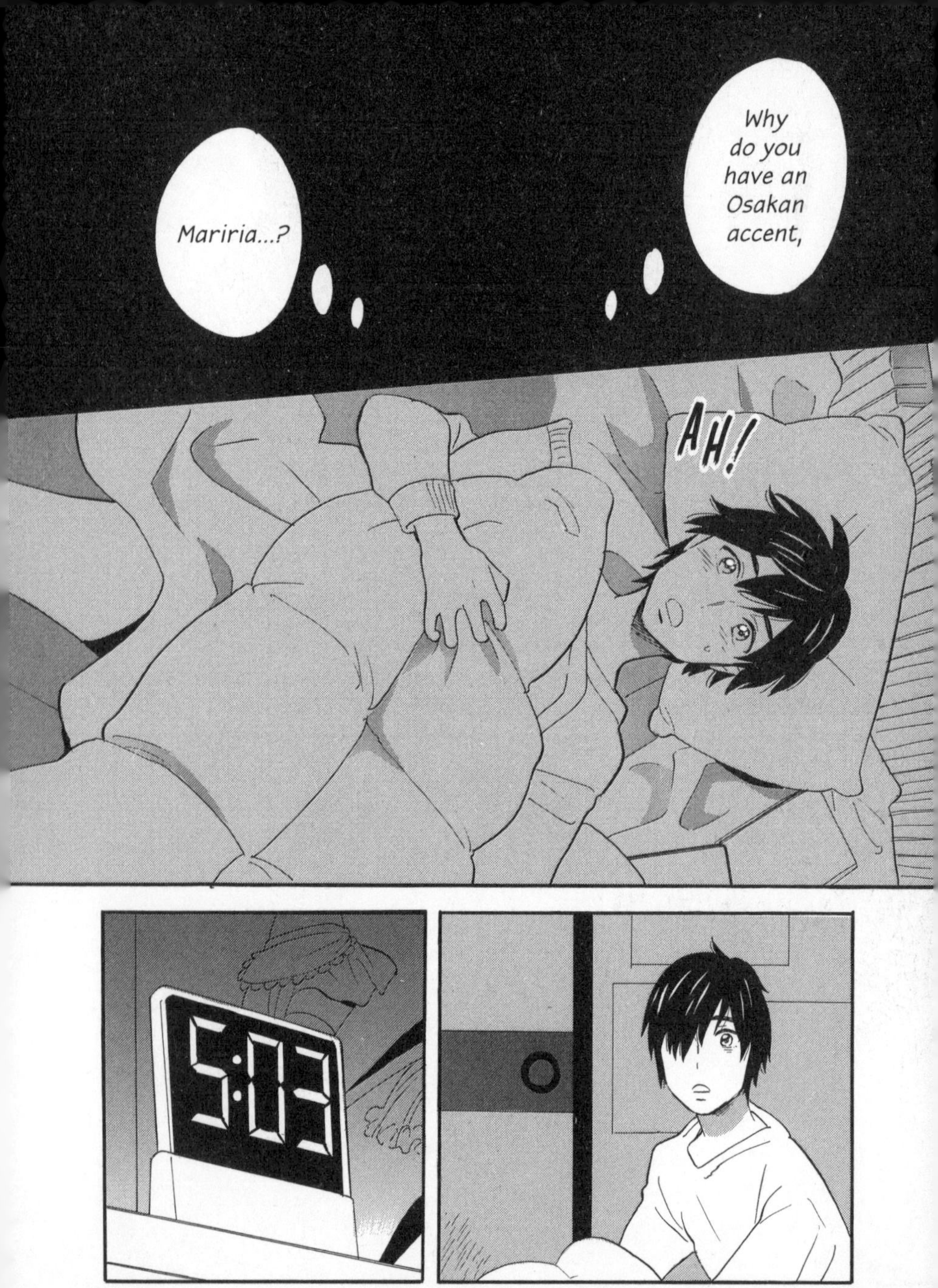
Why do you have an Osakan accent,
Mariria...?
AH!
5:03

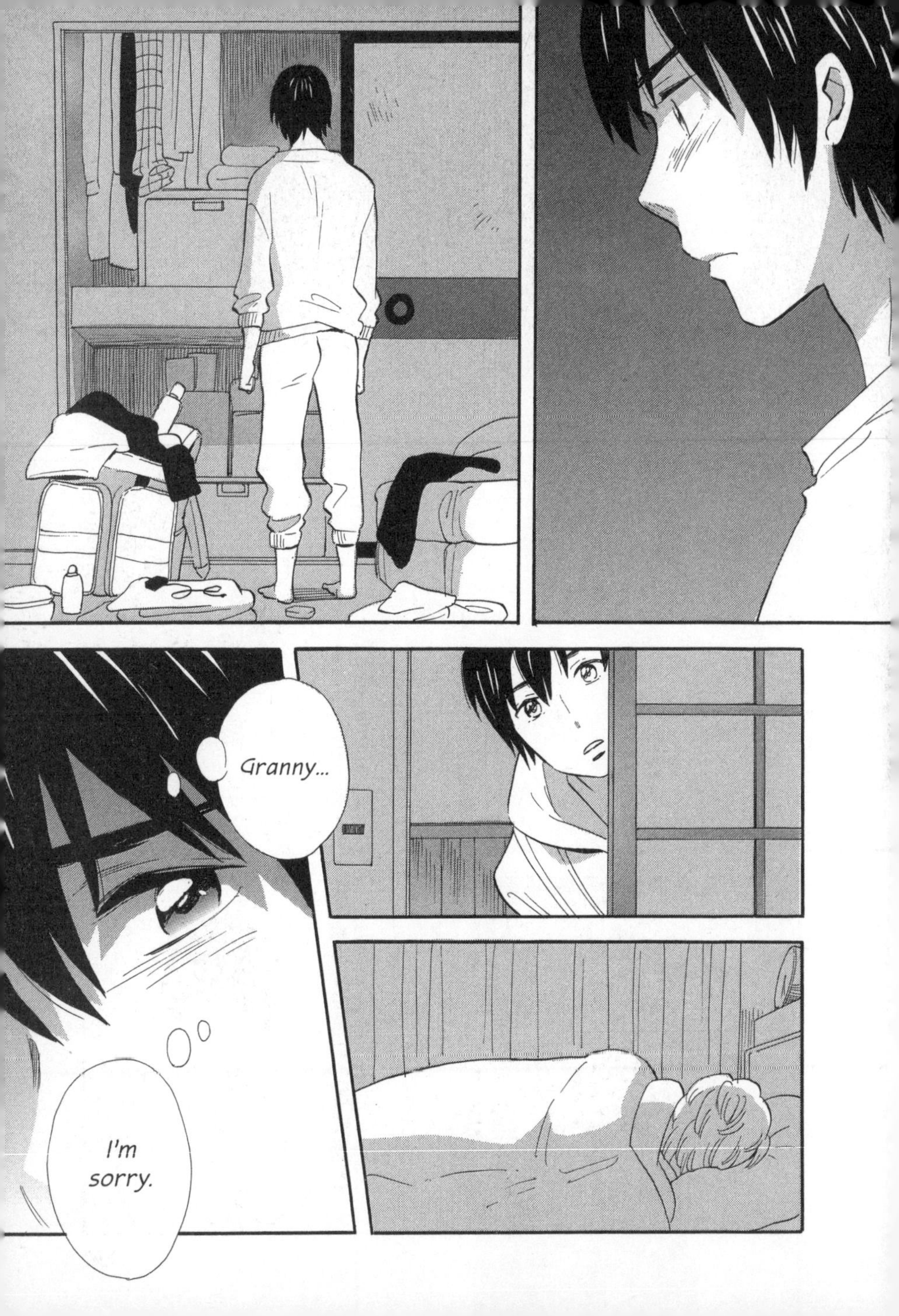
Granny...
I'm sorry.

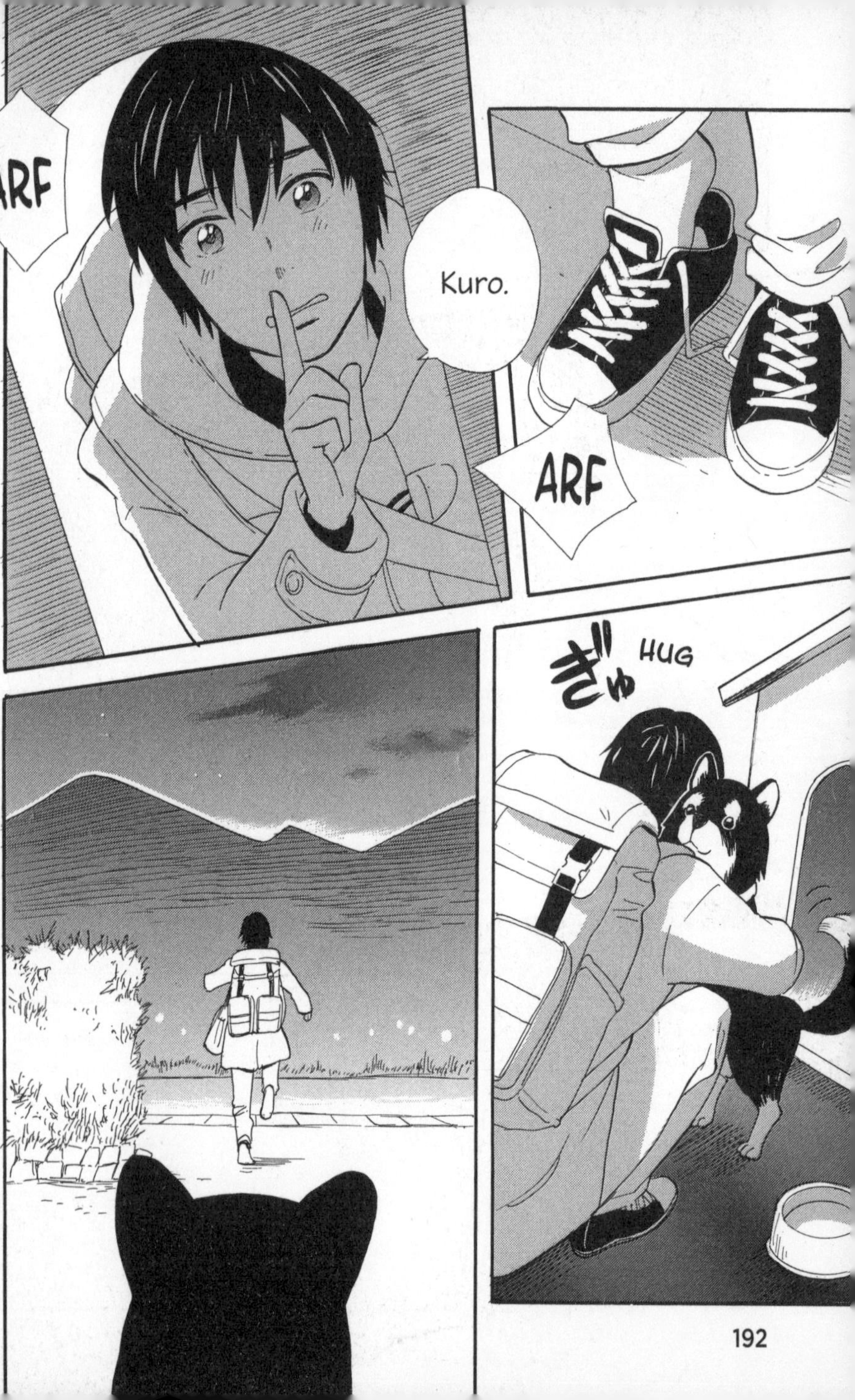
ARF
ARF
Kuro.
ぎゅ
HUG

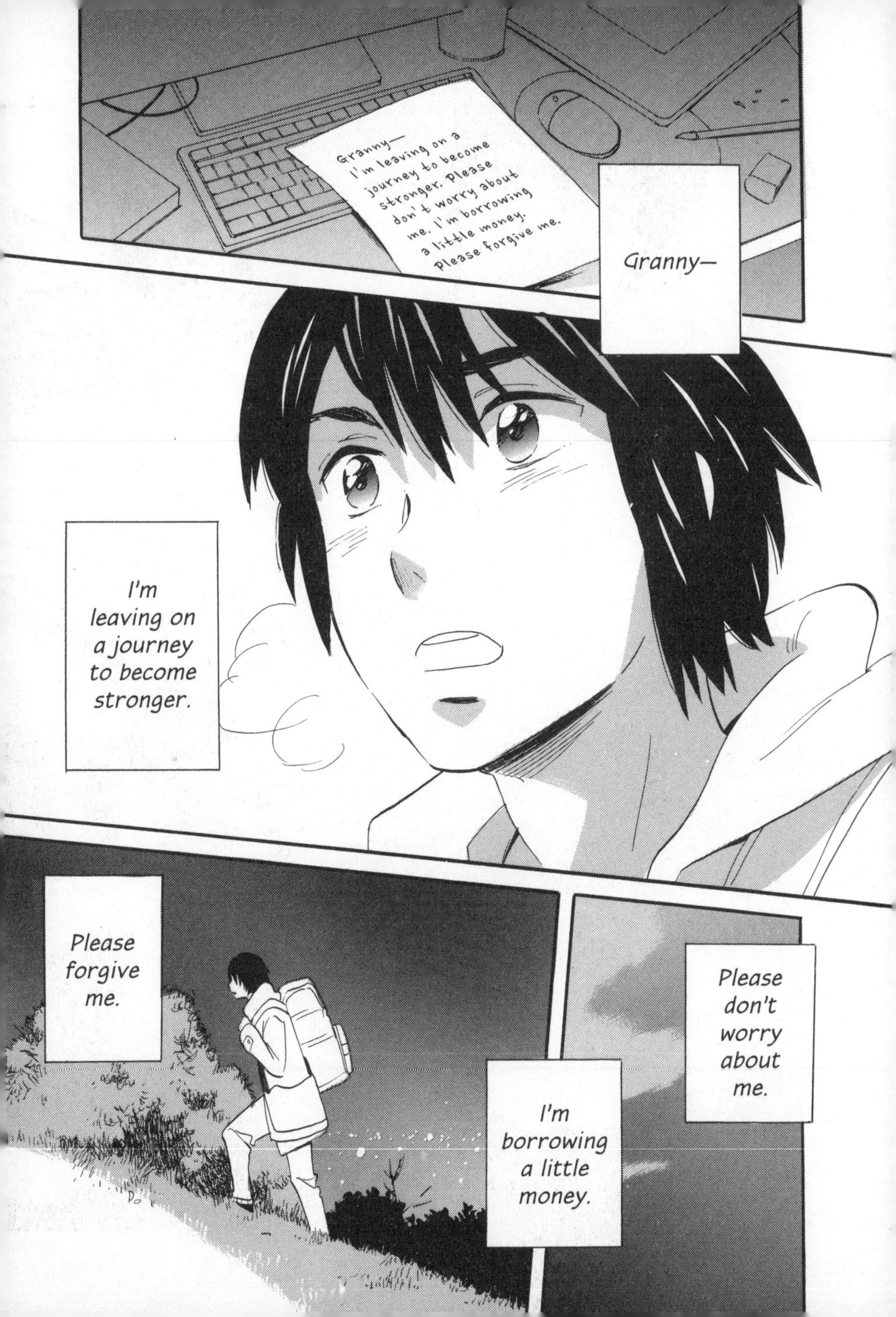

Granny—
Granny— I'm leaving on a journey to become stronger. Please don't worry about me. I'm borrowing a little money. Please forgive me.
I'm leaving on a journey to become stronger.
Please don't worry about me.
I'm borrowing a little money.
Please forgive me.

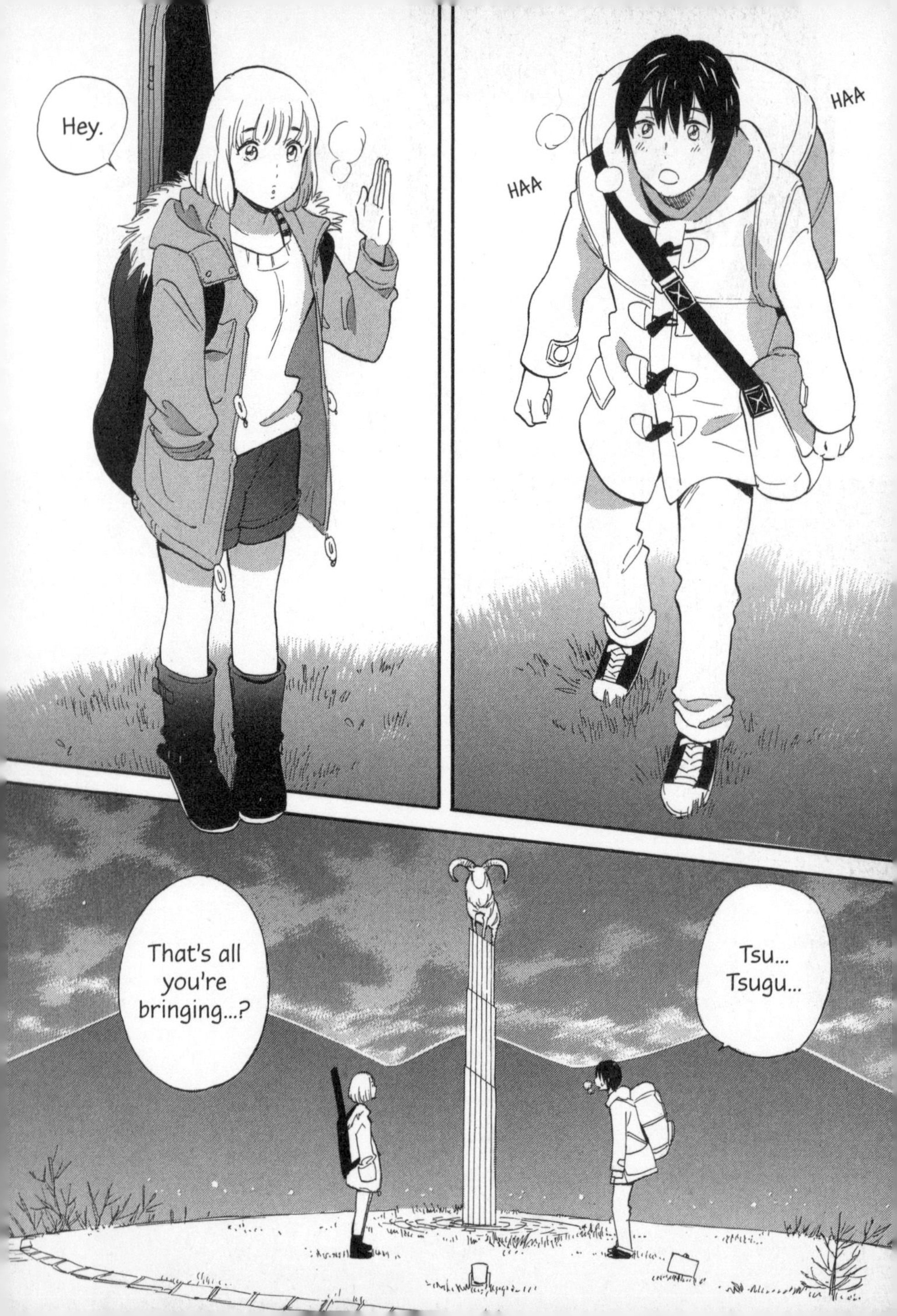
HAA
HAA
Hey.
Tsu... Tsugu...
That's all you're bringing...?

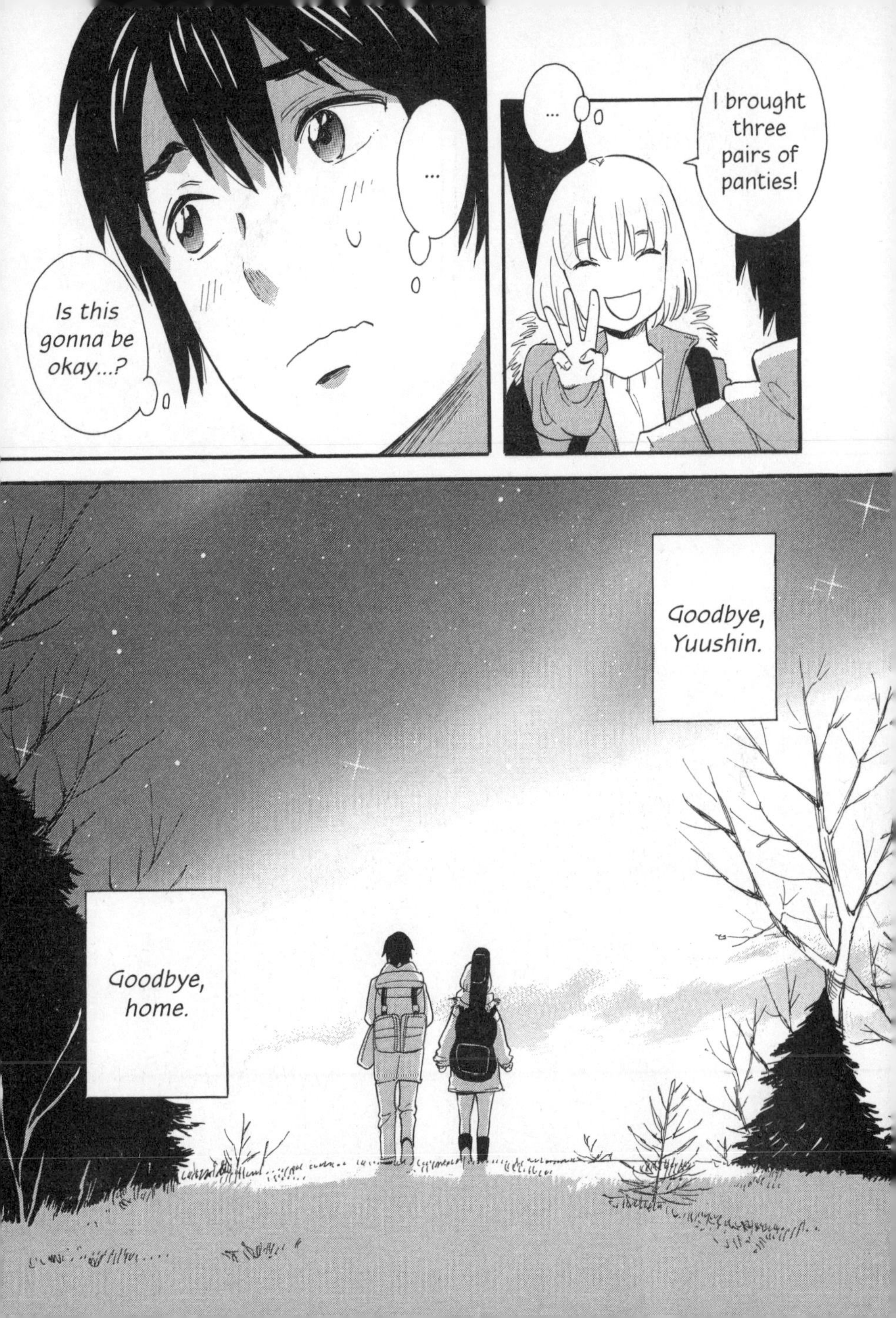
I brought three pairs of panties!
...
...
Is this gonna be okay...?
Goodbye, Yuushin.
Goodbye, home.

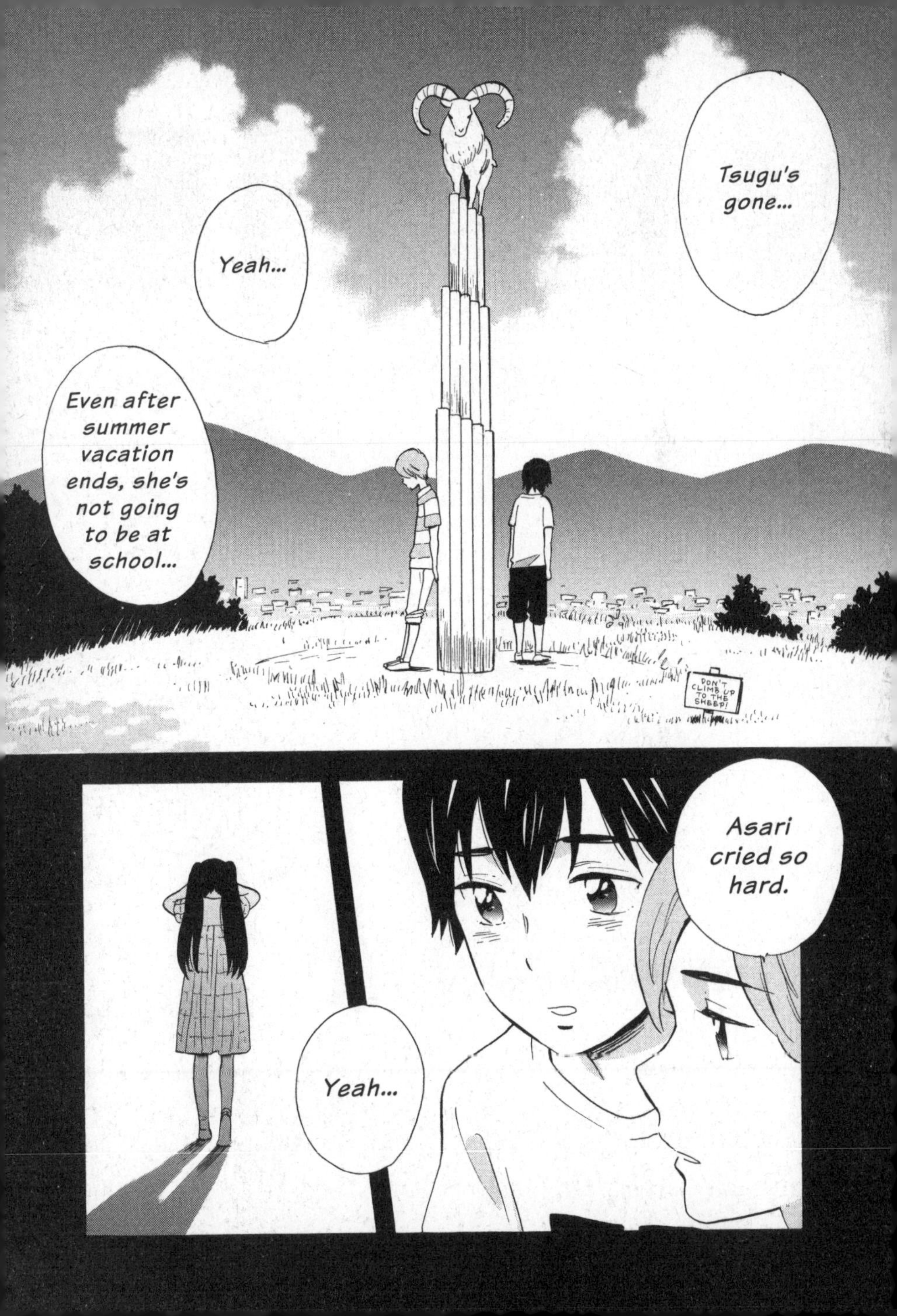
Tsugu's gone...
Yeah...
Even after summer vacation ends, she's not going to be at school...
DON'T CLIMB UP TO THE SHEEP!
Asari cried so hard.
Yeah...

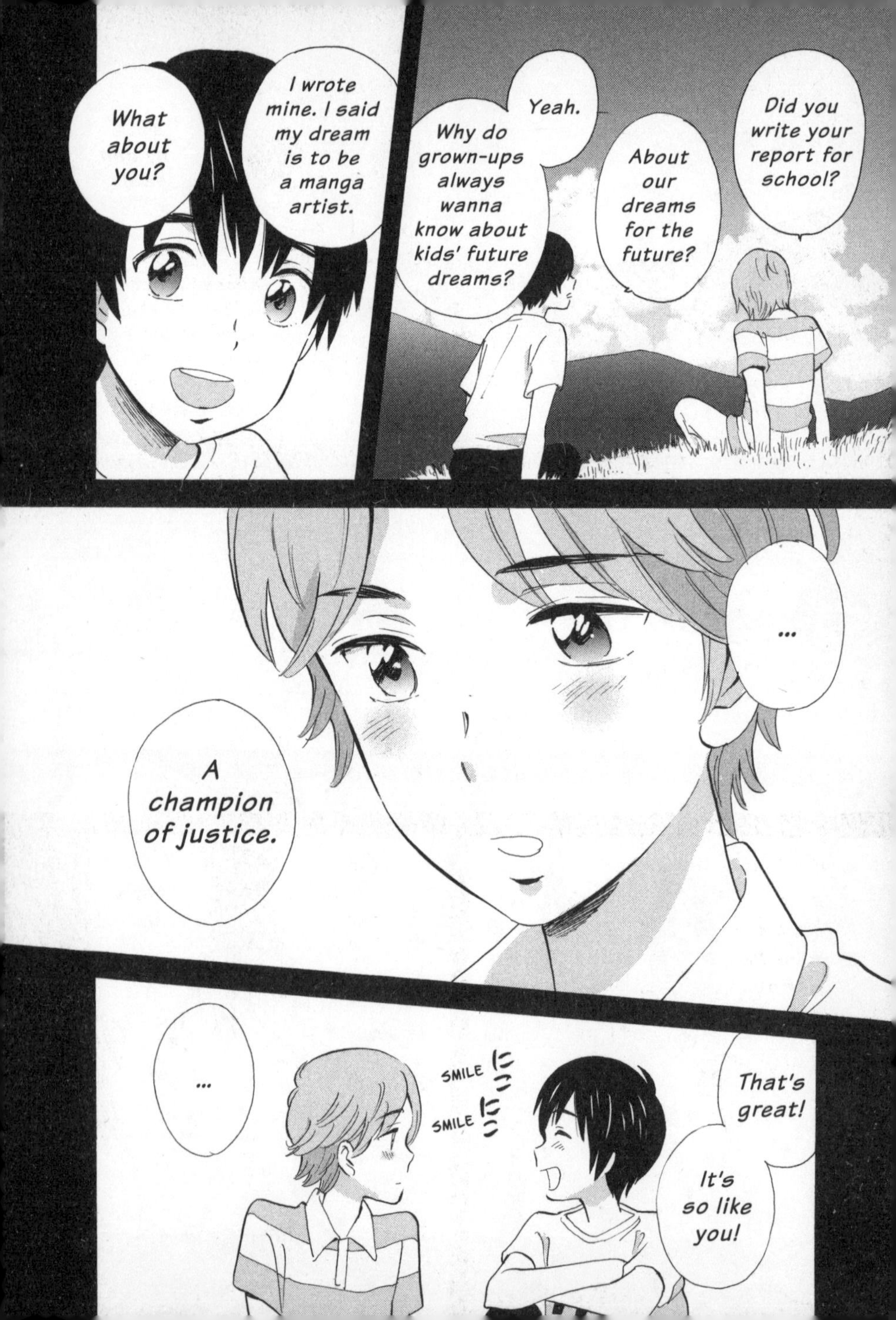
Did you write your report for school?
About our dreams for the future?
Yeah.
Why do grown-ups always wanna know about kids' future dreams?
I wrote mine. I said my dream is to be a manga artist.
What about you?
...
A champion of justice.
That's great!
It's so like you!
SMILE
SMILE
...

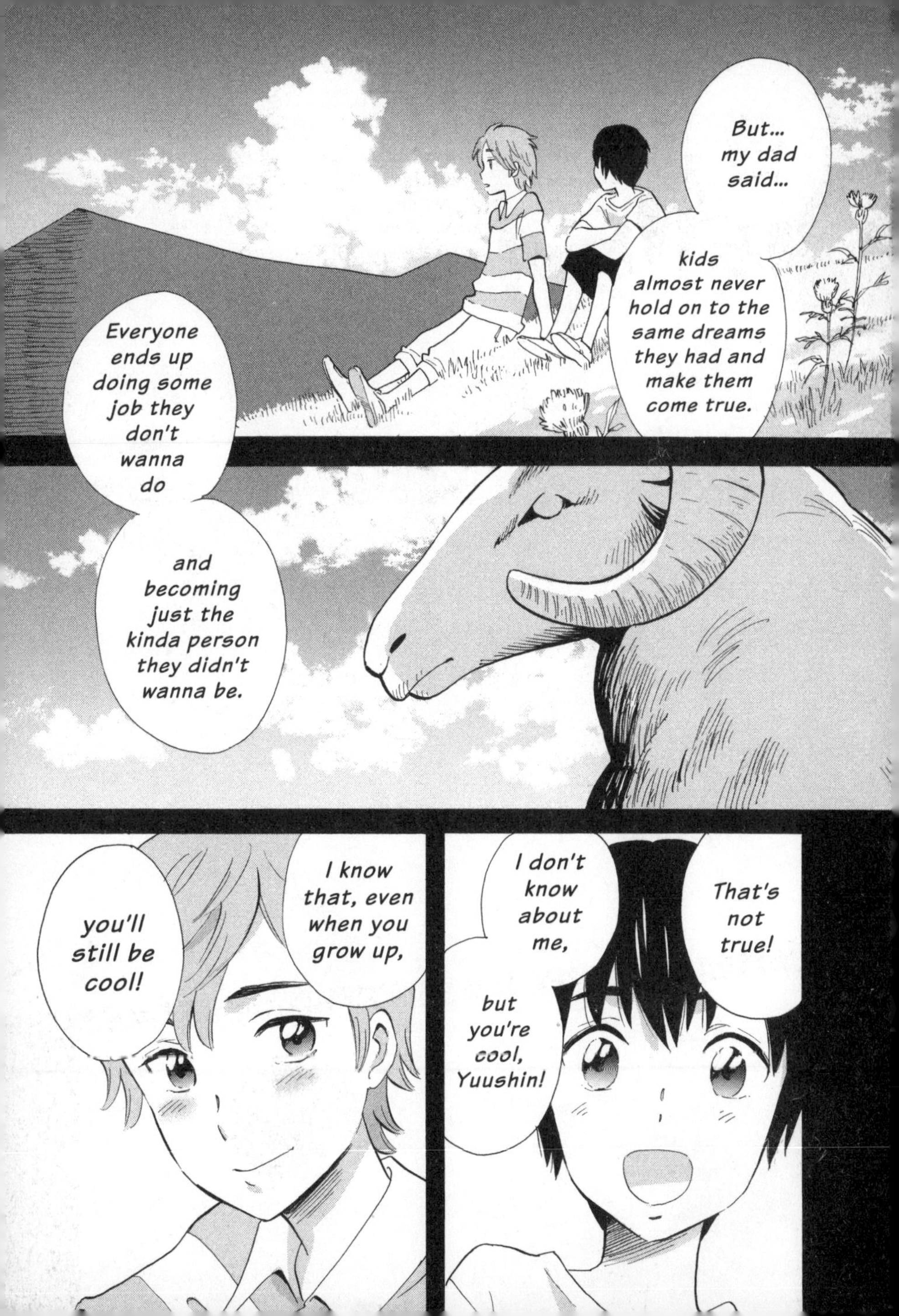
But... my dad said...
kids almost never hold on to the same dreams they had and make them come true.
Everyone ends up doing some job they don't wanna do
and becoming just the kinda person they didn't wanna be.
That's not true!
I don't know about me,
but you're cool, Yuushin!
I know that, even when you grow up,
you'll still be cool!

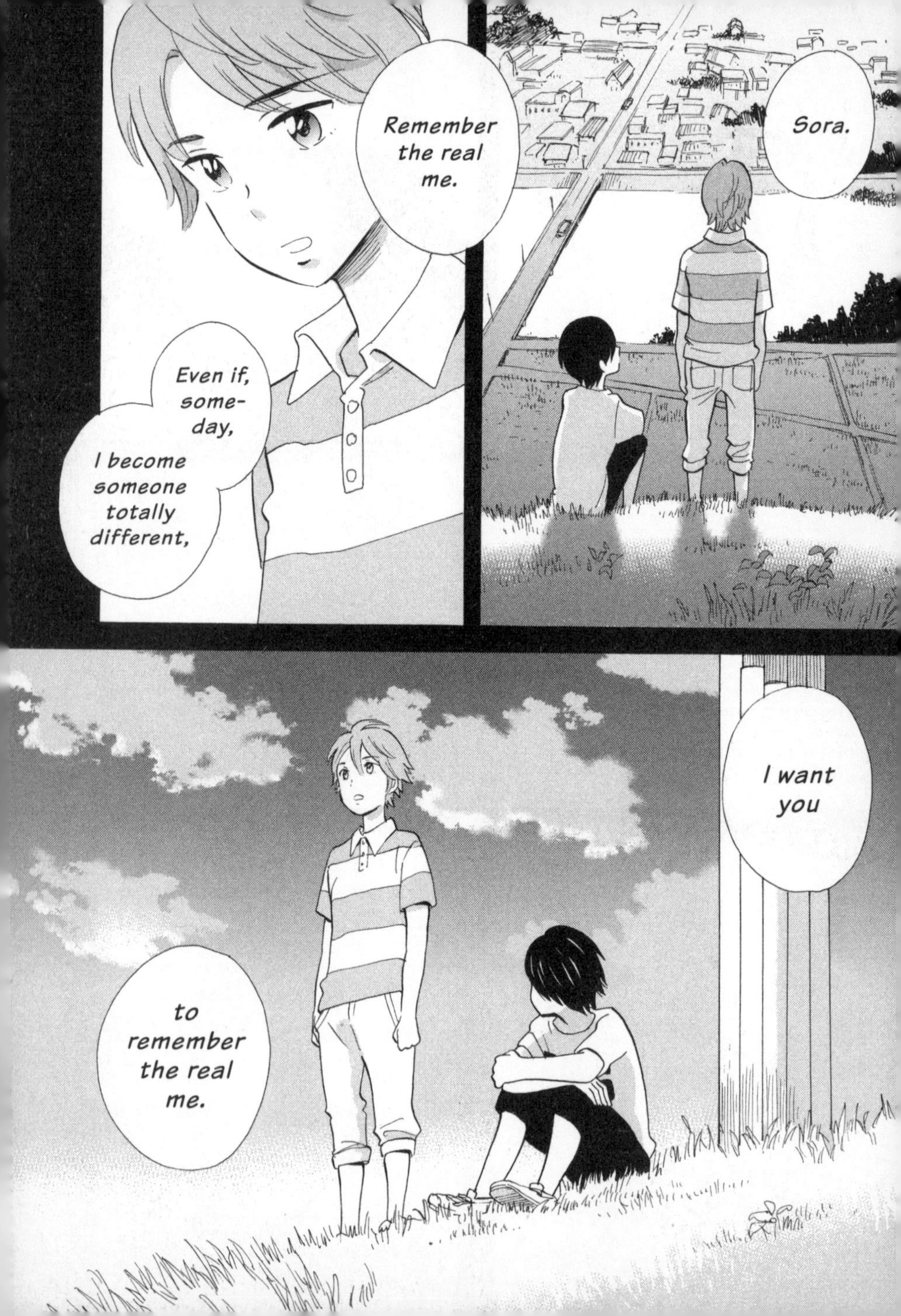
Sora.
Remember the real me.
Even if, someday, I become someone totally different,
I want you
to remember the real me.

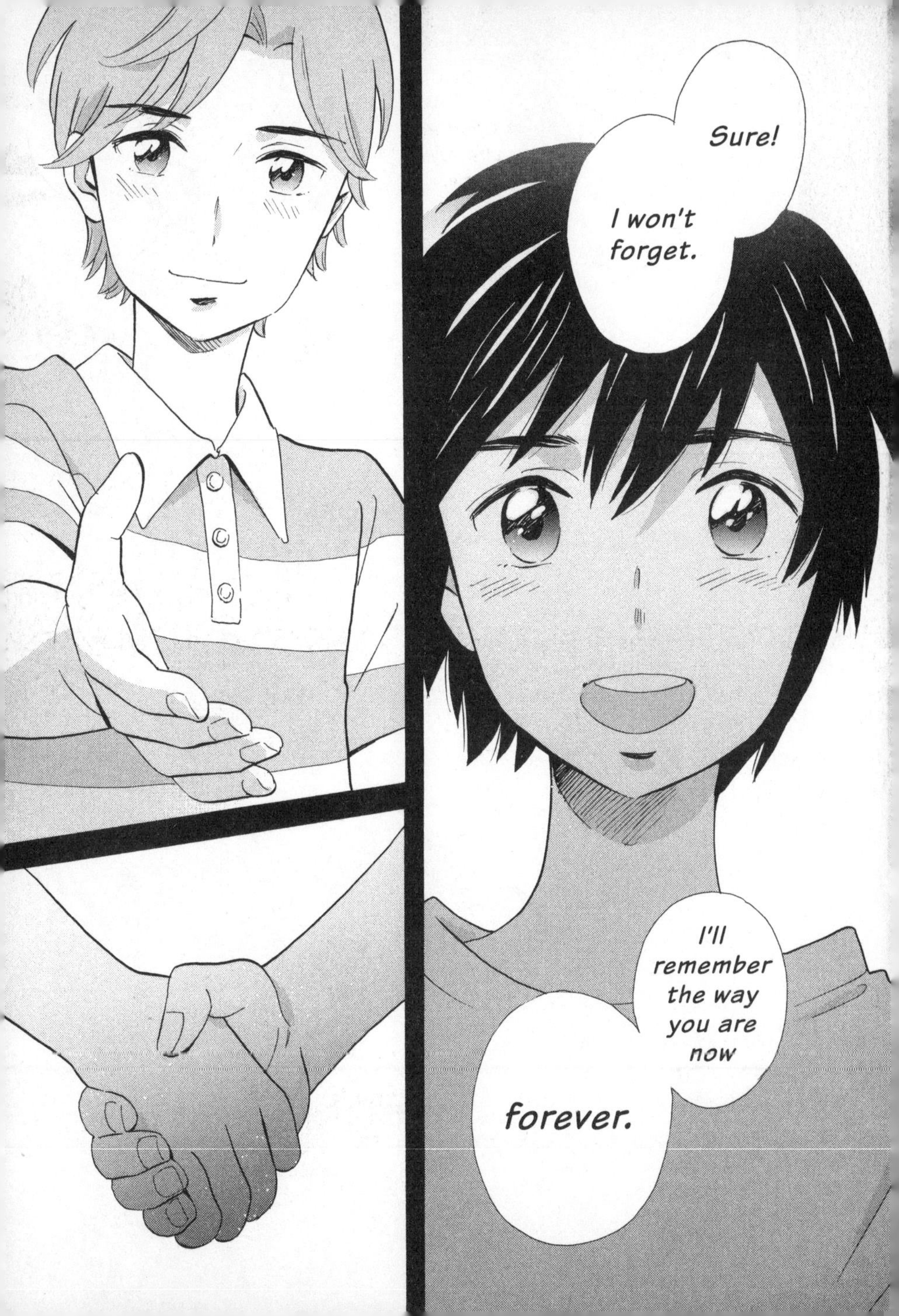
Sure!
I won't forget.
I'll remember the way you are now
forever.

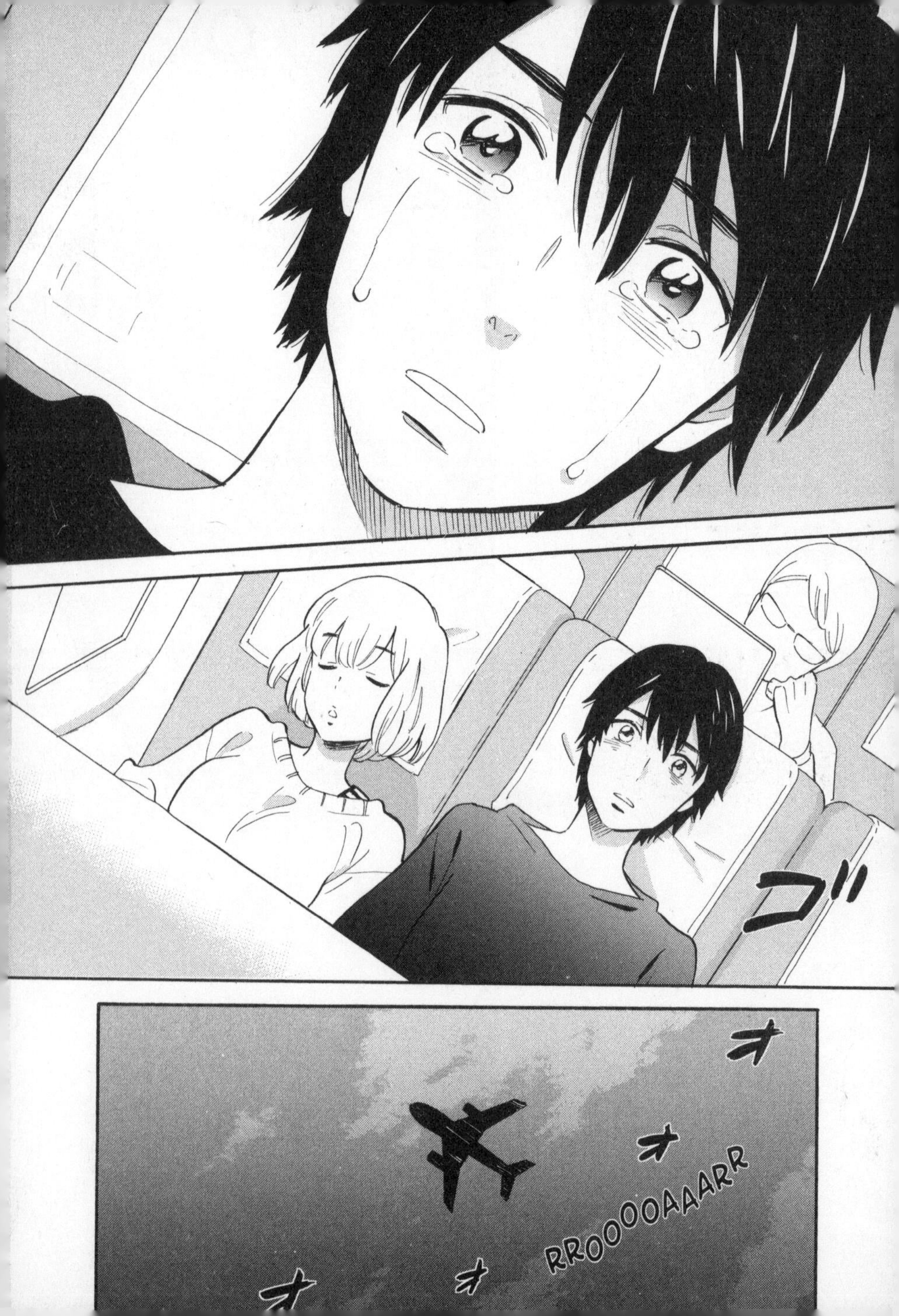
ゴ
オ
オ
RROOOOAAARR
オ
オ

(CHAPTER 6) TOKYO AND POP

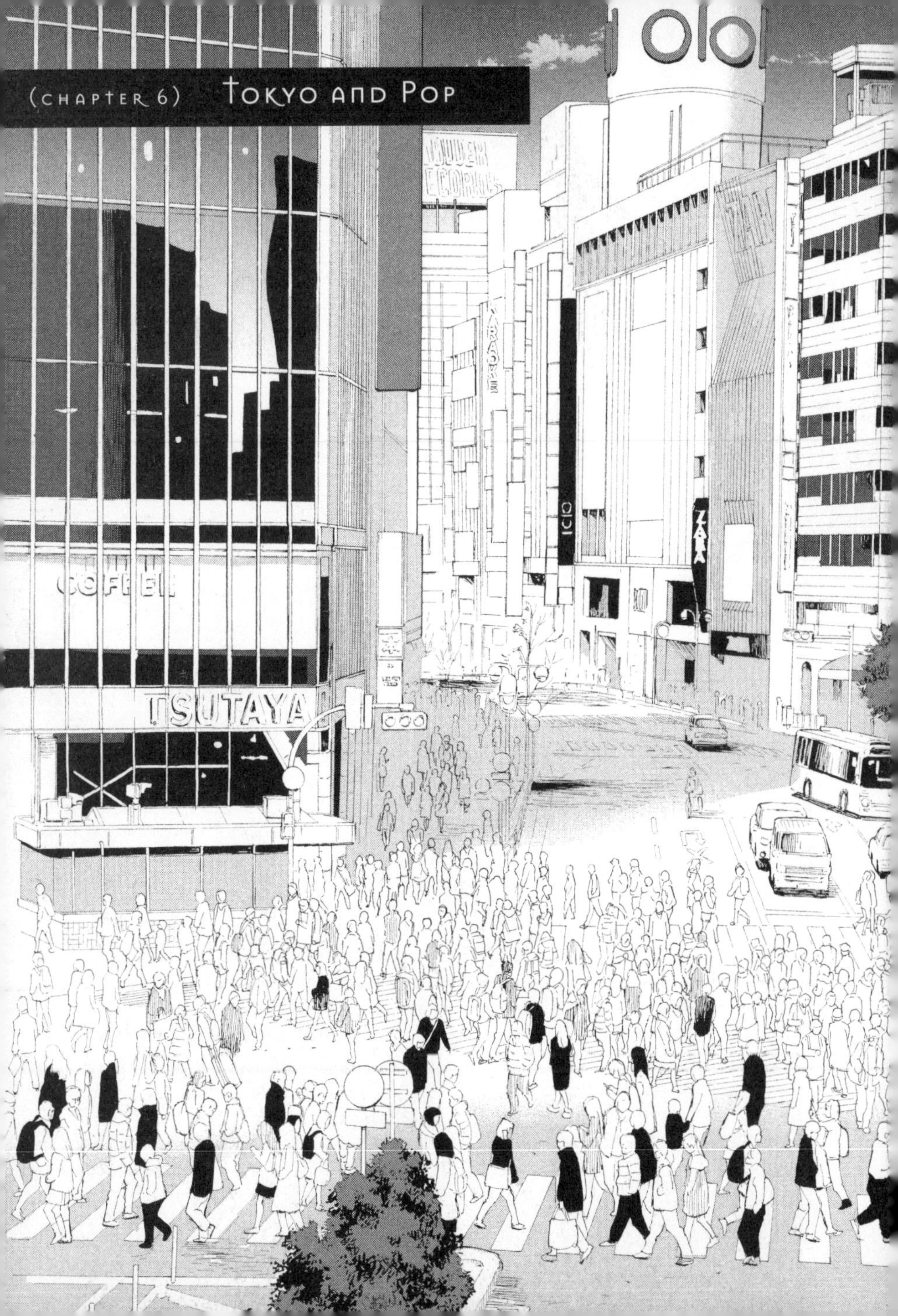
TSUTAYA
ZARA

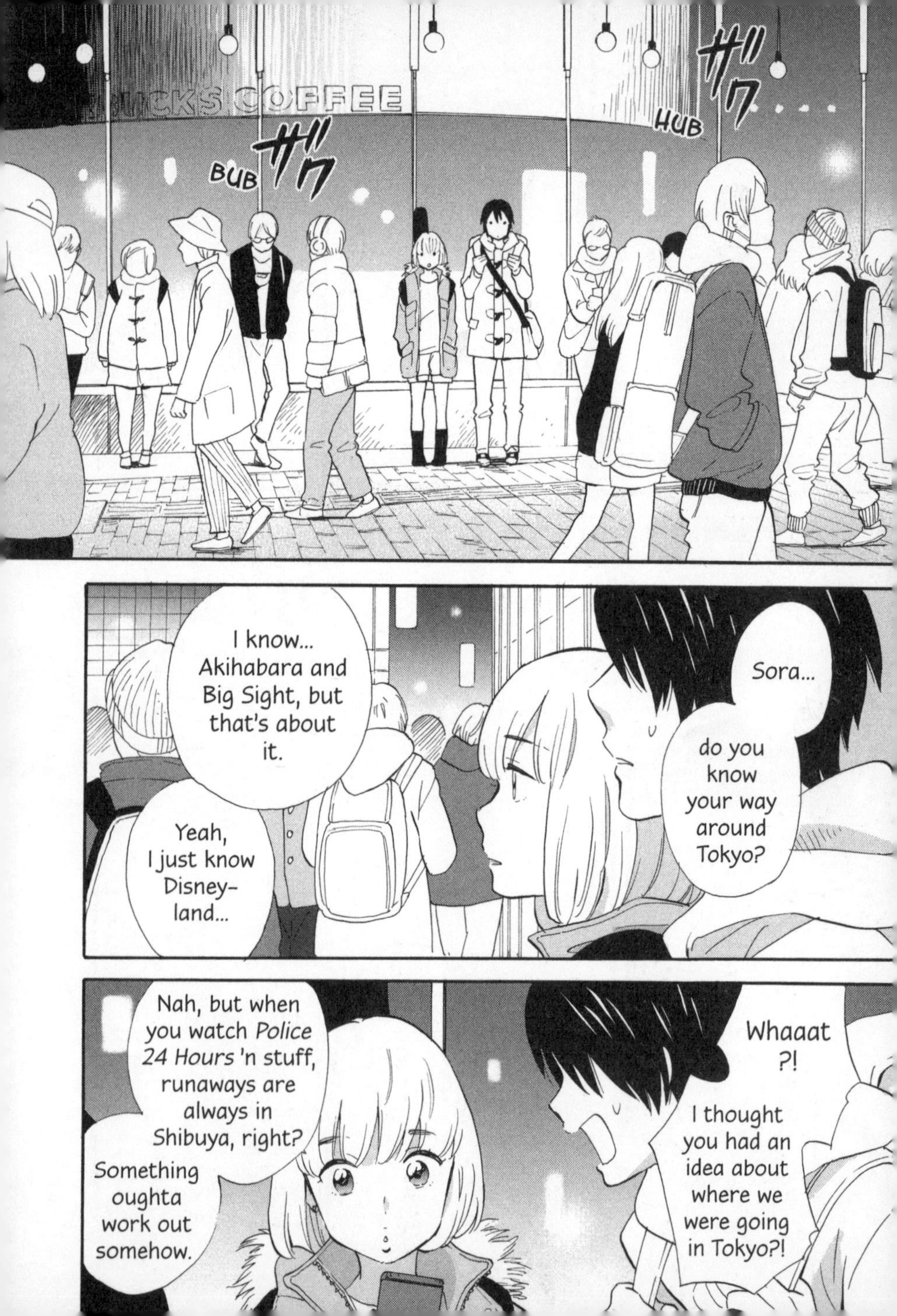

CKS COFFEE
ザワ HUB
BUB ザワ
Sora... do you know your way around Tokyo?
I know... Akihabara and Big Sight, but that's about it.
Yeah, I just know Disney-land...
Whaaat?!
I thought you had an idea about where we were going in Tokyo?!
Nah, but when you watch *Police 24 Hours* 'n stuff, runaways are always in Shibuya, right?
Something oughta work out somehow.

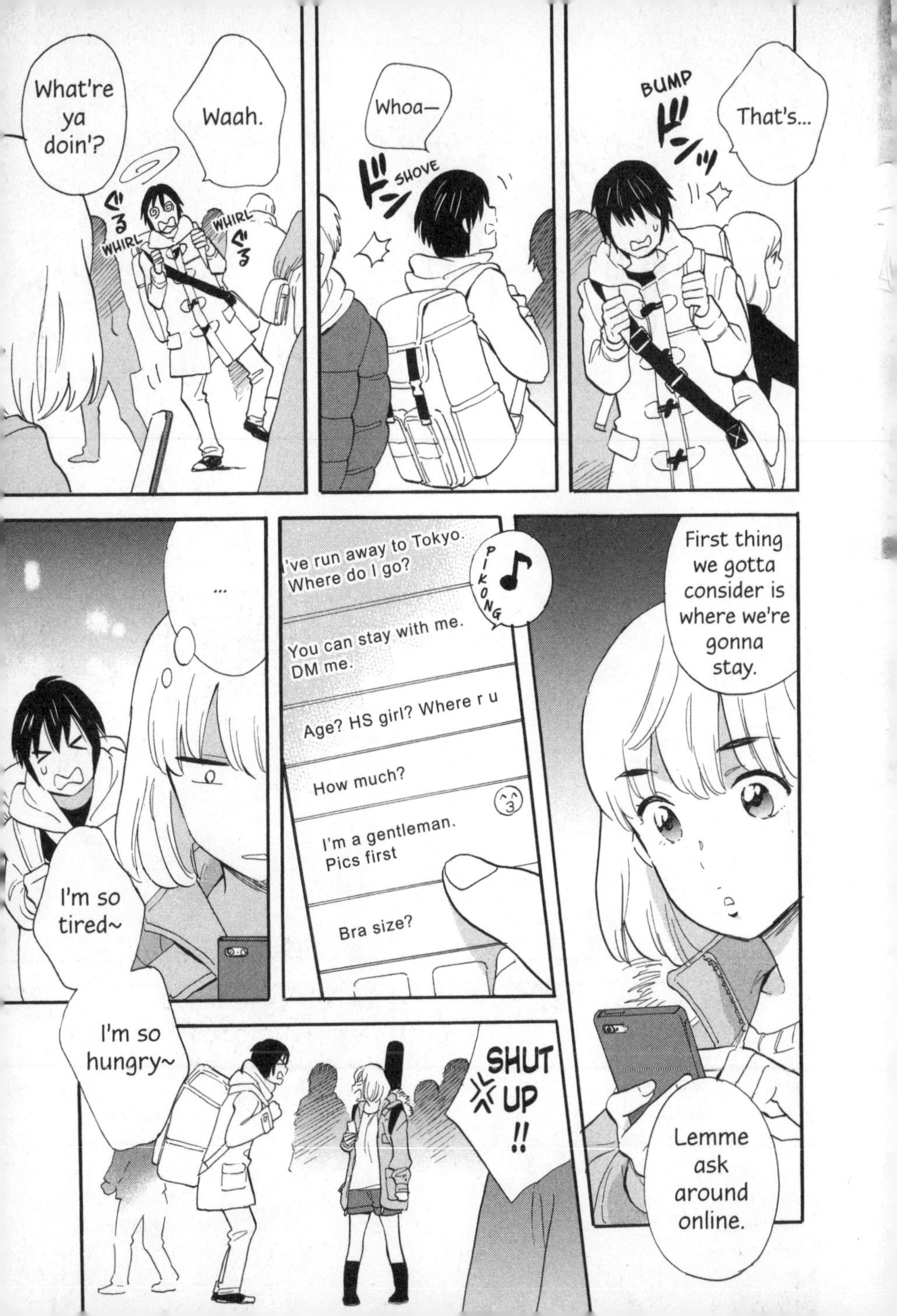
BUMP
ドンッ
That's...
Whoa—
ドン
SHOVE
Waah.
What're ya doin'?
ぐる
WHIRL
WHIRL
ぐる
First thing we gotta consider is where we're gonna stay.
Lemme ask around online.
PIKONG
I've run away to Tokyo. Where do I go?
You can stay with me. DM me.
Age? HS girl? Where r u
How much?
I'm a gentleman. Pics first
Bra size?
...
I'm so tired~
SHUT UP!!
I'm so hungry~

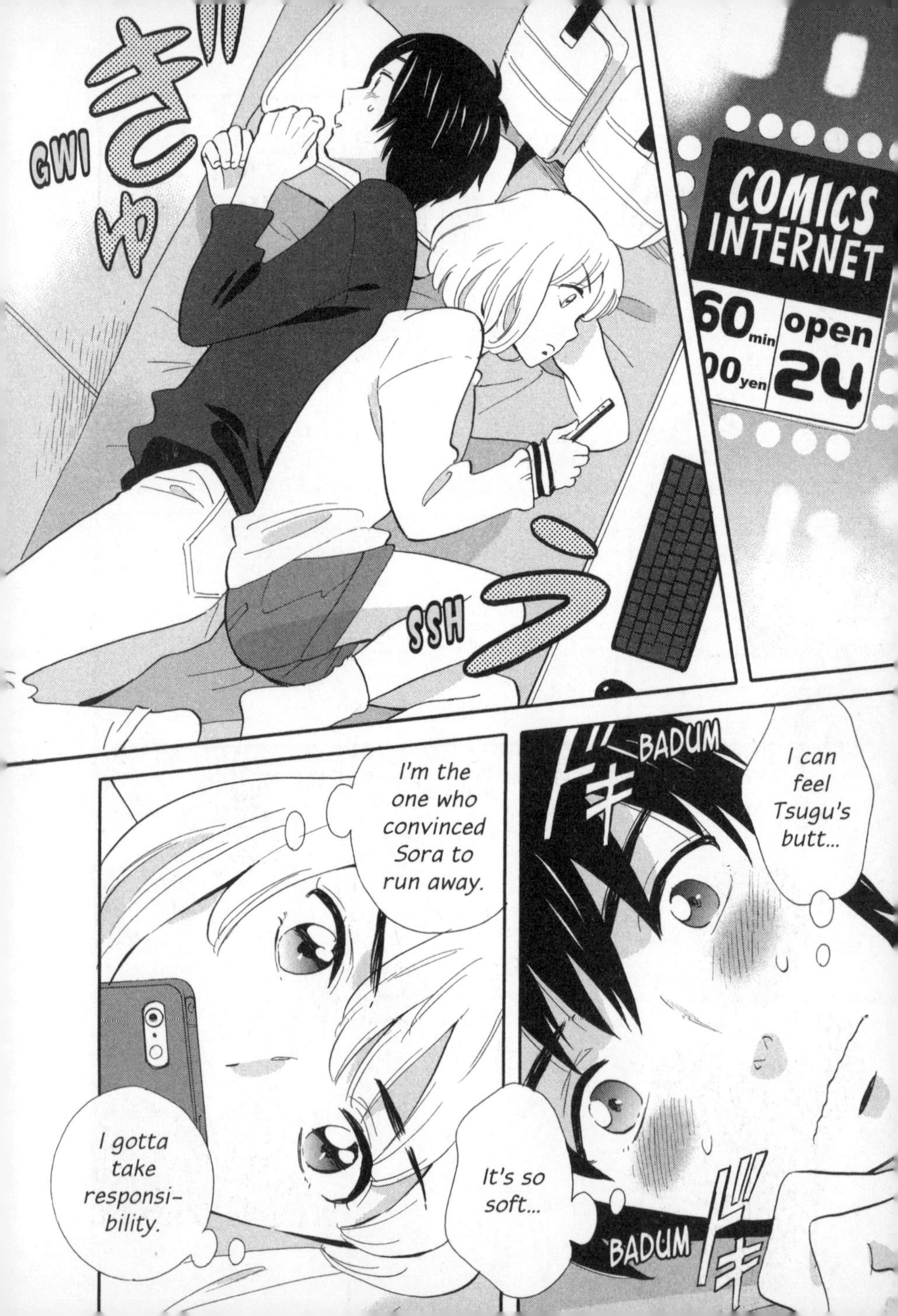

ぎゅ
GWI
COMICS INTERNET
60min
00yen
open 24
つ
SSH
ドキ
BADUM
I can feel Tsugu's butt...
It's so soft...
ドキ
BADUM
I'm the one who convinced Sora to run away.
I gotta take responsibility.

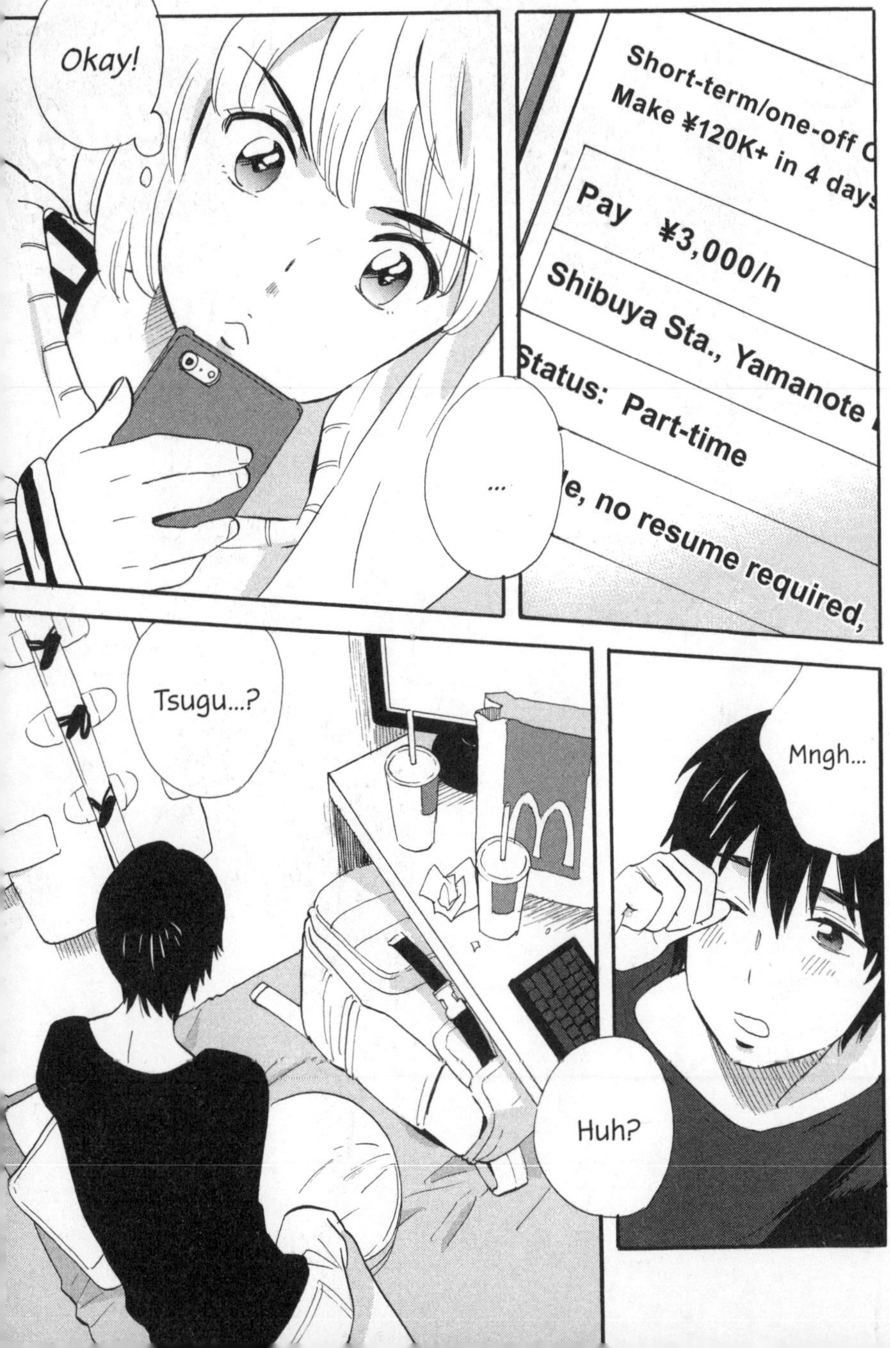

Short-term/one-off
Make ¥120K+ in 4 days
Pay ¥3,000/h
Shibuya Sta., Yamanote
Status: Part-time
no resume required,
...
Okay!
Tsugu...?
Mngh...
Huh?

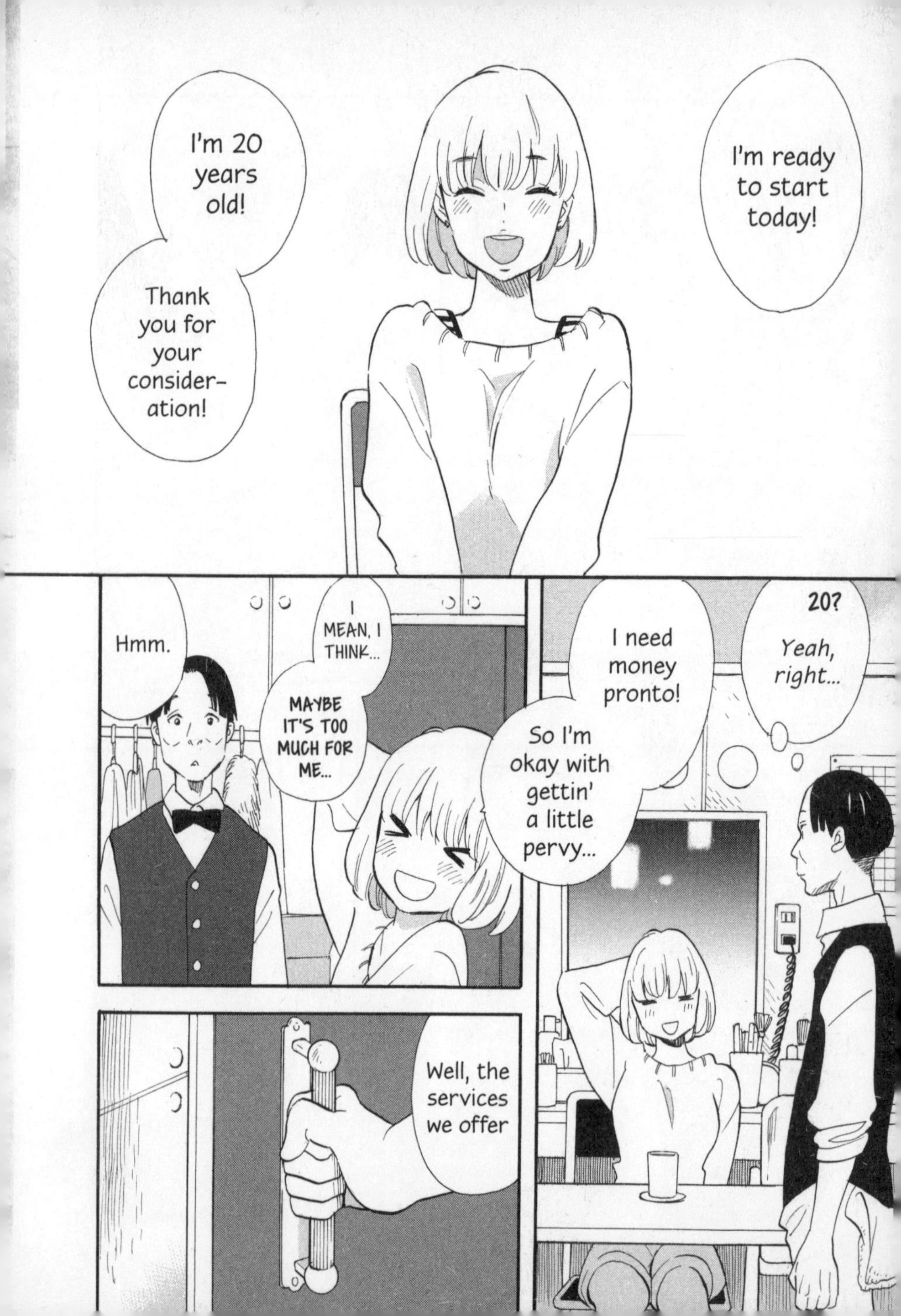
I'm ready to start today!
I'm 20 years old!
Thank you for your consider-ation!
20?
Yeah, right...
I need money pronto!
So I'm okay with gettin' a little pervy...
I MEAN, I THINK...
MAYBE IT'S TOO MUCH FOR ME...
Hmm.
Well, the services we offer

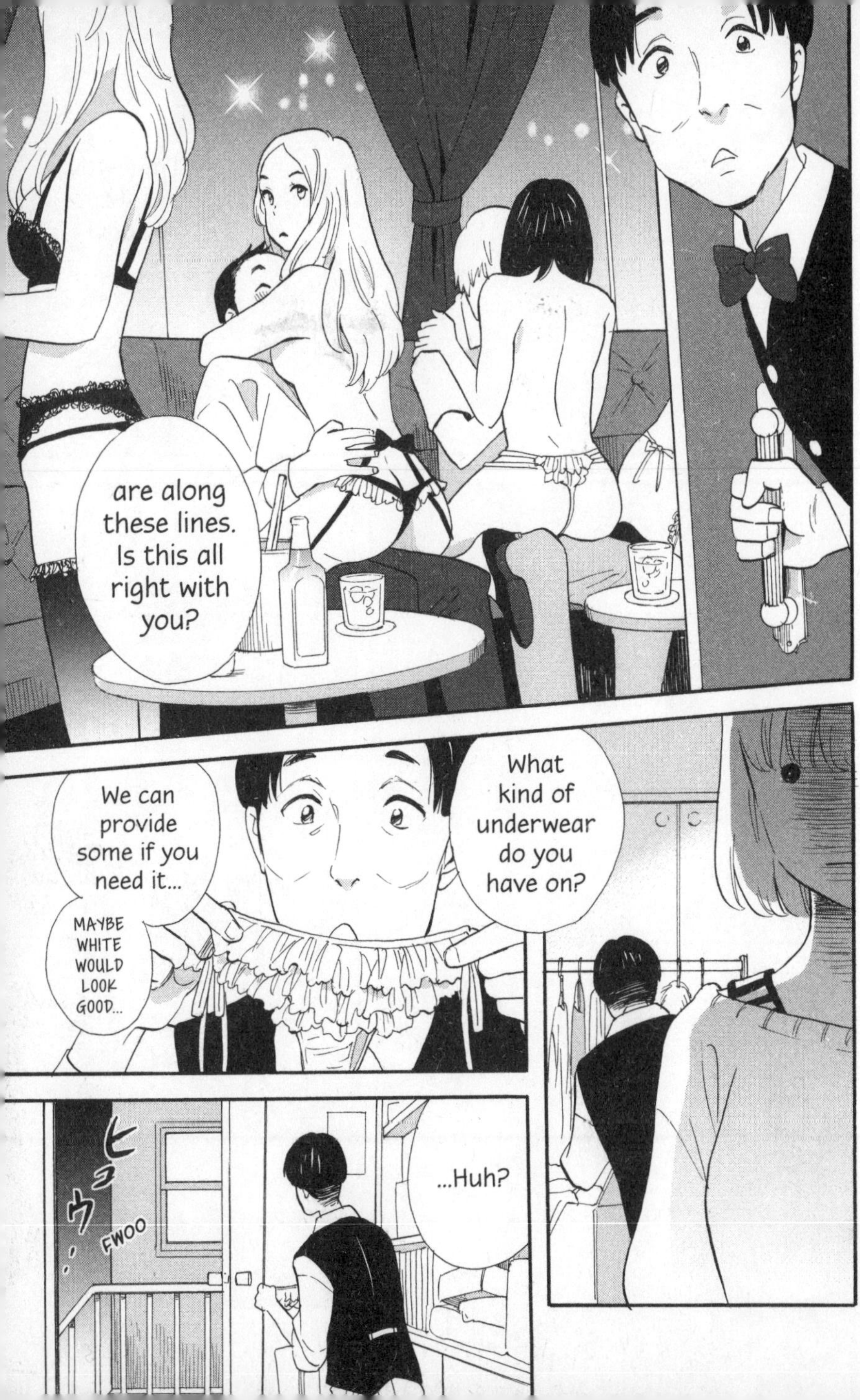
are along these lines. Is this all right with you?
What kind of underwear do you have on?
We can provide some if you need it...
MAYBE WHITE WOULD LOOK GOOD...
...Huh?
ヒュウ
FWOO

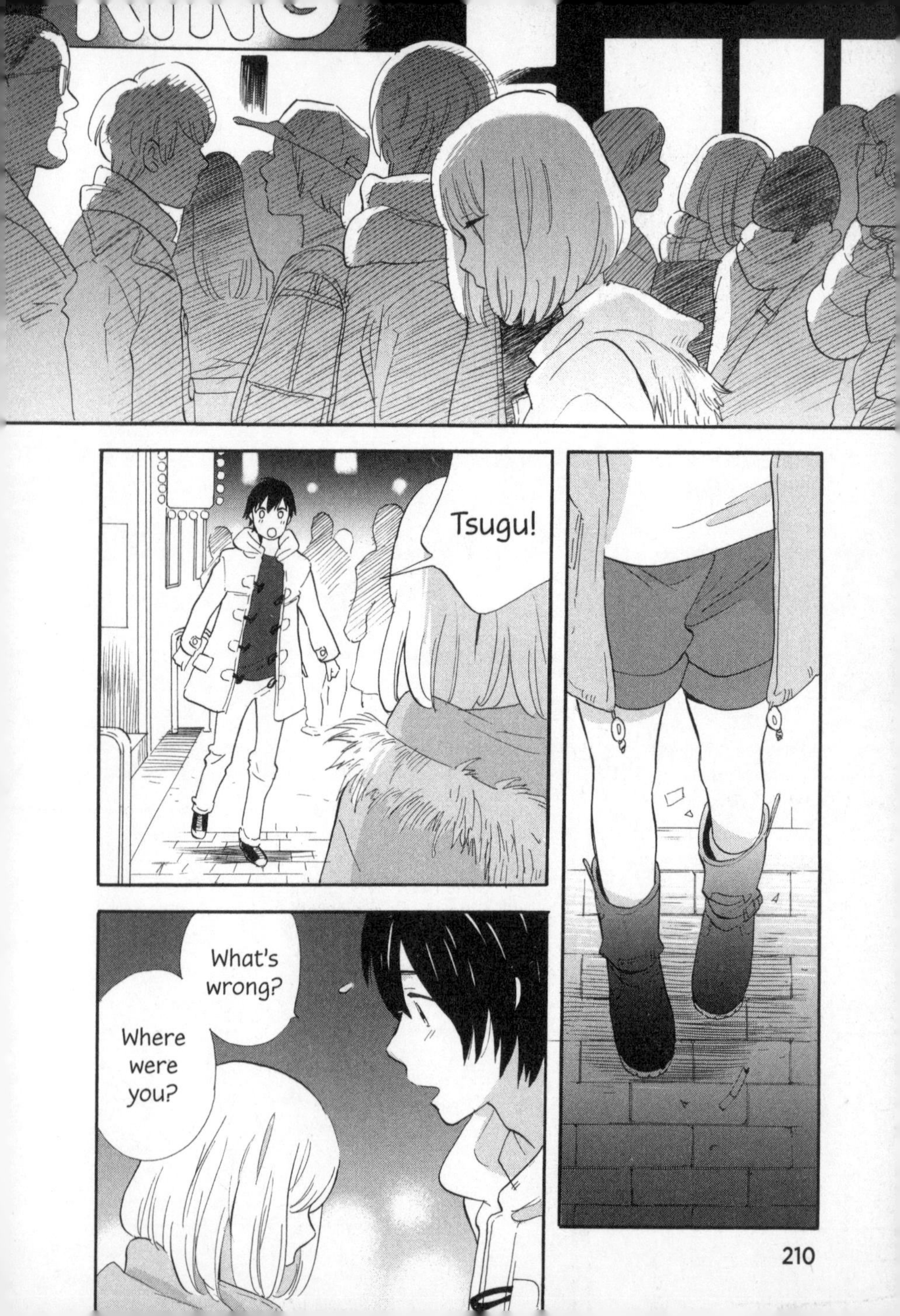
Tsugu!
What's wrong?
Where were you?

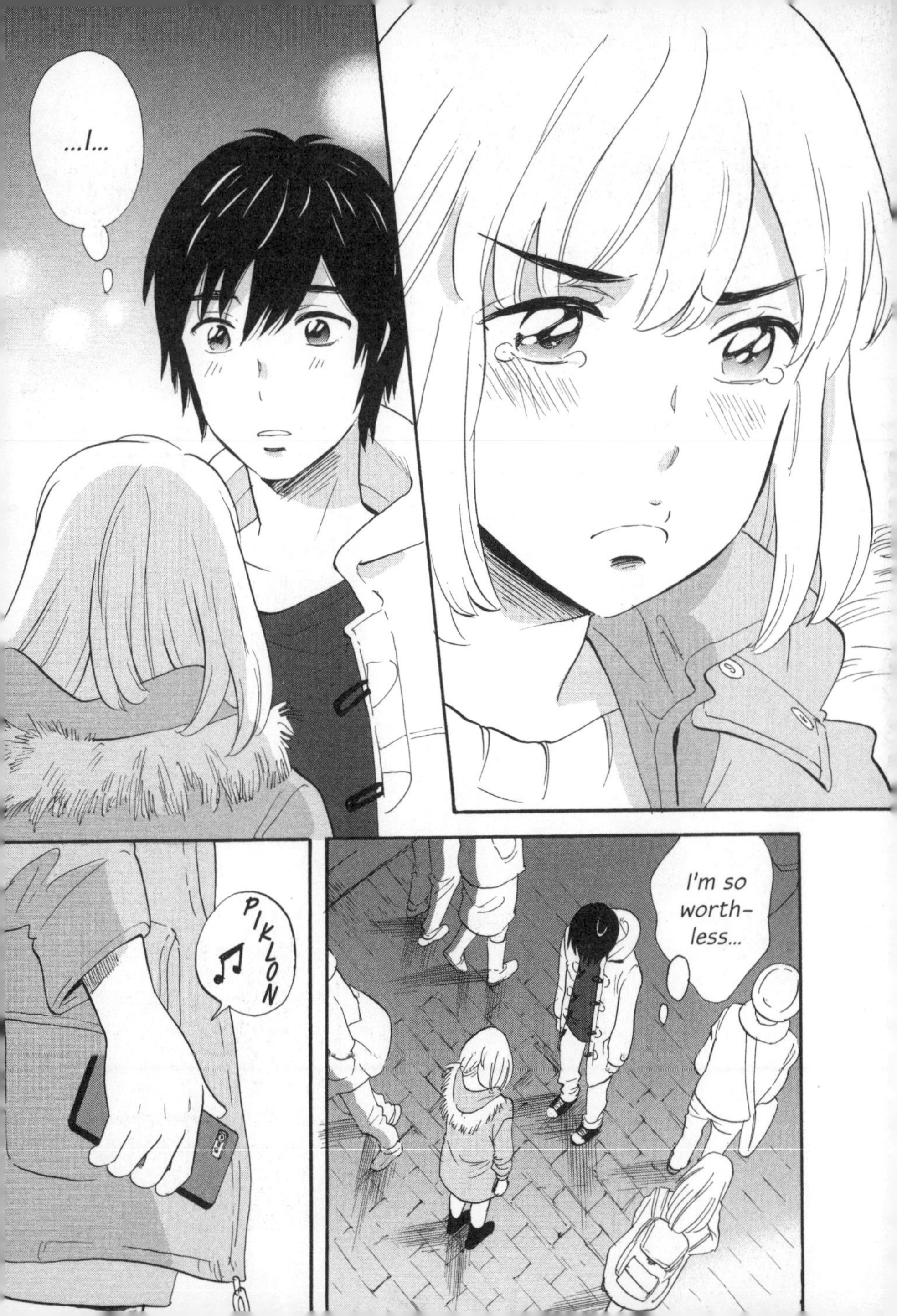
...I...
I'm so worth-less...
PIKLON ♪

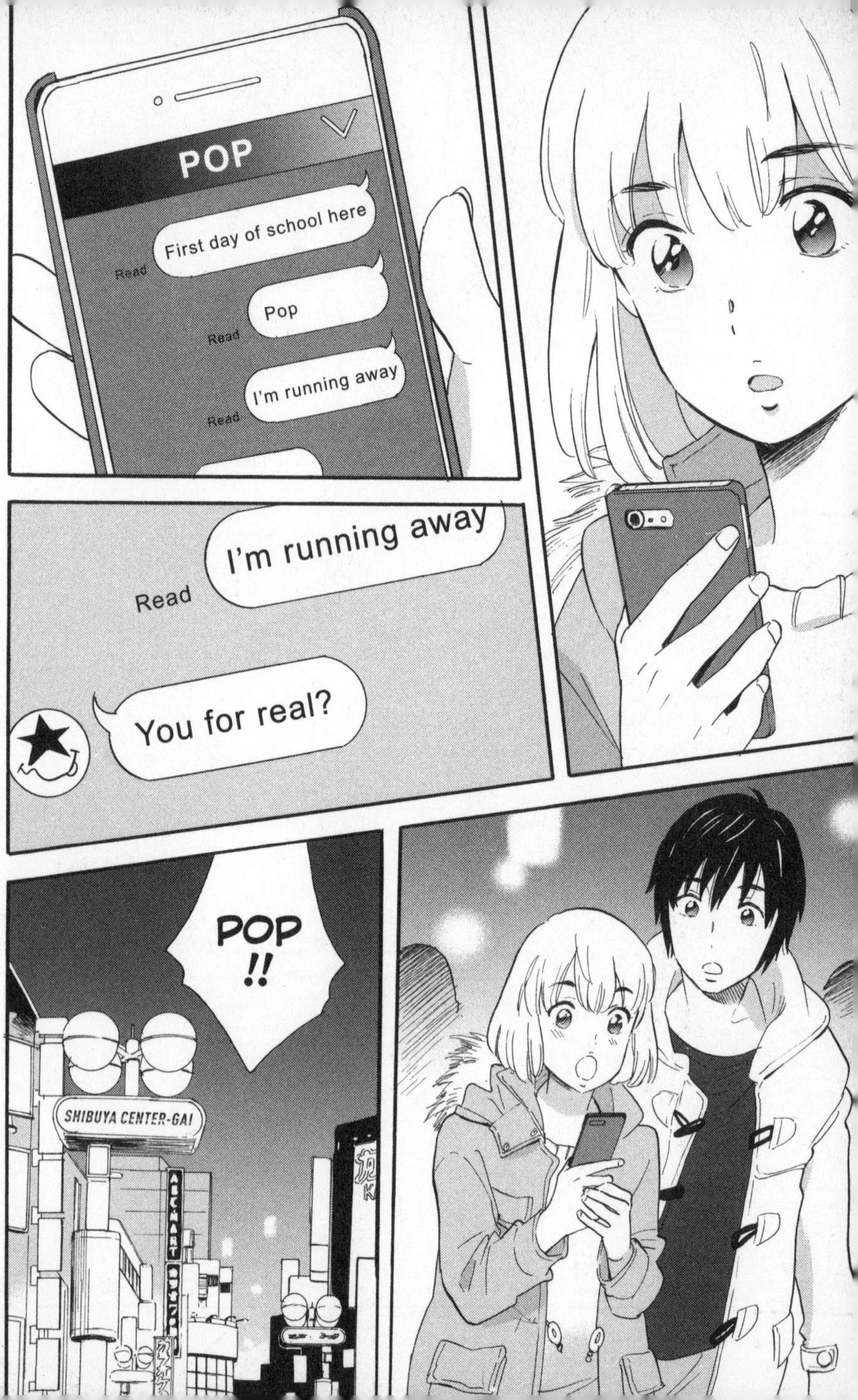
POP
First day of school here
Read
Pop
Read
I'm running away
Read
I'm running away
Read
You for real?
POP !!
SHIBUYA CENTER-GAI

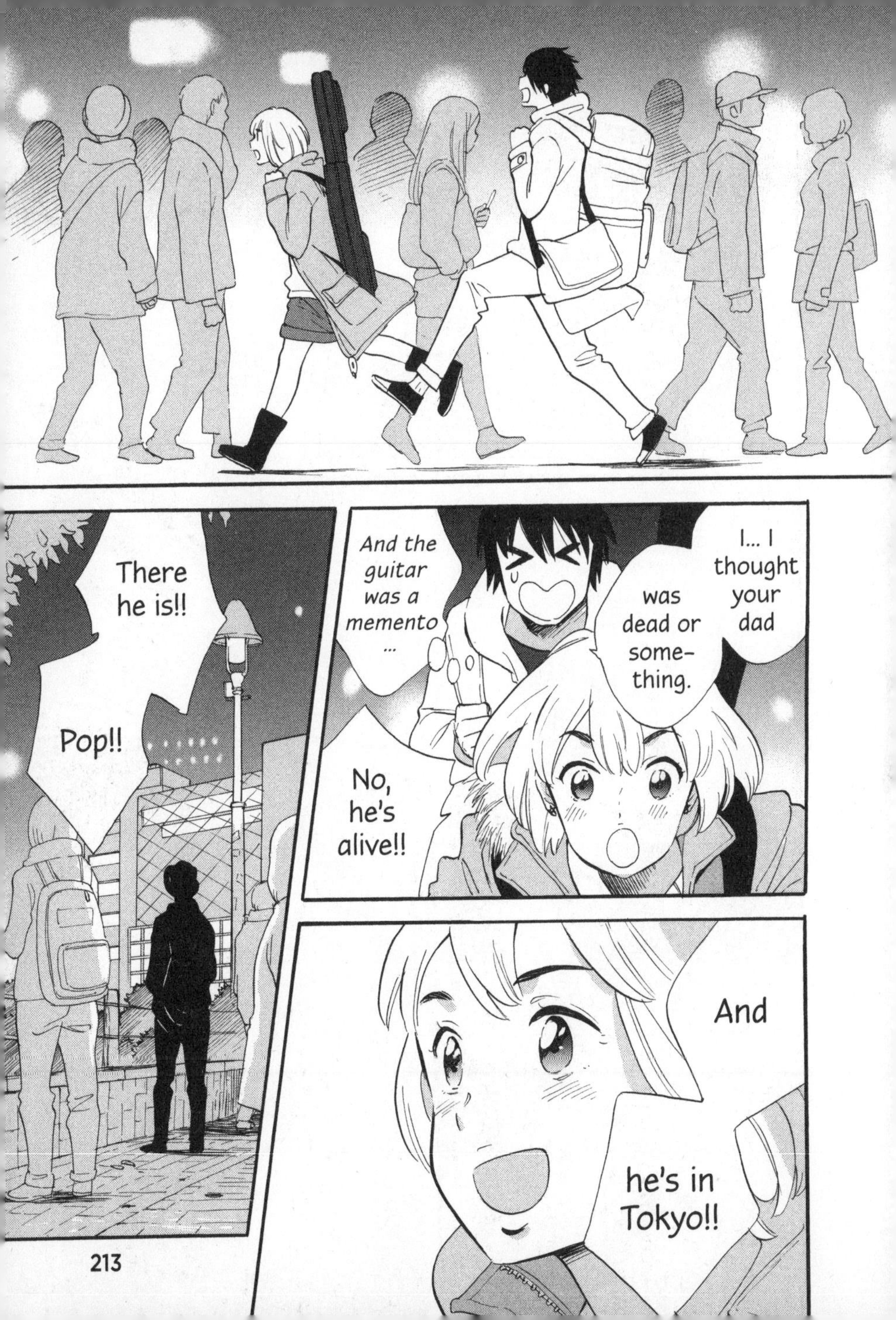
I... I thought your dad was dead or something.
And the guitar was a memento ...
No, he's alive!!
And
he's in Tokyo!!
There he is!!
Pop!!

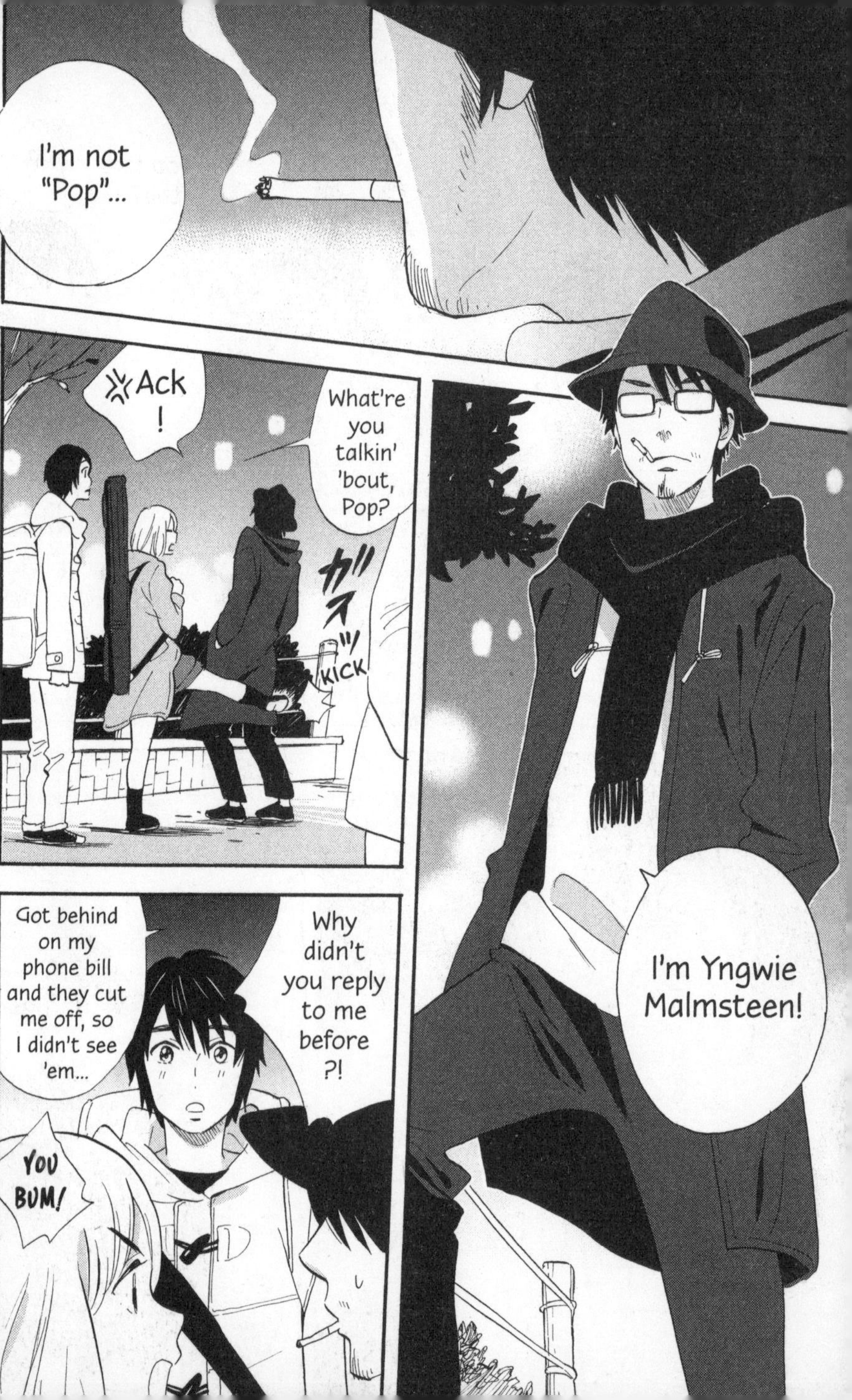
I'm not "Pop"...
I'm Yngwie Malmsteen!
What're you talkin' 'bout, Pop?
Ack !
ガス
KICK
Why didn't you reply to me before ?!
Got behind on my phone bill and they cut me off, so I didn't see 'em...
YOU BUM!

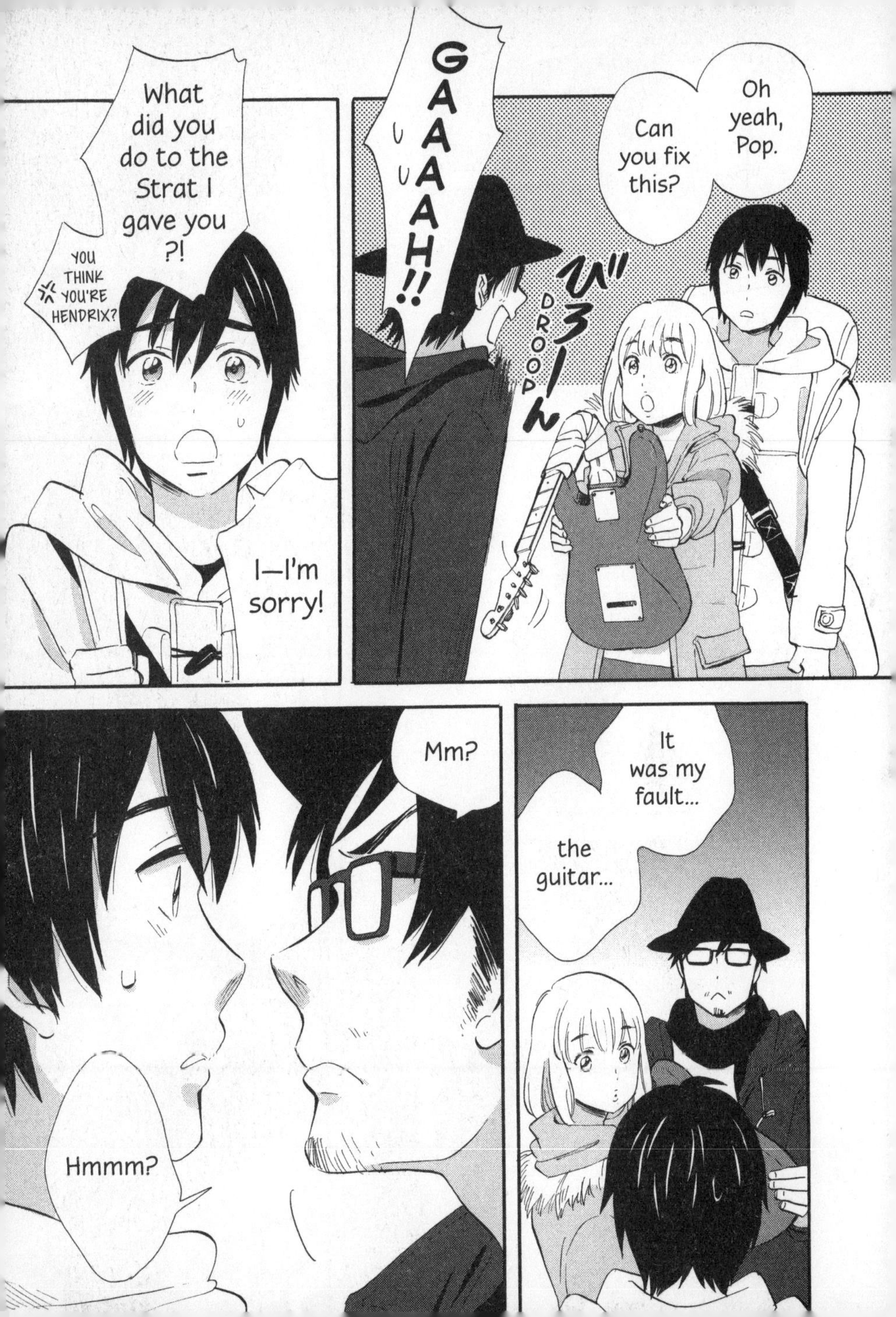
Oh yeah, Pop.
Can you fix this?
GAAAAAH!!
びろーん
DROOP
What did you do to the Strat I gave you ?!
YOU THINK YOU'RE HENDRIX?
I—I'm sorry!
It was my fault...
the guitar...
Mm?
Hmmm?

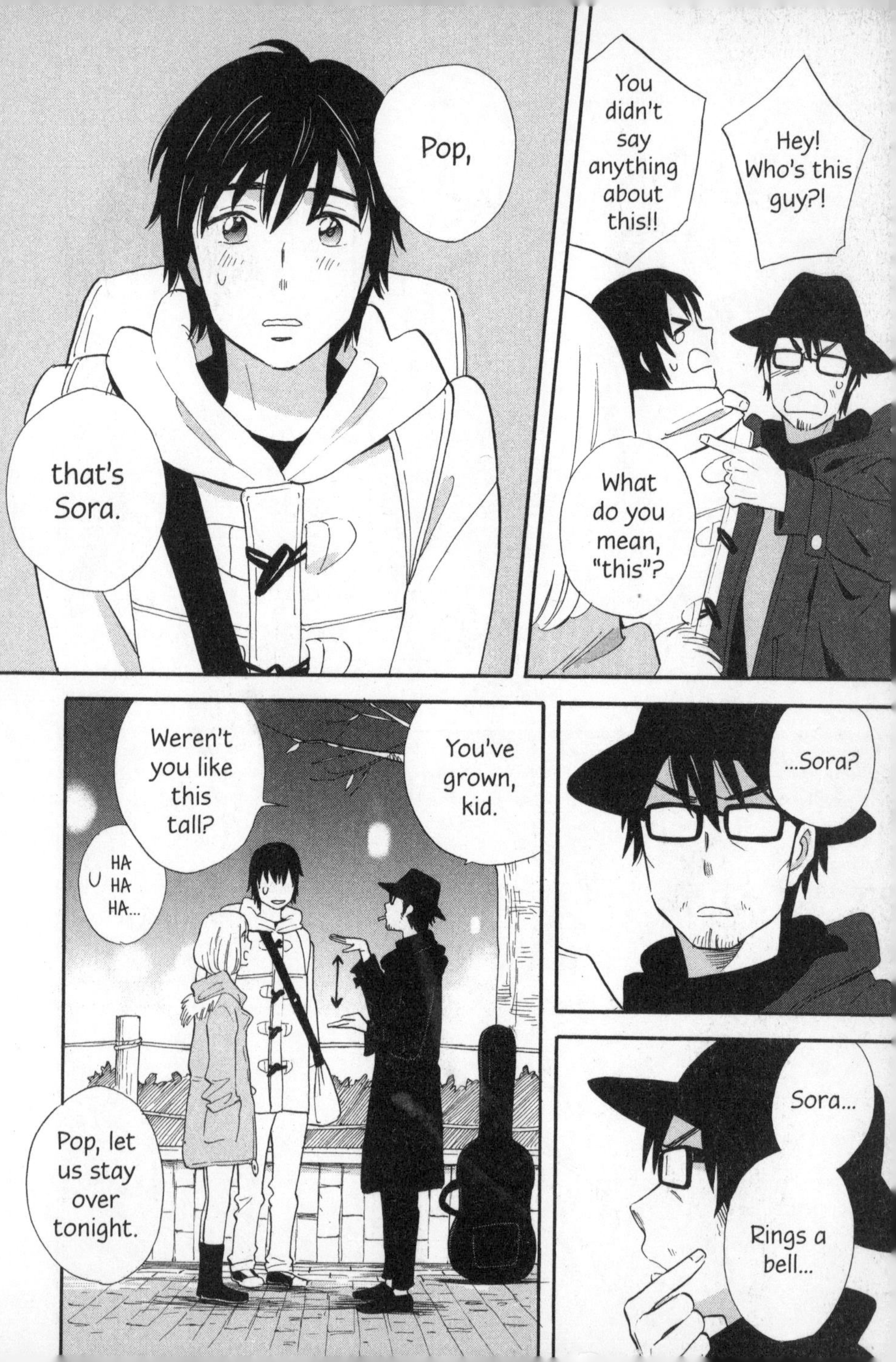
Hey! Who's this guy?!
You didn't say anything about this!!
What do you mean, "this"?
Pop,
that's Sora.
...Sora?
Sora...
Rings a bell...
You've grown, kid.
Weren't you like this tall?
HA HA HA...
Pop, let us stay over tonight.

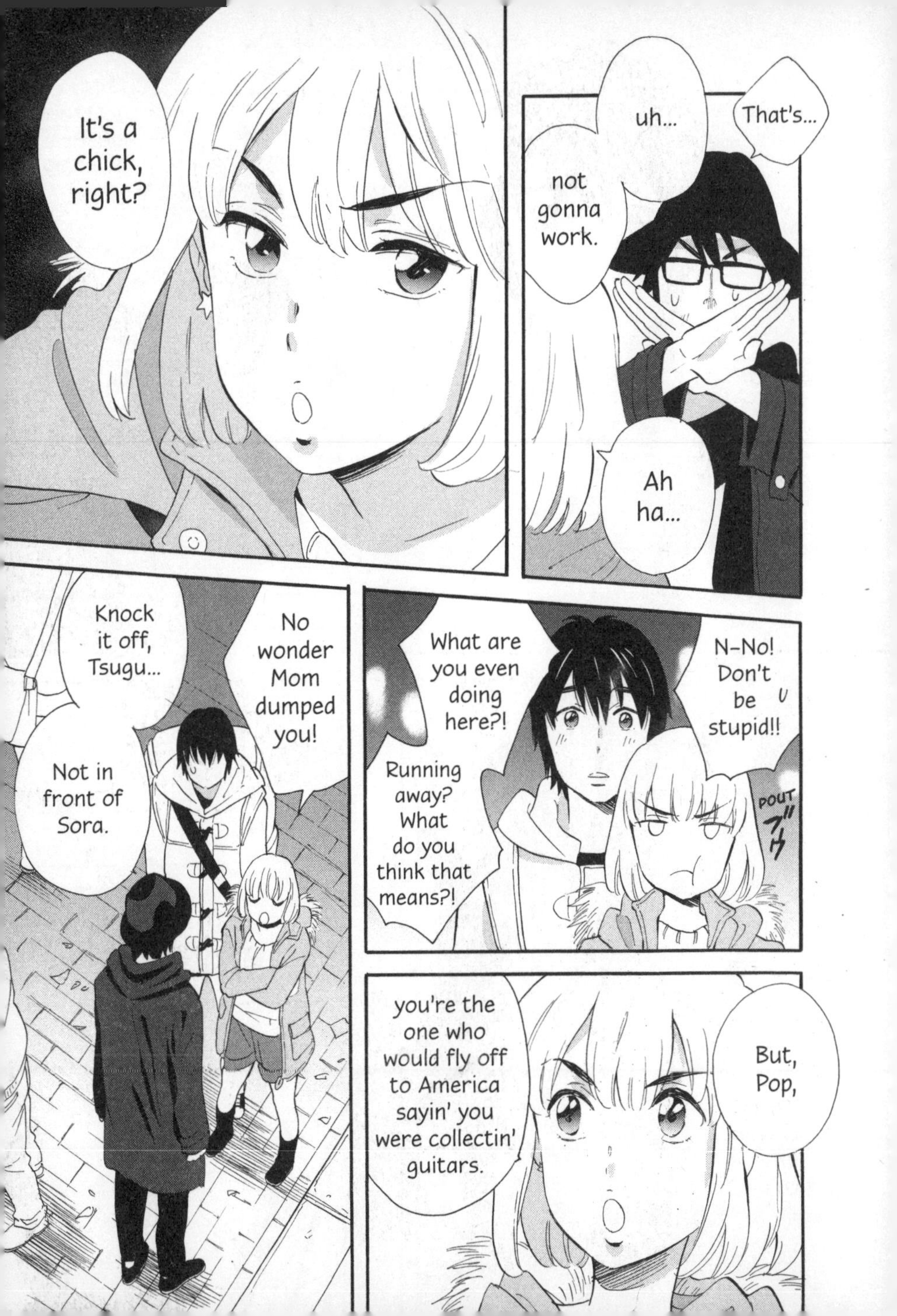
That's...
uh...
not gonna work.
Ah ha...
It's a chick, right?
N-No! Don't be stupid!!
What are you even doing here?!
POUT
Running away? What do you think that means?!
But, Pop,
you're the one who would fly off to America sayin' you were collectin' guitars.
No wonder Mom dumped you!
Knock it off, Tsugu...
Not in front of Sora.

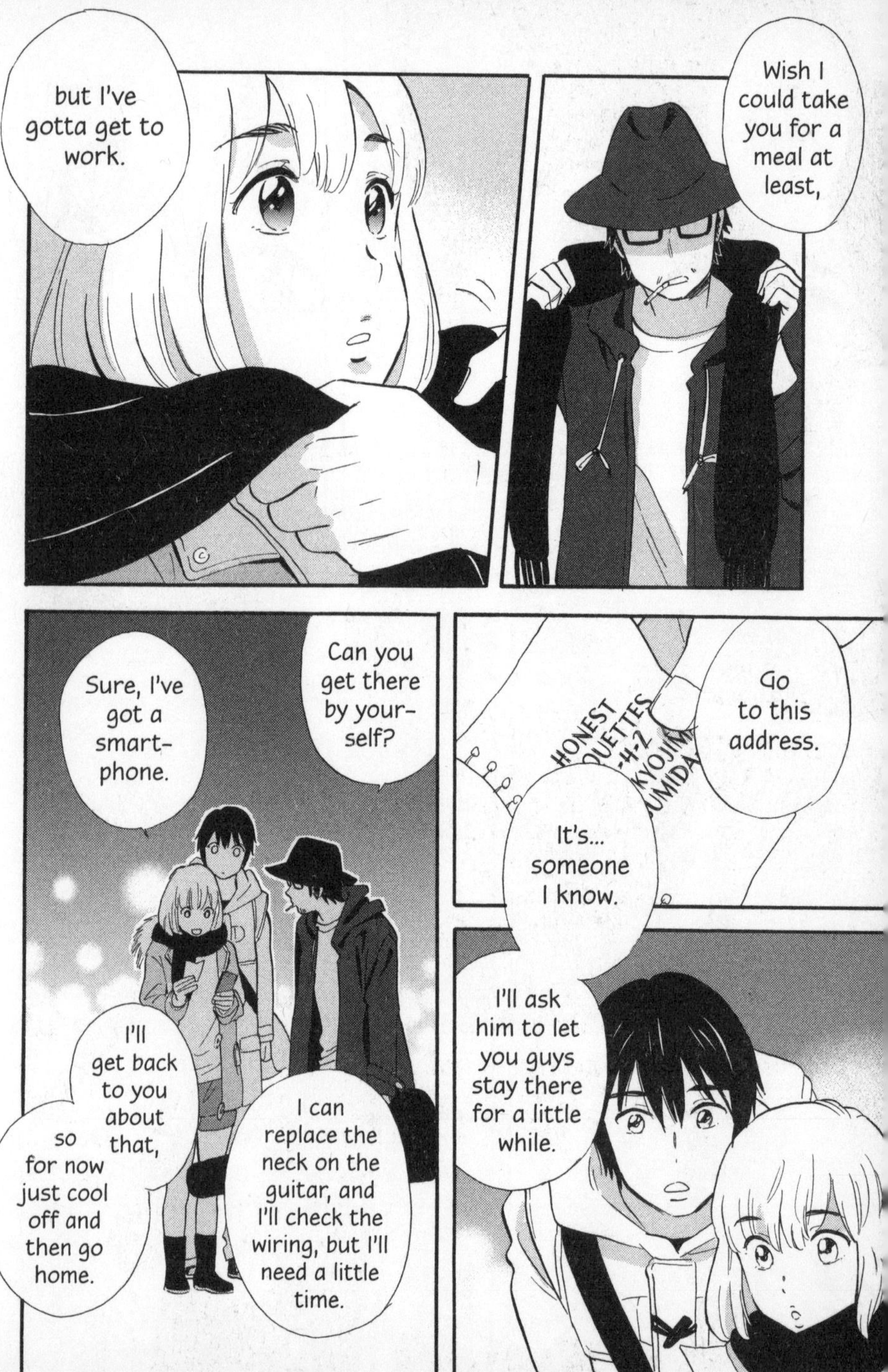
Wish I could take you for a meal at least,
but I've gotta get to work.
Go to this address.
It's... someone I know.
I'll ask him to let you guys stay there for a little while.
Can you get there by yourself?
Sure, I've got a smartphone.
I can replace the neck on the guitar, and I'll check the wiring, but I'll need a little time.
I'll get back to you about that,
so for now just cool off and then go home.

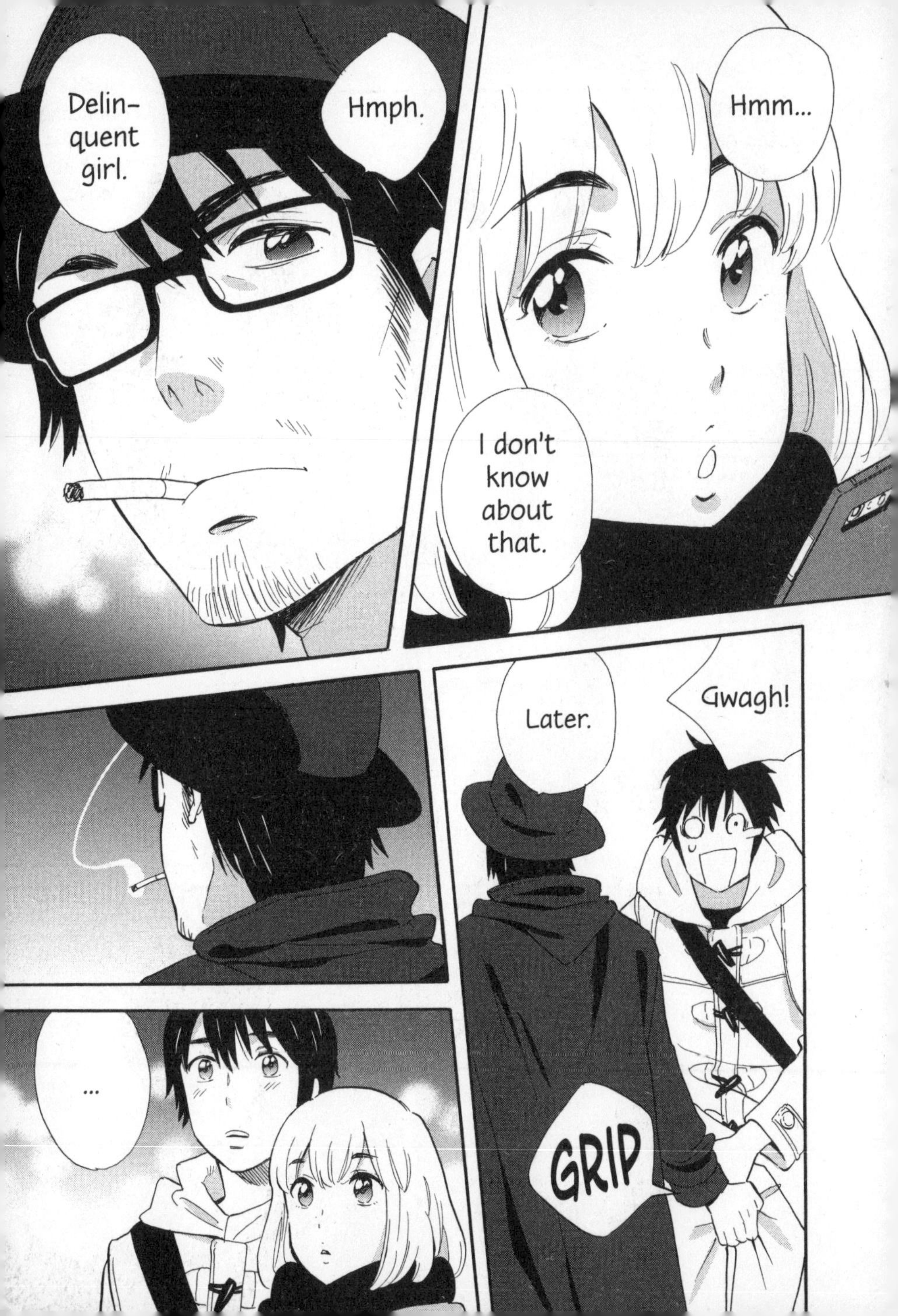
Hmm...
I don't know about that.
Hmph.
Delin-
quent
girl.
Later.
Gwagh!
GRIP
...

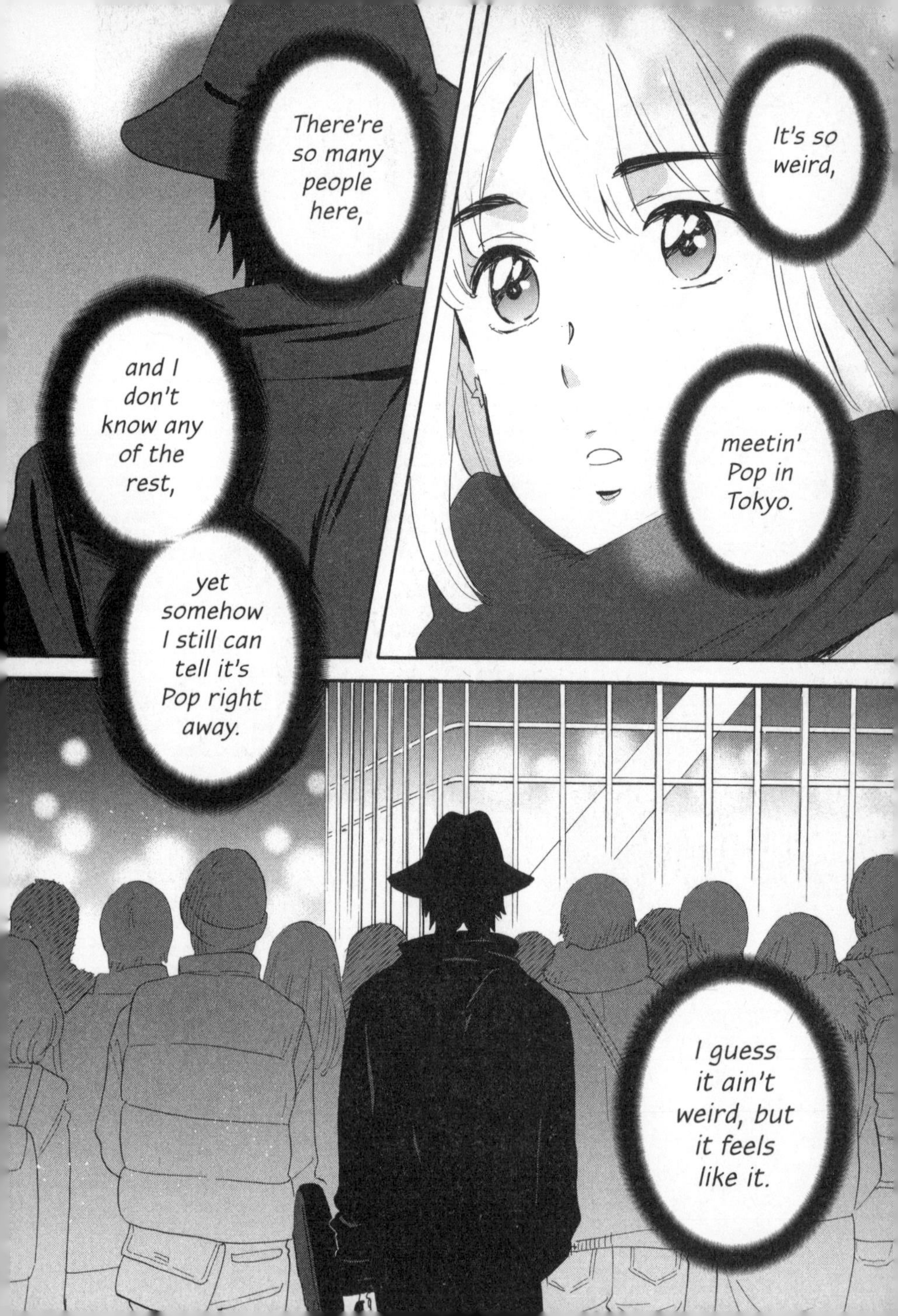
It's so weird,
meetin' Pop in Tokyo.
There're so many people here,
and I don't know any of the rest,
yet somehow I still can tell it's Pop right away.
I guess it ain't weird, but it feels like it.

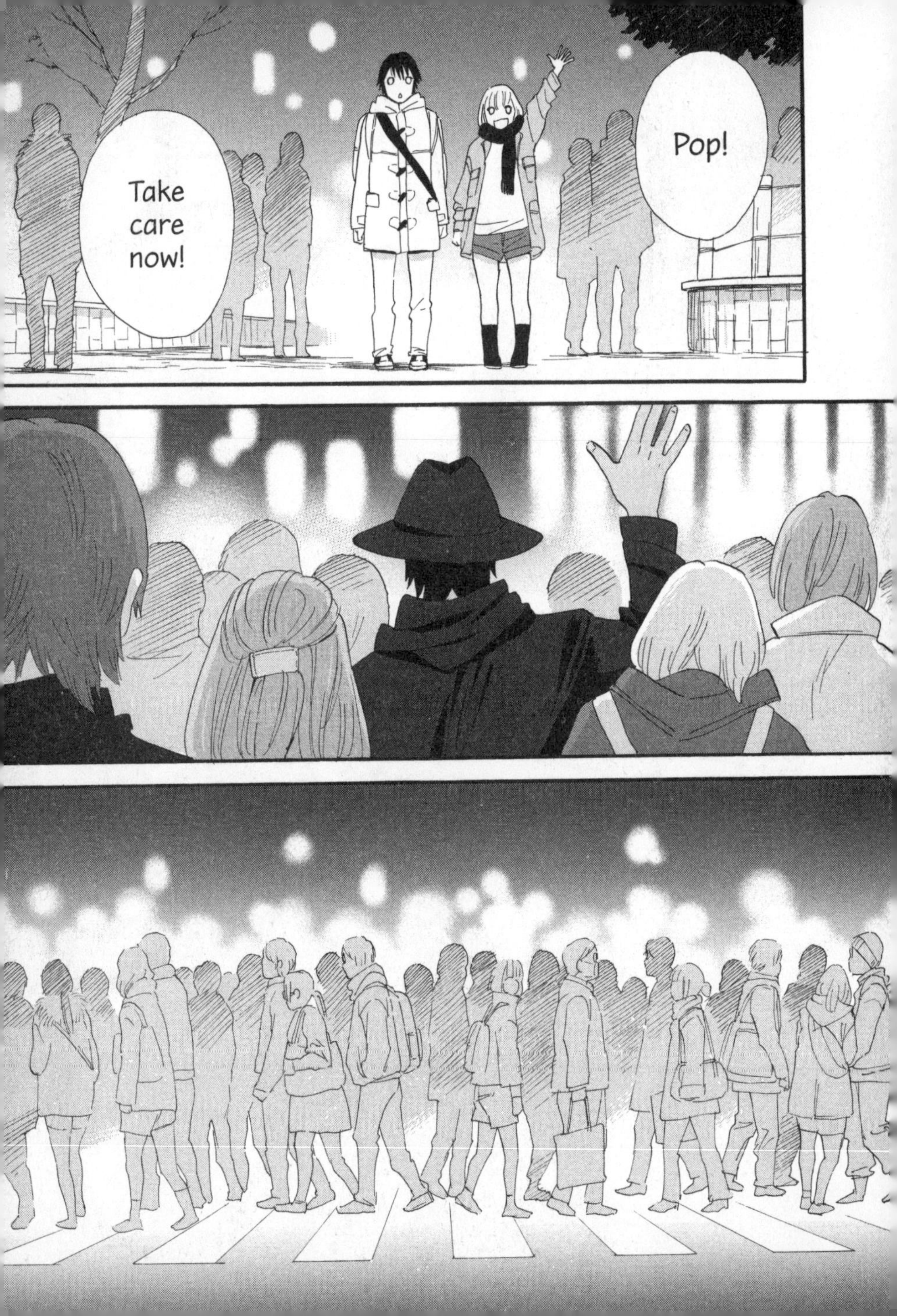
Pop!
Take care now!

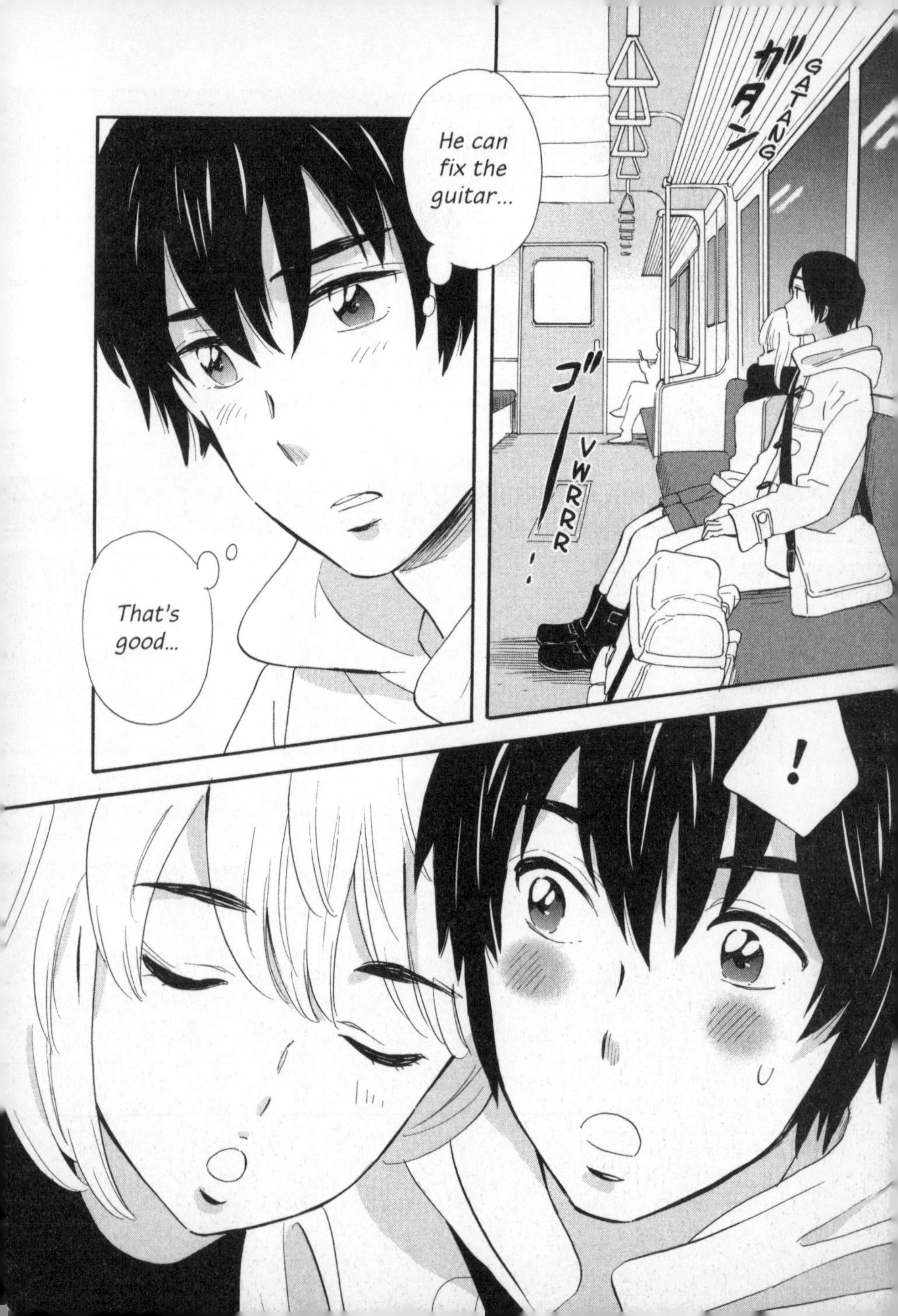
ガタン
GATANG
ゴー
VWRRR
He can fix the guitar...
That's good...
!

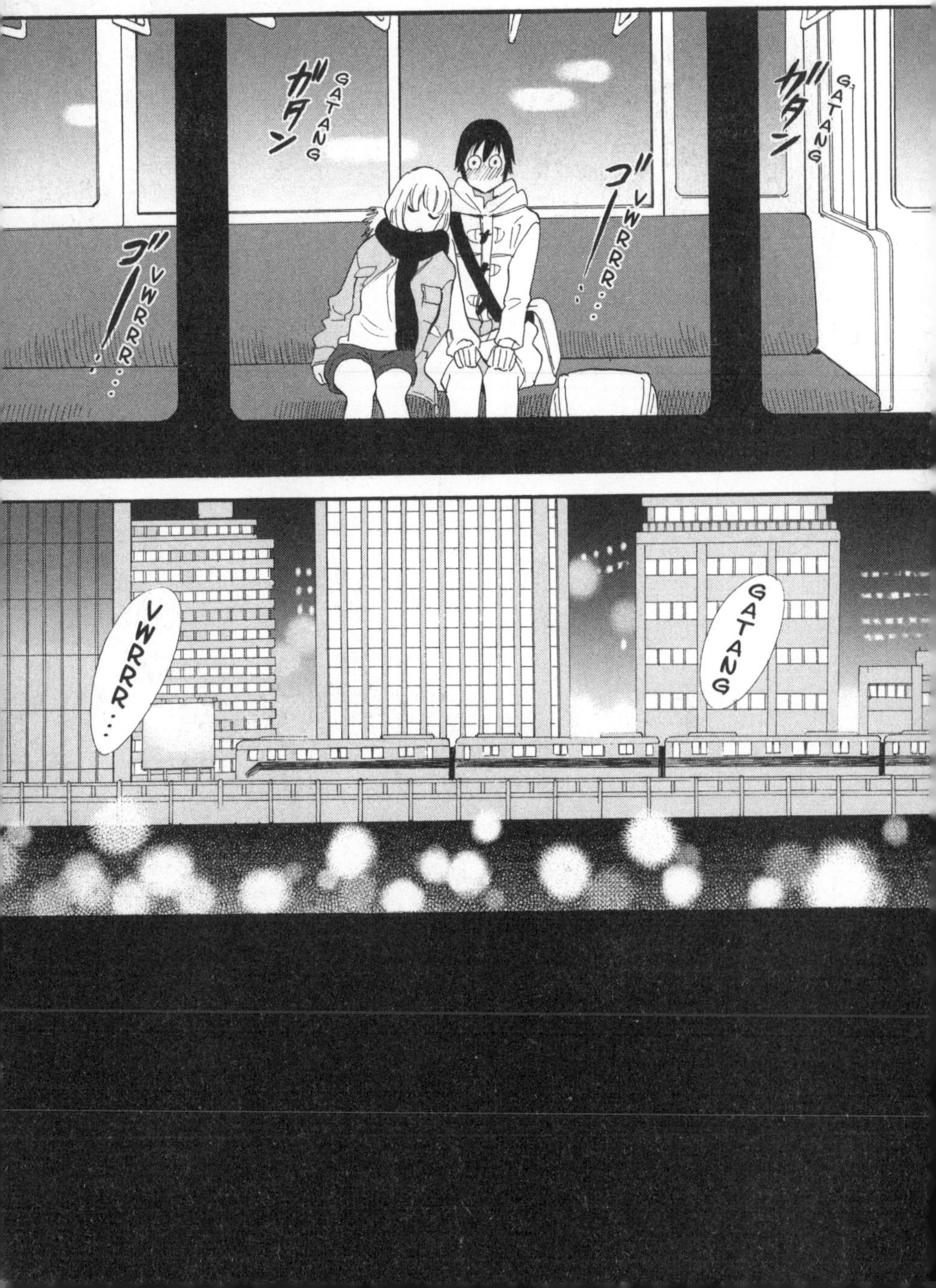
ガタン
G, GATANG
ゴー
VWRRR...
ガタン
GATANG
ゴー
VWRRR...
GATANG
VWRRR...

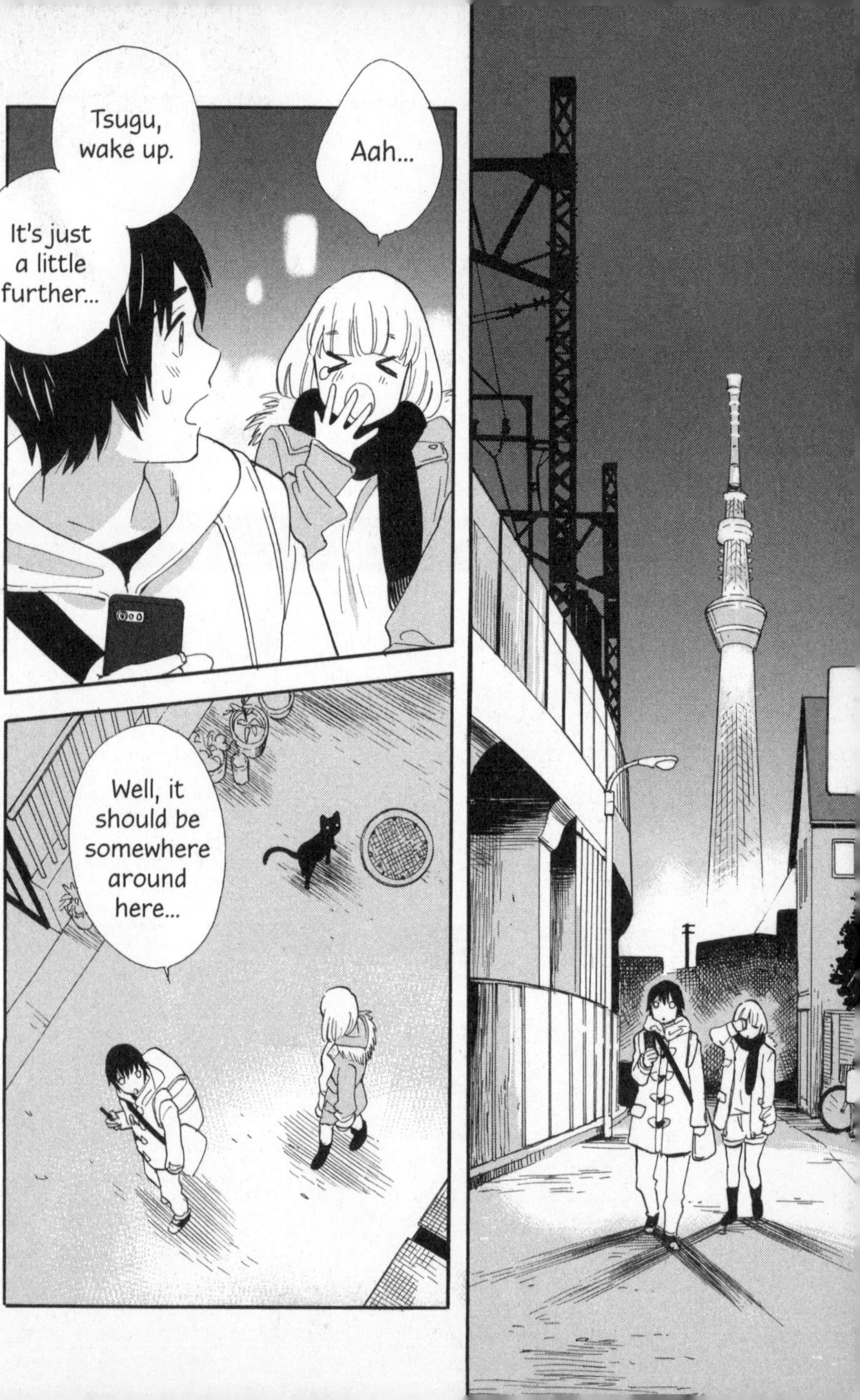
Aah...
Tsugu, wake up.
It's just a little further...
Well, it should be somewhere around here...

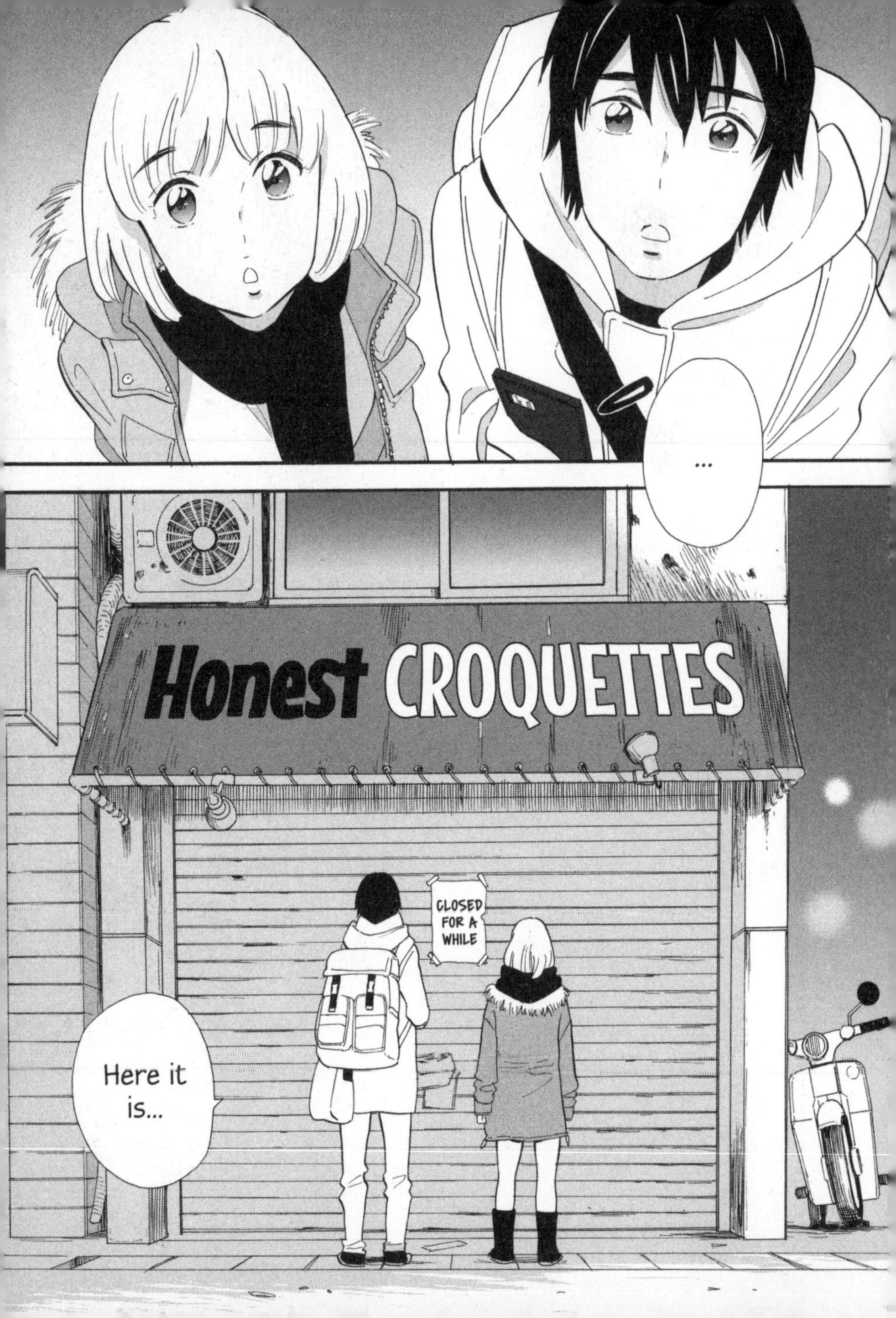
...
Honest CROQUETTES
CLOSED FOR A WHILE
Here it is...

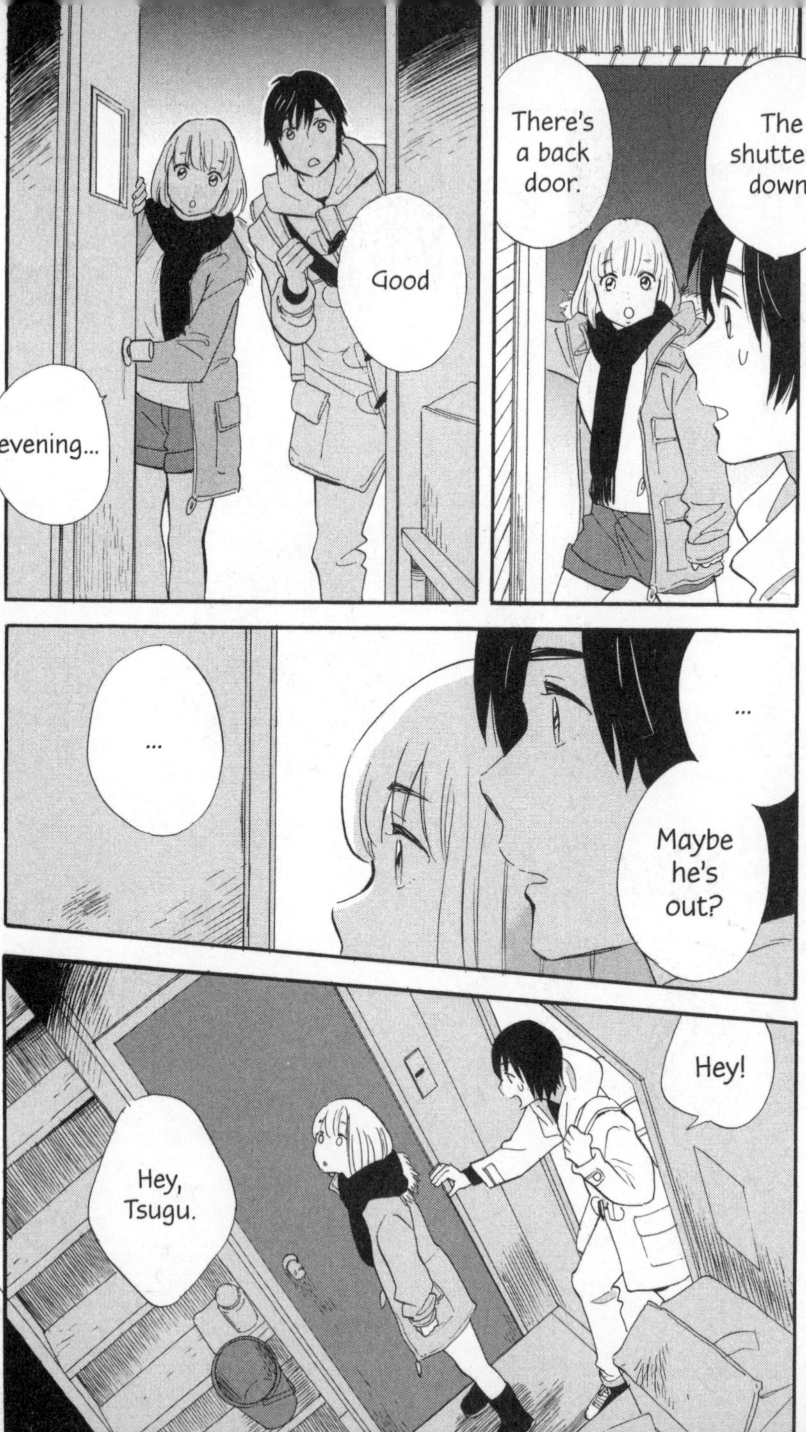
The shutter's down.
There's a back door.
Good
evening...
...
Maybe he's out?
...
Hey!
Hey, Tsugu.

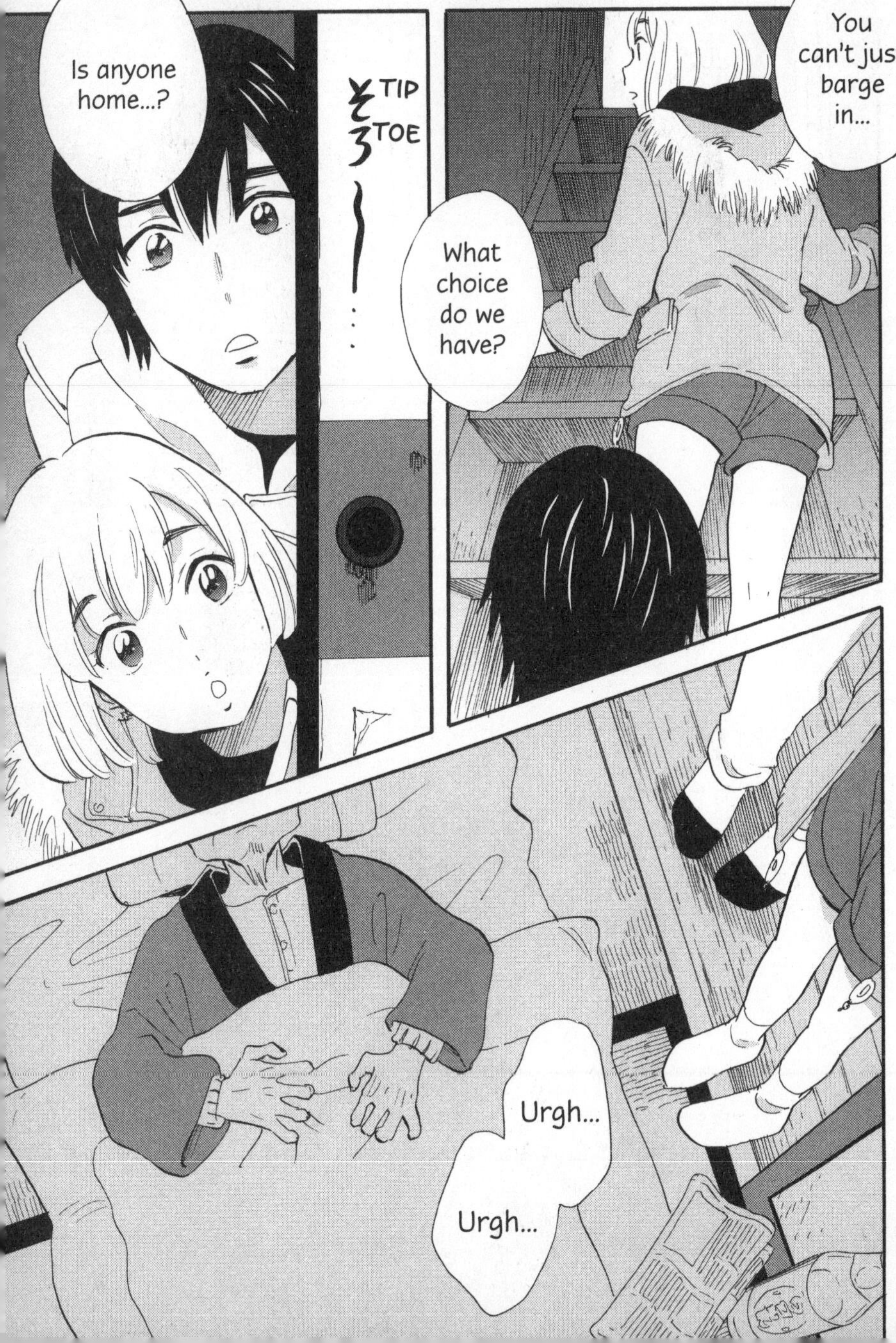
You can't just barge in...
What choice do we have?
Is anyone home...?
そろ TIP TOE
Urgh...
Urgh...

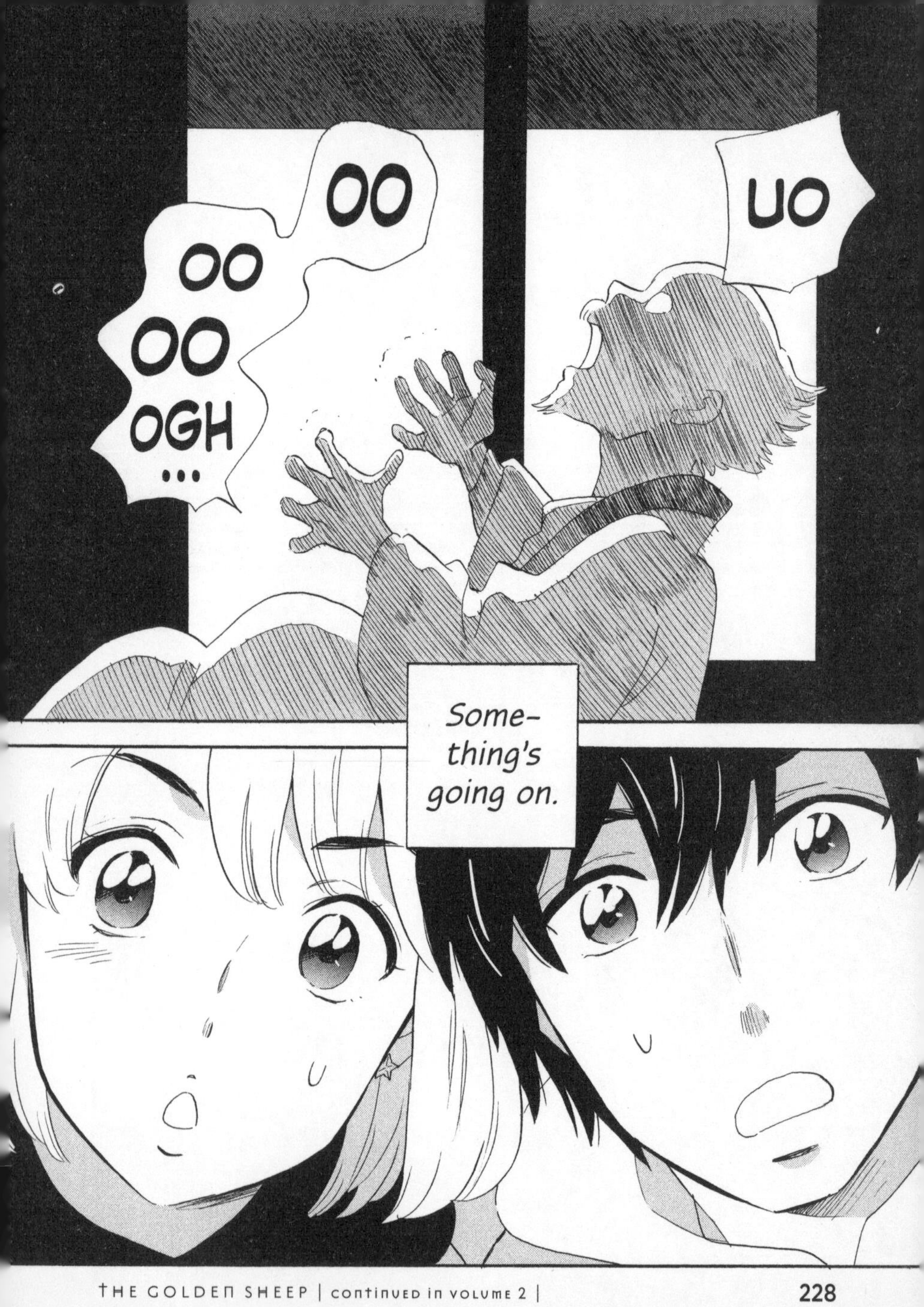
UO
OO
OO OO OGH ...
Some-thing's going on.

THE GOLDEN SHEEP

somehow

Tsugu and Sora end up making croquettes with a **mysterious old man!**

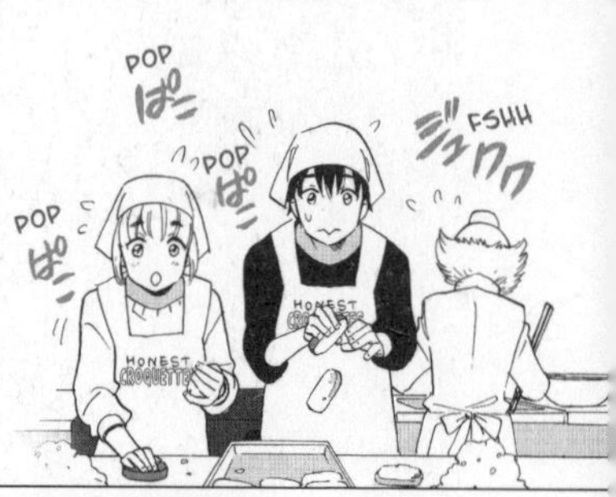
POP
POP
POP
FSHH
HONEST CROQUETTES
HONEST

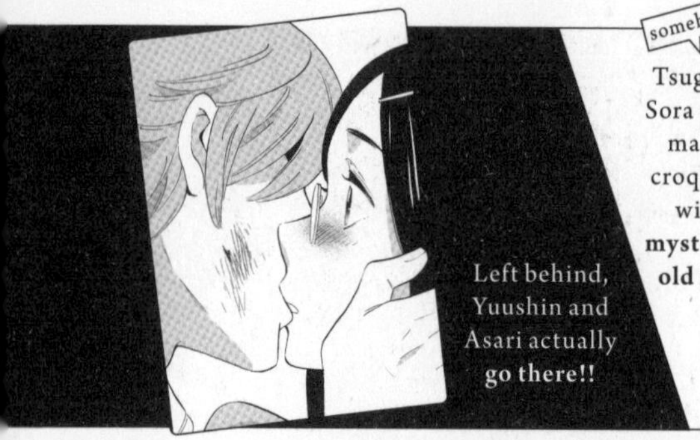
Left behind, Yuushin and Asari actually **go there!!**

Their first date suddenly closes the distance between them.

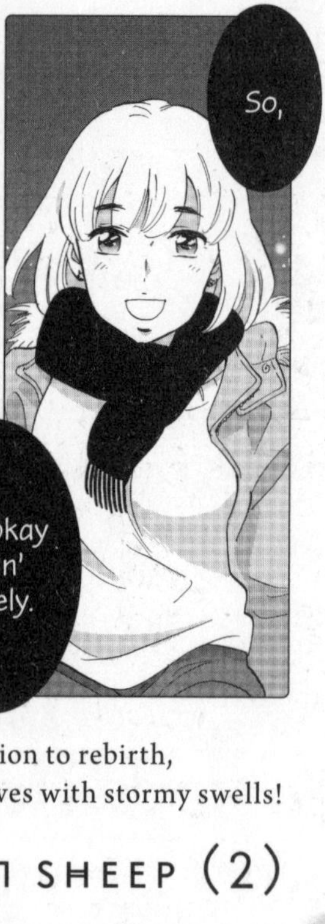
So,

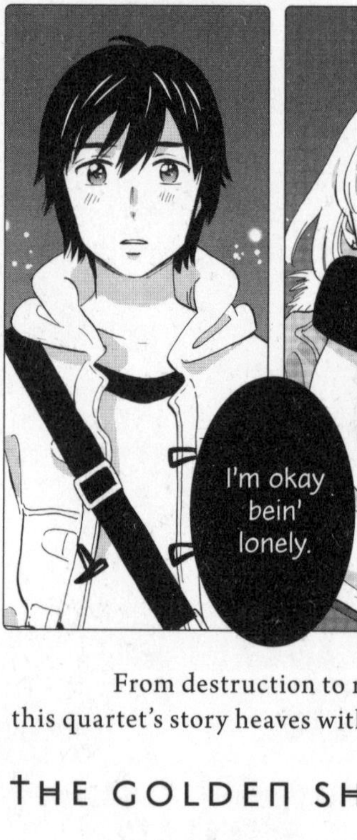
I'm okay bein' lonely.

Spring comes, but where does it lead?

From destruction to rebirth,
this quartet's story heaves with stormy swells!

THE GOLDEN SHEEP (2)

On Sale Winter 2019!

†HE GOLDEⁿ SHEEP I

A Vertical Comics Edition

Translation: Daniel Komen
Production: Risa Cho
           Lorina Mapa

First published in Japan in 2018 by Kodansha, Ltd., Tokyo
Publication rights for this English edition arranged through Kodansha, Ltd., Tokyo
English language version produced by Vertical Comics, an imprint of Kodansha
USA Publishing, LLC.

Translation provided by Vertical Comics, 2019
Published by Kodansha USA Publishing, LLC, New York

Originally published in Japanese as *Kin no hitsuji 1* by Kodansha, Ltd., 2018
Kin no hitsuji first serialized in *Afternoon*, Kodansha, Ltd., 2017-2019

This is a work of fiction.

ISBN: 978-1-947194-80-9

Manufactured in Canada

First Edition

Kodansha USA Publishing, LLC.
451 Park Avenue South
7th Floor
New York, NY 10016
www.vertical-comics.com

Vertical books are distributed through Penguin-Random House Publisher Services.